WITHDRAWN

THE POPE'S MEN

THE POPE'S MEN

The Papal Civil Service in the Renaissance

PETER PARTNER

CLARENDON PRESS · OXFORD
1990

Oxford University Press, Walton Street, Oxford OX2 6DP

Oxford New York Toronto
Delhi Bombay Calcutta Madras Karachi
Petaling Jaya Singapore Hong Kong Tokyo
Nairobi Dar es Salaam Cape Town
Melbourne Auckland
and associated companies in
Berlin Ibadan

Oxford is a trade mark of Oxford University Press

Published in the United States
by Oxford University Press, New York

British Library Cataloguing in Publication Data
Partner, Peter
The Pope's men.
1. Catholic Church. Administration by Vatican, history
I. Title   262.136
ISBN 0-19-821995-4

Library of Congress Cataloging in Publication Data
Partner, Peter.
The Pope's men : the papal civil service in the Renaissance /
Peter Partner.
p. cm.
Includes bibliographical references and index.
1. Civil service—Papal States—History. 2. Popes—Court.
3. Papacy—History. 4. Papal States—Diplomatic and consular
service—History. I. Title.
JN5299.P3P36 1990
354.45'6006—dc20   90-7341
ISBN 0-19-821995-4

Typeset by Downdell Limited, Oxford
Printed in Great Britain by
Courier International Ltd,
Tiptree, Essex

To Adriano Prosperi

Acknowledgements

The suggestion that I write this book came, some years ago, in a letter to the author from Peter Burke, who remarked on the need for a study of 'the pope's servants'. Wolfgang Reinhard has also written of the need for prosopographical work on the prelates of the papal court.[1] Whether I have satisfied either of these scholars, remains to be seen.

Few scholarly books are written without help from others, and this one is no exception. My greatest debt is to Dr Leslie Macfarlane, who has done so much to help and encourage the study of the Vatican Archives by scholars from these islands. Dr Macfarlane read my manuscript in two of its late versions, and gave me invaluable aid of both a detailed and a general sort, and for this I am most grateful.

I am also grateful to Mark Stephenson for astringent and helpful criticism of the first version of the first chapter, and to Dr Michael Haren, who kindly looked through a draft of the biographical appendix, and supplied me with some detailed and precise information from his own work in the Vatican Archives.

Help of a different but no less essential kind came from Dr Julian Havil, who guided my faltering steps through the alien paths of computerized data collection.

I have had generous help from those who work in libraries and archives. I would especially mention Dr Herman Hoberg, in the Vatican Archives, and, in the Archivio di Stato in Rome, Drs Angela Lanconelli, Paolo Cherubini, and Maria Grazia Pastura Ruggiero. The London Library has been as essential to me as ever, and I also remain grateful for the help of the Library of the University of Southampton. Professor Gianpaolo Brizzi showed much kindness in arranging for me to use the facilities of the History Faculty of the University of Bologna.

I have received guidance and stimulus from the published work of scholars interested in this aspect of history. I would especially mention the *Kanzlei der Paepste der Hochrenaissance (1471–1527)* of Professor Thomas Frenz, which, although

[1] *Freunde und Kreaturen: 'Verflechtung' als Konzept zur Erforschung historischer Führungsgruppen Römische Oligarchie zum 1600* (Munich, 1979), pp. 55, 73.

it appeared when my own researches were far advanced, was of the greatest assistance. Professor Frenz also kindly gave permission for the adaptation of part of his invaluable statistical tables. It would also be proper to mention John F. D'Amico's *Renaissance Humanism in Papal Rome* and Barbara McClung Hallman's *Italian Cardinals, Reform, and the Church as Property*, which both deal with topics close to mine.

Professor Judith C. Brown kindly helped me to identify and document Leonardo Salutati of Pescia.

I am most grateful to the British Academy for a generous grant towards the costs of the archival research work preliminary to this study. I am also grateful to Professors Christopher Brooke, John Bossy, and Kenneth Setton, for the interest they have taken in my work, and the support they have at various times given me.

I am grateful to the Editors of the Press for their patience and trouble.

Contents

List of Tables

Abbreviations

AHP	*Archivum Historiae Pontificiae*
AMSM	*Atti e Memorie della R. Deputazione di Storia Patria per le Marche*
Ann.Ist.Ital.-germ.Tr.	*Annali dell'Istituto Storico Italo-germanico in Trento*
Arch. Cam. I	Archivio Camerale, Prima Parte; Archivio di Stato, Rome
Arch.f.Dipl.	*Archiv für Diplomatik*
ASI	*Archivio Storico Italiano*
ASL	*Archivio Storico Lombardo*
ASR	*Archivio della R. Società Romana di Storia Patria*
Atti Acc.Naz. Linc.	*Atti dell'Accademia Nazionale dei Lincei*
Bib.Éc.Ch.	*Bibliothèque de l'École des Chartes*
BIHBR	*Bulletin de l'Institut Historique Belge de Rome*
Boll.Stor.Pis.	*Bollettino Storico Pisano*
BSU	*Bollettino della R. Deputazione di Storia Patria per l'Umbria*
Bull.Sen.SP	*Bullettino Senese di Storia Patria*
CPL	*Calendar of Entries in the Papal Registers: Papal Letters*
DBI	*Dizionario Biografico degli Italiani* (Rome, 1960–)
Div. Cam.	Diversa Cameralia, Archivio Segreto Vaticano
EHR	*English Historical Review*
GSLI	*Giornale Storico della Letteratura Italiana*
Human.Lovan.	*Humanistica Lovaniensia*
Introitus et Exitus	Introitus et Exitus, Archivio Segreto Vaticano
Ital.Med.Uman.	*Italia Medioevale e Umanistica*
JEH	*Journal of Ecclesiastical History*

JWCI	Journal of the Warburg and Courtauld Institutes
Mélanges	Mélanges d'archéologie et d'histoire de l'école Française de Rome
MIÖG	Mitteilungen des Instituts für österreichische Geschichtsforschung
PBSR	Papers of the British School at Rome
Quellen	Quellen und Forschungen aus italienischen Archiven und Bibliotheken
Reg. Vat.	Regesta Vaticana, Archivio Segreto Vaticano
Röm.Hist.Mitt.	Römische historische Mitteilungen
Röm.Quart.	Römische Quartalschrift für christliche Altertumskunde und für Kirchengeschichte
RRIISS	Rerum Italicarum Scriptores, ed. L. A. Muratori. Raccolta degli storici italiani dal Cinquecento al Millecinquecento, new edns. (Città di Castello and Bologna, 1900–)
RSCI	Rivista della Storia della Chiesa in Italia
RSI	Rivista Storica Italiana

1

Introduction

I

This book is concerned with the recruitment, rewards, attitudes, and origins of papal servants. Governments of the fifteenth and sixteenth centuries did not possess a civil service or bureaucracy in the modern sense. In particular, by the sixteenth century most offices in the papal service were sold and were also re-saleable: this was the case with many *ancien régime* governments, and it distinguishes them sharply from modern ones. But although approximate in meaning, the expression 'civil service' seems a permissible way to describe the administrative officials of the Renaissance papal court. Both 'civil service' and 'bureaucracy' are slippery terms, much harder to define exactly than they may seem. Even in the modern world the terms are commonly (but sometimes controversially) applied to bodies very differently constituted. For example, the spoils system distinguishes the US civil service sharply from most European ones, and C. Wright Mills in an influential book, *The Power Elite* (1956), wrote that 'The civilian government of the United States never has had and does not have now a genuine bureaucracy'. Whether this is so or not is of no concern here, but the assertion shows how hard the word is to define.

The book is also to do with the uses of bureaucracy to early modern governments, and with the political price paid by these governments to the oligarchies from which most of their senior officials were recruited. However, the bureaucracies in early modern Europe were not, as a rule, chosen entirely from a single patrician group. To a very limited degree they offered career opportunities to the intellectual élites. This had to some extent been the case for clerks trained in the medieval universities; in the Renaissance period there was a similar opportunity for a small number of men, usually self-educated, who were proficient in the new 'humane studies'. Such men, it has been ironically but accurately observed, were very often law-school drop-outs,[1] who might well have achieved their bureaucratic

[1] A. Field, *The Origins of the Platonic Academy of Florence* (Princeton, 1988), 27.

careers by more orthodox means if they had stuck to the Decretals and the Digest. But they were only a small numeric element in the papal bureaucracy, compared with the conventionally educated clerks who came from noble or patrician families, and who had got advancement by the usual channels of family and regional influence, university doctorates (though these were a minority), and the display of wealth.

The Renaissance papal court was the family of the Roman bishop. He stood at the head of the people of God, which was the community of Catholic Christians of the Latin rite. The pope's aims were the spiritual ones of his office, but the means by which these aims were accomplished were often very worldly. At this time papal policies were determined either by fiscal administrators closely tied to the curial bankers, or by hard-headed church politicians. Papal Rome was an urban, capitalistic environment whose curial administration had much in common with other bureaucratic governments of the period, and was in many respects far less conservative than most royal governments.

The bureaucratic and capitalistic elements in papal government are especially striking to a modern observer because they seem to sit so oddly in a religious context which we are inclined to label as traditional. The Roman Church was a single body of Christians, held together under God's guidance by the sacraments which only a divinely ordained priesthood could administer. Early modern Catholic society was, in some respects at least, based upon like-minded friendship and religious awe. Yet Renaissance papal Rome seems, in respect of its judicial and fiscal organization, to have tended in the quite different direction of a bureaucracy based on rationality and calculation, staffed to a considerable degree by men coming from an entrepreneurial merchant class. Such a government, whose servants are the instruments of an impersonal, collective purpose, contains elements which we are accustomed to think of as modern rather than as traditional.

One way to decide the degree of modernity that we can attribute to this papal civil service is to compare it with contemporary and later bureaucracies. Such comparisons can seldom be direct. For example, the majority of papal civil servants at that time enjoyed the security of tenure which is attributed to modern ones, but the reasons for their security derived more from venality and from the collegiate system than from any concept of a fixed official corps. Most of its officials took an oath of loyalty to the papacy. While not strictly a hierarchy of officials, since the superiority of some offices to others was questionable, the papal court contained a range of official posts, some of which could be held in plurality, but of which many could serve as the rungs of a ladder by which an energetic man could climb to great position.

It is doubtful if the peak of curial ambition, the cardinalate, can be treated as a bureaucratic office in the Renaissance period. Certainly, cardinals tended to grow more directly dependant upon the pope during the Renaissance, but they cannot be viewed, even as late as the seventeenth century, as members of an impersonally directed organization whose goals were fixed by its leader.[2] Another supposed indication of modernity is a bureaucracy which 'goes out of court', and becomes sharply distinguished from the person and household of the ruler. Such a distinction is hard to see in the Renaissance papacy, although it is true that some papal courts and writing offices were physically separate from the papal palace, and could do their work in the absence of the pope; the papal penitentiary is such an example. But the main grace-granting agencies, the signaturae and the consistory, needed the personal presence of the ruler in order to function at all. It is typical of the mentality of the time that when the pope left Rome with some of his officials, he legislated not to preserve the jurisdiction of those left behind, but their privileges as a part of the Roman court.[3]

We should distinguish between a body of officials and an official class; we must also distinguish between sacerdotal and lay status.[4] The papal bureaucracy is interesting as an official class, partly for its origins and connections, partly because of its participation both in priestly and in political power. Although its membership was not confined exclusively to churchmen—for example, papal scriptors and secretaries could be laymen—it was the official instrument of the Roman bishopric, and was concerned entirely with things arising from

---

[2] See C. Weber, *Kardinäle und Prälaten in den letzten Jahrzehnten des Kirchenstaates: Elite-Rekrutierung, Karriere-Muster und soziale Zusammensetzung der kurialen Führungsschicht der Zeit Pius' IX. (1846-1878)* (Stuttgart, 1978).

[3] Chancery rules of Julius II and Leo X, quoted in W. Von Hofmann, *Forschungen zur Geschichte der kurialen Behörden vom Schisma bis zur Reformation* (Rome, 1914), ii. 52 (no. 230) and 60 (no. 257).

[4] From *Max Weber: Essays in Sociology*, ed. H. H. Gerth and C. Wright Mills (New York, 1958), 198–204; O. Hintze, *Soziologie und Geschichte* (Göttingen, 1964), 69 ff.

sacerdotal authority. Most people involved in papal administration were churchmen of some kind, and this was reflected in
their careers; for example, the chamber clerks were automatically appointed papal chaplains if they were in holy orders.
Most highly placed curial churchmen aspired to become a
bishop or cardinal. There were a few hints that status in the
papal bureaucracy could be different from status in the
church: one was Pius II's rule that although papal notaries
(protonotaries) should give place to bishops elsewhere, they
should precede them in the papal consistory.

J. S. Mill held that 'government is always in the hands of, or
passing into the hands of whatever is the strongest power in
society, and that what this power is, does not depend on institutions, but institutions on it'. If we look at the late medieval and
early modern church in the light of this doctrine, we see that
certain sections of the social order had seized control of church
offices, appointments, and incomes in the most vigorous way
possible. In each country a variety of interests, beginning with
the monarchy and the great nobles but encompassing other
parts of society such as the legal officers, the University, and
parts of the merchant class, had entrenched their ecclesiastical
patronage in a way which gave them direct or indirect control
of immense church powers and revenues.

The intimate, manifold links between the ruling sectors of lay
and clerical society make it impossible to understand one
without the other. When we look at the officers of the Roman
court in the fourteenth and fifteenth centuries we cannot
understand them neutrally as international, nor does 'Catholic'
describe them sufficiently. In one century they were predominantly French, in the next predominantly Italian. Any realistic
study of the social context of papal officers must take full
account of the society from which they came, and not confine
itself to the little world of Rome. It is necessary, and an attempt
is made here to do this, to have some idea of the geographical
make-up of the Roman court in European terms, and also to
know the way in which it recruited from the various Italian
regions.

The most important part played by the Roman court in the
European patronage network was to use its papal 'provisions'
to satisfy the huge demands of princes and lesser petitioners
for church offices and benefices. When the various patron
groups could not settle their claims locally, they could make
their wishes known in Rome, conciliate them with those of
other, opposing interests, and have the appointments of their

own clients and nominees proclaimed and legalized by the curia. The Roman court also used its patronage powers to further papal political interests, and to provide for its own officers and servants.

From one point of view the early modern papal bureaucracy was a small part of a coherent clerical ruling group which extended throughout the Catholic world, was inspired by a common ideology, and was directed by a strong central authority. From another point of view it was an amalgam made from a number of ruling groups. The clerical class throughout the Latin Christian world was led by people who formed part of other ruling classes, and whose élites not only supplied the top clerical personnel, but controlled, in one sense or another, large numbers of church benefices and huge amounts of church property. The papal élite was for most of the Middle Ages an élite which overlapped with many other élites. The way in which it overlapped the various Italian élites is one aspect of a general European phenomenon.

II

The political geography of the officers who served the Roman court has on the whole been approached by historians through the cardinals, although some work has been done on the provenance of the lower grades.[5] During the later Middle Ages only a proportion of the clerks who served the Roman bishopric were Romans in the narrow, civic sense; Roman clergy had always been partly recruited from other places, and the foreign element was therefore substantial. The mixed regional origin of the clerks at the Holy See had profound effects on the nature of the institution. Any medieval notable—and most of the senior clerks were notables—carried with him wherever he went the power to spin a social web whose strongest strands were friends and dependants from his own country and family.

From the eleventh century onwards, any cardinal of the Roman Church was likely, therefore, to have a Roman household in which relatives and countrymen predominated. From the Lorrainers and Burgundians of the late eleventh century to the French and Franco-Neapolitan cliques of the late thirteenth, these connections formed a prominent part of the social fabric

5 On the cardinals, A. Paravicini Bagliani, *Cardinali di curia e 'familiae' cardinalizie dal 1227 al 1254* (Padua, 1972). On the court, B. Guillemain, *La Cour pontificale d'Avignon 1309-1376: Étude d'une société* (Paris, 1962 and 1966).

of the Roman court. But the cardinals were not the only Roman prelates important enough to set up regional connections. For example, prominent judges and administrators at the Roman court, such as the protonotaries, resembled the cardinals in often being chosen to represent, either formally or informally, the interests of lay rulers. In the thirteenth century the lower grades of the papal offices, especially of the writing offices, mostly came from Italy. In the second half of that century, of the 168 chancery scriptors whose origins are known only five came from outside the Italian peninsula.[6] At its end, during the pontificate of Boniface VIII (1295–1303), there were no non-Italian scriptors in the chancery at all.[7] The papal court was thus a local industry: as many as three-quarters of the papal-state scriptors came from Rome and the area immediately south of it. These figures refer only to one class of papal functionary, it is true. But it was a numerous one: there were often in the region of a hundred papal scriptors, and at the time these formed about two-thirds of total chancery personnel.[8] It is also true that the scriptors were not bureaucrats according to the classic definition of the great German sociologist, Max Weber, since they took no oath of loyalty on assuming office. Their modern historian says that they can be viewed as contractors for curial business on a monopolist basis rather than as officials.[9] Never-

[6] G. Nüske, 'Untersuchungen über das Personal der päpstlichen Kanzlei, 1254–1304', Arch.f.Dipl. 20 (1974), 39–240; 21 (1975), 249–431.

[7] R. Barbiche, 'Les "Scriptores" de la Chancellerie Apostolique sous le pontificat de Boniface VIII (1295–1303)', Bibliothèque de l'École des Chartes, 128 (1970), 115–87, at 175–6.

[8] Nüske, 'Untersuchungen', pp. 394–429. Under Boniface VIII they numbered only about 50, Barbiche, 'Les "Scriptores"', pp. 170–1. Rome and the papal state provided most of these writers (63% for the period 1254–1404; 73% for Boniface VIII), North Italy (Lombardy, Emilia, and the Veneto) provided a good number of scriptors (19% for the whole period; 12% under Boniface), and the southern kingdom (Regno) rather fewer (8% for the whole period; 12% under Boniface). For Avignon, Guillemain, La Cour pontificale, pp. 321–2, and also B. Schwarz, Die Organisation kurialer Schreiberkollegen von ihrer Entstehung bis zur Mitte des 15. Jahrhunderts (Tübingen, 1972), 39–52. Though about 100 scriptors seems to have been normal in the mid 13th cent. and again in the mid 15th, the number sank under Boniface VIII, and there were several attempts to reduce it to about 70 during the Avignonese period. See T. Frenz, 'Zum Problem der Reduzierung der Zahl der päpstlichen Kanzleischreiber nach dem Konzil von Konstanz', in W. Schlögl and P. Herde (eds.), Grundwissenschaften und Geschichte (Münchener historische Studien, Abt. Geschichtliche Hilfswissenschaften, 15; Kallmünz, 1976), 256–73.

[9] Schwarz, Die Organisation, pp. 72–4; T. Frenz, 'Das Eindringen humanistischer Schriftsformen in die Urkunden und Akten der päpstlichen Kurie im 15. Jahrhundert', Arch.f.Dipl. 19 (1973), 287–418, at p. 306.

theless, they give valuable clues to the way the chancery recruited its staff.

The removal of the papal court from Italy to Avignon (1309–76) profoundly affected its social and regional composition. Its French historian has analysed the Avignonese papal court in its widest sense, understanding it not merely as the sum of papal officers, but as including the household of the popes. He has therefore added the domestic services, such as couriers, bodyguards, marshalsea, and so on, to the other papal officials. French preponderance during the Avignonese period is over-whelming: 70 per cent of all curialists were French, only a little over 23 per cent Italian. Other European areas were feebly represented: curialists from the Empire only 3 per cent, from Spain only 2 per cent, from England one per cent.[10] If the administrative grades of the papal court are considered separately, the situation is slightly different. Sixty per cent of these were French, 32 per cent Italian, 4 per cent from the Empire, 2 per cent in each case from England and Spain. Of the papal scriptors, 54 per cent were French, 41 per cent Italian.[11]

The careers of two types of official at the top of the financial administration and the writing offices respectively, the chamber clerks and the papal secretaries, are studied here. The biographies examined belong to the officials in place between 1417 and 1527. During the earlier Avignonese period these two offices had been divided between Italians and French, with other nations playing a negligible part. In the mid fourteenth century 23 per cent of the chamber clerks were Italian and the rest French, while approximately half the secretaries were French in origin and half Italian.[12]

III

The return of the papal court to Rome in 1376, and the Great Schism which followed in 1378, brought about a duplication, and, after the setting up of the Pisan papal obedience in 1409, something approaching a triplication, of the Roman bureau-cracy. The territories from which the three competing popes

---

[10] Guillemain, *La Cour pontificale*, pp. 449–77.

[11] Scribes of French origin to fill these places were evidently hard to find: in 1365 Pope Urban V wrote to the papal legate in Italy to ask him to recruit scribes of suitable competence from southern Italy to serve in the Avignonese writing offices. Quoted by Guillemain, *La Cour pontificale*, p. 330.

[12] Guillemain, *La Cour pontificale*, 283–5, 297–300.

drew their officers were unlike those of earlier times. Even the
Avignonese obedience (the dioceses which accepted the rule of
Pope Clement VII and his successors) was discontinuous in
many respects from the earlier 'Avignon Papacy', especially
following the flight of Benedict XIII to Perpignan in 1408; after
this the Iberian character of Benedict's obedience became very
marked. Nor was the Roman obedience of Urban VI (1378–89)
and Boniface IX (1389–1404) a restoration of the regional
pattern set by Boniface VIII at the beginning of the century.
Urban and Boniface established a firm hold by certain Neapolitan magnate families on the Roman court: from this time the
Brancacci, Caraccioli, Tomacelli, and their affinities became
the controlling factions of the Roman court.[13] In the Pisan
obedience of John XXIII (1410–15) another Neapolitan family,
the Cossa, was added to the rest.

We do not have detailed analysis of the geographical provenance of the curial staff of the various obediences during the
Schism. The numbers of curialists in each of the Avignonese
and Roman/Pisan obediences were probably no lower in each
court than in the entire Roman court before the Schism: the
number of curialists therefore at least doubled. We know, for
example, that almost a hundred scriptors from the Pisan
obedience were carried over into the court of Pope Martin V
(1417–31) after the end of the Schism. By 1420 Martin V was
employing almost 150 scriptors, or half as many again as the
maximum number that had been reckoned permissible, and
double the number allowed at some points in the fourteenth
century when popes were trying to restrict the growth of curial
staff.[14]

Martin V was the first Roman pope to have been elected
since Boniface VIII. When he entered Rome on 28 September
1420 Martin began to effect a restoration which was just as
much a restoration as that which took place after 1815 at the
end of the Napoleonic period. French domination over the
government of the Roman Church, almost absolute for much of
the fourteenth century, was ended, and French participation
in papal administration was drastically and permanently
reduced. We may see this as a victory of Italian élites over
French ones, in which the prize was the great financial and

---

[13] A. Esch, 'Das Papsttum unter der Herrschaft der Neapolitaner: Die
führende Gruppe Neapolitaner Familien an der Kurie während des Schismas
1378–1415', *Festschrift für Hermann Heimpel*, ii (Göttingen, 1972), 713–800.

[14] Frenz, 'Problem' (1976), pp. 256–62; cf. Schwarz, *Die Organisation*,
pp. 40–7.

social advantage of control of the curial patronage machine. The papacy continued to be an international organization, but one dominant nation replaced another in its government. The 6:4 ratio of French officers to others in the Avignonese chancery was replaced by a 6:4 ratio in favour of the Italians to others, during the period 1471–1527.[15]

In the years following the restoration of church unity under Martin V, the main means of effecting Italian control was the almost complete adoption of the officials of the Pisan obedience into the bureaucracy of the new papal regime. The Pisan officers had been largely Italian in provenance. Martin V had been a cardinal of the Pisan obedience of John XXIII, and after his accession the officials remaining from the court of John XXIII tended to see themselves as the legitimate possessors of office.[16] Matters were not as simple as that, and some compromises had to be made with the officials of other papal obediences. Some attempt had been made in 1415, when Gregory XII submitted to the Council of Constance, to protect the tenure of his officials. This agreement was not recognized by the Pisan officials, who protested fiercely and often successfully against the intrusion of members of other groups.

At the top of the official hierarchy François de Conzié, Martin V's chamberlain, and Jean de Broniac, his vice-chancellor, had started in the Avignonese obedience but had transferred to the Pisan one.[17] Only in the case of the apostolic treasurer did Martin V envisage having three senior officials sharing the same post, each drawn from a different obedience. But even in this case it was understood that the Pisan treasurer, Antonio Casini, would actually exercise the treasurer's office, while the other two appointments were nominal.[18] No agreement about the tenure of officials had been made with the Avignonese obedience, and very few Avignonese officials were received into Martin's court: possibly two Avignonese clerks of the chamber were received by Martin, but one stayed with de Conzié in Avignon and so never came to Rome, and the other

[15] T. Frenz, *Die Kanzlei der Päpste der Hochrenaissance (1471-1527)* (Tübingen, 1986), 240.

[16] Von Hofmann, *Forschungen*, i. 112–13.

[17] For de Conzié see M. Dykmans, 'D'Avignon à Rome: Martin V et le cortège apostolique', *BIHBR* 39 (1968), 203–309, at pp. 256–8; P. Partner, *The Papal State under Martin V: The Administration and Government of the Temporal Power in the Early Fifteenth Century* (London, 1958), 132.

[18] L. von Mitteis, 'Curiale Eidregister', *MIÖG*, Ergbd. 6 (1901), 413–48, at p. 448; E. von Ottenthal, 'Die Bullenregister Martins V. und Eugens IV.', *MIÖG*, Ergbd. 1 (1885), 401–589, at p. 494; Partner, *Papal State*, p. 137.

was employed on missions in France. Three of Gregory XII's chamber clerks were received into Martin's chamber, but only after protests on the part of the Pisan clerks.

Even the Pisan official most deeply compromised in the last few months of John XXIII's stay at Constance, when John was seeking to defy the Council, was excluded from office only in the first part of Martin V's pontificate. This was Stefano Geri da Prato, Bishop of Volterra and John XXIII's secret treasurer. The Florentines pleaded on his behalf with the new pope, and although he was not restored to his old place at the registry of apostolic letters, which was a sensitive appointment concerned with household finances, he was eventually given the dignified appointment of councillor of the apostolic chamber.[19]

The Council of Constance was the great crisis of the late medieval papacy: subsequent councils did not produce such intractable problems. Martin V's acute difficulties in absorbing the officials of the various obediences of the Schism were not repeated after the defeat of the Council of Basle (1431–7) and of the schismatic pope elected by its supporters, Felix V. A couple of talented ex-secretaries of the Council, Pietro da Noceto and Aeneas Sylvius Piccolomini, were given office in Rome after the collapse of the conciliar party in 1449, and so were one or two other former Basle officials such as the Spaniard, Jacob Gerard. To extend patronage to such men was an act of grace: the Council of Basle had been utterly defeated and its servants did not have the claim on the Roman bureaucracy which those of Gregory XII had in 1417. By the mid fifteenth century, patronage in Rome had little to do with the great movements of politics and opinion in the universal church. However, the Council of Ferrara-Florence (1438–9) occasioned some changes in the staffing of the papal bureaucracy. Besides receiving an important bishop like the orthodox Greek Bessarion, Eugenius IV employed as secretaries Greeks (Nicholas Sagundinus of Siponto and George of Trebizond) and Italian Hellenists (Cristoforo Garatone and Giovanni Aurispa).

The great trend of the fifteenth century was towards the localizing and regionalizing of the patronage of the Roman Church in favour of privileged groups among the Italian clergy.

---

[19] He died in 1435. See Baix, *La Chambre apostolique*, pp. CCCXL-XLI; C. Guasti, 'Gli avanzi dell'archivio di un pratese vescovo di Volterra', *ASI*, 4th ser., 13 (1884), 20–68; *I commissioni di Rinaldo degli Albizzi*, ed. C. Guasti, i (Florence, 1864), 229; P. Partner, 'Camera Papae: Problems of Papal Finance in the Later Middle Ages', *JEH* 4 (1953), 55–68, at pp. 64–5; Partner, *Papal State*, p. 133.

The process was not smooth: on many occasions at the beginning of a pontificate there was a little revolution in which the former pope's most intimate and trusted servants were driven from court. This can give the misleading impression of a patronage revolution which dislodged everyone of importance. But the spoils system of the Roman court was considerably less radical than it seems. Though in each pontificate the balance of power between the various clienteles changed, most papal officers were fairly sure of employment under another pope, even if uncertain of further advancement.

The decline of the French element in the Roman court was one of the main features of court life after the return to Rome in 1420. Of the seven French cardinals of the first year of Martin V only one was still alive at his death in 1431, and only three had been created to replace those lost. Of the twenty-nine cardinals created or published by Eugenius IV (1431–47) only four were French. The defeat of the Council of Basle may be accounted a defeat for the French faction at the Roman court; moreover, the victory of the Aragonese Alfonso the Magnanimous in the struggle for the southern Kingdom meant defeat for the Franco-Angevin faction at the Roman court by 1443. To some extent the eclipse of the French was balanced by the rise of the Catalans, which culminated in the election of Alfonso Borgia as Calixtus III in 1455.[20]

The composition of the College of Cardinals had profound, though indirect, effects on the selection of papal officers at the lower levels. One of the most important objectives of any cardinal resident in Rome was to place his dependants in the papal bureaucracy. The decline of the French and the rise of the Catalan elements in the administration can be traced just as much in the lower levels of the Roman court as in the higher ones. Still, it will not do to minimize French power in Rome. The careers of Cardinal d'Estouteville and of other French clerical magnates in the fifteenth and early sixteenth centuries testify to the contrary, and without such power the Council of Pisa could never have assembled in 1511.[21]

[20] See J. F. Broderick, 'The Sacred College of Cardinals: Size and Geographical Composition (1099–1986)', *AHP* 25 (1987), 7–72, at pp. 36–44. According to Broderick's figures, 52% of 'Renaissance' (1447–1513) cardinals were Italian, and 18% French. For the Catalans see J. Rius Serra, 'Catalanes y Aragones en la corte de Calixto III', *Analecta Sacra Tarraconensis*, 3 (1927), 193–330.

[21] See G. Bourgin, 'Les Cardinaux français et le diaire caméral de 1439–76', *Mélanges*, 24 (1904), 277–318. For Guillaume d'Estouteville see P. Ourliac, 'La Pragmatique Sanction et la légation en France du Cardinal d'Estouteville', *Mélanges*, 55 (1938), 403–32; A. Schiavo, *Il palazzo della Cancelleria* (Rome,

Just as, in the Avignonese period, about 40 per cent of papal curial officials had come from outside France, so in the period 1471–1526 about 40 per cent of all papal chancery officials came from outside Italy. The proportion of Italians to others varied in different parts of the papal bureaucracy. In some offices, such as those of the minor penitentiaries who had to hear penitents from every quarter, a mixture of nationalities was essential. In the main writing offices—the chancery, apostolic chamber, secretariat—Italians enjoyed the lion's share, with a proportion which increased as the importance of the office increased. In the judicial offices things were more evenly balanced, though the proportion of Italians perhaps rose later in the fifteenth century. But what, above all, sharpened the grip of Italians on the offices of the Roman court was the practice of selling them. Under Martin V and Eugenius IV the only office to be widely sold was that of scriptor, but after mid-century the practice spread to other offices, first to the abbreviators, and then to the great new colleges of venal offices set up by Sixtus IV (1471–84) and Innocent VIII (1484–92).

In financing the purchase of offices and benefices the Italian clerks enjoyed great advantages; above all, it was easier for them to obtain the use of family capital for such purposes. The revenue obtained from capital invested in offices was on the whole higher for Italians than for other clerks, because, once entrenched in the Roman court, it was rather easier for an Italian to get papal provision to benefices from which he could draw an additional income. In Italy after the Schism the general reservations of benefices made by the Pisan popes were maintained. The important distinction was between bishoprics and abbeys valued at an annual assessment of over 200 florins, for which the procedure was expedited through the papal consistory, and benefices of lesser value, which were impetrated by petition through the referendaries.[22] In the papal state the dioceses were directly subject to the Holy See and papal power to appoint was unimpeded. In the Regno a

1964); R. H. Trame, *Rodrigo Sánchez de Arévalo 1404–1470: Spanish Diplomat and Champion of the Papacy* (Washington, 1958), 137; C. W. Westfall, 'Alberti and the Vatican Palace Type', *Journal of the Society of Architectural Historians*, 33 (1974), 102–3.

[22] See E. Göller, *Der liber taxarum der päpstlichen Kammer: Eine Studie über seine Entstehung und Anlage* (Rome, 1905), 27–35; E. von Ottenthal, *Die päpstlichen Kanzleiregeln von Johannes XXII. bis Nicolaus V.* (Innsbruck, 1888), 173–4, 175, 189–90, 213–14, 224. D. Hay, *The Church in Italy in the Fifteenth Century* (Cambridge, 1977), 12, is not quite exact on this topic.

number of bishoprics and abbeys were exempt, and the powers of the crown were an obstacle to papal provision in many cases. For different historical reasons there were impediments to the free use of papal provisions to benefices in Venetian and Milanese territories.[23] But, in spite of these limitations, a clerk holding responsible office in the Roman court stood a very good chance of adding to his dignity and income by provision to minor benefices, by grants of major benefices in administration or in *commendam*, by pensions charged on the benefices of others, or by promotion to the episcopate. If his influence was strong he might also obtain promotion to benefices outside Italy. Naturally enough, Italian clerks who wished to defend and extend the church patronage which they enjoyed in individual Italian dioceses sought to accomplish this aim either by getting office for themselves or their close relatives in the Roman court, or by acquiring influence in the court in some other manner. It comes as no surprise to learn that of 172 canons of the cathedral chapter of Florence between 1417 and 1500, at least 94 (55 per cent) either held office in the Roman court or were closely connected with it in some way. Similar patterns have been found for the clergy of early fifteenth-century Genoa, for that of early sixteenth-century Lucca, and, indeed, for the entire body of Italian clergy in the sixteenth century.[24]

IV

Faced by this phenomenon of an upper clergy which seeks to strengthen its control of patronage by finding office or influence in the papal court, we look for a general explanation of the class from which it comes. The fifteenth and sixteenth centuries were a period of great change in the social structure of much of the Italian peninsula. The major families which had

[23] P. Prodi, 'The Structure and Organisation of the Church in Renaissance Venice: Suggestions for Research', in J. R. Hale (ed.), *Renaissance Venice* (London, 1973), 409–30.

[24] R. Bizzocchi, 'Chiesa e aristocrazia nella Firenze del Quattrocento', *ASI* 142 (1984), 191–282; idem, *Chiesa e potere nella Toscana del Quattrocento* (Bologna, 1987); M. Berengo, *Nobili e mercanti nella Lucca del Cinquecento* (Turin, 1974 repr.), 87–99, 357–77; B. Nogara, D. Puncuh, and A. Roncallo (eds.), *Suppliche di Martino V relative alla Liguria*, i. *Diocesi di Genova*, Atti della Società Ligure di Storia Patria, NS, 13 (87, 1973). And, generally, B. McClung Hallman, *Italian Cardinals: Reform and the Church as Property, 1492–1563* (Berkeley, Los Angeles, and London, 1985).

almost everywhere monopolized power over communal institutions to the detriment of the popular elements were seeking to consolidate and in some places to transform their control of social and political life, often in ways which changed a covert into an overt dominating status. In some places these families accepted the title of patricians, in others they preserved the denomination of citizens until they changed it to some kind of explicitly noble rank.[25]

The history of these new dominations, or extensions of old dominations, is imprinted deeply upon the history of the church. In the struggle of competing families to consolidate their positions, church patronage was one of the obvious weapons to use, not only for the economic reasons outlined above, but also because high church office conferred dignity and status both on its holders and on the families to which they belonged. Office in the papal court had a special place in this pattern, and the question of access to the Roman court and effective representation in it was important for the strategies of most prominent families and factions. The Medici are the most obvious example.

Church benefices were thus treated as part of a family's patrimony, and were transferred from one member of a family to another by 'resignation', usually on the part of uncle to nephew.[26] In this way bishoprics, abbeys, and major benefices were retained in the control of a single family for very long periods, sometimes exceeding a century. The possession of office in the papal court was an important auxiliary in the technique of family control of church property. Roberto Bizzocchi has shown this with especial force for the case of Florence. But the incentive was even more powerful in the case of clerks originating in the papal state.

There were two main paths by which new men could hope for advancement in the Roman court: the long-established one of accomplishment as a teacher or practitioner of canon or

[25] M. Luzzati, 'Familles nobles et familles marchandes à Pise et en Toscane dans le bas moyen âge', in G. Duby and J. le Goff (eds.) *Famille et parenté dans l'Occident Médiéval* (Rome, Collection de l'École Française de Rome, 1977), 275–96; also Berengo, in the same work.
[26] P. Prodi, *Il sovrano pontefice: Un corpo e due anime: La monarchia papale nella prima età moderna* (Bologna, 1982), 324: English trans. *Papal Prince—One Body and Two Souls: The Papal Monarchy in Early Modern Europe* (Cambridge, 1988). See also G. Alberigo, *I vescovi italiani al concilio di Trento* (Florence, 1959); D. Hay, *The Church in Italy*, pp. 18–20; B. McClung Hallman, *Italian Cardinals, passim*; Bizzocchi, *Chiesa e potere*.

civil law, and the very recent one of fame acquired for learning in the humanities. Distinction in legal knowledge continued to be in the Renaissance, as it had been in the Middle Ages, the most solid foundation for a career in the Roman court for those who lacked a secure patronage base. In some papal offices legal qualifications were obligatory, as for example in the rota or in the signaturae of grace and justice, and in the cases of consistorial advocates, referendaries, of the auditor of the apostolic chamber, and so on. In other offices such qualifications, although not essential, were desirable, as in the cases of chamber clerks, and of major abbreviators of apostolic letters.

By contrast, although there was one specifically humanist post in the papal librarianship, prowess in the humanities was seldom rewarded by any administrative office other than that of apostolic secretary. This distinguished and lucrative post could lead to the very top of the clerical hierarchy, but there were very few such jobs to be had. The total number of secretaries appointed in the seventy years following Martin V's accession in 1417 was eighty-eight, and of these a number was transient, supernumerary, or honorific. Of these eighty-eight secretaries about thirty-seven (42 per cent) could be described as well known for their accomplishment in the humanities, and of these thirty-seven perhaps ten (11 per cent of the whole) came from families which could not be described as notable. The situation changed sharply after the institution of the venal college of secretaries in 1487. The total number of secretary positions increased to thirty, but no poor man could afford to buy the office, which cost 2,500 ducats under Alexander VI and 4,500 ducats under Leo X. Only the domestic secretaries, who were personal intimates of the pope, and of whom there were only one or two, made no payment for their post.

So after 1487 the chances for poor humanists to get responsible office in the Roman court decreased sharply. Of 161 secretaries identified after 1486 and before 1527 only two or three were Italian humanists of non-notable family. Two who had successful careers were of humble social origin and of German extraction: the humanist Jacob Questenberg and the half-Venetian Francesco Argentini. Clerks of humble origin rose in papal service through their legal abilities, but in the chamber the number of such men was very small. The doctorate in law was expensive, and rich students obtained it much more easily than poor ones. Some chamber clerk lawyers came from well-known legal dynasties; among the secretaries the legal dynasts were less prominent, but not unknown. We must conclude that in the High Renaissance papal Rome was not a place where careers were open to all the talents.

Patronage and clientage are in many ways as interesting for the limits placed on them as for their ramifications. The Roman court raises in our minds the kind of questions which we ask about all bureaucracies of the *ancien régime*. We wish to know whether they were monopolized by established connections, what those connections were, and if there was room within the organizations to promote talented administrators who compared with the rest were basely born. Besides looking for indications of social mobility, we seek some idea of the flexibility of the patronage system, and the extent to which its permanent vested interests were affected by the rather frequent changes in papal leadership. That the pope was usually an elderly man, likely to be replaced after not too long a reign by someone else from a quite different family, distinguished the papacy from most other contemporary governments.

Beneath the senior civil servants of the papacy whose names find a place in our books marched a large army of junior officials, many of whom must have been disappointed in their hopes of promotion. There were a hundred scriptors of apostolic letters, who had to buy their places even before the advent of the colleges of venal offices. In spite of their numbers the scriptors could be men of some importance: the office was held (though in their case in plurality) by powerful and dignified officials, and even some scriptors who held no other papal office seem to have become rich and respected men. There were also in the Roman court at any one time 150 notaries of various sorts, and by the end of the period a hundred solicitors of apostolic letters, sixty minor abbreviators, eighty-odd scriptors of briefs. The duties of some of these offices were light, but none were yet sinecures.

In spite of restricted career prospects, from the late fifteenth century almost all the minor officials had to buy their posts, and cumulatively the capital they advanced to the government was substantial: by the end of the period the total capital value of all offices was in excess of a million and a half florins. Even at the lower levels the price of offices was high enough to ensure that the officers could not, save in exceptional circumstances, be drawn from poor families. The relations of the papal government with this lower bureaucracy lay somewhere between a modern government's relations with its civil service trade unions and its relations with investors in the national debt. Indications of the collective point of view of the lower officers of the papal court are hard to find, but in the Counter-Reformation period we can discover a pointer in the protest made to Pius IV by officials in the papal penitentiary who feared for the loss or reduction of the incomes attached to their posts due to the proposed reforms of 1562: 'We appeal to your holiness to protect the interests of the officers who have sold their patrimony to buy offices which lie under your protection.'[27] In this appeal for the interests of minor as well as of major capitalists, we are perhaps coming near to the spirit of the Roman court.

V

There were two phases in the transformation of the ruling group of officials in the Roman court: first, the substitution of Italian for non-Italian officials in the papal bureaux, and second the growth of a clerical office-purchasing class among the Italian notables. The aim of the latter was to consolidate the control exercised by magnates over local church benefices and revenues by the purchase of papal offices. Can these arrangements be seen as a kind of permanent representation at the papal court on the part of the Italian oligarchs, tempering the absolute power of the papacy and making it in some respects a republic to which the privileged Italian gentry had access? This was the view expressed by the Venetian curialist Giovanni Francesco Commendone, writing in the Roman court in the mid-sixteenth century. He viewed the Roman court as a career open to all the talents. 'In fact', he wrote, 'the door is open to all'.

In the same way that in popular regimes any citizen is eligible for office, and may aspire to any rank, the magistracies being filled by lot from all conditions of men, so in the same way in this [papal] republic persons of low origin, sometimes unworthy individuals, have had high office conferred on them, they being as it were embarked in a ship with all their patrons and kinsfolk; and the evidence for this is the wide freedom of speech which officials enjoy in Rome, and the industrious manner in which courtiers at the Roman court seek to curry favour with everyone.[28]

[27] E. Göller, *Die päpstliche Pönitentiarie von ihrem Ursprung bis zu ihrer Umgestaltung unter Pius V.*, ii 2 (Rome, 1911), 133–4.

[28] G. F. Commendone, 'Discorso sopra la corte di Roma', British Library, Add. MSS 29,444, fo. 43^v; Add. MSS 8401, fo. 7^v. I have not yet seen the edn. by D. Rota (Bergamo, 1983).

Of course, Commendone took an exaggeratedly Venetian and republican view of Rome. The idea of entire freedom of speech in the secretariat of Paul IV makes the eyes open wide. And any view of these matters which fails to take into account the role of the cardinals is bound to be defective. Nevertheless, the idea of the Roman court as a sort of plutocratic republic is not entirely nonsensical. A well-known example of the speculative purchase of high office at the Roman court is that of the purchase of the post of auditor of the apostolic chamber by the Borghese family, for Orazio Borghese, in the late 1580s.[29] Having risked their whole capital and plunged into debt to buy the job, the family faced ruin when Orazio died prematurely. Only the gracious concession of the post to Orazio's brother Camillo Borghese saved the family fortunes, and set Camillo on the path which was to lead him swiftly to the cardinalate and to his election as Pope Paul V.

The main changes in the social composition of the Roman court were probably complete by 1527. Administrative reforms were made in the Counter-Reformation period, but these did not much alter the way in which officials were recruited, nor the class from which they came. On the other hand, the growth of a noble caste in Italy was slow, and was still in its earlier stages in 1527; it was not complete before the early seventeenth century. By the eighteenth century it became possible to speak of a tacit alliance between the Italian nobility and the papacy. The change in social terminology becomes quickly clear to anyone who reads the biographical compilations of eighteenth-century antiquarians which deal with holders of office in the Roman court in the Renaissance period. Their biographers, writing three centuries later, call numerous papal secretaries, treasurers, and protonotaries 'noble', even though in the fifteenth century the families of these men would not have claimed such a status. Usually, however, if the family survived to the eighteenth century it had become noble. The mere title of one biography of a Maffei, a non-noble family in the fifteenth century, makes the point. It is Benedetto Falconcini's *Vita del nobil'uomo e buon servo di Dio, Raffael Maffei detto il Volter-rano*, published in 1735 about a subject who died in 1522. The instance of the chamber clerk Antonio Fatati, who died in 1484, may also be mentioned. Fatati's venerated remains were described in the eighteenth century by Bishop Prospero

---

[29] W. Reinhard, 'Ämterlaufbahn und Familien Status: Der Aufstieg des Hauses Borghese 1537–1621', *Quellen*, 54 (1974), 328–427, at pp. 346–64.

Lambertini as those of a 'patrician of Ancona': no such social description would have been applied to him in his lifetime, in spite of his coming from a notable family.

People often think of the Roman court as an institution with peculiar characteristics, quite different from those of other governments. But in most respects papal government was subject to the same forces that affected government elsewhere. In Rome, as in many other parts of Europe (for example, in France), it was a time when not only the big local leaders but also those of more modest status spent a great deal of effort in seeking power and place at the court, and in buying offices from the court when the opportunity offered.

There were some special features of the Roman court, apart from its priestly nature. The papacy gave Italy the nearest thing to a social and political focus that was available at that period. The papacy was, of course, a force in Italian politics; this aspect of affairs has often been described, though in the writer's view mistakenly, as a reason for calling the papal monarchy of the time a 'Renaissance principate'. But the social dimension of the Roman bishopric was just as important as its participation in the struggle for regional power and influence. Local leaderships in various parts of the peninsula handled their relations with the Roman bishopric in very similar ways. In dealing with the bureaucracy of the Roman court, we are led directly to the strategies of kindred aggrandizement practised by the Italian notable families. This is not a sort of government peculiar to the Roman circumstances; historians have come to similar conclusions about other Italian governments. As has often happened since the expression 'Italy' has had any meaning, papal politics were managed by men whose interests and points of view can be properly understood only by looking at their Italian context.

2

The Roman Court and the Papal Civil Service

I

The Roman court was the household of a bishop, the ceremonial court of a ruler, and the centre of government of the universal church and the papal state. In practice these functions were not clearly distinguished for the officers concerned: some, like secret chamberlains and registrators, or the datarius, were household as well as administrative officials; and others, like the chamber clerks, could also be papal chaplains or papal state officers. The distinction between household and administration was nevertheless present to contemporaries; for example in a physical distinction between the 'palace' (*palatium, palazzo*) and the 'court' (*curia*). Early in the fifteenth century rules were proposed to govern the costume worn by chamberlains and prelates going to and from the palace and the court.[1] A physical separation certainly obtained between the Vatican Palace and the chancery, which lay near the Theatre of Pompey on the other side of the Tiber. The papal 'family' contained the domestic secretaries but no others; it could also include laymen such as the banker who acted as 'apostolic depositary'. But, large as it became in this period, the papal *familia* excluded most administrative officials of the curia. The lines were sometimes blurred; honorary membership of the papal household was granted to people then termed *continui commensales* of the pope, but this privilege did not allow them to live in the palace as part of the papal household.

Describing the administrative services of the Roman court is a daunting task, and one not made easier by the big changes of the late fifteenth century.[2] It is perhaps best to begin with the

---

[1] C. Guasti, 'Gli avanzi', *ASI* 13 (1884), 347.

[2] I have followed Von Hofmann, *Forschungen*, and also H. Bresslau, *Handbuch der Urkundenlehre für Deutschland und Italien* (3rd edn., Berlin, 1958), 287–322. For the consistory see Partner, *Papal State*, p. 133, and L. Pásztor, 'Le cedole concistoriali', *AHP* 11 (1973), 209–68. For the *custos cancellariae* see Von Hofmann, *Forschungen*, i. 48–53, ii. 78–9.

papal consistory, which had no permanent staff of its own, but whose operation involved all the main authorities and services of the court, including the cardinals. The Consistory was in effect the main papal council, and it could have diplomatic functions such as the reception of envoys, but its ecclesiastical ones concern us here. Procedure for papal provision to bishoprics and abbeys assessed at an annual value of over 200 florins was expedited in consistory. A cardinal would act as proposer of the promotion, and would receive an appropriate gift (*propina*). The vice-chancellor's secretary was responsible for making out the consistorial certificate (*cedula*) once the grant had been made; it was registered by the powerful master of chancery, the *custos cancellariae*. Only on presentation of these certificates could the bulls of conferment be drawn up. The consistory was attended not only by the cardinals but by the vice-chancellor, apostolic chamberlain, treasurer, chamber clerks, rota judges, referendaries, protonotaries, consistorial advocates, and so on. A distinction was made between public and secret consistories. At the latter not only were promotions made, but the administrative business of the College of Cardinals in its collegiate aspect was transacted, to decide which cardinals should participate in a particular 'distribution' of its financial profits.

Since the time of the early medieval Reform papacy much of the business had been done through the apostolic chancery. However, the later Middle Ages saw great changes. Since the Great Schism parts of the procedure for conferring benefices had been taken away from the chancery and new powers in the matter given to offices connected with the papal household. Of these the most important were the signatura and the dataria, which both took shape in the late fifteenth century. By these means powerful household officials invented new procedures which financially benefited both the new officers and the pope. In the signatura the 'domestic referendaries' obtained the papal signature for petitions which he conceded personally; though later he also allowed them to be granted by others under special commissions. In the same period other household officials belonging to the dataria received fees for the registration of bulls and for the grant of special graces and dispensations; they also administered the sale and resale of venal offices. At the beginning of the fifteenth century the datarius had been an obscure minor official responsible for dating petitions; at its close he had become one of the main papal officers, and his bureau had assumed key importance in papal finance.[3]

These important new household offices were located in the Vatican Palace. Though the oldest and probably still the largest of the papal bureaux, the chancery was no longer situated on the Vatican hill.[4] Instead it was to be found on the opposite side of the river, often in premises connected with the cardinal vice-chancellor. From Calixtus III's time until 1521 it was to be found in the palace later called Sforza-Cesarini; it was then moved to the palace now termed the 'Cancelleria'. The vice-chancellor of the Roman Church remained a very important and wealthy officer; he was invariably a cardinal. Especially important was the thirty-five years' tenure of the office by Rodrigo Borgia, the subsequent Alexander VI (vice-chancellor 1457-92, pope 1492-1503). Beneath the vice-chancellor a substitute (locum tenens), normally a bishop, assisted in the everyday running of the chancery; the custos has already been mentioned.

The seven notaries of the Holy See (known as participating protonotaries) were dignified officers who until Pius II's time claimed precedence over bishops in curial protocol; their duties related to the grant of consistorial benefices and to the issue of letters of justice, and they took very substantial fees. The honorary rank of protonotary was often granted to clerks within or without the Roman court; it was much sought after because of its dignity and because of the exemption from the jurisdiction of the ordinaries which went with it.[5] The abbreviators were the most numerous and important class of upper chancery official.[6] The most responsible, the dozen de parco

---

[3] For the signatura see Von Hofmann, Forschungen, ii. 131-4; Katterbach, Sussidi per la consultazione dell'Archivio Vaticano, ii. Referendarii utriusque Signaturae (Vatican City, 1931), XII-XVI. For the dataria see also L. Célier, Les Dataires du XVe siècle et les origines de la Daterie Apostolique (Paris, 1910), and P. Partner, 'Papal Financial Policy in the Renaissance and Counter-Reformation', Past and Present, 88 (1980), 17-62.

[4] Von Hofmann, Forschungen, ii. 130. See also A. Schiavo, Il palazzo della Cancelleria (Rome, 1964).

[5] Von Hofmann, Forschungen, i. 56-67.

[6] B. Schwarz, 'Die Abbreviatoren unter Eugen IV.', Quellen, 60 (1980), 200-74; id., 'Abbreviature officium est assistere vicecancellario in expeditione litterarum apostolicarum: Zur Entwicklung des Abbreviatorenamts etc.', in E. Gatz (ed.), Römische Kurie, kirchliche Finanzen, Vatikanisches Archiv: Studien zu Ehren von Hermann Hoberg (Miscellanea Historiae Pontificiae, 45-6/ii; Rome, 1979), 789-824. And also Schwarz, Die Organisation, especially pp. 67-8. On what follows, see also the work of A. Fuller, in the Introduction to CPL 16 (1986).

maiore who assisted the vice-chancellor, saw to the drafts or minutes of bulls. Some sixty others *de parco minore* or *de prima visione* had charge of other stages of the bulls. The chancery scriptors, already mentioned above, were a numerous class whose writing offices were not located in the chancery, where they had no common writing bureau. They engrossed papal bulls, each taking the work back to his own house. To distribute and supervise the work there were the *distributor* and *rescribendarius*. The *registratores litterarum apostolicarum* also had duties to distribute and check chancery work, especially registry copies: they also had important taxing functions. The petitions on which the bulls were based had, however, already passed through the hands of the referendaries. Other checks on the operation of the chancery were operated by the corrector of apostolic letters (in the fifteenth century also a referendary) and by the auditor of the *audientia litterarum contradictarum*. The latter, though a key official in the Middle Ages, had lost much of his former importance by the sixteenth century.

The referendaries were an important group of officials, closely connected with the papal household, who in the fifteenth century took to themselves some important sections of chancery business.[7] From the time of Pius II one or two domestic referendaries were important in the concession of papal graces; later these domestic referendaries were closely connected with the dataria, and worked in the signaturae of grace and justice. They were qualified lawyers whom the popes authorized to read and sign certain categories of petition. Under Martin V these related only to benefices of lower value, but the categories were periodically enlarged. Such referendaries undertook confidential household financial business earlier in the fifteenth century, until the datarius gradually took their functions over.

In the papal penitentiary officials tended, as they did in the chancery, to extend the competence of the office and to widen the discretion they possessed to grant graces to supplicants.[8] The apostolic penitentiary was a great official, always of cardinal's rank. The minor penitentiaries were not just employed at St Peter's, but in some other Roman basilicas and churches as well. Penitentiary scriptors could be laymen, but

[7] Von Hofmann, *Forschungen*, i. 26–7, 70–80, 95–7, 231–2; ii. 131–4; Katterbach, *Sussidi*, ii, XII–XVI at n. 3.

[8] Göller, *Päpstliche Pönitentiarie*, *passim*; Schwarz, *Die Organisation*, pp. 115–25.

more often were clerical pluralists who also held office in the chancery and elsewhere. In the earlier fifteenth century complaint about the functioning of the penitentiary was most often concerned with the 'correctors', who under Eugenius IV expanded their competence and were assigned 'assistants' on the model of the abbreviators de parco minori in the chancery. There were complaints about the behaviour and communal life led by the minor penitentiaries, which occasioned their reform.

In spite of disquiet about some aspects of the penitentiary, its competence and jurisdiction were progressively extended until they reached a maximum under Pope Sixtus IV. The period from his pontificate (1471–84) until the Sack of Rome in 1527 is reckoned as the most important in the history of the office.[9] The penitentiary was closely linked with the main financial offices, and in special cases its petitioners were made to come to terms and make a settlement with the chamber, or in later times with the dataria. In lesser cases they paid in the penitentiary according to a fixed scale.

The apostolic chamber, like most of the main papal bureaux, assumed the main lines of its final shape during the thirteenth century.[10] It was the chief financial agency of the papacy, responsible for financial transactions with monasteries and with other churches, and also for many important parts of the administration of the papal state, including its finances. It supervised and controlled the apostolic collectors sent to look after the fiscal interests of the papacy in the Catholic world, and it controlled the treasurers of provinces of the papal state. The apostolic chamberlain was invariably of cardinal's rank; beneath him a vice-chamberlain and an apostolic treasurer ran the financial administration. A banker chosen to run the main chamber account was classified as a papal household official, known as the depositary; he co-operated with the clerks of the chamber in keeping and auditing the main account books.

The chamber clerks, normally seven in number from the time of Eugenius IV, were the principal administrative officers of the bureau. They were supervised by the vice-chamberlain and the treasurer. Besides doing the financial business they played an important part in the drawing up and registration of certain categories of bulls, notably those referring to benefices con-

    [9] Göller, Päpstliche Pönitentiarie, ii/1. 14–15.
    [10] Partner, Papal State, pp. 130–5; id., 'Papal Financial Policy'; M. G. Pastura Ruggiero, La reverenda Camera Apostolica e i suoi archivi (secoli XV–XVIII) (Rome, 1987), 53–8.

ferred in consistory and those concerned with the running of the papal state. In this aspect of their work they co-operated closely with the secretaries. In financial matters they worked with the confidential financial officers of the papal household in many things, at first with the secret treasurers, and later, after the household financial business had been consolidated in these new bureaux, with the officers of the two signaturae and of the dataria. The chamber clerks kept the accounts relating to the obligations and settlement of dues arising from benefices conferred by the Holy See, namely the payments known as annates and common services. It was the duty of the chamber to see that bulls authorizing the conferment of a benefice were not released until the proper payments had been made.

The chamber clerks also had to co-operate with the clerk of the College of Cardinals, who shared the 'common services' revenues with the chamber. Each month a duty chamber clerk known as the *mensarius* was appointed. The notaries and, under them, the four scriptors of the chamber drafted, corrected, and engrossed the correspondence carried out in the name of the chamberlain, who had his own seal. They also engrossed bulls sent through the chamber, whose drafts had been prepared by the secretaries and chamber clerks. The chamber also supervised the running of the registry of petitions, though there was some competition with the chancery over this, and eventually the business fell under the control of the dataria.

The chamber was collectively organized as a college, and it possessed an internal administration to distribute the fees among its members. It was operated under a papal statute, of which the earliest known version is that of Eugenius IV, of 1444, although earlier *libri pitaphii* of a comparable nature existed in the chamber before this time. Meetings of the chamber were presided over by the chamberlain or vice-chamberlain, and attended by the treasurer, by one or two senior officials known at various times as 'councillors', 'assistants', or 'presidents', by the chamber clerks, and by the main legal officers of the chamber (auditor, fiscal advocate, fiscal proctor, advocate for poor litigants). The banker serving as apostolic depositary also had his place in sittings of the chamber. The expression 'president' was used with varying meanings at various times, sometimes, apparently, to indicate the vice-treasurer or other senior official who was not a chamber clerk; but from the time of Innocent VIII onwards (1484–92) it was often used to indicate the chamber clerks themselves, on the occasions when they sat ('presided') in the chamber.

The apostolic secretaries did not collectively form a special bureau until their reorganization under Innocent VIII in 1487. They were, however, among the most powerful and well-remunerated of curial officials, and they formed an important link between the chamber, the chancery, and the small group of powerful familiars who surrounded the pope. They were of relatively recent origin: the practice of employing secretaries to transmit papal commands (often in the form of a new type of papal letter known as the brief) originated in the second half of the fourteenth century.[11] Their institutional link with the apostolic chamber was almost as strong as that with the chancery. Bulls dispatched *per cameram* [*secretam*] (i.e. granted in the secret chamber of the pope) went through the hands of the secretaries, though they were not sent through the *Camera Apostolica*. The secretaries did deal with the bulls registered in the apostolic chamber. But the earlier connection of the secretaries with the chancery was not severed, and several types of chancery bull (such as those for the concession of notarial office, for portable altars, and for other miscellaneous matters) were initiated by the secretaries, and brought them their share of the appropriate chancery tax. Secretaries frequented the chancery premises as well as the apostolic palace; it was in the chancery 'in the midst of the Theatre of Pompey' that a celebrated brawl took place between two secretaries, George of Trebizond and Poggio Bracciolini, in 1452.[12] The official dress worn by the secretaries was until 1487 the same as that of the chamber clerks.

The secretaries prepared, engrossed, and dispatched the class of papal letters known as briefs, using for the purpose from the late fourteenth century onwards a new papal privy signet ('the fisherman's ring'). In the earlier fifteenth century

---

[11] D'Amico, *Renaissance Humanism in Papal Rome* (Baltimore and London, 1983), pp. 252–3; Partner, *Papal State*, p. 205. See also, Kraus, 'Die Sekretäre Pius II', pp. 25–80; id., 'Secretarius und Sekretariat: Der Ursprung der Institution des Staatssekretariats und ihr Einfluß auf die Entwicklung moderner Regierungsformen in Europa', *Röm.Quart.* 55 (1960), 43–84; T. Frenz, 'Die verloren Brevenregister 1421–1527', *Röm.Quart.* 57 (1977), 354–65; id., 'Das Eindringen' (1973), 287–418, and (1974), 384–506; id., 'Armarium xxxix, vol. 11 im Vatikanischen Archiv: Ein Formelbuch für Breven aus der Zeit Julius II.', in *Hoberg Festschrift*, i (1979), 197–213; Schwarz, *Die Organisation*, pp. 60, 112, 180; Pitz, 111–12, 173 ff. The bull setting up the college of secretaries is in *Magnum Bullarium Romanum*, i (Luxemburg, 1727), 441–5.

[12] Von Hofmann, *Forschungen*, ii. 155–62.

these briefs were of a mainly political nature, and it is with this type of correspondence, usually executed in a humanist script, that the secretaries are most frequently associated. But these political functions brought them little in the way of fees, and their activities were far from being limited to them. Their aim, like that of all curial officers, was to increase the scope of their activities in ways that gave them a bigger share of the taxes from petitioners.

The secretaries often intervened in the concession of graces which, because of their personal standing with the pope, they could secure for a supplicant when other curialists could not. Such concessions often had to do with matters which the chancery could not obtain, or had been granted in a deficient form, or with petitions made verbally and without written supplication. All these the pope could grant in person and by word of mouth at the instance of a secretary.[13] The grants could be executed as bulls passing 'through the secret chamber' or as briefs 'without signature' (meaning that these briefs did not pass through the referendaries of the signatura). The number of petitions thus granted through the secretaries was large, and from Nicholas V onwards (1447-55) there were complaints laid against the practice. A report of the trial of Bartolomé Flores, the domestic secretary of Alexander VI sentenced for corruption in 1497, claimed that in his five year period of office as domestic secretary he had issued some 3,000 briefs of this kind. Proposals for reform of the curia mentioned both the improper intervention of the secretaries in handling petitions which should have gone to the Signatura in the normal way, and the arbitrary and excessive fees charged by the secretaries.[14]

In everything which concerns the secretaries the importance of the reorganization of 1487 is capital. Before Nicholas V the only distinction among secretaries was between those fully participating in the revenues and those who were supernumerary. The latter were termed so either because they had been granted an expectancy of a secretary's place which had not yet materialized, or because they were ambassadors or councillors representing foreign powers, who had been given the title as an honorary distinction.

From the time of Nicholas V there were one or two 'domestic'

13 D'Amico, *Renaissance Humanism*, p. 26; J. Burckardi, *Liber Notarum* (RRIISS xxxii/1), ii. 54-6, 114; Von Hofmann, *Forschungen*, ii. 124, 159.

14 M. Tangl, *Die päpstlichen Kanzleiordnungen von 1200-1500* (Innsbruck, 1894), 404; Von Hofmann, *Forschungen*, i. 155-62; ii. 158-9, 242.

secretaries who were especially privileged household companions of the pope, serving continually in the Vatican Palace. The first true domestic secretary was Pietro de Noxeto, the former companion of Aeneas Sylvius Piccolomini. Pietro, like Aeneas Sylvius, obtained power and influence under Nicholas V, although unlike Aeneas he did not manage to keep it. Calixtus III (1455-8) reduced the number of participating secretaries to six, or eight including the domestic secretaries.

The power and influence enjoyed by the domestic secretaries forced the rest of the secretariat to change its nature. After Pius II not only did the political influence of the ordinary participating secretaries drop sharply, but their work changed. In effect they received financial compensation for their loss of political status. The first stage was to give such secretaries more business in the form of briefs 'with the signed petition enclosed' (breve supplicatione interclusa); this change took place under Paul II (1464-71). It greatly increased secretarial activity, but made it far more concerned with the routine bestowal of benefices. Under Sixtus IV secretarial control of the secret bulls was much diminished by the setting up of the abbreviator de curia, who had charges of the drafting of secret bulls and of those which went 'through the palace and through the chamber'.

The separation of the office of secretaries with confidential political functions from the rest was formalized by Innocent VIII when he set up the college of thirty secretaries in 1487. At the same time Innocent raised a large sum of money by the sale of twenty-four new secretaryships; the bull mentions a total purchase price for these jobs of 62,400 gold florins.[15] The secretaries were henceforth authorized to resell their office on payment of a resignation fee of 100 florins. New incomes were assured to the new college from taxes on officials in the papal state, so as to assure the profitability of the investment for the purchaser.

From this time onwards only the domestic secretaryships can be treated as important political posts; the other secretaries became mere administrative officials. Powerful political figures often purchased secretaryships (for example, Gianbattista Ferrari, the datarius and one of the most prominent men under Alexander VI), but these were investments. The venal secretarial posts were no longer the springboards for political power that the earlier secretaryships had been. The

[15] Magnum Bullarium Romanum, i. 445.

new arrangements favoured secretaries who had been sent away from the Roman court on mission; they were now enabled to draw the full secretaries' portion for a year, and this aspect of the 1487 reform was praised by Giacomo Gherardi (at that time a secretary away on mission).

The emergence of the domestic secretaries and of the signaturae showed the ability of powerful household officials to reshape the old curial structure in order to respond to changes in the internal balance of power. An even more striking instance was the emergence of the dataria. Earlier popes had managed their household finances through secret treasurers whose relations with the rest of the papal financial organization had been floating and vague.[16] The sources from which these secret accounts drew their main money supply tended, naturally, to be offices filled by men who were also the confidential servants of the pope. Such an office was that of the registrar of apostolic letters, which controlled the taxes for the authentication and registration of bulls, and usually transferred the monies to the secret accounts. By the time of Eugenius IV confidential chamberlains also received monies from such sources as special compositions for spiritual graces, and payments for the sale of offices. An early account of this kind, belonging to a confidential chamberlain, is that kept by Francesco Dal Legname of Padua early in the pontificate of Eugenius IV.

All these monies flowed into secret accounts kept by the secret chamberlains, over which the apostolic chamber exercised only a very general form of audit and control. Similar accounts to those of Francesco Dal Legname were later kept by Bartolomé Regas for Calixtus III and by a papal nephew for Pius II. Under the latter pope for the first time these financial functions began to fall under the influence of the datarius, an official whose nominal duties lay in the chancery, to inscribe a date upon petitions which had been conceded. The earlier datarius had not been a household official, but his duties brought him into close contact both with the petitioners and with other key officials such as the masters of the register of petitions and the referendaries.

Using the central position which they occupied in the granting of papal favours, successive datarii made themselves into the official with whom a petitioner had to come to terms, if a money payment was going to be due for the concession of a

---

[16] Partner, 'Camera Papae'.

grace. At the same time, by means which are very obscure, the datarii intruded themselves into the financial business of selling offices, taking the place in the chain which had previously belonged to one of the secret chamberlains. The secret treasury administered previously by the secret chamberlains continued to exist, but was downgraded to a cash account which drew upon the dataria for its funds. The latter took business both from the apostolic chamber and from the penitentiary; petitioners who might formerly have made a composition with one of these offices now made them with the dataria.

The dataria represented a rather casual combination of administrative functions, but one which proved to have great potential power, perhaps above all because it came into existence at the moment when the sale of offices was becoming one of the linchpins of papal finance. At the end of the fifteenth century the datarius was a powerful but still much-resented figure. He was not yet the head of a major organization, but still only one of a number of papal canon lawyers who had thrust themselves between the pope and his petitioners. His function as the salesman of papal offices gave him great advantages. The big loans which the papal government launched through the sale of new offices in the early sixteenth century made the officer responsible for these funding operations into one of the great men of the papal court. The dataria lost its shadowy outlines and became a recognized and organized government office, which from 1517 onwards had its own rights over the papal registry of bulls.[17]

Thorny legal questions could emerge at any stage of the examination and decision of a petition submitted to the pope, and also during the preparation of the bull or brief in response to a petition which had been granted.[18] If it had been granted in a legally deficient form, the defect could sometimes be supplied by modification of the clauses; the addition of these *clausulae* could add a formidable supplement to the costs of securing a papal grant. The matter was often raised in discussion of desirable reforms of procedure in the curia. The organization of papal judges to deal with such matters was complex. Jurisdiction lay in many cases either with the referendaries who sat in the signatura or in the 'audientia litterarum contradictarum'. The most ancient and distinguished body of papal judges was that of the rota, composed of the auditors of the sacred palace.

[17] N. Storti, *La storia e il diritto della Dataria Apostolica dalle origini alle nostre giorni* (Naples, 1969), 77; N. del Re, *La curia romana* (Rome, 1970), 443–4.
[18] For the *registratores* see M. Haren's Introduction to *CPL* xv (1976), 18–38.

Cases were frequently referred to them under a papal commission, although they also possessed the kind of jurisdiction technically referred to as 'ordinary'. The apostolic chamber had an auditor to hear cases arising out of its work, or which came in appeal from the papal state. This was one of the most important judicial posts, often going to a lawyer of high professional renown.

II

The pope's servants were also employed on matters which could take them far from the Roman court. The papal state had its own bureaucracy, which was closely entwined in many ways with the staff of the Roman court. It was divided into provinces, some of which were classed as 'legations'. The cardinal legates who headed these legations cannot, at this stage of their history, be accurately described as civil servants. In the late fifteenth century the cardinals were still calling for an autonomous role in the government of the papal state, and they made this wish known in some of the electoral capitulations required of popes at their election.[19] Not all areas of the papal state were continuously under the control of cardinal legates, however: some were ruled by rectors or governors who answered directly to the pope. Moreover, from the early sixteenth century onwards, cardinal legates began to become absentees, exercising their office through vice-legates or governors while they remained in Rome.

On the whole, the top administrative personnel of the papal state below the rank of cardinal legate were drawn from the pool of officials in Rome. The lion's share of these appointments went to those in the service of the apostolic chamber, the main administrative organ dealing with the papal state. The senior posts available were those of governor, vice-legate, or treasurer (the last went almost invariably to someone from the financial offices, or to a lay banker). But apostolic secretaries were also sometimes chosen for administrative posts in the papal state,

[19] Partner, *Papal State*, pp. 161–86; id., *The Lands of St Peter: The Papal State in the Middle Ages and the Early Renaissance* (London, Berkeley, LA, 1972), 425–40; id., 'Legations', *New Catholic Encyclopedia* (1967). For the electoral capitulations see J. Lulvès, 'Päpstliche Wahlkapitulationen', *Quellen*, 12 (1909), 212–35; J. A. Watt, 'The Constitutional Law of the College of Cardinals: Hostiensis to Johannes Andreae', *Mediaeval Studies*, 33 (1971), 127–57; U. Mannucci, 'Le capitolazioni del conclave di Sisto IV, 1471', *Röm.Quart.* 29 (1915), 73*–90*.

and some appointments were made from officials in other parts of the curia. The key factor in papal state appointments was the grant of leave of absence from the Roman post, sometimes with loss of its emoluments during absence, sometimes not. One of the most important temporal power posts was that of Governor of Rome, which possessed some jurisdiction over curialists, and required the holder to maintain a confidential relationship with the pope.[20]

But the number of papal state posts open to the industrious and rapacious curialist was large. The chamber clerk Giovanni Tommaso Scioni of Rieti, for example, was the holder of half a dozen important curial posts between the pontificates of John XXIII and Eugenius IV. Not content with these, he not only leased pasture lands which he owned in the Viterbo area to the papal superintendent of pasture (*doganerius*) but in 1425 did not scruple to get the office of pasture superintendent for himself. He was treasurer of the patrimony of St Peter in Tuscia at the time, and thus was in two ways the official controller of the area he had a personal interest in exploiting.

Curialists could be sent elsewhere than to the papal state. Almost any senior papal servant could be sent to Catholic powers inside or outside Italy as a papal envoy: secretaries perhaps had an advantage in obtaining such appointments. Papal practice in these matters was in a state of transition. The dispatch of the legate *de latere* with extensive powers of negotiation and jurisdiction was quite possible until the sixteenth century was far advanced. Such a legate would normally be a cardinal. But the dispatch of a papal nuncio, an envoy of lesser status and usually possessing lesser negotiating powers, was less costly and often more convenient. The office of papal collector, a financial official sent out to parts of Catholic Europe to collect the dues of the apostolic chamber, was far from obsolete, although the sums collected were much smaller than earlier. In the later Middle Ages these collectors had generally been drawn from the staff of the apostolic chamber. But in the later fifteenth and the sixteenth centuries the collectors were drawn from a wide circle of curialists, and they had not necessarily had much to do with financial business before their appointment.[21]

20 N. del Re, *Monsignore Governatore di Roma* (Rome, 1972).

21 For the English collectors see M. Monaco, *Il 'De Officio Collectoris in Regno Angliae' di Pietro Griffi da Pisa (1469-1516)* (Rome, 1973), 200–22, and W. E. Lunt, *The Financial Relations of the Papacy with England, 1327-1534* (Cambridge, Mass., 1962), 693–713.

Probably the most frequent title under which clerks were sent as papal representatives was that of commissioner, *commissarius*. The legal idea of a commissioner derived in church law from the delegation of jurisdiction from a superior to an inferior; such commissions were much used in papal jurisprudence. The commissioner was an institution of most late medieval countries, including England, though neither in England nor among students of the papacy has it received the attention it deserves from scholars.[22] In the fifteenth century the commissioner could be a papal officer who accompanied papal armies as a political and sometimes also a financial supervisor. Similar officials were appointed to the armies of Venice and elsewhere.[23] But the commissioner could be appointed to other administrative and financial special missions, particularly in the papal state. This use of the commission for judicial, military, and administrative purposes can be paralleled elsewhere, for example in England; it also foreshadows later developments in France and Prussia.

The appointment of the commissioner with the powers of rector in the papal state is a form of delegated power to be found from the time of Martin V onwards. Often the commission applied to a single aspect of government, such as settling a dispute between two cities; commissioners could also conduct special inquiries such as that in the city of Cesena after it passed from the rule of the Malatesta family to that of the church. An extension of the same principle was the annual appointment of clerks of the chamber to a judicial travelling assize of the papal state, a practice which began in 1506. These commissioners, often appointed to exact particular

---

[22] See, in general, *Historical Essays of Otto Hintze*, ed. F. Gilbert (New York, 1975), 267–301. The chancery regulations of Martin V refer to commissioners in the context of delegated jurisdiction: Von Ottenthal, *Päpst, Kanzleiregeln*, p. 230.

[23] For papal commissioners see G.-L. Lesage, 'La Titulaire des envoyés pontificaux sous Pie II (1458-1464)', *Mélanges*, 58 (1941-6), 206–47, at 229, 244-5; J. Petersohn, *Ein Diplomat des Quattrocento: Angelo Geraldini (1422-1486)* (Tübingen, 1985), 34-5, 92-3; C. Penuti, 'Aspetti della politica economica nello stato pontificio sul finire del '500: Le "visite economiche" di Sisto V', *Ann.Ist.Ital.-germ.Tr.*, 2 (1976), 183–202; Prodi, *Il sovrano pontefico*, p. 112. For Venetian procurators M. Mallett, 'Venice and its Condottieri, 1404-54', *Renaissance Venice*, pp. 121–45. Giovanni Vitelleschi as papal army commissioner, Vat. Arch., Arm. 39, vol. 7a, fo. 101, and see Partner, *Lands*, p. 406. For procedure, M. Sciambra, G. Valentini, and I. Parino, *Il 'liber brevium' di Callisto III* (Palermo, 1968), 116, commissioners sent to collect a crusading tenth in 1457, 'si presentino coi conti, come sempre i commissari'.

taxes, became such a normal feature of papal state government that common usage began to apply the term to them
rather than to any other commissioners. But, as so often
occurs, the commissioners began to give rise to just the sort of
abuse they had originally been appointed to stop, and the institution had to be overhauled in the second half of the sixteenth
century.[24]

The protean nature of the commissioner's office, and the
frequency with which a single officer might be given commissions, are illustrated by an anecdote related about Andrea de'
Spiriti, a chamber clerk referred to above. He was said 'to have
been sent as commissioner to the provinces, regions, and
places of Italy, to the Signoria of Venice, to the Duke of Ferrara
. . . to the Emperor, to the King of Hungary, etc. So that I saw
and counted about fifty papal bulls, all commissions.'[25]

Yet a further area in which papal commissioners were employed was that of building and planning, a function of such
papal agents from the time that Martin V and Eugenius IV used
them to look after the repairs of the Roman churches. A prominent later example was Nicholas V's trusted confidential
agent, Nello da Bologna, who began by supervising the logistic
arrangements for the Jubilee of 1450, and was responsible for
the Roman building and town-planning projects of the rest of
the pontificate: a similar function was executed for Sixtus IV
by Jeronimo de' Giganti.[26] These officers were, of course,
laymen and not clergy.

The College of Cardinals cannot be excluded from a review
of the Roman court. The cardinalate was the summit of all
curial ambition. The cardinals, especially in the papal
Consistory, acted not only as a papal council or senate, but also

[24] The reform of the papal state commissioners, 29 May 1567, in P. A.
de Vecchis, Collectio Constitutionum Chirographorum et Brevium (Rome, 1732),
i. 88-9. The earlier institution of an eyre of chamber clerks, 1506, in Magnum
Bullarium Romanum, i (1727), 473-4. For commissions authorizing chamber
officials to make compositions for arrears and settlements with persons guilty of
criminal offences, see that granted to Ludovico Agnelli and Niccolò Calcaneo,
10 June 1482, in J. Schlecht, Andrea Zamometić und der Basler Konzilversuch
vom Jahre 1482 (Paderborn, 1903), 124*-5*. For Cesena see I. Robertson, 'The
Return of Cesena to the Direct Dominion of the Church after the Death of
Malatesta Novello', Studi Romagnoli, 16 (1965), 123-61, at p. 146.

[25] Cronache e Statuti della città di Viterbo (Florence, 1872), 102 n.

[26] For Nello da Bologna, see A. Gottlob, Aus der Camera apostolica des
15 Jahrhunderts (Innsbruck, 1889), 40-1; G. Burroughs, 'Below the Angel: An
Urbanistic project in the Rome of Nicholas V', JWCI 45 (1982), 94-124, at pp. 98,
111. For Jeronimo de' Giganti see E. Müntz, Les Arts à la cour des papes
pendant le XVe et le XVIe siècles, iii (Paris, 1882), 180.

as the most important committee for the conferment of papal benefices. For every 'consistorial benefice' there was a *cardinalis ponens*, who proposed the successful candidate and was awarded a fee (*propina*) for his pains. A further fee had to be paid to the cardinal's secretary, and this additional heavy tax was much resented.[27] Not surprisingly the post of cardinal's secretary, though a private and not a papal one, was a frequent stepping-stone to major office in the papal court.

The College of Cardinals had much in common with the other colleges of papal officials in the Roman court, but it preceded them historically, and, indeed, probably served to some extent as their model. Like the other colleges, the cardinals had a machinery for dividing the corporate revenues which accrued to them. The most important income was their half-share in income from 'common services' charged on bishoprics and major abbeys conferred through Rome. The amount of this share depended on the number of cardinals resident in Rome at the time of the 'division'. Appointment as legate *de latere* (which normally attracted a salary) lost the legate the right to share in the divisions. To administer the finances of the college there was a cardinal chamberlain; under him a clerk of the College of Cardinals was responsible for the paperwork to be executed with the officials of the apostolic chamber.[28] The post of clerk to the college often served as a springboard for a career in the financial administration. The most striking example is that of Leo X's main financial official, Cardinal Francesco Armellini, who became clerk of the college when already a chamber clerk.

The constitutional position of the cardinals was intermediate between the oligarchic aspirations they had shown in the later Middle Ages and the quasi-bureaucratic position which they came to occupy after the Counter-Reformation. Spasmodic attempts to control the papal monarchy by constitutional pressure were made by means of the electoral pacts or capitulations imposed upon several fifteenth-century popes at the time of their electoral conclave. Eugenius IV, Pius II, Paul II,

[27] Von Hofmann, *Forschungen*, i. 263.

[28] See A. V. Antonovics, 'A Late Fifteenth-Century Division Register of the College of Cardinals', *PBSR* 35 (1967), 87–101; Baumgarten, *Untersuchungen und Urkunden*. An example of a career apparently based on tenure of this office is that of Enrico Bruni, later apostolic secretary, treasurer-general, and Archbishop of Taranto. Paolo Emilio Cesi was another holder of the office to become a cardinal, but it is doubtful if its tenure was of much importance to his career, which was based on family influence in the curia. See below.

and Sixtus IV accepted such pacts, but none observed them, and one or two repudiated them.[29] Office-holding and patronage were mentioned in these electoral pacts; in particular the cardinals showed their dissatisfaction with the way in which the popes used patronage powers in the papal state. The electoral pact imposed upon Sixtus IV required him to share nominations to papal state appointments between his own dependants and those of the cardinals. There was also a demand that each cardinal be conceded the control of a papal state stronghold, preferably one which would also be useful as a summer residence.

The tendency was not, however, for cardinals to increase their constitutional power, but rather for their role to be reduced to that of great pensioned courtiers. This was especially noticeable in the demands, made in electoral pacts from 1458 onwards, that cardinals who failed to obtain 4,000 gold florins a year from the combined revenues of their benefices and of their share in the divisions of the College of Cardinals should be paid a papal pension of 100 florins a month. By the time of Sixtus IV these pensions were paid to eight or nine cardinals, that is to say to about a third of the number of cardinals normally in residence at the papal court.

Cardinals drew pensions not only from the pope but from many other sources. As 'cardinal protectors', representing the interests of a town, government (whether Italian or outside Italy), or religious order at the Roman court, cardinals attracted other payments. Finally, every cardinal expected to receive a large income from absentee tenure of benefices held by him in plurality. Such benefices could include bishoprics held in administration and abbeys held on a temporary basis *in commendam*. A cardinal could be authorized to impetrate for a number of benefices up to a maximum of several thousand florins annually, in a given church province. However, cardinals often found it hard to acquire legal title to benefices of the full value which they had been allowed to petition for, and even when they had title, they often found it difficult or even impossible to recover the revenues due to them. An easier course was to charge with

---

[29] P. Partner, 'The "Budget" of the Roman Church in the Renaissance Period', in E. F. Jacob (ed.), *Italian Renaissance Studies: A Tribute to the Late C. M. Ady* (1960), 256–78, at pp. 263–4; id., 'Papal Financial Policy', 56. For the context, H. Jedin, 'Vorschläge und Entwürfe zur Kardinalsreform', in *Kirche des Glaubens Kirche der Geschichte*, ii (Freiburg, Basle, and Vienna, 1966), 118–47; D. S. Chambers, 'The Economic Predicament of Renaissance Cardinals', *Studies in Medieval and Renaissance History*, 3 (1966), 289–313.

pensions the bishoprics or benefices which they resigned.[30]

The claims of the cardinals to some form of collegiate sharing with the pope in the government of the church under divine law distinguished them from all other papal officers. During the vacancies of the Holy See which followed the death of a pope, this collegiate right took a visible and practical form. The cardinals of this period cannot be treated simply as bureaucrats. Only a minority, for example, can be said to have led careers in the Roman court which led to their promotion to cardinal's rank. Of 285 cardinals living between 1417 and 1527, 110 instances (39 per cent) can be found of clerks who might be said to have had a career in the Roman court before the cardinalate. Reginald Gregoire, examining a rather shorter period, found the much lower proportion of 25 per cent among the cardinals of the period 1417–1503.[31]

This state of affairs may be compared with the earlier one of the Avignonese period, when only 32 among the 134 promotions to the cardinalate (23 per cent) were from officials of the curia, and with the later period of 1593–1667, when 163 promotions among 276 (59 per cent) were from serving curialists.[32] Only in relatively modern times—and then for a restricted period—was the cardinalate quite definitely a career for curial bureaucrats. In the period 1846–78 124 cardinals had had curial careers (66 per cent) as compared with 65 who had not.[33] The secular trend in a wide and general sense was towards the bureaucratization of the cardinals, but although the trend is visible in the Renaissance period, it still had far to go.

III

The number of effective working officials in the Roman court is

[30] McClung Hallman, *Italian Cardinals*, pp. 38–46. For the earlier period D. Brosius, 'Die Pfründen des Enea Silvio Piccolomini', *Quellen*, 54 (1974), 271–327, gives a good idea of 15th-cent. practice.

[31] R. Gregoire, 'Il sacro collegio cardinalizio dall'elezione di Sisto IV all'elezione di Giulio II (1417–1513)' [sic, for 1471–1503?], *Società Savonese di Storia Patria: Atti e Memorie*, NS, 24 (1988), 209–32, at p. 229.

[32] Guillemain, *La Cour pontificale*, p. 196; P. J. A. N. Rietbergen, 'Pausen, Prelaten, Bureaucraten: Aspekten van de geschiedenis van het Pauschap en de Pauselijke Staat in de 17e Eeuw', doctoral thesis (Nijmegen, 1983), 101. A section of this thesis has been published, 'Problems of Government: Some Observations upon a Sixteenth-Century "Istruttione per li governatori delle città e luoghi dello stato ecclesiastico"', *Mededelingen van het Nederlands Instituut te Rome*, NS, 6 (1979), 173–201.

[33] C. Weber, *Kardinäle und Prälaten in den letzten Jahrzehnten des Kirchenstaates*, ii. 617–19.

hard to calculate. The commonly quoted figure of 2,000 venal offices open to purchase under Pope Leo X (1513–21) gives no idea of the number of officers with active duties, and since even offices with active duties could be held in plurality, there is little doubt that the figure multiplies the real number of officers several times. The traffic in offices which changed hands by resignation was intense. Fewer than a third of the offices were vacated on account of the death of the holder, and there is some reason to think that the average tenure of an office in the late fifteenth or early sixteenth century was about 7.5 years. An officer who remained in an office until his death extinguished its value for his heirs; a more prudent management of the office as an investment was to sell it during life. An office could also be vacated on account of promotion to another office or dignity legally incompatible with it: typical instances were those of promotion to a bishopric or to the cardinalate.

It is possible to make conjectures about the number of officials from the number of offices. In the first half of the fifteenth century the total number of offices was probably below 500, and the total number of officers, because of absenteeism and pluralism, somewhat smaller. After the creation of the big *vacabili* colleges of lower priced offices (100 *sollicitatores* in 1482, 104 *collectores taxae plumbi* in 1497, 101 *scriptores archivii* in 1507, 141 *praesidentes Ripae* in 1509) the number of offices shot up very steeply, but the number of effective officials did not increase in the same proportion. For the early sixteenth century we can estimate the stable population of Roman court officers by using dataria figures which give the number of transactions in offices and the number of occasions on which offices were vacated by the death of the office-holder. If we apply the standard death rate generally used by demographers for comparable populations to the number of such deaths, we can get some idea of the actual number of officers as opposed to the number of official posts.

A document drawn up in the dataria records the traffic in offices between November 1503 and July 1514.[34] It lists 336 *resignationes*, 224 *vacationes* (i.e. offices vacated through the death of the holder), and 45 *promotiones*. During this period the number of offices was rising from about 700 at the beginning to about 960 at the end. We know from figures gathered from a large number of papal appointments by Von Hofmann, and covering the longer period of 1455 to 1521, that the death rate

[34] Von Hofmann, Forschungen, ii. 175–6.

among papal officers in 1503–14 was somewhat above normal; we may therefore adjust the standard death rate upwards slightly. If we apply to the annual mortality of 21.3 officers in 1503–14 a standard death rate of 38 per thousand, we may conclude that the stable population of officers in the Roman court in that period was about 560, including absentee sine-curists like the *praesidentes Ripae*.

We can only guess at the stable population of Roman court officers in the earlier fifteenth century, when the proportion of pluralists and sinecurists was much lower. Perhaps the total number of officers was below 500. This, if it was the figure, is still substantially above the numbers in the Avignonese papal court of the fourteenth century, when pluralism was lower and absenteeism rare; at that time the number of administrative officers varied between 250 and 300.[35] Thus the number of officers may have doubled between the fourteenth and the sixteenth centuries: a steep increase, but not so large as that which historians have sometimes loosely conjectured, failing to distinguish between the number of offices and the number of officers.

We can thus arrive at some conjectural figures for the number of papal administrative officials, and we must, as we do this, distinguish the latter from the papal household or *familia* with which they overlapped. There can easily be confusion between the two, because when contemporaries referred to the *corte romana* or the 'palace', they often had in mind not the administrative services but the *familia*. Among the domestic prelates of the household there were likely to be several key figures of the administration: the domestic secretaries, the papal treasurer, the datarius, and perhaps other personally trusted papal servants who might be secretaries or chamber clerks. Besides the domestic prelates the household contained other 'lords' and also a swarm of chamberlains (*cubicularii*) and stewards, and to each of these might be attached a little herd of followers. The whole papal household numbered perhaps 150 persons in the mid fifteenth century, but had increased to 600–700 under the Medici popes of the early sixteenth. But though the *familia* was located in the papal palace, it was neither the *palazzo* nor the *curia*. For example, the secretaries were guaranteed a common room in the *palazzo* by the bull of 1487, but they were not treated as part of the papal *familia*; this privilege was reserved for the confidential or domestic secretaries.

---

[35] Guillemain, *La Cour pontificale*, pp. 444–9.

IV

Having acquired some idea of what the papal administration was, it may be useful to ask which elements in the papal administration might be described as in some sense modernizing. Max Weber's philosophy of history, as applicable to Western Europe and North America, pivoted on the idea of a rationalizing mentality which imposed bureaucracy on government, thus moving it from the traditional to the modern form. We do not have to accept all his ideas, but they have proved valuable in helping historians to compare social organizations and governmental systems. In considering how his theories can be applied to practice it is necessary to distinguish between means and ends. Governments did not use bureaucratic methods so as to be more rationally consistent, as some historians have implied. The aim of bureaucratic government, as Weber frequently emphasized, was to exercise power more effectively over the subjects.

The papal bureaucracy of this period owed its development not to the desire of the popes to impose a rational rule of law, but to their desire to interpret canon law in a way which would enlarge their discretionary powers in dealing with petitions. Some conciliarist canon lawyers of the late fifteenth and early sixteenth centuries, like Cardinal Giovanni Antonio di Sangiorgio and his pupil, the chamber clerk Giovanni Gozzadini, objected strongly to the arbitrary elements in Renaissance papal jurisdiction. But their objections went unheard, because the interests opposed to reform were so powerful. The administrative changes in papal ways of dealing with petitions had been accompanied by a shift in the distribution of power which conferred new authority on certain officers, such as the datarius, the referendaries, the secret chamberlains, and gave them the means to get new riches.

If we see papal bureaucracy as a way by which the late medieval and Renaissance popes sought to impose their power over the church, and to fight the intrusive claims of kings and princes, it becomes easier to understand, even if its supposed modernity becomes thereby a little questionable. It has been remarked that the papal court was modern in its high degree of literate expression, in its orderly (or supposedly orderly) system of hearing lawsuits in appeal, in its exact definition of departmental administration, in its insistence on academic qualifications for some officials, and in its denying privileged status to officials of noble lineage (though the formulae did make noble lineage a ground for privilege in the conferment of benefices).

But there were some private and (in the phraseology of Max Weber) patrimonial elements in the Roman court which pointed in a different direction. For example, the secretaries and chamber clerks, like many other papal officials, relied to a large extent on the fees paid them by supplicants. Apostolic scriptors swore no oath of loyalty to the pope and received no fixed stipend, relying on fees paid them for executing documents in their own private offices. Above all, the sale of offices was a practice incompatible with modern bureaucracy. Venality tended to convert office into what Max Weber termed a 'benefice'. In addition, a particular papal institution (also noticed by Weber) which had no direct equivalent in lay governments was that of the papal cardinal-nephew endowed with vast administrative powers.

Whether we can say that such papal administrations were modern, or more modern than earlier ones—and it is the comparative use of the adjective which is critical—is a thorny question. One difficulty is the extreme laxity with which most historians have had to treat these categories, in order to make them make sense. For example, most of the *ancien régime* governments sold government offices, and in France the commanding heights of administration were still largely in the hands of people who had purchased their offices as late as the time of the French Revolution.[36]

Yet the existence of venality is only one factor in the equation. In most governments, including the papal one, what has been said of English early modern offices obtained: 'Sale, or rather purchase, was only one of several ways of entering office, and it seldom operated in isolation from any of the other factors: patronage, family connexion, special abilities and qualifications, reward for merit or service.'[37]

[36] C. B. A. Behrens, *Society, Government and the Enlightenment: The Experiences of Eighteenth-Century France and Prussia* (New York and London, 1985), 173-4. See also Hintze's comment on venality of office in France, *Soziologie und Geschichte*, pp. 87-9, which seems to be contradicted by R. Mousnier, *La Venalité des offices sous Henri IV et Louis XIII* (Paris, 1971), 310, 439. On this topic the remarks of W. Fischer and P. Lundgren, in C. Tilly (ed.), *The Formation of National States in Western Europe* (Princeton, 1975), 497, seem to me to be rather disingenuous.

[37] G. Aylmer, *The King's Servants* (London, 1961), 237. For late medieval secretaries in England and Scotland, see Partner, 'William of Wykeham and the Historians', in Custance (ed.), *Winchester College: Sixth-Centenary Essays* (Oxford, 1982), 6-7; L. J. Macfarlane, *William Elphinstone and the Kingdom of Scotland* (Aberdeen, 1985), 407 ff.

The presence of what is usually thought of as modernity in the papal administration, and the dangers of assigning modern qualities to it uncritically, can be found in the history of the secretaries. The secretary was a general phenomenon of late medieval and Renaissance government. From the mid fourteenth century onwards these trusted confidential servants bypassed the cumbersome procedures of the medieval chanceries and transmitted their royal masters' commands in new forms which differed greatly from the normal chancery ones. The history of the office showed the kind of discontinuity later to be found in that of the papal secretaries. In England William of Wykeham, for example, was royal secretary and keeper of the privy seal in the mid fourteenth century, but the history of the privy seal soon branched off from that of the secretaries. There was similarly uneven development of the secretarial office in the late medieval kingdom of Scotland.

There are many common characteristics in the way the secretarial office developed in different parts of Europe. In England, in France, in Aragon, and in the kingdom of Naples, the secretary was a powerful new official, usually with some connection with the household. The fifteenth-century royal secretaries in Naples were organized in a very similar way to the papal secretaries in Rome, including the two domestic secretaries; and in Naples also honorary secretarial posts were created for distinguished humanists.[38]

If the modernization of government really is some sort of recognizable process, then the question of the continuity of development of the key modernizing offices is bound to present itself. In the papal case the first century of the history of the secretaries shows considerable continuity.[39] They were the immediate agents of the papal will; the duty of the secretary was to accompany the pope and to accept letters from him wherever he was and at whatever time he chose. There were, as has already been indicated, important changes in the mid

---

[38] See A. Ryder, The Kingdom of Naples under Alfonso the Magnanimous: The Making of a Modern State (Oxford, 1976), 218–37.

[39] Kraus, 'Secretarius und Sekretariat' (1960); id., Das päpstliche Staatssekretariat unter Urban VIII. 1623-1644 (Rome, Freiburg, and Vienna, 1964); P. Richard, 'Origines et développement de la Secrétairerie d'État Apostolique (1417–1823)', Revue d'Histoire Ecclésiastique, 11 (1910), 56–72, 505–29, 728–54; R. Ançel, 'Le Secrétairerie pontificale sous Paul IV', Revue des Questions Historiques, NS, 30 (1906) [vol. 79], 408–70; K. M. Färber, 'Der Brevensekretär Cesare Glorierio: ein Beitrag zur Geschichte der kurialen Sekretariate in der zweiten Hälfte des 16. Jahrhunderts', Quellen, 67 (1987), 221–81.

fifteenth century. The 'participating' secretaries, who until
that time had shared the duties and the fees more or less
equally, were pushed to the margin of political influence by the
exclusive right of access to the ruler which had been gained by
the domestic secretaries. Paul II (1464–71) notoriously refused
to see the participating secretaries until some weeks after his
accession.

The way was then open for the big increase in routine work
accorded the participating secretaries, and for the setting up
of the college of secretaries in 1487, which formalized the distinction between the political role of the domestic secretaries
and the administrative role of the participating ones. But the
appearance of the venal college of secretaries in 1487 is by no
means the only hiatus in the history of the office. Had the
domestic secretaries remained the effective political agents of
the papal will, we would perhaps be able to talk of a process of
steady modernization in government. This was not the case: the
office of domestic secretary was destined, in the long run, to
suffer the same fate of shunting from the main lines of power
and access to power that had befallen the participating secretaries earlier.

Under Leo X the major change was towards the drafting and
engrossing of a very large part of the correspondence of the
Holy See in Italian instead of in Latin. This applied especially
to the correspondence and instructions given to the papal
envoys, the *nunzi*, but also to a wide variety of other correspondence and instruments. The changes demanded an
increased number of papal servants to produce the minutes
and final copies of these vernacular documents. None of these
new officials were, in the curial sense of the expression,
secretaries: that is, they did not belong to the college of secretaries, nor did they possess a secretary's *locus*. On the one hand
the pope's cousin, Cardinal Giulio de' Medici, who was also
vice-chancellor, supervised a large amount of the diplomatic
correspondence, though in his capacity as a Medici prince
rather than in his capacity as vice-chancellor. His chief execu-
tant for this correspondence was usually Pietro Ardinghelli,
who is often called a papal secretary by contemporaries, but
never held such a title. On the other hand Bernardo Dovizi,
another Medici creature, was made papal treasurer and
cardinal, and was given a further part of the Italian correspondence to execute at the orders of the pope himself. Neither
Dovizi nor his assistants were termed 'secretaries', though in
some respects they fulfilled this function. Finally, two 'domestic'

secretaries (Pietro Bembo and Jacopo Sadoleto) were appointed for the Latin correspondence of secret bulls and briefs.

The correspondence run by Cardinal Giulio de' Medici pointed towards the development, later in the century, of the secretariat of the papal cardinal-nephew (though Giulio was cousin and not nephew). When Giulio himself became Pope Clement VII in 1523, though the general shape of the Italian diplomatic correspondence was retained, the means of executing it were modified. Sadoleto was reappointed domestic secretary, but to his duties were added those of carrying out much of the Italian diplomatic correspondence in the vulgar tongue with the nunzi. That the chief minister of Clement VII was in effect Gian Matteo Giberti, under Clement the papal datarius, but formerly the secretary of Cardinal Giulio de' Medici, had other effects for the papal diplomatic correspondence. Giberti's letters in his own name, directed both to papal nunzi and to foreign princes, form an integral part of the papal correspondence.

These discontinuities in the history of the papal secretariat are minimized by its historians, but they are of the first import- ance in assessing its early modern growth.[40] If there was a revolution in government in the papal secretariat of the six- teenth century, it is to be connected, not with the impersonal power of the papacy, but with the change to the use of Italian in papal political correspondence, and with the power assumed by the papal relatives in controlling this correspondence. Nothing happened in the history of the papal secretariat which can easily be compared with the development of the omnicompetent English secretaries of state. In the end the history of the papal secretariat illustrates the flexibility of monarchic power, and its ability to transform institutions according to its needs, and not the steady growth of a modernizing institution.

Chronologically the later history of the papal secretariat lies outside the scope of the present work. However, it is necessary to mention the phenomenon of the cardinal-nephew authorized to deal with all papal business, on which the later papal secret- ariat was based. This development was not a manifestation of the power of the state, but of the power of a familial institution which had become parasitic on the government. Recent histor- ians have emphasized the inseparability of nepotism from

---

[40] A similar objection to the one made here against historians who want to see linear progress in the development of governments and societies is made by J. Wormald, Lords and Men in Scotland: Bonds of Manrent, 1442-1603 (Edinburgh, 1985).

papal government during the whole early modern period.[41] We may agree, and we must add that it is impossible to term the institution of the cardinal-nephew a modernizing one, although its offshoot, the papal Segretariato di Stato, has by most historians been called modernizing.

It may be that the idea of modernization is not really applicable to societies which preceded the Industrial Revolution. The concept of modernization makes little sense unless modern society can be contrasted with something called 'traditional society'. But traditional society—and this was one of the main weaknesses of Weber's original thesis—is a vague and insubstantial concept. The vulnerability of this aspect of Weber's ideas has been admitted by some distinguished sociologists.[42] The concept of progressive modernization of government seems to be very difficult to apply to concrete examples in early modern Western Europe, although this was the historical context for which Weber invented it.

There are other conceptual difficulties. The unimaginative loyalty of some sociologists to Weber's 'ideal types' has led to the absurdity of people talking about 'regression' from these ideal types (for example, from a developed bureaucracy), so that in their eyes a government may be deemed more modern at an earlier stage of its development than at a later. Such an analysis is inadmissible for the papal government, as for any other.

The papal government of the sixteenth and seventeenth centuries was typical of its period in the way in which it combined archaic, patrimonial ways of running a government with managerial methods which in some respects looked forward to more modern times. It presents a special difficulty for the theory of modernization, in that its ideological basis was something which has to be defined as traditional, even

---

[41] Particularly by W. Reinhard, in 'Nepotismus: Der Funktionswandel einer päpstgeschichtlichen Konstanten', *Zeitschrift für Kirchengeschichte*, 86 (1975), 145–85, and 'Papa Pius: Prolegomena zu einer Sozialgeschichte des Papsttums', *Von Constanz nach Trient: Beiträge zur Kirchengeschichte . . . Festgabe für August Franzen* (Paderborn, 1972), 261–99; see also M. Laurain-Portemer, 'Absolutisme et népotisme: La Surintendance de l'état ecclesiastique', *Bib.Éc.Ch.*, 131 (1973), 487–568. Also G. B. Scapinelli, 'Il memoriale del p. Oliva S. J. al card. Cybo sul nepotismo (1676)', *Rivista di Storia della Chiesa in Italia*, 2 (1948), 262–73.

[42] See especially S. N. Eisenstadt, 'Studies of Modernization and Sociological Theory', *History and Theory*, 13 (1974), 225–52. G. Stokes, 'How is Nationalism Related to Capitalism?', *Comparative Studies in Society and History*, 28 (1986), 591–8, is also relevant.

though its methods have very often been as modern, or more so, as those of other contemporary governments. That, perhaps, is only a problem for those who care to make it so.

3

Why Did Men Become Papal Officials?

I

The papal court offered the chance of promotion to the highest rank in Christendom. No pope of the period was other than a cardinal on election, and only Adrian VI (1521–3) was not attached to the papal court at the time of his becoming pope. Thirty-nine per cent of cardinals of the period had been promoted to the sacred college from an official post in the Roman court, and to the ambitious clerk such posts were desirable for this supreme career opportunity, apart from the other chances they afforded. Fifteen per cent of papal secretaries and chamber clerks taken as a whole became cardinals. The secretaries Aeneas Sylvius Piccolomini and Alessandro Farnese each became pope, one as Pius II and the other as Paul III (1534–49). The outstanding example of the successful curialist is Rodrigo Borgia, who spent thirty-five years in the post which comes closest to that of head of the papal civil service, the vice-chancellorship, before his election as pope in 1492.

The ways to preferment in the Roman court were various, and men did not as a general rule advance from low to high office by sequential promotion. No *ancien régime* bureaucracy followed such a system, and the papal court was normal for its time in that high office was more often achieved through influence and patronage than through ability and long devotion to duty. Nevertheless, some men of not particularly distinguished family, lacking great wealth or princely position, began in the lower offices of the court and worked their way over a period to high ones, or at least to key and lucrative positions in the bureaucracy. Such careers were far from being the norm, but they can be found. I have fixed, as examples of this career pattern, upon twenty-two secretaries and chamber clerks, or 6 per cent of the whole group.[1]

The sample therefore gives some idea of the sequential

---

[1] The sample consists of: Ludovico Agnelli (d. 1499), Petrus Altissen (d. 1491), Enrico Bruni (d. 1509), Jacopo Cardelli (1473–1530), Rinuccio d'Arezzo (Castiglione) (1395–1457), Angelo Cesi (1450–1528), Angelo Colocci (1474–1549),

careers open to active men who began without exceptionally powerful patronage, and who survived long enough to work their way to responsible office. A common element in the careers under consideration was their length: the average sojourn in the Roman court of the twenty-two officers was thirty-three years. It should not, however, be supposed that these men worked their way up the curial ladder by virtuous bureaucratic practice: like everyone else, they had to get the right kind of patronage at the right moment. Angelotto Foschi de Berta, for example, a none-too-scrupulous member of a powerful Roman family, was already a very successful curialist during the period of the Schism who came into his own as a member of the Colonna clique surrounding Pope Martin V, and was made cardinal under Eugenius. Giovanni Battista Ferrari, on the other hand, was a financial operator who borrowed from his brother to buy his first offices in the Roman court: he spent some time in lower offices before suddenly achieving great power as the major-domo of Alexander VI.

The sample excludes people who began their career in the Roman court on the highest rungs of the ladder, notably by appointment as secretary, chamber clerk, or major abbreviator. Two who are known to have served for a long period as secretaries of cardinals before getting a papal office (Giacomo Gherardi, for sixteen years the secretary of Ammanati, and Leonardo Dati, the secretary of Giordano Orsini and subsequently of other cardinals) have been included, and there were probably others who had the same sort of advantage. I have excluded officers whose first positions had an element of personal service to the pope: an office such as that of secret chamberlain was not prominent, but potentially, like anything which admitted the holder to close personal contact with the pope, it was a powerful position.

The most common posts in which these men started their careers were that of apostolic scriptor or minor abbreviator (eighteen out of twenty-two, or 81 per cent). One (Juan Gerona) began as a scriptor in the apostolic chamber, two (Bruni and Maffei) started as notaries of the chamber, and one (Colocci) as a scriptor of briefs. Two were laymen: the consistorial advocate

Leonardo Dati (1408–72), Angelotto de Foschi de Berta (1378–1444), Giovanni Battista Ferrari (1445–1502), Domenico Galletti (d. 1501), Niccolò Garigliati (d. after 1500), Angelo Geraldini (1422–86), Jacopo Gherardi (1434–1516), Juan Gerona (d. 1494), Gerardo Maffei (d. 1466), Fernando Ponzetti (1444–1527), Thomas Regis (Le Roy) (d. 1524), Falcone Sinibaldi (d. 1492), Andrea Spiriti (d. 1504), Antonio Jacopo Veneri (1422–79), Giovanni Veneri (d. 1490).

Angelo Cesi of Narni and the papal secretary Gerardo Maffei of Volterra. Both the last were the founders of clerical dynasties: the rise of the Cesi was the more spectacular, because of the cardinalate acquired by Paolo Cesi in the early sixteenth century, and the subsequent promotion of the family to ducal rank by the popes. But the Maffei also acquired a solid and durable position as magnates, based on the advancement of their members at the papal court. However, none of the sample could be said to be of humble extraction: all were of middling to prominent patrician status if from the cities, or else of minor noble status. Five of the twenty-two (Rinuccio d'Arezzo, Colocci, Dati, Gherardi, Ponzetti) were distinguished humanists in their own right, and at least four (Agnelli, Foschi, Regis, Sinibaldi) were closely connected with humanist circles as patrons or correspondents.

Of the officers with clerical status, seven became bishops and three (Ferrari, Foschi de Berta, Antonio Jacopo Veneri) cardinals. Among the whole sample of 364 secretaries and chamber clerks, 34 per cent became bishops and 12 per cent cardinals, so in the smaller sample the figures of 32 per cent to become bishops and 14 per cent to become cardinals are compatible ratios. Among those who acquired high office in the course of the twenty-two sequential careers, Andrea Spiriti became vice-chamberlain under Alexander VI, and Falcone Sinibaldi treasurer-general under Innocent VIII. Enrico Bruni, Angelo Colocci, and Fernando Ponzetti also held the post of treasurer-general: Ponzetti managed things so that when he was appointed cardinal in 1517 he resigned the treasurer's office to his own nephew. This was not a bad career for a medical doctor with literary interests.

Others starting on lower rungs of the ladder later acquired less-known offices which were nevertheless lucrative and of key importance in the curial system. Several were masters of the registry of Bulls (also termed the registry of apostolic letters). They included Juan Gerona, who occupied the post from 1476 to 1487, and Angelo Colocci. Two others in this post, the Spaniard, Petrus Altissen, and the north Italian nobleman, Niccolò Garigliati, were complained of for their conduct of the office. Altissen was a notable clerical pluralist who held six offices at the time of his death in 1491, and was thought to have left over 20,000 ducats in movables besides his real property. Although he was dead, and Garigliati was in charge of the registry at the time of a curial reform inquiry in 1497, Altissen and another official, Franceschino de Suno, were accused of having grossly and systematically overcharged the fees due to the registry of bulls: their regulations were satirically termed by their critics the *leges Altissinanas et Sunanas*. Garigliati, naturally enough, denied the irregularities. However, he seems to have resigned from the curia within two or three years of the complaints. Rinuccio d'Arezzo, the humanist and Hellenist teacher of Poggio and Valla, held for a time the similarly lucrative office of *custos* of the chancery, and so did Nicholas V's domestic secretary, Pietro da Noceto.

The regional distribution of the officers in the smaller sample is not glaringly different from that in the larger. There is a smaller proportion of non-Italians (one Spaniard, one Frenchman, one German, or 13.6 per cent), a much smaller ratio than the 23 per cent in the main sample. Eight of the twenty-two came from the papal state, six were Tuscans, and one Neapolitan, if we count Ponzetti as a Neapolitan and not as the Florentine which he claimed to be. Two came from Piemonte, and one each from Mantua and Modena. It is noticeable that no Venetian clerks appear to have worked their way up from the ranks of the papal curia by long service. On the whole (though there were exceptions) those Venetian clerks who chose the papal curia as a career came from powerful patrician families and enjoyed powerful curial patronage; they therefore began their curial careers near the top of the tree.

Table 1 shows the dates by which members of the group occupied selected offices. It will, however, be noticed that by the last decade of the century officials who already occupied high office were buying minor offices as investments; Alexander VI's favoured official, Giovanni Battista Ferrari, for example, purchased a scriptorship in 1495 when he was already one of the most powerful men in the papal court. It must also be remembered that by the end of the fifteenth century the venality of the offices made it possible for clerks to buy their way into positions in a manner which had been difficult to do earlier without flagrantly breaching canon law. The career of Angelo Colocci is an example of the attainment of high office by the systematic and skilful investment of large sums in the venal offices. Between 1499 and 1510 Colocci invested between 14,000 and 15,000 ducats in offices, recouping 5,000–6,000 ducats through resales by 1511. Colocci had moved straight into the top of the market, and he occupied not less than two key curial posts in plurality from 1504 onwards.[2]

[2] Ubaldini, *Vita di Mons A. Colocci* (1969); *Atti del Convegno di Studi su Angelo Colocci. Jesi. 13-14 sett. 1969* (Iesi, 1972); *DBI* (unsigned); Frenz, *Kanzlei*,

TABLE 1. Sequential careers: Dates of holding offices

	Notary of chamber	Scriptor	Abbreviator	Secretary	Chamber clerk
Agnelli		1468		1487	1478
Altissen		1480	1476	1487	
Bruni	1476			1487	
Cardelli		1493	1497	1504	
Cesi		1512	1503	1503	
Colocci	1502		1499	1504	
Dati	1465		1455	1455	
Ferrari		1495	1471	1497	
Foschi de Berta	1405		1414	1425	1414
Galletti		1475	1459	1491	
Garigliati		1464	1450	1485	
Geraldini				1455	
Gerona	1468	1457?	1464	1479	1486
Gherardi			1464	1457	
Maffei	1436	1457?			
Ponzetti		1485	1485	1499	1500
Regis	1498	1500		1521	
Rinuccio d'Arezzo		1440		1450	
Sinibaldi		1445	1448	1455	1465
Spiriti	1458–64?		1458–64?		1470
Venieri, A. J.		1443		1457	
Venieri, G.		1461		1487	1451

II

The fees collected by a chamber clerk were from the beginning of the sixteenth century reckoned as the biggest regular fee income gained by any collegiate officer of the Roman court, more than that gained by other important groups like the proto-notaries and the major abbreviators, and outstripped only by the fees of the great officers of state, and by two or three key chancery officials.[3] The office was reckoned to be worth 400 ducats a year at a date between 1487 and 1497, 600 ducats under Julius II, and 800 ducats annually in 1514. Its annual value was maintained or increased under Leo X and his two successors. This was reflected in the price paid for the office, which rose from 4,000 ducats in 1495 to 5,000 in 1505, and to an asking price of 10,000 in 1514; it was conventionally reckoned as worth 14,000 ducats in 1525, but a sum of 10,000 ducats was actually paid for a clerkship in the following year. It seems, therefore, that the conventional idea of the return on the capital invested in the office was in the region of 8 per cent. The fees charged by the chamber clerks must have been rising steeply throughout this period, since the price of the office was due in gold, and the fees were payable in silver, which was depreciating steadily in terms of gold.

The biggest problem for any supplicant in the Roman court was that each fee had to be negotiated separately with the office responsible: there was no standardized tariff, even in the statutes of the various offices. This is also a difficulty for the historian, and there is no readily accessible source to tell us how the fees due to a fifteenth-century chamber clerk were made up. We know that the chamber clerks took a share (normally the college of clerks took a fourteenth part) in the lesser services (*servitia minuta*) which were adjoined to the common service paid on a bishopric or abbey, and also took the *sacra*,

p. 282. Frenz rightly puts a question mark against the appointment of Colocci as master of the registry in the papal chancery in 1492, when he was 18. This was one of the main chancery posts, and a very technical one; it is most unlikely that Colocci held such a post at that age, and if he had his biographer, Ubaldini, would have noted it. My calculations of money paid for offices by Colocci are from Frenz and from Fanelli's edn. of Ubaldini. See also Von Hofmann, *Forschungen*, ii. 83.

[3] Von Hofmann, *Forschungen*, i. 269–89; ii. 163–76, 209–52. There is also a list of offices and their value under Innocent VIII or Alexander VI, in P. Imbart de la Tour, *Les Origines de la Réforme*, ii (2nd edn., Melun, 1946), 41 n.

a 5 per cent payment on the chamber's half of the common service. At the beginning of the fifteenth century the distributions of these dues to the chamber personnel took place daily.[4]

We also know that the clerks charged on the bulls which were sent through the chamber: the most important charge was the *ius cappellani* (which presumably referred to the normal appointment of chamber clerks as apostolic chaplains) called the *devolutum*, which was a 4 per cent charge said to have been conceded in 1437 on bulls sent through the chamber. This was replaced in 1516 by a 3 per cent charge on all annates and common services, and by a heavy 10 per cent charge on all churches and monasteries which could be said to have been conceded as papal 'graces': the last may be presumed to have been provided in consistory.[5] The definition of what was and what was not a 'grace' must have been to a large extent arbitrary, and this element of additional uncertainty shows how devoid of system or principle the taxation of supplicants was. The 1516 changes were part of Leo X's supposed reform of the curial tax fees, a reform whose main effect was a steep increase in the charges. It was, of course, in the interests of the papal government to increase curial charges, the so-called *regalia* of the papal officials, so as to support the price at which the offices were sold.[6]

Other payments due to the clerks of the chamber were the *jocalia*, which included a payment of 40 ducats for bulls for

[4] U. Kühne, *Repertorium Germanicum*, iii (Berlin, 1935), 30*.

[5] For the fees due to the chamber clerks, see Von Hofmann, *Forschungen*, i. 264, 268; ii. 61, no. 260; J. Hergenroether, *Leonis X. Pontificis Maximi Regesta* (Freiburg i.B. 1884), 352, no. 5612 (the abortive attempt to abolish the 'devolutum', made in 1513). The 1516 rules are in Div. Cam. 63, fo. 159, and Div. Cam. 65, fo. 183. The passage referring to the 10% tax on graces is the most important (Div. Cam. 65, fo. 183): 'Sed loco deuoluti tres pro centenario annatarum et communium eis per nos concessos et in recompensatione dicti deuoluti de annatis vero debitis tempore vacationis, non autem sperans uel eventualibus que eueniente casu dumtaxat exigi possint.' [For the prohibition against charging for papal concessions which the petitioner 'eventually' failed to secure, see Von Hofmann, *Forschungen*, i. 264, ii. 249.] 'Idemque in reliquis iuribus eis debitis servari voluimus, ut ante conditionibus eventuum vel fructibus vere debitis peti non possint, sed obligatio principalis cum cautione sufficiat, et pro gratiis faciendis tam communium quam annatarum non ultraque ad rationem decem pro centenario a quibuscumque personis cuiuscumque qualitatis et dignitatis, preterquam a sancte Romane ecclesie cardinalibus, a quibus nihil capere possint, ab eorum vero fratribus et nepotibus tres pro centenario, dumtaxat pro dictis gratiis, que vere gratie dici merentur capiant, et non ultra.'

[6] See the discussion in Partner, 'Papal Financial Policy', *Past and Present*, 88 (1980), 23–4. For Leo X's 'reform', see Von Hofmann, *Forschungen*, i. 273 ff.

perpetual plenary indulgences, 12 for grants of temporalities, 40 for the setting up of a cathedral church with its annexed dignities, 6 ducats for the concession of a right of patronage, 50 for a bull of privilege for a religious congregation, and so on. The clerks and their nephews and familiars also had the right to have bulls made out in their interest sent free through the curia. The clerks also enjoyed the right to have two loads of salt delivered to them annually by the *doganerio* of the Roman salt monopoly.[7]

The fees due to the secretaries were also substantial; the income enjoyed from his post by a secretary in the mid fifteenth century was in the region of 250–300 florins annually. Secretaries invested appreciable sums in Roman and Florentine banks: Cincio Rustici placed his money in the Florentine Monte Comune, and George of Trebizond, at the end of a twelve-year tenure of the office, had over 4,000 florins placed in Roman banks, besides investments in real property.[8]

The secretarial office was made venal in 1487 at an issuing price of 2,600 ducats. However, from 1487 the income of the secretaries did not depend exclusively on fees paid by supplicants to the Roman court, but included an element derived from a new tax imposed on all office-holders in the papal state, payable from the moment that even the expectancy of the papal state office was granted. An annual return for the college of secretaries of at least 8,000 ducats was guaranteed from this tax in the bull setting up their college. It may be conjectured that this did not represent a realistic anticipation of the yield of the new tax, but a papal guarantee of a minimum return on the investment. Since a collegiate income of 8,000 ducats would have produced an income of 266 ducats for each secretary if the income was shared between thirty secretaries, it seems that the intention was to guarantee a minimum return of 10 per cent on the investment. It was an ingenious idea to finance the

---

[7] For the free expedition of bulls, see A. Clergeac, *La Curie et les bénéfices consistoriaux* (Paris, 1911), 135–6; Von Hofmann, *Forschungen*, ii. 31. For the salt concession see L. M. Bååth, 'L'Inventaire de la Chambre Apostolique de 1440', *Miscellanea Archivistica Angelo Mercati* (Vatican City, 1952), 135–57, at 146 n., and the printed mandate in L. M. Bååth, *Acta Pontificum Svecica: Acta Cameralia*, ii (Stockholm, 1957), 581–3.

[8] For Rustici, L. Berthalot, 'Cincius Romanus und seine Briefe', *Quellen*, 21 (1929–30), 209–55, at p. 239; for Trebizond, Monfasani, *George of Trebizond*, p. 114. For income, F. R. Hausmann, 'Die Benefizien des Kardinals Jacopo Ammanati-Piccolomini: Ein Beitrag zur ökonomischen Situation des Kardinalats im Quattrocento', *Röm.Hist.Mitt.* 13 (1971), 27–80, at p. 36; J. Petersohn, *Ein Diplomat*, pp. 39–40.

papal deficit at a difficult moment, and it is not surprising that Innocent VIII paid a substantial bonus to the curialist who suggested it.[9]

The income from fees paid in the Roman court to the secretaries came from bulls going through the chancery connected with the grant of the notariate, with portable altars, and with some associated matters. It also came from the *taxa quinta* on bulls dealt with in the chamber, and the taxes due on briefs. With the taxes on briefs was associated the new tax, payable at six-monthly intervals by all office-holders in the papal state, which was backed up by powers of visitation granted to the secretaries. Secretaries and their familiars were also entitled, like the chamber clerks, to the free dispatch of bulls through the curia.

Expectancies ('supernumerary' places) for the office of secretary were probably granted in some numbers by Calixtus III in the middle of the century; however, there is no proof that money was paid for the office at this period. The prices paid for secretarial places after 1487 show that the revenue of the office must have kept up handsomely: by 1505 places were changing hands for more than 3,000 ducats, and by the pontificate of Leo X the price paid was usually 5,000 ducats or more, though the market occasionally dropped. Income must have been raised substantially above fifteenth-century levels to justify this almost twofold increase in the price, since interest rates went up at the time of heavy borrowing by the two Medici popes.[10]

The domestic secretaries enjoyed, as the other secretaries did not, the right to fees on the briefs sent without signature (*absque signatura*). This right could be exploited by a clever or unscrupulous domestic secretary to yield an enormous personal income, and this is the explanation of the very large fortunes with which some domestic secretaries were credited. That the fees charged by the domestic secretaries were discretionary and not fixed is confirmed by a remark of the former secretary Gaspar of Verona that Leonardo Dati, as domestic secretary under Paul II, exacted much lower fees than previous holders of the office had been wont to demand. The real position of the

---

[9] Von Hofmann, *Forschungen*, i. 154–7, ii. 46; Frenz, *Kanzlei*, pp. 220–3; *Magnum Bullarium Romanum*, i (1727), 441–5; O. Tommasini, 'Nuovi documenti illustrativi del diario di Stefano Infessura', *ASR*, 12 (1889), 1–36.

[10] For Medici borrowing see Partner, 'The "Budget" of the Roman Church', pp. 265–74; id., 'Papal Financial Policy', p. 25. For the prices of secretarial places see Frenz, *Kanzlei*, p. 223.

domestic secretaries differed so widely from that of the rest of the secretaries that it is misleading to treat them as belonging to the same class of official; they did not belong, for example, to the college of secretaries.[11]

III

Although it usually meant the investment of larger sums for their purchase, to hold two or more offices was one of the most obvious ways to improve status and revenue in the Roman court. Of 2,200 office-holders of the period 1471–1527 investigated by Frenz, 400 (18.2 per cent) held two offices, 180 (8.2 per cent) held three, and 110 (5 per cent) held four.[12] Typical patterns of office-holding among chamber clerks and secretaries may be seen in Table 1 above, which deals with a sample of 22 persons, and in Table 2 which deals with the whole group of 364 persons. It is noteworthy that the smaller sample, which is based on long and successful careers, includes five of the twenty-five examples of people who combined the offices of secretary and chamber clerk (6.9 per cent of the whole group).

Among the chamber clerks the most common office to be held in plurality was that of apostolic scriptor, which was venal from the very beginning of the period. Among 141 chamber clerks 36 held the office of scriptor (25.5 per cent), 9 that of major abbreviator (6.4 per cent), and 28 that of minor abbreviator (19.8 per cent). Among the 249 secretaries 118 also held the office of apostolic scriptor (47.3 per cent) and 53 that of minor abbreviator (21.3 per cent). As has just been mentioned, 25 persons held the offices of both secretary and chamber clerk.

Secretaries who were not bishops were entitled by the bull setting up their college in 1487 to apply for the honorary rank of apostolic protonotary, which, although inferior to the six participating protonotaries, was an honourable office conferring valuable privileges in canon law and the right to wear a distinctive curial dress. The participating protonotaries were powerful men who, after their office became venal, had to buy it for 3,500 ducats or thereabouts.[13]

---

[11] Such as the gains attributed to Leonardo Grifo (D'Amico, *Renaissance Humanism*, p. 33) and Bartolomé Flores (above, p. 27). Similar gains were attributed 'sine cuiusquam querimonia aut aliquo suo crimine' to Pius II's domestic secretary, Gregorio Lollio, RRIISS iii/16. 50.

[12] *Kanzlei*, p. 241.

[13] For protonotaries, see Frenz, *Kanzlei*, pp. 203–4; Von Hofmann,

It must be emphasized that many of these offices were incompatible one with another, and that they were not all held simultaneously, although up to three or four of a compatible nature were quite frequently held by a single person, often with a specific papal dispensation if the plural holding was not covered by chancery rules. With papal permission offices could be resigned, and thus sold or transferred to a relative. After the death of a holder a relative might be allowed to succeed, as in the case of the Roman layman Pietro de' Leni, who was allowed to succeed his younger brother Luca, a former canon of S. Maria Maggiore, as a chamber clerk in 1486. A typical case involving resignation by a living member of the family to another was that of the Venetian brothers, Andrea and Pietro Conti. Andrea was made chamber clerk in 1439, but resigned to be taxator of the registry of bulls in 1440. His brother succeeded him on his resignation as taxator in 1448, then resigned (i.e. sold) this office to become a chamber clerk in 1455, retaining the clerkship until his death in 1465.[14]

A better-known example of the succession of son to father in the curia is that of Gaspare Biondo, son of the well-known humanist Flavio Biondo, to whom his father resigned his office of chamber notary in 1463, and who was allowed to succeed to Flavio's office of apostolic secretary after the latter's death in the same year. He was allowed to succeed to the father's office of chamber notary without payment, since Flavio Biondo had possessed the office since 1432 without selling, resigning it, or exercising it, but it is unknown whether the same concession was made for the office of secretary. Gaspare Biondo later resigned the office of chamber notary to his brother Francesco in 1483; this was connected with his own advancement to chamber clerk in 1481. He occupied both the secretary's and the chamber clerk's offices until his death in 1493, when his *locus* of secretary was extinguished in pursuance of an arrangement made when the college of secretaries was set up in 1487. A similar example is that of the well-known Sigismondo de' Conti, secretary from 1481, and the domestic secretary of Julius II, who was also the historian of the papal court. A

Forschungen, i. 56–67, ii. 22, 24–5, 52, 66, 143–5. P. M. Baumgarten, *Aus Kanzlei und Kammer: Erörterungen zur kurialen Hof- und Verwaltungsgeschichte in 13, 14, und 15 Jahrhundert* (Freiburg i.B., 1907), 322–33; G. V. Marchesi Buonacorsi, *Antichità e eccellenza del protonotariato apostolico* (Faenza, 1751).

[14] For the practice of 'resignation' see McClung Hallman, *Italian Cardinals*, pp. 20–1, 33–4; Hay, *Church in Italy*, pp. 18–19.

TABLE 2. Offices held by chamber clerks and secretaries, 1417-1527

	Chamber clerks	Secretaries		Chamber clerks and secretaries
	1417-1527	1417-1527	1471-1527	1417-1527
Chamberlain	1	1	1	1
Treasurer	11	10	10	16
Vice-chamberlain	7	2	2	9
Vice-treasurer	9	3	2	9
Apostolic collector	9	3	1	9
Auditor of chamber	5	2	1	7
Notary of chamber	5	9	9	12
Solicitor of apostolic letters	5	34	34	39
Councillor of chamber	2	1	0	2
Depositary of chamber	1	4	0	5
Datarius	4	9	9	13
Auditor of rota	2	1	1	3
Referendary	15	19	12	33
Clerk of Sacred College	6	4	3	10

TABLE 2. (Cont.)

	Chamber clerks	Secretaries		Chamber clerks and secretaries
	1417–1527	1417–1527	1471–1527	1417–1527
Apostolic scriptor	36	118	79	154
Scriptor of penitentiary	9	18	11	27
Corrector of apostolic letters	1	1	2	2
Major abbreviator of apostolic letters	9	27	18	36
Minor abbreviator of apostolic letters	28	78	53	90
Scriptor of briefs	3	16	16	19
Taxator of apostolic letters	12	5	1	16
Protonotary	17	26	21	36
Secret chamberlain	7	11	9	19
Registrar of apostolic letters	7	19	13	25
Consistorial advocate	1	1	1	2
Other offices	21	37	21	51
Clerk of chamber	140	25	22	140
Secretary	25	249	169	249

secretary's place for Sigismondo's son Giovanni Francesco (by then 34 years old, and a curial official since 1490) was found in 1511, and the son occupied it until his death in 1534.

When the right of regress (*resignatio cum pacto de retro emendo*) was added to the right of resigning the office in favour of someone else, the concession was so much more valuable, since it increased the flexibility of the financial arrangements. Such a concession enabled the master of the registry of bulls, Niccolò Garigliati, who has been mentioned above, on his promotion to Bishop of Ivrea in 1485 to resign his curial offices when he became a bishop as the regulations required, but then to return and to repurchase them, thus combining his bishopric with his former official functions in the curia.[15] This must have been the mechanism by which many of the curial bishops flouted the rule which required them to resign curial office on promotion. Garigliati continued as master of the registry of bulls for a further fifteen years after becoming Bishop of Ivrea.

There was, finally, the far from unimportant question of dress, protocol, and status. The offices of secretary and chamber clerk were senior and important: in the earlier fifteenth century both wore the same court dress. Both, if clerks, had the right to nomination to other dignified posts: the chamber clerks to be papal chaplains, the secretaries (after 1487) to be honorary protonotaries. The last honour was certainly considerable, and gave the right to wear a dress like that of the bishops, save for the facing being black instead of green. The chamber clerks had the right to attend the papal consistory, at which the only other officials present were the auditors of the rota and the participating protonotaries. They also attended the meetings of the apostolic chamber itself, which are discussed below. The secretaries, by contrast, had no corporate organization until they were organized in a college in 1487: following this, they had the right to a common room in the apostolic palace. Finally, from the pontificate of Leo X onwards, the secretaries, together with the papal scriptors and *sollicitatores*, enjoyed the additional status of Palatine Count (Count of the Lateran Palace), which in the case of the secretaries gave the holder the right to create notaries, to legitimate bastards, and to confer doctorates.[16]

[15] Frenz, *Kanzlei*, p. 414; Von Hofmann, *Forschungen*, ii. 82, 117; Eubel, *Hierarchia*, ii. 187; Gherardi, *Dispacci e lettere di Giacomo Gherardi*, p. 246; P. Paschini, *Il carteggio fra il card. Marco Barbo e Giovanni Lorenzi* (Vatican City, 1948), 128, 'dimissis officiis cum pacto de retro emendo'.

[16] Von Hofmann, *Forschungen*, ii. 56, 62 (authorization for secretaries, 8 May 1517), 64.

There was also the possibility of the appointment of any clerk whose work brought him into personal contact with the pope, or who enjoyed exceptionally powerful patronage, being appointed a papal familiar or papal chamberlain, other forms of status which conferred dignity and legal privileges. That these were far from empty dignities is made clear from the way in which his promotion to papal chamberlain was referred by Giacomo Gherardi, and by Sigismondo de' Conti's choice to be depicted in the robes of papal chamberlain in the Raphael painting which became known as the 'Madonna of Foligno'.

IV

The quest and the market for benefices occupied the energies of most senior officials in the Roman court. Membership meant the enjoyment of access to the richest source of clerical patronage in western Latin society. Mere occupancy of office gave no automatic access to favour, although certain offices did under the papal chancery rules enjoy special privileges in the conferment of benefices. The way to success depended above all upon favour, whether from a cardinal or other great man, or from the pope himself. It also depended upon a good knowledge of the intricate chancery rules and the canon law which lay behind them, and upon the cunning and the business sense to handle practice in what was in effect a highly competitive stock market. Speed was essential: the way in which clergy would attend or spy upon the deathbed of any clerk whose demise would place benefices upon the market was notorious. The volume of business in benefices which passed through the Roman court was enormous. When a new pope succeeded to the papal throne, the number of supplications for benefices conceded on his first day would normally run into thousands.

There are some technical problems connected with the privileged markets in benefices and in offices whose solution remains difficult. The main one is that of brokerage. It is almost certain that both these markets created brokers, who introduced buyers and sellers and took commission on the transaction. But the clandestine nature of the market makes it difficult to know who these brokers were: it is probable that most were themselves clergy with office in the Roman court. They are the 'very special friends' which the procedural manuals advised the aspiring clerk to find in the Roman court, but who these friends were, in a particular case, is usually hard to determine. Some, especially those who served ultramontane patrons, were proctors in the Roman court: an instance is the Spanish clerk, Juan of Gerona, who served the English crown.

The curial description for those who solicited benefices for others, especially benefices conferred in consistory, was *sollicitatores*. It is clear from the identity of the three main *sollicitatores* who negotiated the setting up of their venal college in 1482 that these men included some of the richest and most distinguished curialists. Sinolfo dei Conti Ottieri di Castel Lotario was a powerful chamber clerk (later also a secretary); Petrus Altissen one of the top chancery officials; Francesco da Noceto was another influential secretary.[17]

Banks dealing in the Roman court probably also handled some of the intermediary business, but until their accounts have been examined with this problem in mind it will be hard to pronounce upon it. The draft reform of the Roman court for Pius II criticizes the practice of bankers who solicit the promotion of bishops or abbots, which suggests that some of this lucrative brokerage came their way. It is noticeable that banks were not to be forbidden to solicit for minor benefices.[18] Probably the banks and some of the other brokers managed investments in the benefice market on behalf of outside investors: their investment income could be assured by the grantee of the benefice reserving a pension payable to the

---

[17] Frenz, *Kanzlei*, pp. 458–60. For *sollicitatores*, whom he says were not officials in the strict sense until 1482, see Von Hofmann, *Forschungen*, i. 134–8. For brokerage in French public finance in the 17th cent., see D. Desert, *Argent, pouvoir et société au Grand Siècle* (Paris, 1984), especially pp. 341–68, and also S. Kettering, *Patrons, Brokers, and Clients in Seventeenth-Century France* (New York and Oxford, 1986). See also V. Burkolter, *The Patronage System: Theoretical Remarks* (Basle, 1976), pp. 22–3; J. Boissevain, *Friends of Friends: Networks, Manipulators and Coalitions* (Oxford, 1974). I did not come across B. Schimmelpfennig, 'Der Ämterhandel an der römischen Kurie von Pius II. bis zum Sacco di Roma (1458–1527)', in I. Mieck (ed.), *Ämterhandel im Spätmittelalter und im 16. Jahrhundert* (Berlin, 1984), 3–41, until too late to use it here. For *specialissimi amici* in papal practice, see R. Bizzocchi, *Chiesa e potere nella Toscana del Quattrocento* (Bologna, 1987), 107; and see also Partner, 'William of Wykeham and the Historians', in R. Custance (ed.), *Winchester College: Sixth-Centenary Essays* (Oxford, 1982), 29–30. Also P. N. R. Zutshi, 'Proctors Acting for English Petitioners in the Chancery of the Avignonese Popes', *JEH*, 35 (1984), 15–29.

[18] Raymond de Roover did not examine this possible aspect of banking practice, nor has Melissa Meriam Bullard yet turned her attention to it. There is a prohibition against merchants soliciting the promotion of abbots or bishops in the second draft of the Reform statutes of Pius II: Von Hofmann, *Forschungen*, ii. 230.

investor on its fruits.[19] In the venal office market there was a publicly recognized arrangement for small investors to make joint investments in the so-called *societates officiorum* for the purchase of offices to which clerical functions were not attached.

The wholesale concessions made by the pope to favoured courtiers, to take up benefices in a given diocese or church province up to the value of a sum which might be extremely large, give the impression that papal provision to a benefice was a much simpler and easier affair than it really was. It was necessary, after getting such a general concession, to identify benefices which appeared to be vacant and liable to papal provision, and then to obtain the appropriate provision from the papal machine. Other claimants might appear and fight their claims in the papal courts, and the litigation connected with provision to a single benefice might well continue for many years before a clerk got unopposed entry. The obstacles to the provision might come from the local regional clergy who claimed the benefice by election of the chapter or in some other way, but they might equally come from elsewhere in the Roman court.

The chancery rules gave specific advantages to some classes of papal officials, including secretaries and chamber clerks, in the provision to church benefices in Italy. Even so, few papal provisions went through automatically and without opposition, unless the clerk concerned had spent infinite time and money on identifying, conciliating, and compensating the opposition. Many benefices were so burdened with pensions incurred in the course of buying off the opposition that their real was far inferior to their apparent value.

Once a benefice was obtained, a clerk resident in the Roman court was very likely to farm its revenues. He was impeded by a constitution of Paul II from farming the revenues for a term of longer than three years, though this ordinance had only placed the practice on a more permanent and legalized basis than before.[20] That the sale or farm of benefices was a normal way for a clerk to endow his family may be illustrated from the life of the chamber clerk Fabiano Benci of Montepulciano, who

[19] Von Hofmann, *Forschungen*, i. 188–90; C. Bauer, 'Die Epochen der Papstfinanz: Ein Versuch', *Historische Zeitschrift*, 138 (1927), 457–503, at p. 488.
[20] McClung Hallman, *Italian Cardinals*, pp. 66–80; *Magnum Bullarium Romanum*, i (1727), 384.

was praised by his biographer, Agostino Patrizi, for his gener-
osity in paying the dowries of his nieces, daughters of a Pucci.
His correspondence with Lorenzo de' Medici reveals that he
financed the dowries from benefices, in a complicated operation which required the help of the Medici and of their banking
manager, Giovanni Tornabuoni.[21]

Whether income from benefices was bigger or smaller than
income from curial office depended entirely on the status,
patronage, and luck of the curialist concerned. Since income
from the benefices was raised outside Rome, sometimes in a
distant country, it was clearly a more difficult source of
revenue to control. The effort of obtaining patronage and
pursuing litigation in order to obtain and exploit a benefice
was likely to be far greater than the effort expended in obtaining a curial office: perhaps greater than the effort involved in
fulfilling the duties of a curial officer. One or two officials
whose careers have been looked into by curious modern historians seem to have drawn a better and more secure income
from office than from benefices, but the question is impossible
to resolve. Most senior curial officials tried to secure benefices;
few seem to have decided that they were not worth the time,
trouble, and expense which getting hold of them and exploiting
them undoubtedly required.

An example is Angelo Geraldini, who when he was papal
secretary and major abbreviator of apostolic letters drew
approximately 600 florins annually from his offices, but only
about 150 florins from his benefices. A similar distribution of
income can be found for the period in which they were secretaries for Jacopo Ammanati and Aeneas Sylvius Piccolomini.
Under the Medici popes the pickings from benefices may
have grown: the chamber clerk and papal governor, Giovanni
Gozzadini, enjoyed an estimated income of 700 ducats annually
from benefices at his death in 1517 (though the real income
was probably smaller, and his salary as governor and chamber
clerk probably larger). By the seventeenth century the situation had not changed greatly: the salary paid Fabio Chigi for
his offices after 1639 was financially much more important
than what he drew from benefices, although one of these was a
bishopric.[22]

[21] Patrizi's 'Life' in J. Mabillon, Iter Italicum, i (Paris, 1687), 254. For the
correspondence with Tornabuoni and the Medici see Bizzocchi, Chiesa e potere,
pp. 142–3, where Benci is not identified by name, but as 'il chierico della
Camera Apostolica originario di Montepulciano'.

[22] For Geraldini, Petersohn, Ein Diplomat, pp. 38–41; see also Hausman, 'Die

V

The career paths of chamber clerks and apostolic secretaries show some broad differences. There was a tendency among chamber clerks to secure either internal promotion in the hierarchy of the chamber, or appointment (on a temporary or secondment basis) to the office in the papal state. However, the first of these career paths, the chamber itself, was also open to some extent to secretaries. The one official of the sample to become apostolic chamberlain was Alessandro Farnese, the future Paul III, who had been an apostolic secretary when he shot to prominence as treasurer and cardinal, as a young man favoured by Alexander VI.

Of the secretaries who were also chamber clerks, six became papal treasurer. Five other secretaries, however, who were never chamber clerks, nevertheless became treasurer, and only six treasurers were former chamber clerks who had never been secretaries. It is curious, too, that the office of apostolic depositary, which was a technical financial post normally held by a banker but occasionally given to a papal clerk, was more often held by a secretary than by a chamber clerk.

The papal state offered some opportunities to the secretaries, some of whom (like the humanist Niccolò Perotti, whose career as a papal governor ended in disaster) followed prominent careers in its government, but the chamber was so directly involved in papal-state administration that its clerks naturally assumed far more posts there than were filled by officers from other parts of the papal administration. Of the chamber clerks 35 per cent became papal governors, commissioners, or the holders of an equivalent papal state office; the comparable figure for secretaries is only 13 per cent. In addition, 14 per cent of chamber clerks, and only a negligible proportion of secretaries, became papal state treasurers.

On the other hand, diplomatic missions to lay rulers, usually in the capacity of *nunzio*, were much more often filled by secretaries than by chamber clerks. The *nunzi* were the

Benefizien', pp. 36–7; D. Brosius, 'Die Pfründen des Enea Silvio Piccolomini', *Quellen*, 54 (1974), 271–327, at pp. 273 ff. For Fabio Chigi, see K. Repgen, 'Die Finanzen des Nuntius Fabio Chigi: Ein Beitrag zur Sozialgeschichte der römischen Führungsgruppen in 17. Jahrhundert', in E. Hassinger, J. H. Muller, and H. Ott (eds.), *Geschichte Wirthschaft Gesellschaft: Festschrift für Clemens Bauer* (Berlin, 1974), 229–80.

nucleus of a future papal diplomatic service, and the secretaries made up a good part of that nucleus. The office of apostolic collector, which in the pre-Schism period had sometimes doubled as a financial and diplomatic post, was from the mid fifteenth century used less, and less frequently with a diplomatic emphasis. The offices could be doubled, as they were by the apostolic secretary, humanist, and Hellenist, Lianoro Lianori, when he was sent to Castile as *nunzio* and apostolic collector in 1467.

The treasurer's and vice-chamberlain's offices were extremely dignified and powerful posts at the top of the chamber hierarchy. The latter office was on the whole confined to specialists, whose careers ended in the chamber. The treasurer, on the other hand, was a key financial officer who enjoyed the personal confidence of the pope, and who could normally look forward to further favour and distinction. Of the seventeen treasurers referred to in Table 3, five became cardinals, and one became pope. Falcone Sinibaldi, the treasurer under Innocent VIII, was a brilliant if unscrupulous man who had been thought since his youth to have been destined for the red hat: his death in 1492 was ascribed by an unfriendly chronicler to rage that the accession of Alexander VI deprived him of the hope of the cardinalate. The only treasurers of this group not to become bishops were the Pisan Guiniforte Buonconti, treasurer for a couple of years until his death in 1462,

TABLE 3. *Papal state and chamber appointments of secretaries and chamber clerks* (% of total no. of posts in parentheses)

	Posts held by secretaries	Posts held by chamber clerks
Chamberlain	1 (0.4)	0
Treasurer	10 (4)	11 (7.9)
Vice-chamberlain	2 (0.8)	7 (5.0)
Vice-treasurer	3 (1.2)	9 (6.5)
Apostolic collector	3 (1.2)	9 (6.5)
Auditor of apostolic chamber	2 (0.8)	5 (3.6)
Notary of apostolic chamber	9 (3.6)	5 (3.6)
Depositary of apostolic chamber	4 (1.6)	1 (0.7)
Papal state customs officer	1 (0.4)	3 (2.2)
Papal state governor, etc.	18 (7.2)	24 (17.5)
Papal state treasurer	3 (1.2)	19 (13.7)
Papal state commissioner	14 (5.6)	24 (17.5)

and Buonconti's successor, Antonio Laziosi of Forlì, the former dean of the chamber clerks.

The list of treasurers promoted to cardinal illustrates the greatly increased importance of financial policy after the 1480s. The treasurers made cardinals under Alexander VI (Alessandro Farnese, Adriano Castellesi, Francesco Loriz) were the first examples of such promotion since Martin V's treasurer, Antonio Casini, had been made cardinal in 1426. Julius II promoted his shady treasurer, Francesco Alidosi, to the rank of cardinal, and Leo X gave similar promotion to Fernando Ponzetti and Bernardo Dovizi (Bibbiena). Not until 1529 was the office of treasurer again given to a technician. In the last case the new treasurer owed his appointment to the influence of a curial banker: he was Francesco del Nero, the creature of the then all-powerful apostolic depositary, Filippo Strozzi.[23] This was the beginning of a new tendency: by the end of the sixteenth century the treasurer's office was thought of as more appropriate to a merchant than to a prelate.

VI

Under Martin V and Eugenius IV the typical chamber clerk led a strenuous life, which could frequently take him from his post in Rome to be treasurer or rector of provinces which were only with difficulty controlled by their papal lord. Night marches and sieges of remote hill towns were often his lot. Such careers were led by able lawyers such as the Perugian Benedetto Guidalotti, by Bartolomeo Bonizzi of Orvieto, and by the lawyer and distinguished humanist Francesco Pizzolpassi, who ended his life as Archbishop of Milan. Until mid-century chamber clerks served commonly in these papal state offices: the well-known Bolognese lawyer and chamber clerk, Jacopo Mucciarelli, for example, served as treasurer of papal provinces under Nicholas and Calixtus.

Later in the century, though chamber clerks continued to fill similar offices in the temporal power, the obligation to carry out these sometimes thankless tasks in the papal provinces fell on rather fewer of their number. For example, Antonio Laziosi of Forlì, who served long enough to become dean of the chamber clerks under Paul II, spent little time in such posts, as

[23] M. M. Bullard, *Filippo Strozzi and the Medici: Favour and Finance in Sixteenth-Century Florence and Rome* (Cambridge, 1980), 127, 159, 170, and see also my review in *Renaissance Quarterly*, 35 (1982), 88.

did his contemporary Guiniforte Buonconti of Pisa, who ended as apostolic treasurer. However, chamber clerks with supernumerary status who were waiting for a permanent participating clerkship willingly took administrative posts in the papal state. An example is Jacopo Feo of Savona, a supernumerary chamber clerk who was governor of the Patrimony and Perugia on different occasions and died while Governor of Cesena and Bishop of Ventimiglia (1467). Similar careers were led by Antonio Fatati, the only chamber clerk to be formally beatified for his sanctity of life, who had served as treasurer general of the Marches in 1449–53, before becoming bishop of his native city of Ancona in 1463, and by Andrea Pili of Fano, a supernumerary chamber clerk who died while Bishop of Recanati and lieutenant-general of the Marches in 1476.

Some had their own reasons for preferring temporal power posts. The chamber clerk Stefano Nardini of Forlì, who made a great career, first in the chamber and then as cardinal and Archbishop of Milan, spent a great deal of time in papal state positions, being at various points Governor of Campagna and Marittima (1453–4), Governor of the Patrimony (1455–6), lieutenant and treasurer of the Marches (1456), and Governor of Rome (1462): he seems even to have returned for a time to the relatively humble duties of Governor of the Patrimony while a cardinal (July–October 1483). It is possible that this zeal was connected with Nardini's anxiety to advance the careers of his relatives: he had a turbulent nephew, Pierpaolo, whom he had made lord of Carbognano and Giulianello in the Roman Campagna, and who came to a bad end after his murder of the papal castellan of Soriano in 1489, five years after the uncle's death.

Another chamber clerk who, late in the fifteenth century, seems to have thought a career in the temporal power to have been well worth while, was the cultivated Mantuan, Ludovico Agnelli. Agnelli was Governor of the Patrimony before his nomination to chamber clerk in 1478; he was also vicar-general of the Marches in 1486, when he failed to subdue the revolt of Osimo. After various diplomatic missions, he was made Governor of Viterbo for Cardinal Juan Borgia in 1498, having previously been created Archbishop of Cosenza. The pope allowed him to retain his clerkship as well as the archbishopric, and he was thus still a chamber clerk on his death in Viterbo (supposedly through poison administered on behalf of Cesare Borgia) in 1499. It may not be accidental that both Nardini and Agnelli were accused of abuse of power in their papal state posts.

Accusations of partiality against papal governors were, however, very frequent, and were sometimes upheld by the pope. This happened to the papal secretary and humanist Niccolò Perotti, whose career as a papal governor was twice interrupted by his removal, either because he had taken sides among the factions or because of his poor financial management. But he still went on to a third governorship in the important city of Perugia.

By the early sixteenth century the chamber clerk had become much more likely to spend most of his career in Rome. The provincial treasuries were often entrusted to lay bankers, and the provincial governorships became part of a rather different patronage structure. As an exceptional move a chamber clerk and former datarius, Giovanni Gozzadini, was sent to govern the newly acquired papal cities, first of Piacenza and then of Reggio, under Julius II and Leo X. Gozzadini was murdered while Governor of Reggio in 1516, so the precedent was not encouraging. Antonio Pucci, nephew of the powerful Lorenzo Pucci, was given a lengthy and important mission as *nunzio* in Switzerland in 1517.

But by the early sixteenth century, when they were not performing their traditional duties in the management of the 'spiritual' finances, the chamber clerks were almost entirely taken up with the central administration of Rome and of the papal state. Every working day, the *mensarius* read the incoming correspondence of petitions, complaints, and lawsuits relating to a huge range of temporal power matters. He referred each for action or decision, either to a fellow chamber clerk, or to the chamber auditor or other judge, or, if the gravity of the matter required it, to the pope. The remaining cases were dealt with by the *mensarius* himself. The volumes of the *libri decretorum* of the chamber dating from Julius II's pontificate, which happen to have been preserved, strikingly show how most of the temporal power business was channelled through the chamber. They also argue for a much tighter central control of the papal state than had obtained in the fifteenth century.[24] Chamber clerks also assumed important duties in

[24] Arch. Cam. I, 289–90, 289, fo. 1b. 'Liber ordinarius propositionum et occasionum siue ordinationum Camere Apostolice clericorum qui presidium successiuis diebus cameralibus emanatarum et manu clerici pro ipse mensarii uel in eius locum subrogati scriptarum, ad futuram earum memoriam. Et per me Jo. Gozzadinum et dictis clericis et presidentibus nostris, nunc pro isto primi mensem Januarii MDVIII mensarium.' See also Pastura Ruggiero, *La reverenda Camera Apostolica*, pp. 53–4.

the running of the City of Rome, notably the presidency of the grain office (the office of the annona) and the presidency *delle Strade*. Gozzadini's career as a provincial governor was by this time unusual for a chamber clerk.

VII

The pattern of earlier secretarial careers was very different. Until the mid fifteenth century at least, the office of secretary meant serving the pope in a sensitive political capacity; it also meant access to his person. This did not mean, early in the century, that the secretary was an obvious candidate for political missions. The place for the secretaries of Martin V and Eugenius IV was by the pope with their pens at the ready: though available to be sent as papal envoys, they were still in effect considered as extensions of the papal chancery. Moreover, if they were laymen it was sometimes more difficult to send them with ambassadorial or quasi-ambassadorial functions. Biondo Flavio was, it is true, sent on an important mission to treat with Francesco Sforza at Carcarella in 1434, as soon as he entered papal service, and was employed on two or three other similar missions during the course of his career. But these missions were rather exceptional ones, undertaken at a time of political crisis for the papacy. The same could be said for his colleague, Antonio Loschi.[25]

In mid-century the position of the secretaries changed quite rapidly. The office was bestowed more frequently, often in a more or less honorary capacity, as for example it was conferred upon Aeneas Sylvius Piccolomini when he was already a high-ranking diplomat in imperial service. Whether honorary or not, secretaries were from this time onwards much more frequently in holy orders. One of the earliest secretaries to be sent on major diplomatic missions was the Hellenist Cristoforo Garatone, who was made Bishop of Coron after being sent as ambassador to Constantinople in the period preceding the Council of Florence. He was finally dispatched with the crusading army in 1448, and was killed at the Battle of Kossovo. It was an important, if a rather discouraging precedent.

Rather than with Garatone, a new secretarial career pattern

[25] See the biography in *DBI* by R. Fubini. For the treaty of Calcarella see Partner, 'Florence and the Papacy in the Earlier Fifteenth Century', in N. Rubinstein (ed.), *Florentine Studies: Politics and Society in Renaissance Florence* (London, 1968), 381–402, at p. 394.

became evident with the rise of Bartolomeo Roverella (1406–76) to power and office. Roverella came from an ambitious family of small nobles in Adria in the Ferrarese region. His career began as a chaplain with legal qualifications in the household of the humanist chamber clerk and papal state official Scipione Mainenti, Bishop of Modena. In Rome Roverella attracted the attention of the Patriarch Vitelleschi, and secured an appointment as secret chamberlain to Pope Eugenius. This kind of confidential access to the pope was a key to fortune: within a short time he became a papal secretary, and then Bishop of Adria (1444) and in the following year Archbishop of Ravenna. He kept the secretaryship only a few months after becoming bishop, but it was an important stage in his rise to power. The rest of his career was a mixture of senior diplomatic and papal state appointments, which led to his becoming cardinal in 1461.

The best example of the secretariat as a springboard to a diplomatic career in the second half of the century is Angelo Geraldini (1422–86), whose life has recently been the subject of an excellent study.[26] Geraldini came from a probably quite obscure merchant family in Amelia, in papal Umbria: his trying to fake a relationship with the Irish Geraldines suggests that he had little genealogy to boast about. Originally a protégé of Cardinal Domenico Capranica, he first entered the Roman court as an abbreviator in 1450, obtaining appointment as a secretary in 1455. He was rector of the papal Comtat Venaissain from 1458–61, and from the latter part of Pius II's pontificate was an important papal envoy (occasionally also a papal state governor) who undertook several delicate missions: in modern terms, he was a trouble-shooter. Like many papal envoys, he depended for advancement quite as much on the patronage and support of the courts to which he was accredited as on that of the pope: his most critical relationship in the first part of his career was with the Duke of Milan, who gave him unstinted support until an attempt to make him Archbishop of Genoa failed. A second patron, more compliant than Sforza in his willingness to give high office to Geraldini's close relations, was the Aragonese King of Naples, and Geraldini also managed to exploit the Castilian government to his own advantage.

Geraldini's office of secretary was held only for a year or so, and he relinquished it when he embarked upon his not inconsiderable efforts on behalf of himself and his family: the contemporary family historian boasted that no other family in

[26] Petersohn, *Ein Diplomat*; Frenz, *Kanzlei*, p. 283.

Europe had accumulated so many official positions. Geraldini did not, however, attain the red hat: he was unsuccessful here where another papal state clerk, his exact contemporary, who also filled important *nunzio* positions, was successful. Antonio Jacopo Venieri (1422–79) was a member of a prominent family of the March of Ancona which had been powerful in the apostolic chamber since the pontificate of Eugenius IV. His uncle, the Archbishop of Ragusa, had had the doubtful honour of being the last papal legate accredited to Constantinople, in 1453. Venieri, like Geraldini, was an influential *nunzio* in Castile; but the former went on to the highest honours, becoming cardinal in 1473.

There were also secretaries who accepted the temporary post of papal *nunzio* accredited outside the Roman court, but who expected to return in due course to their secretarial posts in Rome. The best documented case of this quite common phenomenon is Giacomo Gherardi of Volterra (1434–1516). Gherardi established himself in the Roman court during the sixteen years he served as secretary to Cardinal Jacopo Ammanati. Appointed as a participating secretary in 1479, he retained the post at least until 1506. This was in spite of many years of absence from the Roman court, either while serving as papal *nunzio*, or in the service of the Medici in Volterra or Florence. Gherardi's correspondence in the time he was *nunzio* in Florence and Milan (1487–90) is one of our best sources for the practice and point of view of the secretaries at this period. The tutor of Giovanni de' Medici, he received his reward from Leo X with his appointment as Bishop of Aquino in 1513.

From the time of the collegiate reorganization of secretaries in 1487, and the systematic sale of all the secretarial posts except those of the domestic secretary, it is doubtful whether any career pattern for the secretaries can be said to have existed. After 1487 the office became a prestigious investment for the rich curial clerk, one which he might well sell within a relatively short time, and which he was likely to execute through deputies. The list of secretaries from 1487 is a roll-call of the rich and powerful, but it has little to do with the writing of the pope's important political correspondence: this was the business of the domestic secretaries.

VIII

Knowledge of the law was very important indeed to the chamber clerk, and very useful, though not essential, to the secretary. The whole papal court depended, in the end, on right judgements being delivered in canon law matters. The complex business of the papal provision to benefices, resignation from such benefices, and the clandestine traffic in benefices, all depended on the interpretation of canon law. Legal qualifications, however, were a step to greater things, and chamber clerks and secretaries did not as a rule look for careers as judges in the Roman court. Five chamber clerks and two secretaries became auditor of the apostolic chamber, while three chamber clerks and one secretary were at some point auditors of the Rota. Even so, in one or two instances a Rota auditor resigned this post to become a chamber clerk.

But from the second half of the fifteenth century there was one key and lucrative post in the Roman court which required good legal knowledge, and which both chamber clerks and secretaries were anxious to fill, that of a referendary. The referendaries stood close to the pope at a vital point of the consideration of petitions and the distribution of patronage; they were also much involved in the work of the dataria. Fifteen chamber clerks (10.7 per cent) and twelve secretaries (4.8 per cent) became referendaries.

One of the most natural objects of the ambition of a clerk in papal service was to trim his dress with green and to become a bishop. A bishopric was in itself a possible aid to further promotion: an important post as *nunzio* or commissioner was more likely, in certain circumstances, to go to a curial bishop than to a simple clerk. On the other hand, the rules regarding promotion to bishop meant that many offices and benefices were ruled incompatible with the bishopric, and unless the

TABLE 4. *University degrees of chamber clerks and secretaries* (% given in parentheses)

	Chamber clerks	Secretaries
License in Arts	5 (3.5)	4 (1.6)
Master	8 (5.8)	7 (2.9)
Doctor in Canon Law	50* (35.4)	39† (16.2)
Doctor in Civil Law	28* (19.8)	20† (8.3)
Doctor in Theology	2 (1.4)	3 (1.2)

* Six chamber clerks were 'utriusque' (qualified in both canon and civil law).
† Ten secretaries were 'utriusque'.

bishop-elect had enough credit with the pope to get dispensation to continue to hold the incompatible offices, he risked promotion into penury. The revenues of a bishopric—to which he was unlikely, in the normal course of events, to pay more than a courtesy visit—were infinitely variable, and even an apparently well-endowed see could be impoverished by the pensions with which previous incumbents had charged its revenues.

Fifty-six chamber clerks (40.2 per cent) became bishops at some point of their career: of these, only four (2.9 per cent) were bishops before their appointment as chamber clerk. Seventy-four secretaries (29.5 per cent) became bishops at some point: of these as many as thirty (12 per cent) were already bishops at the time of nomination to secretary. In the period 1417–87 the office of chamber clerk gave an even greater chance of promotion to bishop. In the earlier period forty chamber clerks were appointed who became bishops (29 per cent of the whole sample), whereas only twenty-three secretaries appointed before 1487 (9.2 per cent of the whole sample) became bishops. This lower figure reflects the rather high proportion of laymen among secretaries in the period before 1487.

Resignation of office on promotion to a bishopric was enforced on many occasions. Twenty-one chamber clerks resigned their office of clerk on these grounds (about half of those who became bishops while still chamber clerk). The proportion of resignations by secretaries (twenty-one) is the same, when account is taken of the many secretaries who were already bishops before appointment. In the later period it was common for secretaries who had been promoted to bishop to resign their office and subsequently to repurchase an equivalent secretary's place, probably by exercising a right they had acquired before promotion.[27]

It was customary for the pope to issue an especially favoured clerk with a dispensation to retain his curial offices, on promotion to bishop. For example, Bartholomé Regas was given a dispensation by Calixtus III to retain all his curial offices (of vice-treasurer, custos of the chancery, chamber clerk, scriptor, and lector) on promotion as Bishop of Barcelona, until he gained possession of the see: in the event he kept chamber clerkship and scriptorship until his death twenty years later.

[27] Instances of bishops who reacquired one or more loci as secretary after resigning on promotion: Enrico Bruni (Frenz, Kanzlei, p. 345), Rafaello Ceva (ibid. 437), Giuliano Cibo (ibid. 391), Domenico Galletti (ibid. 317), Agostino Spinola (ibid. 292).

This was not an innovation of the mid-century: under Martin V Angelotto Foschi had retained possession of his chamber clerkship after promotion to the see of Anagni in 1415, and Benedetto Guidalotti also retained his clerkship after promotion to the see of Valva-Sulmona in 1427. By the end of the century it was normal for both secretaries and chamber clerks to be empowered to retain these offices on promotion to a bishopric, unless there were special circumstances: what had been the exception became the rule.[28]

At first sight the opportunities for promotion to the greatest prize of all, the cardinalate, appear to have favoured the secretaries. Sixteen chamber clerks (11.3 per cent) became cardinals over the whole period, and thirty-five secretaries (14.5 per cent) achieved the same dignity during their lifetimes (though some not until after 1527). However, if the period 1417–86 is separated from the later one, a very different pattern appears. In the earlier period nine former chamber clerks became cardinals, and only four former secretaries. The system of buying secretarial posts from 1487 onwards meant that any rich and ambitious clerk in the Roman court could invest in a secretary's office for a time, while he was on his way to the cardinalate and actually doing other things. Of the thirty-one former secretaries who achieved the red hat after 1487 (from whose number came 15.7 per cent of the cardinals promoted between that date and May 1527), only the four domestic secretaries (Podocataro, Bembo, Benedetto Accolti, and Sadoleto) can be said to have made a career as papal secretary: the rest were primarily investors in the office.

The thirty-one secretaries appointed after 1486 who became cardinals each spent on average six years in the secretarial office, which is just over a year below the norm for tenure of the office in the period. Many, if not most of them, are likely to have exercised the secretary's office through deputies. Marino Caracciolo held his secretary's place for thirty years, most of which he spent outside the Roman court on diplomatic missions. Giandomenico De Cupis showed his appreciation by buying (in his own name) a second secretary's place, and Agostino Spinola purchased two extra places.

It would be as sensible to talk of these clergy pursuing a career as papal secretary as it would be to talk about a major stockholder in Imperial Chemical Industries pursuing a career in industrial chemistry. This group of men were investors in

[28] See Von Hofmann, *Forschungen*, i. 210–14.

bureaucracy, and were not, in respect of their investments, bureaucrats. Their career patterns demonstrate that a substantial proportion (roughly 15 per cent) of those whose business acumen and patronage expertise took them as far as the cardinalate thought that the revenues, access opportunities, and dignity of the secretary's office made it a sound investment.

It seems that some recent discussion of 'Why men became cardinals' has underrated the need for wealth as a means of getting to the top of the Roman court, and that, in the later Renaissance period at least, two of the most important requisites for attaining this dignity were large cash resources, and a sound investment strategy. It is true that not all cardinals got their promotion through their wealth, and that some cardinals had difficulty in finding the money to support the standard of life which their high office required. But a majority of cardinals were wealthy and it is likely that they owed their promotion in part to their earlier prosperity. The same was true of high officers in other Renaissance courts.[29]

How men grew rich at the papal court was described candidly in 1438 by the Florentine humanist Lapo da Castiglionchio, who had spent two years in the Roman court and purported to think he was about to commence a fat career there, though the real intention of his tract may be satirical.

There are as many ways to wealth in the Roman court as there are offices there, ways not just to a modest competence but to riches. The wealth acquired by cardinals and protonotaries is known to all—no question about the pope himself! Equally obvious is the wealth of the chamberlain, in whose jurisdiction is the whole court, and all the provinces, towns, and their populations of the papal state. What kind of profits go to the vice-chancellor, to the referendaries, the secretaries, the papal chamberlains, the chamber clerks, the auditor of the chamber? What do the curial advocates make, the proctors, pleaders, officers of the signatura, apostolic scriptors? There are many others, enjoying the countless sources of wealth which allow any of these folk to live comfortably and splendidly in the court without any other source of income.

Asked by his interlocutor in the *Dialogue* whence all this money comes, he replies that it all comes from the petitioners to the

[29] See e.g. D. Girgensohn, 'Wie wird man Kardinal? Kuriale und außerkuriale Karrieren an der Wende des 14. zum 15. Jahrh.', *Quellen*, 57 (1977), 138–62. A good appreciation of later Renaissance practice is in W. Reinhard, 'Ämterlaufbahn und Familienstatus'. For financial stringency among Renaissance cardinals, see Chambers, 'The Economic Predicament of Renaissance Cardinals'.

Roman court, and that all their fees and gratuities are in the end divided in common among the curial officers.[30]

IX

If some men achieved the peak of clerical ambition through a career in the Roman court, others failed or for other reasons withdrew. The total is hard to reckon with accuracy, because of the possibility that papal officials recorded here only once or twice may have had careers in other posts whose records have been overlooked. But it seems that sixty-three officers in the sample withdrew from the Roman court at one stage or another (17.2 per cent of the total). Of these about half (8.7 per cent of the total) had careers which appear not to have lasted longer than one or two years. Others withdrew after long curial careers, the longest of which was forty-six years. The average length of service of those recorded as withdrawing was 6.2 years.

Perhaps some gave up the quest for princely favour, and went back to live on whatever benefices they possessed. This would not have been a difficult decision for someone like Carlo de' Medici, Cosimo's illegitimate son (1430–92), who after a brief spell as chamber clerk in Rome returned to Tuscany, and ended his days as Provost of Prato. But the more likely explanation for withdrawal is a decision to seek favour and fortune elsewhere, with another prince.

Some French and German papal officers returned to their native lands, though few Spaniards seem to have done so. The Englishman Adam Moleyns seems to have held a supernumerary post as chamber clerk at some time between 1435 and 1439, but there is no indication that he seriously pursued an official career at the papal court, and it is probable that he was more interested in the prestige of the title of chamber clerk (he also secured appointment as apostolic protonotary) than in actually exercising the office. Two or three of the French and German officers who went home were bishops returning to their sees. Johannes Atzel, for example, after short service as a chamber clerk went in 1426 to his bishopric of Verdun, where he died in 1472.

But the curial bishop who returns to his see and remains

---

[30] R. Scholz, 'Eine humanistiche Schilderung der Kurie aus dem Jahre 1438', *Quellen*, 16 (1914), 108–53, at pp. 134–5.

there indefinitely to carry out his episcopal duties is a rare bird. Antonio Fatati, who was beatified in the eighteenth century, devoted himself to episcopal duties from his translation to Ancona in 1463 until his death in 1484: the withdrawal of Gian Matteo Giberti from the Roman court to his see of Verona in 1528 is well known, as is the contemporary withdrawal of Jacopo Sadoleto to his see at Carpentras.

Nine or ten other curial bishops in the sample returned to their sees, some because they had fallen into disgrace at court. Gaspare Colonna returned to his see of Benevento after the death of his uncle, Pope Martin V, in 1431, and the subsequent rebellion of the Colonna against Eugenius IV. Tommaso Piccolomini went to Soana on his promotion to the bishopric in 1467, but this was almost certainly the means adopted by Paul II to get rid of him. The miserable Ventura Benassai, a lay curial banker and chamber clerk who got himself made Bishop of Massa, went there after he had been broken for corruption in 1504. Bartolomeo Bertini got papal permission to go to his see of Valva-Sulmona in 1437, but continued to enjoy half the proceeds of his curial office. Andrea Buondelmonte was resident in his see of Florence after he had acquired it simoniacally in 1532, but his character suggests that he was not impelled by a religious sense of duty in doing so. Niccolò Sandonnini, who had had a long curial career, is said to have resided in his see of Lucca from appointment until death, because his flock intervened to stop him accepting any more papal appointments. Leonardo Salutati seems to have gone to his see of Fiesole on appointment in 1450 and to have remained there until his death in 1466—his longevity, indeed, apparently embarrassed the Florentine regime, which had other plans for the disposal of the bishopric.

It may be assumed that influential Tuscans like Giovanni Acciaiuoli and Antonio Francesco Tornabuoni, who both briefly had supernumerary posts as chamber clerks, belonged to the same class as Carlo de' Medici, and had plenty of other strings to their bow if a career in the chamber proved difficult or uncongenial. It is unknown why Giovanni Boscoli, a relative of the curial bankers of the same name, should have briefly held the title of chamber clerk, gone to Bologna as an important papal envoy in 1431, and then after one or two other curial missions returned to Florence to practice as a lawyer.

Another of the half-a-dozen or so clergy with supranumerary appointments as chamber clerks who for one reason or another left the Roman court was Antonio Capodilista. This was a jurist in the suite of Cardinal Ludovico of Treviso who left Rome to return to his native Padua, where he was a canon of the cathedral and where his family was rich and powerful. The Capodilista had held fiefs in the Paduan countryside since the fourteenth century, and during the lifetime of Antonio acquired a member who devoted himself to the genealogy of the family. In the sixteenth century they gave their name to one of the most luxurious and beautiful villas of the Veneto.

X

Literary laymen did not find it easy to get a foothold in the Roman court as papal officials, in spite of the few brilliant careers enjoyed by lay papal secretaries. Competition among humanists for the papal secretary office was ferocious, and some of the most distinguished scholars of the fifteenth century emerged defeated from this struggle. Francesco Filelfo (1398–1481) tried for years to secure a place among the secretaries, but the hostility of some of the existing secretaries denied it to him, and all he got was a temporary pension and the grant of the mere title of secretary from Pius II.

Another striking example of the difficulties of making headway in the Roman court is the career of the distinguished Tuscan humanist, theologian, and encyclopaedist, Raffaele Maffei of Volterra.[31] Maffei belonged to a family with very strong connections indeed with the Roman court, and was the son of Gerardo di Giovanni, who held important office in both the chamber and the chancery, and the brother of Antonio, another curial officer and a prominent Riario dependant who paid for his loyalties with his life during the suppression of the Pazzi conspiracy. Other family connections made good curial careers, but Raffaele, whether from moral scruple or from lack of careerist competence, never secured any office above that of papal scriptor and of notary of the Roman court, which was a not-too-costly sinecure. The only two members of the Maffei family to secure bishoprics were both Franciscans. Similar frustrations to those which were perhaps experienced by Raffaele attended the curial career of Alessandro, the younger brother of the more successful papal secretary, Paolo Cortesi.[32]

Some eminent humanists employed as papal secretaries

---

[31] D'Amico, *Renaissance Humanism*, pp. 82–5 and *passim*; Frenz, *Kanzlei*, p. 438.

[32] D'Amico, *Renaissance Humanism*, pp. 73–6.

abandoned the post or lost it, even after a distinguished curial career. The most striking example is Poggio Bracciolini, who seems to have fallen out of favour in the Roman court early in the pontificate of Nicholas V, perhaps because of some of the fierce literary and personal quarrels with other secretaries. So in 1453, after a curial career of half a century, he left Rome in order to take up the prestigious and well-paid post of Chancellor of Florence, which he then occupied for five years until his retirement. An equally distinguished example is that of the poet and literary scholar Pietro Bembo, who served as one of the two domestic secretaries of Leo X throughout the pontificate, but failed to get any preferment under his successor Adrian VI, and in 1521 left the Roman court, to which he did not return until his appointment as cardinal in 1539.

The career of Jacopo Sadoleto provides both parallels and contrasts with that of Bembo. Sadoleto started from a lower social position than Bembo; as the son of an Estense law professor, he lacked the prestige and political clout of a Venetian noble. But, once installed with him as domestic secretary, he used the advantages of office to better effect than Bembo did his. Above all, he was willing, as Bembo was not, to accept ordination, and thus to enable himself to acquire the bishopric of Carpentras in 1517. After Leo's death in 1521 Sadoleto waited a few months in Rome to see if preferment was forthcoming from the new pope; when none came he retired to his diocese of Carpentras—which was not in France, but was a part of the papal enclave of Comtat Venaissin. On the accession of Clement VII in 1523 Sadoleto was called out of retirement at Carpentras to become domestic secretary to the new pope. Only weeks before Rome fell in 1527 Sadoleto obtained the pope's permission once more to return to his diocese of Carpentras: it may be that the leave granted was only a short one of three months, but in the event his absence was prolonged for a term of years, and his post of papal secretary was never resumed.

The distinguished humanist who was granted an honorary secretarial place was a different case. The Milanese humanist Lodrisio Crivelli was one of these; he got the honorary secretarial title from Pius II, and used the connection when he fled to the Roman court during his quarrel with Francesco Sforza in 1463/4, but he never secured (and perhaps never sought) a permanent secretarial place in Rome. Crivelli's place was in Milan, the only court where he had real political importance.

All in all, the tenacity with which men pursued careers in the

Roman court is evidence enough of the opportunities it offered. Lapo da Castiglionchio, at that time in his early thirties, wrote that he had so far spent two years there, and that he looked forward to spending the rest of his life there. Even when old and ill, men hung grimly on to their official posts in Rome, and there seems to be little evidence of a pattern of retirement. Papal officers might build stately houses and buy estates in their home areas with the proceeds of office in the Roman court, like Angelo Geraldini of Amelia, or the Rizzoni family of Verona,[33] or Battista Bagarotti of Piacenza, the brother of the Milanese chancellor. But they did not on this account give up their posts in the Roman court, although they might, if their position there was strong, spend more time in their place of origin without abandoning their Roman offices.

As for abandoning the Roman court to follow a religious vocation, the phenomenon was practically unknown. Francesco Coppini, the Bishop of Terni and former chamber clerk, died as a monk in the monastery of S. Paolo fuori le Mura, but this was only because he had been sent there in disgrace after his supposed misbehaviour during his legation to England in 1461. Filippo Baronci of Pistoia, former secretary, scriptor, and abbreviator, gave up all three offices to 'enter religion' in 1427, but this was in order to assume the comfortable post of preceptor of the hospital of S. Spirito in Sassia in Rome.

---

[33] See D'Amico, *Renaissance Humanism*, pp. 71-2; Von Hofmann, *Forschungen*, i. 46, 125 and ii. 38, 136, 235, 257.

4

Recruitment, Organization, and Performance

I

In late medieval and early modern societies, promotion to office in church or state was usually due to patronage, or to what contemporary Englishmen would have called 'good lordship'. Behind the client's link with his patron there often lay the further bonds of a common regional origin (in English terms, the lord and his dependant were 'countrymen'), and perhaps also of kinship. The protection offered by the lord and the service returned by the client were normally given within this framework, and most advancement was due at least in some measure to links of this nature.

It would be foolish, however, to disregard the success of the popes in overcoming the negative effects of the prevailing clientelism, and in getting the best men to serve their cause. The papal government ran its secretariat, finances, and propaganda through some of the most able minds of the day, turned to its own account many of the great advances in the arts and sciences, and kept Rome, in spite of the struggle with the princes and the drift towards schism, the main centre of religious power and cultural identity. Place-seeking was one of the chief occupations of the Roman court, perhaps the chief, but a government of sordid jobbers could not have achieved such lofty aims.

There was very little formal policy in the Roman court about the way its members should be recruited. The earlier, fourteenth-century requirement that papal officials should be tonsured clerks and not laymen was applied with far less rigour during the Schism (1378–1417), because of the need to sell curial posts. The post of scriptor could easily be executed by laymen, and so was sold freely to them, even if they were married, and even if they were to work in the penitentiary.[1] Almost half the secretaries were laymen in the period from

---

[1] Von Hofmann, *Forschungen*, ii. 146–7. For the scriptors see Schwarz, *Die Organisation*, pp. 131–7.

1417 until the setting up of their college in 1487 (forty-three out of eighty-eight). The year 1487 marked a watershed in this as in other matters: from that time onwards, although the one or two domestic secretaries were still quite often laymen, the other secretaries (who were, of course, in a big numerical majority) were normally all clerks.

It was exceptional, however, for the office of chamber clerk to be conferred on a layman. The custom that chamber clerks should also be papal chaplains made such an appointment difficult. There seem to have been only two instances of laymen who became participating chamber clerks, and remained laymen throughout their chamber careers. One was Gaspare Biondo, son of a married layman-secretary. Gaspare succeeded to his father's posts of chamber notary and secretary in 1463, and obtained the clerkship, with dispensation to hold it in plurality with the offices of secretary and scriptor, in 1483. The other was the Roman notable Pietro Leni, who succeeded to the chamber clerkship of his brother Luca (who had been a canon of S. Maria Maggiore in Rome) in 1486, and remained a chamber clerk until his death in 1493.

Ventura Benassai was also a layman, a curial banker, at the time of his appointment as chamber clerk in 1499. It is uncertain whether he took clerical orders at this time, or at some slightly later date before his nomination (which gave rise to some scandal) as Bishop of Massa in 1501. Similarly, Franco Giberti, whose main distinction is to have been the father of the reforming bishop Gian Matteo Giberti, began his career in the Roman court as a lay merchant, but took orders at some point before his appointment as chamber clerk in 1511. It was therefore unusual, though by no means unknown, for a chamber clerk to be a layman. The remark by Paris de Grassis in 1504 that the chamber clerks were 'more laymen than clerks' referred to their way of life rather than to their personal status.[2]

There was no specific examination of literacy or morals for chamber clerks, unless they were also apostolic scriptors (such examinations were in theory required for the scriptor's post). Assurances about the candidate's moral qualities (de qualitatibus ac moribus vite sue) had to be given when a secretary was first formally received into the college.[3] The nomination to a clerkship or to a secretary's post was nominally by the pope's

[2] Von Hofmann, Forschungen, i. 217 n.
[3] Schwarz, Die Organisation, pp. 131-7.

wish, and often (though not invariably) expressed in a bull. In the procedure after 1487 the nominee had to present his bull of nomination to the college before admission. There is no indication that the candidate for the office submitted a petition for it, as he would have done for a scriptor's place.

II

The Reform proposed by the cardinals in 1423 said that the chamber clerks should be distinguished and serious persons (*viri insigni et graves*): earlier, at the Council of Constance, it had been said that chamber clerks ought to be doctors or licentiates in law.[4] There was, however, no formal requirement that chamber clerks should be legally qualified, and some of them were not (see Table 4). However, the fact that the apostolic chamber was a court of law which was authorized to decide cases in the absence of the chamberlain, and without reference to the court of the auditor of the chamber, meant that some legal knowledge was essential to a chamber clerk. The rule was that major lawsuits (*causae majores*) were not to be assigned to papal commissioners for decision, unless the commissioners were licensed in canon or civil law, or had the appropriate doctorate. However, the jurisdiction of the chamber was not that of commissioners.[5]

Able lawyers were certainly attracted to the chamber. Of the chamber clerks serving in the first half of the fifteenth century, seven at some time held the post of auditor of the apostolic chamber, which normally went to someone of considerable legal ability. Many chamber clerks, such as Gozzadini of Bologna, Capodilista of Padua, Roselli of Arezzo, came from dynasties of well-known lawyers. Niccolò Sandonnini de Luca (1435–99) was a clever lawyer who served in Cardinal Bessarion's household, was chamber clerk and secretary, and became Bishop of Modena and subsequently (when Borso d'Este refused to let him into his first see) of Lucca. Others, such as Francesco Pizzolpassi of Bologna and Domenico Capranica, had distinguished careers which were enabled to some extent by their legal ability. A well-known jurist of the later period was Ieronimo Ghinucci of Siena (d. 1541), later cardinal, who was an important figure of the Medici courts, and was both

---

4 Partner, *Papal State*, pp. 138–40.
5 Ibid., pp. 147–9.

chamber clerk and secretary; a comparable career was led by Lorenzo Pucci (1459–1531), another canonist, and a former law teacher at the University of Pisa, who passed through the apostolic chamber on his way to the red hat. The post of chamber clerk was competed for by established law teachers from the universities, and some chamber clerks taught law in the Roman University. Giovanni Gozzadini (1477–1517) is an example of both these categories.

Law teachers like Gozzadini and the Paduan Suliman de' Sulimanni (d. 1468), or the future Cardinal Stefano Nardini who had been Rector Citramontanarum and Reader in the Codex at Bologna in 1444–5 and came to Rome in 1449, went from the University to careers in the Roman court in which they remained until death. But it would be wrong to think of teaching posts in the University simply as one of the gates for entry into papal service: law teachers could go in and out of both careers as best suited them. An example is the Bolognese lawyer Luigi de' Garsi (d. 1450), who became a scriptor in the Roman court in 1418, probably while the papal court was in Mantua and waiting to proceed to Bologna. He taught law in Bologna from 1419 onwards; he was also a canon of the cathedral. He became a chamber clerk in 1427, and was *mensarius* periodically until 1430. He was a Rota auditor by 1431, and a deputy for the auditor of the chamber in that year and in 1434. He worked spasmodically in the chamber after that date, but in 1440 he evidently returned to Bologna, working as vicar of the bishop's court, and teaching the Decretals in the University. In 1446 he went back to Rome, became auditor of the chamber, and finally resigned his post of participating chamber clerk to Guiniforte Buonconti. He became Bishop of Rimini in 1449, and died in 1450, leaving a collection of manuscripts to the Dominicans of Bologna.

Towards the end of the period chamber clerks with legal degrees seem to have become rather less frequent. It is possible that some of the clerks of Leo X and Clement VII, such as Niccolò Gaddi, Bonifacio Cattaneo, Cristoforo Barocci, and Thomas le Roy, possessed law degrees, but they are not normally so described, and the same goes for the Ponzetti, uncle and nephew, and for Franco Giberti. Most of these later chamber clerks were above all financial entrepreneurs, as the criticism made by Paris de Grassis implied.

III

In the first half of the fifteenth century the secretaries were not as a rule lawyers, though under Martin V quite a few important secretaries, such as Bartolomeo Aragazzi of Montepulciano, Antonio Loschi, and Cencio de' Rustici, were so qualified. Petrus de Trilhia, a clerk who had passed as papal secretary from Benedict XIII to John XXIII and then to Martin V (in whose court he was also a chamber notary), left the Roman court in 1425 and taught law in the University of Bologna: he subsequently appeared at the Council of Basle.

The laymen-secretaries thus could also be lawyers, and it is noticeable that someone who worked as close to the secretaries as Leon Battista Alberti was qualified in canon law. Lorenzo Valla, however, is not known to have had a law degree, even though he came from a dynasty of canon lawyers. Few of the domestic secretaries of the second half of the century and the opening years of the following century had legal qualifications, either. The rise of Bartolomeo Roverella as secretary under Eugenius IV and his successors was helped by his canon law abilities, and under Paul II Leonardo Dati, the Florentine humanist and domestic secretary, had a doctorate in civil law. But for the one or two secretaries who worked closest to the pope, a legal qualification was unusual; only three of the eleven fifteenth-century domestic secretaries seem to have had one.

For clerks of the later period holding the venal office of secretary in the college set up in 1487, a degree in law was common. The reason for this was not that the secretarial work demanded a legal qualification, but that the type of rich and ambitious curialist who invested in a secretary's place after 1487 was likely to have come to the Roman court equipped with a degree in canon law. Some clerks who held secretarial places, like Benedetto Accolti (1497–1549), were among the well-known canonists of the day; but their legal abilities had little to do with the execution of the duties of the secretarial post. The German humanist and papal secretary Jacob Aurelius Questenberg (1465–1524) was a notable example of the legally qualified ultramontane who makes a successful career in the Roman court.

It was inevitable that the Roman court should seek to recruit able humanists to indite its correspondence and conduct its propaganda: from this point of view the mastery of a revived

TABLE 5. *Chamber clerks and secretaries with humanist connections or activities* (% given in parentheses)

	Chamber clerks	Secretaries
Author of Neo-Latin work	7 (5.0)	37 (15.3)
Correspondent of humanists	20 (14.3)	60 (24.9)
Well-known Greek or Latin scholar	19 (13.6)	43 (17.8)

Latin vocabulary and syntax was only an extension of the old *ars dictaminis* which had always led to promotion in Rome. As the Englishman Samuel Pepys remarked two centuries later, the man educated in humane studies possessed the 'knowledge how to tell a man's tale', so that he could use his wits to get advancement. The most natural office for the accomplished humanist to seek in the papal court was that of secretary, but there were many other offices where humanists were to be found. It was natural that besides their ordinary curial work some humanists should produce propagandist works magnifying the Holy See and expounding its policies. The earlier humanist secretaries played a less direct role in papal propaganda than might be imagined; in the second half of the fifteenth century the contribution of the humanists to the papal publicist effort was much greater, as is discussed below.

The aura conferred by a scholarly reputation could also be important to governments anxious for the prestige of hiring such folk, and in the first half of the fifteenth century the princely courts competed to employ the most eminent humanists. The renowned Gasperino Barzizza, for example, was offered a secretaryship by John XXIII, and actually swore the papal secretary's oath to Martin V, but never in fact worked in Rome; he preferred to work as a secretary to Filippo Maria Visconti. The way these men expected to move from one court and one city to another can be illustrated from the career of Antonio Loschi of Vicenza, who began his political career in the Milanese chancery, moved to the papal court early in the century, but can be found under Martin V remarking to the Florentine envoy that he was thinking of transferring his investments to the Florentine Monte Comune and coming to live in Florence. This may have been a feeler put out to see how much the Florentine government might be willing to pay for his services; in the event, he stayed in the Roman court until his death in 1441.

An awkward character and the habit of making enemies could deny the most distinguished humanist any permanent preferment as a papal secretary, as Filelfo's career shows. Francesco Filelfo was one of the best-known literary scholars in Italy, but the determined opposition of the resident papal secretaries blocked his advancement from honorary to effective status. However, as has been said in an earlier chapter, over 40 per cent of papal secretaries in the period 1417–87 could be described as competent humanists. From Eugenius IV to Paul II the little group of humanist-secretaries in the Roman court constituted one of the liveliest intellectual gatherings in Renaissance Italy. Biondo and Poggio, Aurispa, George of Trebizond, and Valla, were among the most original and informed minds of their time.

That the outside world thought of the papal secretaries as a group of men remarkable for their scholarly and literary pursuits is attested by the literary competition for poems on the theme of 'true friendship' written in vulgar Italian, which took place in Florence on 22 October 1441, and was known as the *Certame coronario*. The nine literary pundits chosen as judges in this competition, which was organized by Leon Battista Alberti on behalf of Piero di Cosimo de' Medici, were the secretaries of Pope Eugenius IV, then present in the city. In the allocution he pronounced for the occasion Alberti remarked that the papal secretaries had been chosen as judges to honour their pontifical master, and also because they all professed *studii d'umanita*.[6]

This acknowledgement of the competence of the secretaries as literary judges, made in the Florentine literary circle by someone who held office in the papal court at the time, is more convincing evidence of the way in which they were generally regarded than the *ex parte* claims made for the secretaries made by two of their number, Jacopo Gherardi and Sigismondo de' Conti, thirty years later. Gherardi and Conti were at that time defending the rights of the secretaries to distinction and prominence in the Roman court and their claim to precedence over the consistorial advocates in curial protocol. To support their case they asserted the special rhetorical skills which their humane studies were said to confer upon the secretaries,

---

[6] G. Gorni, 'Storia del Certame Coronario', *Rinascimento*, 2nd ser., 12 (1972), 135–81; J. R. Berrigan, 'Leonardo Dati: "Hiemsal Tragoedia": A Critical Edition with Translation', *Human.Lovanen*. 25 (1976), 84–145.

and the weighty political duties which the popes assigned to them.[7]

The progress of the classicizing spirit in the Roman court can be seen in the increasing use of humanist handwriting in papal official documents; this phenomenon has been studied by a very competent scholar.[8] His conclusions were that the influence of the new hands was to be found as much in the apostolic chamber as in the engrossments made by the secretaries and their amanuenses; he used as a main source the audit notices made by the chamber clerks in the chamber account books. The increasing influence of the humanist hands took hold of the Roman court in three main thrusts, of which the first took place under Eugenius IV, and especially during the sojourn of the court in Florence, the second under Pius II, and the third, the final one, under Sixtus IV. But his most interesting conclusion was that the influence of humanism on the curia showed itself less in its impact on the handwriting—though that was considerable—than in its influence on the style of the documents.

By the pontificate of Sixtus IV both the Roman court and most other Italian courts were already so penetrated by humanism that the presence of well-known classical scholars there had ceased to be remarkable, or in itself more than a secondary asset to the prestige and political effectiveness of princely policy. From this time forth, a measure of learning and accomplishment in classical Latin came to be taken for granted as the equipment of someone who aimed at promotion on the political wing of the papal court. Special distinction in Latin or Greek scholarship could improve a man's position in the papal court, but it tended to be viewed as ornamental rather than useful. The archaeological and historical interests of an official like Angelo Colocci, for example, were more in the nature of aristocratic diversions than aids to promotion.

There is often a doubt in a particular case whether the secretarial office was bestowed on a humanist as a true employment or as an honourable sinecure. For example, although Giannozzo Manetti, the biographer of Nicholas V, was given the office by Nicholas and confirmed in it with participating status by Pius II, there is no sign that he actually worked as a

---

[7] For the defences of the secretaries by Gherardi and Conti, see D'Amico, *Renaissance Humanism*, pp. 31–2. At the time of writing the defence, Sigismondo de' Conti was employed in engrossing the secretarial briefs, but was not himself a secretary. His lament over making the office venal in 1487 is quoted by Pastor, v. 353.

[8] Frenz, 'Eindringen', pp. 491–2.

secretary for either. Nor is there any indication that Aeneas Sylvius Piccolomini worked as a papal secretary after his appointment in 1446 or its confirmation in 1447, though in his case the nomination was not made primarily because of his humanist talents, but to honour the emperor's servant and envoy. There is, similarly, no indication that the Milanese humanist Leodrisio Crivelli actually exercised his secretarial office in the Roman court.

In 1471 Gherardi and de' Conti had been unknowingly singing the swan song of the old papal secretariat. After 1487 able humanists continued to serve the pope in the confidential role of domestic secretary, but the venality of the secretarial office meant that its old scholarly distinction had gone for ever. Sigismondo de' Conti himself lamented when the office was made systematically venal that 'Henceforth this office, which had hitherto been bestowed as a reward for industry, faithfulness, and eloquence, became simply a marketable commodity.' However, the lament of Conti disregarded the fact that the number of secretaries had been recklessly multiplied by Calixtus III some twenty years earlier. The other advocate of the secretarial cause in 1471, Gherardi, writing to the pope in 1488, expressed (perhaps hypocritically) pleasure that the number of secretaries had been increased, and also—more sincerely, since it was to his own profit—his satisfaction that absentee secretaries could henceforth draw their salaries![9]

After 1487 a good capacity for business continued to be indispensable to a chamber clerk, who was one of the main executive officers of the Roman see. But the office of secretary (saving that of domestic secretary) could henceforth be discharged entirely by substitutes, and secretaries' places were subsequently purchased by or on behalf of people who could not possibly have executed the office themselves, or could have exercised it only with difficulty. Eight bishops or archbishops bought places in the first secretarial college of 1487; most must have exercised the office through substitutes.

Far more anomalous appointments followed; in the papal financial crisis of 1521 there were several strange ones. Agostino Chigi, son of the banker, who was appointed papal secretary in 1521 and died in the same year, was only 5 years old at the time of appointment. Three lay bankers were allowed to acquire secretary's places in their own names: they were the

---

[9] Gherardi's reaction to the venal college: 'Laetor auctam dignitatem et numerus secretariorum, et ea in re absentis servi rationem haberi' (Dispacci, p. 56).

Florentine Battista Puccini, the Roman manager of the Altoviti bank; the Genovese Tomasso Salvagi; and the well-known Anton Fugger. All these appointments were, of course, connected with loans made by the bankers concerned to the Holy See. In two cases the banker concerned was granted two secretary places, though with an obligation to resign one of them within a year.

The nomination of children to a secretary's place was not confined to moments of papal financial need. In 1502 the 9-year-old Giandomenico de Cupis, the son of Julius II's former mistress, Lucrezia dei Normanni, was given a secretary's place. De Cupis was the future bishop and cardinal, whose positive qualities seem to have emerged only rather later in his life: the dying Julius II refused to grant him the red hat in 1513, describing him as *un putto ignorante*.

The most remarkable sale of a secretary's place was that to the hospital of S. Giovanni in Laterano, which was allowed to make the purchase for 600 ducats in 1502. The terms were that the hospital should enjoy the place in perpetuity, thus effectively reducing by one the number of secretarial places for sale. It was to enjoy all the income of a place, with the exception of revenues concerned with monastic congregations.

IV

Some of the more striking distinctions between Renaissance and modern bureaucracies can be drawn from the evidence of the age of entry into papal service as a Roman court officer. Dates of birth are known for ninety-seven officials in the survey, or 26.6 per cent of the total. The dates of birth of secretaries are in better supply than those of chamber clerks, because the literary figures among the secretaries have attracted more scholarly attention than the purely clerical officials. No less than forty-two of the ninety-seven officials (43.2 per cent) for whom birth dates are known could be termed 'humanists'. In consequence, although chamber clerks number 38.5 per cent of the main survey, and secretaries 66.2 per cent, the chamber officials account for only 28.9 per cent of those whose birth date is known, and the secretaries 79.3 per cent (the apparent discrepancy comes from the eight secretaries in the smaller sample who were also chamber clerks).

It is also possible to look at the age at which officials reached the senior dignities of chamber clerk or secretary. In forty-four

TABLE 6. *Age on appointment to papal office, 1417–1527* (% of known cases given in parentheses)

Age	No. entering papal civil service	No. appointed as chamber clerk	No. appointed as secretary
5–19	10 (10.3)	0	5 (6.5)
20–29	33 (34.0)	9 (32.1)	13 (16.9)
30–39	24 (24.7)	8 (28.6)	22 (28.6)
40–49	21 (21.6)	6 (21.4)	20 (26.0)
50–59	7 (7.2)	4 (14.3)	13 (16.9)
60 +	2 (2.1)	1 (3.6)	4 (5.2)
TOTAL	97	28 (28.9)	77 (79.3)

cases (45.4 per cent), no earlier appointment in papal service is known before the official was made chamber clerk or secretary. There is no significant difference in such cases between the offices of chamber clerk, thirteen (46 per cent) of whom in the sample of twenty-eight are not known to have held an earlier papal appointment, and that of secretary (thirty-one or 40.2 per cent). Two factors which affect the extremes of Table 6 are the venality of the secretarial and chamber clerk offices in the later part of the period, and the practice of rewarding elderly humanists with a papal secretaryship. As has been mentioned above, Agostino Chigi, the 5-year-old son of the banker, was bought a secretaryship in 1521; Giovanni Usumari had been made apostolic protonotary in 1490 at the age of 10, and papal secretary at the age of 15. At the other end of the scale the humanist Giovanni Aurispa is first found as a papal secretary aged over 60, in 1433, and Johannes Copis, who had entered the papal court by 1479, bought a place as chamber clerk in 1526, when in his late 80s.

About a third of papal officers had entered papal service aged between 20 and 29. One difference between the Renaissance and modern career structures is evident: 30.9 per cent of the sample entered the Roman court over the age of 40. On the other hand, careers in the Roman court were not short. The average lifespan of the officers in the sample was 61.2 years.[10]

10 This figure is strikingly confirmed for the canons and other beneficed clergy in St Peter's, 1477–1599, who are estimated to have had an average survival to 61 years by P. Schmidtbauer, 'Prolegomena zu einer Sozialgeschichte des Kapitels von St. Peter im Vatikan', *Röm.Hist.Mitt.* 28 (1986), 243–301, at p. 269.

Once men acquired a Roman court post they were, because of the exceptional patronage opportunities, unlikely to leave the court unless they fell drastically out of favour, or unless they came from very powerful families which could fulfil their expectations elsewhere. If the assumption (not an entirely correct one) is made that all officers who entered the Roman Court remained there until death, the average length of career in the Court would be twenty-eight years. Amending the calculation to take account of the 17 per cent who left the Roman court at some stage is difficult, but perhaps an average length of career of twenty-four years would be nearer the mark. The long, sequential careers of the group discussed at the beginning of Chapter 2 above were not, therefore, exceptional. One factor tended to lengthen the effective time spent in the Roman court: a good many clerks had worked in it as secretaries or dependants of cardinals or curial bishops for a number of years before they got appointments as papal officers.

V

Admission to the office of chamber clerk was a business which placed rather more emphasis on entry into a privileged corporation than on entry into government service. Having secured papal nomination (which, at least from the mid fifteenth century, was usually by the issue of a bull), the aspirant clerk swore allegiance to the Holy See between the hands of the chamberlain, vice-chamberlain, or his lieutenant, and also paid a sum known as the *jocalia* of which the greater part went to the chapel of the chamber clerks, and the rest to their corporation. The oath was that of a papal chaplain: apart from promises of fidelity the chaplain swore to defend and maintain the Roman papacy and the regalia of St Peter and other rights of the Roman Church. He also swore to carry out faithfully the business and commissions (*negocia et officia*) committed to him by the pope or the chamberlain, to look faithfully after whatever goods were entrusted to him by the chamber, and to avoid all fraud in this respect.[11] The oath could be administered anywhere by a competent person; on different occasions it was sworn in the papal antechamber, in the chamberlain's house, in a chapel in S. Maria Maggiore, in the Camera del Papagallo

---

[11] G. Tellenbach, 'Beiträge zur kurialen Verwaltungsgeschichte im 14. Jahrhundert', *Quellen*, 24 (1932/3), 150–87, at p. 180.

in the Vatican Palace, in the vice-chamberlain's garden, in the apostolic chamber.

The second and more important step was the reception of the candidate by the corporation of the chamber. Since the financial interests of the other chamber clerks were vitally involved, this was no empty ceremony, but a closely watched and sometimes bitterly contested business. On one occasion, as is related below, the chamberlain tore the robes of office from the neophyte clerk and sent him away. The procedure took place in the apostolic chamber at a formal session of the chamber. The new clerk was robed in the rochet and cape of office. He swore to observe all the privileges of the other lords of the chamber, principally the constitution of Eugenius IV which limited the number of chamber clerks to seven participating members (he might have already sworn this to the chamberlain or vice-chamberlain, but in that case he would usually repeat the oath). If he was a supernumerary clerk he normally recognized that this was his status, and often promised (if that was the case) not to lay claim to any of the revenues of the office. If his new colleagues were satisfied about his status and intentions, they gave him the kiss of peace, and 'received him into the consortio of the other chamber clerks'. He was then conducted to his stall, wearing his new robes. If he had become a participating chamber clerk, he was said to have been given the place (datus fuit sibi locus).

Until the last two decades of the fifteenth century, when supernumerary places for chamber clerks were suppressed, the essential distinction was between a participatory and a supernumerary place. Under Martin V the number of chamber clerks had been high, especially because of pressure from the various obediences. In 1418 there had been fifteen chamber clerks, in 1420 thirteen, in 1425 fifteen, and in 1430 at the end of the pontificate there were still ten. According to the 1438 bull, clerks who had been nominated above the statutory number of seven were to be content with the name, dress, and standing of chamber clerk, but they received no revenues and had no other rights. In due course, when a place fell vacant, the pope would name either the most senior, or another of the supernumeraries whom he thought fit. The supernumerary post was thus an expectative right, though one given without guarantee of its fruition. In this way the pressure exerted by the corporation on the popes to preserve the restricted number and hence the individual revenues of its members had been successful.

But administrative practice did not always fit in with these careful arrangements to defend property rights. When chamber clerks were sent on missions away from the curia, someone had to do the job they had been performing in Rome. This usually meant that one of the supernumerary clerks would perform the work. Should he be paid for it directly from corporation revenues, and at what stage, if any, of his activity as a substitute did he acquire a changed legal status? Earlier rules made on the subject had had to do with the rights sometimes accorded to named chamber clerks to continue to draw their share of the corporation revenue, even when they were absent from the Roman court on mission. Other less privileged clerks, who were absent from Rome or were not working in the chamber, were excluded from participating in its income.[12]

There was a dispute in 1444 about the work done in the chamber as a substitute on behalf of absent clerks by the supernumerary clerk, Petrus de Sanctolaria, whom the pope required to be admitted to the full rights of chamber clerk. A compromise was reached, by which Petrus de Sanctolaria was allowed to draw the emoluments of an absent participating clerk when he performed the absentee's duty, though the absent clerk drew his own salary for the whole month in which he left the curia, and the whole month in which he returned. Similar exceptions in favour of other named supernumerary clerks were made in 1450–1 and later.[13] In 1455 this practice was denounced by Calixtus III in a bull which mentioned the importunity, ambition, and avarice of the multitude of supernumeraries, forbidding them further to receive the revenues of

[12] Partner, *Papal State*, pp. 217–18 (3 Dec. 1425). An earlier order had authorized Benedetto Guidalotti to continue to draw his share of chamber clerks' revenues even when not in residence in the Roman court, Div. Cam. 6, fo. 173b, 12 Aug. 1420.

[13] 4 Sept. 1444, Arch. Cam. I, vol. 1713, fos. 16b, 20b. Petrus de Sanctolaria secured a participating place, Div. Cam. 6, fo. 78b, 30 Aug. 1446; see also Reg. Vat. 435, fo. 2b (9 Feb. 1448). The ordinance of 4 Nov. 1450, Div. Cam. 26, fo. 179, was made by the chamber clerks sitting alone. '[Five named chamber clerks] camere apostolice clerici inter se de eorum unanimi consensu statuerunt et ordinaverunt quod de cetero nullus clericorum debeat facere aliquem mensem seu aliquod exercitium officii huiusmodi clericatus exercere vel gerere nisi sit de septem numerariis unus verus et intra numerum septenarium comprehensus, et non aliter ... De quia tunc ordinatione expresse excipi voluerunt dominum Jacobum de Mozarellis dicte camere clericum quem de speciali gratia voluerunt posse huiusmodi officium exercere loco domini Jacobi Turlono.' Similar provisions to participate while he was doing the work of an absent clerk, in favour of the supernumerary Jacopo Feo of Savona, 27 Oct. 1451 (Div. Cam. 26, fo. 209).

absent portionary clerks, and ordering also that they should thenceforth attend only the formal part of sittings of the chamber, leaving the room when judgements were to be deliberated. One wonders, reading the indignant language of this bull, whether the portionary chamber clerks had not already been made to pay something to remain in their places. But, in spite of Calixtus's bull, two months after its issue he made arrangements for a favoured and important clerk appointed over the quota of the seven participant clerks, Pedro Climent the *soldanus* and depositary, to enjoy the revenues of absent chamber clerks in precisely the manner which the pope had a few weeks earlier so vehemently denounced.[14]

The resistance of a powerful chamberlain to papal conferment of participatory status on a supernumerary clerk, when the chamberlain's consent had not been obtained to a papal appointment to a place, is strikingly shown by an incident told in Vespasiano da Bisticci's life of the Spanish curialist Juan Margarit, later Cardinal Moles. Margarit had been a supernumerary chamber clerk since January 1450; the pope named him in October of that year to the place left vacant by Pietro de Sanctolaria (who had had a participating place from 1446 until his death). On 2 October Cardinal Antonio de la Cerda transmitted the papal order to the chamber that Margarit was to be admitted to full participating status. According to Vespasiano, Margarit on the pope's order went to the chamber to be admitted, and the chamberlain (Cardinal Ludovico da Treviso) tore the official robes of a chamber clerk off his back after he had assumed them. Margarit returned to the pope to complain, and Nicholas V upheld him against the chamberlain ('Scarampo'), with whom the pope had a violent scene. The chamberlain withdrew his opposition and humbly apologized, and the record shows that three days later Margarit was admitted to the full office with the consent of the three chamber clerks present. The incident was subsequently used by Nicholas V (not the firmest of popes) as evidence that he was capable of controlling an over-powerful official like Ludovico da Treviso.

A slight suspicion hangs over Calixtus III, but it is uncertain that either supernumerary or portionary posts as chamber clerk were systematically sold before Sixtus IV: a reform proposal made by Cardinal Carafa in the last decade of the

[14] Reg. Vat. 467, fo. 3, 7 July 1455; having been sworn in as chamber clerk two days earlier, Pedro Climent was taken to the apostolic chamber to be received as a clerk, but met there with the protest of the dean of the chamber clerks, Nichola Delavelle, and of his colleagues, that Climent had been appointed

century remarks that clerkships of the Chamber were not sold before Sixtus. They were certainly sold and were also resaleable by 1483, as Sixtus's bull of that year makes clear.[15] The price paid for the chamber clerk's office rose steeply, from 5,000 ducats or less in the last decade of the fifteenth century, to 10,000 in the second decade of the sixteenth. This was a huge price, more than double that paid for any other collegiate office in the Roman court.

The full sitting of the apostolic chamber was required at least twice weekly. It was presided over by the chamberlain (or, more often, by the vice-chamberlain or lieutenant). Under him sat the treasurer, the councillors if such officials had been appointed, the portionary chamber clerks sitting under the senior clerk or dean, the fiscal auditor, the *advocatus pauperum*, and the other fiscal officials. By 1438 the 'councillors' had disappeared. As one of the main papal official bodies and tribunals the chamber affected a very dignified air. Its members were the *domini de camera* and it was usual to refer to the clerks as 'presiding' in the formal meetings. Early in the sixteenth century the popes deputed to one of the chamber clerks the running of the Roman grain supply organization, the annona, and he became known as the 'president' of the annona. The same title was later given to other chamber clerks placed in charge of the Roman mint, of the urban services *delle strade*, and of various indirect urban taxes. Because they 'presided', the appellation of 'presidents' of the chamber was sometimes given to chamber clerks during the late fifteenth century and later, but this was only a title of dignity, and did not refer to any specific office unless the clerk concerned also had the duty of 'president' of one of the Roman urban supervisory bodies.

The changed emphasis in the early sixteenth century, when the apostolic chamber was responsible for the running of the papal state in a far more direct way than hitherto, can be read in the new statutes issued to the chamber in 1518 by Leo X.[16] These are far more specific than those of Eugenius IV. They require the chamber clerks to be diligent and exigent in the

over the 'septenarium'. Climent swore to observe the privileges, and on 12 July a compromise was found under which he was to substitute for Stefano Nardini while the latter was absent from the Roman court. On 10 Sept. Calixtus issued a bull confirming this arrangement, and extending it to cover the substitution by Climent for other absent chamber clerks; Rius Serra, *Regesta iberico de Calixto III*, p. 316. For the earlier bull of 8 May, see Von Hofmann, *Forschungen*, ii. 19; *Magnum Bullarium Romanum*, i (1727), 362-3.

[15] The bull of 3 July 1483 in Von Hofmann, *Forschungen*, ii. 41-2. Carafa's remark, ibid. 238.   [16] *Magnum Bullarium Romanum*, i. 586-92.

regular audit of the accounts of provincial treasurers and customs officials, to be severe in prohibiting the custom of making payment of their salaries to subordinate papal state officers in discounted cloth and goods instead of in cash, to inspect the fortresses to ensure that the proper numbers of garrison troops were maintained, to ensure that papal state officials did not act oppressively or abuse their powers in respect of the subjects. The execution of the last duty is enabled by a clause which gives chamber clerks the right of direct access to the pope's person to report such abuses, and also requires them to report once monthly either to the pope in person or to the chamberlain. Nothing could show the high status of the chamber clerks in the Roman court more clearly.

VI

The links between the secretaries and the chamber clerks were close. This may be gathered not only from the plural offices of the twenty-five secretaries who were also chamber clerks, but from the basic rules governing the status of the two offices. The secretaries swore an oath which resembled that of the chamber clerks in the obligation to obey the instructions of the chamberlain and not those of the vice-chancellor. It also obliged the secretaries to observe the custody of whatever was committed to their care by the apostolic chamber.[17] The subordination of the secretaries to the chamberlain arose from their responsibility for letters written in the apostolic chamber, which were one of the main sources of their income before the changes of the late fifteenth century. The bull of appointment installed the new secretary in the 'number and *consortium*' of the secretaries,[18] which was a similar wording to the installation of a chamber clerk, but there is no trace of a formal ceremony of reception before 1487. From 1488 the bull of appointment did not in theory make a secretary, but after papal nomination the neophyte secretary was obliged to present himself in person before the college of secretaries, and to be examined on his qualifications before formal admission was given. It is very doubtful whether this injunction was observed in the case of children who secured papal nomination. Earlier in the century the secretaries wore the same formal dress as the

17 Von Ottenthal, 'Die Bullenregister', 471 n.; M. Tangl, *Kanzleiordnungen*, p. 47.

18 Von Ottenthal, loc. cit. A later bull of appointment (1496) is printed by L. Célier, *Les Dataires*, pp. 139–40.

chamber clerks; after 1487 they wore that of the protonotaries.

There was no college of secretaries until one was set up by Innocent VIII as he made the office venal in 1487; nor were the secretaries governed by a body of statutes until after that date. That the statutes which we possess in a sixteenth-century version were not given at the same time of setting up the college is shown by the language used in the bull of establishment, which says that the collection of revenues of the new college is to be arranged in whatever way the secretaries collectively decide (*communi voto*). From that time, however, the secretaries had the same kind of regime as the other colleges, such as the chamber clerks, abbreviators, and scriptors.[19] Under the statutes given them at some time after 1487 they appointed a chaplain from outside their numbers, held prescribed religious services, and were, from one point of view, a religious fraternity. As with the chamber clerks, they were obliged to organize and attend the funeral ceremonies of deceased colleagues of their college. They elected 'defenders' (*defensores*) to administer the organization of the college, and 'receivers' (*receptores pecuniarum*) to administer its revenues. The day-to-day accounts of the college were run by a registrar (*registrator*). They appointed four *mensarii* monthly to carry out the duties of the office, two to sign the bulls, and two to sign the consistorial briefs: the rest of the thirty members of the secretarial college were forbidden, if they were not among the *mensarii*, to carry out any of the duties assigned to the secretaries. They were assigned a room in the apostolic palace to execute their duties.

Before 1487 (and probably for a period after that date) the secretaries lacked any such formal organization, though it may be conjectured that some of the later administrative machinery, such as the officials in charge of receiving and dividing the secretarial revenues, had existed, perhaps in a different form, from an earlier date in the history of the office.

From the late fourteenth century there had been a theoretical limit of six to the number of secretaries. This limit was overstepped by all popes from Martin V to Calixtus III. They sometimes appointed secretaries in an apparently honorary capacity (for example, as a dignity granted to some secretaries of princes who had been sent on temporary missions to the Roman court). That the number of secretarial posts was

---

[19] Frenz, *Kanzlei*, pp. 220–3; Von Hofmann, *Forschungen*, i. 148–57. The bull of 31 Dec. 1487 (Von Hofmann, *Forschungen*, ii. 46) is in *Magnum Bullarium Romanum*, i. 441.

exceeded under Martin V is not surprising: eighteen secretaries swore obedience between 1417 and 1421 alone, eleven of these from different obediences. Martin V subsequently appointed at least five more secretaries. On the other hand, the number of actual working secretaries under Martin was not large: seven to nine in the first years of the pontificate, then six, and from 1429–31 only four.[20]

The limit on the numbers of secretaries was exceeded by Nicholas V, and yet more so by Calixtus III, who, it was claimed by the writer of the entry referring to him in the *Liber Pontificalis*, appointed as many as fifty secretaries, among them 'notaries and mechanics (*operarios*) and ignorant fellows'. This charge seems exaggerated: twenty-nine secretarial appointments by Calixtus have been recorded, but most of these are of men who are known to have been of some distinction, and certainly were not ignorant mechanics. However, perhaps half a dozen of his nominees are not otherwise known as papal officials, and it may be among these that the offending appointments were to be found. Calixtus III seems to have granted secretaryships which were in fact expectancies of the office and carried no right to its revenues, though this is seldom mentioned in the bull of appointment. The supernumerary nature of the secretaryship conceded is mentioned in the bulls of Leonardo Dati in 1455, and of Andrea of Trebizond (son of the secretary George), in 1457, both with the expectation of the first free secretarial place. Andrea obtained a participating place in the same year, but it was cancelled, and he did not finally get a substantive promotion until 1466. Dati signed as a secretary under Calixtus, but does not seem to have obtained a participating place until Paul II made him domestic secretary in 1464. In appointing the Englishman John Lax as secretary in 1455, Calixtus specifically set aside papal constitutions concerning a fixed number of secretaries.

Calixtus certainly aroused opposition among the secretaries by the number of his appointees, and he tried to compensate them by formally reducing the number of 'participating' secretaries to six, besides one or two 'domestic' secretaries who did most of the political correspondence. Calixtus's bull states its cause to have been the low remuneration which the secretaries were receiving—'little or nothing', it says—as a result of the excessive number of appointments, and the same cause is given

[20] Von Ottenthal, 'Die Bullenregister', pp. 478–9. For subsequent pontificates see Frenz, 'Das Eindringen'; Pitz, *Supplikensignatur*, pp. 111–12; Kraus, 'Die Sekretäre'.

for the reduction in the reference to Calixtus's cutting secret-arial numbers in the 1487 bull of Innocent VIII (*ob tenuitatem emolumentorum*). The apparent inconsistency in Calixtus's legislating to reduce the number of participating secretaries, while at the same time increasing the number of appointments, could be explained by a policy of selling the expectancies to the office, but there is no positive evidence that such sales took place. Similar complaints about the grant of secretarial office to unworthy persons were made soon after the death of Calixtus III by Giovanni Battista Bracciolini. Even earlier, under Nicholas V, Giovanni Battista's father, Poggio, had ironically complained that the pope had already appointed enough secret-aries to make a cohort to frighten the Turks.[21] Calixtus III's bull did not much reduce the actual number of secretaries engaged in drawing up papal documents; there were, for example, twelve functioning papal secretaries under Pius II.

When the college of secretaries was set up in 1487, the offices of the six existing participating secretaries remained with their holders, and twenty-four new posts were sold, making a total of thirty, without the domestic secretary or secretaries. The pope promised, in setting up the new college in 1487, to extinguish the 'old' offices of the six participating secretaries who had held the office before 1487, as they died or withdrew, and not to resell them, so that the total number of secretaries would eventually sink to twenty-four. This promise was only partly and at long intervals observed by Innocent VIII's successors, so that only four of the six secretarial places had been extinguished by 1521: there was still controversy about the remaining two as late as the 1570s.[22]

VII

Until Innocent VIII's pontificate the revenues of chamber clerks and secretaries were drawn from the bureaucratic trans-actions in the papal court for which they were responsible. Making the offices venal changed the principles underlying their remuneration because it became important to the papal government to support the revenues of the venal offices (and hence the price to be set upon them), if necessary by assigning to them sources of papal income which had no administrative connection with the normal execution of the office concerned.

[21] Giovanni Battista Bracciolini's 'Life' of Domenico Capranica, in E. Baluze, *Miscellaneorum lib.III* (Paris, 1680), 268. See also Von Hofmann, *Forschungen*, i. 150 n.; Pastor, *History*, ii. 203 n.   [22] Frenz, *Kanzlei*, pp. 220–1.

The most obvious instance of such assignments accompanied the establishment of the college of secretaries in 1487. At that time the pope assigned to the new college of secretaries in perpetuity the proceeds of a tax to be imposed on all appointments to a wide variety of public offices in the papal state— governorships, rectorates, podestà, commissioners, treasurers, chamberlains, chancellors, castellans, tax farmers, and so on. The offices concerned were listed and valued in an official assessment drawn up for the purpose, and the tax was to be collected at six-monthly intervals.[23] He also gave to the secretaries in perpetuity, to be exercised by one of their number, the important office of visitor and auditor of the fortified places in the papal state, and of supervisor of the arrays of troops.

These important concessions were the first occasion on which the farming of papal state offices were geared into the credit structure of papal finance on a generalized basis. Clearly, the existing revenues of the secretaries, drawn from the fees paid them in the Roman court, had been insufficient to support the price which Innocent VIII had decided to place upon the new secretarial posts. It was, therefore, necessary to find other sources of revenue which would sufficiently compensate those who purchased the office for the capital sum they advanced to the pope for the transaction. Regular payments continued to be made to the college of secretaries by provincial treasurers until the end of the sixteenth century and beyond, though the nature of the assessment changed in the later period.

Although the normal revenues of a clerk of the chamber were far higher than those of a secretary, and were able to justify a much higher purchase price for the chamber clerk's office, it was in the end found that the collective revenues of the chamber clerks had to be supplemented in the same way as those of the secretaries—that is, from the papal state. The process by which this occurred is obscure. In 1502, following a series of quarrels between the Umbrian communes of Spoleto and Terni, Alexander VI withdrew the small region of the 'Terra Arnulphorum', the hilly zone behind Cesi and over the river Nera, to the north-east of Terni, from papal administration, and placed it under the direct control of the apostolic chamber.[24] There would have been nothing unusual in this, had

23 *Magnum Bullarium Romanum*, i. 441–5; Tommasini, 'Nuovi documenti'.

24 29 Apr. 1502, *Magnum Bullarium Romanum*, i. 463–4. For the area, see Partner, *Lands of St Peter*, pp. 427–8; Guiraud, *État pontifical*, pp. 163–6; Esch, *Bonifaz IX.*, pp. 493–6.

the clerks of the chamber merely assumed charge of the area as papal commissioners. In the initial grant the normal papal revenues arising in the area were reserved, some for the payment of the castellan of the fortress of Cesi, the main papal stronghold of the area.

Evidently the concession of Cesi and the Terra Arnulphorum to the chamber clerks did, in spite of the cautious wording of the 1502 bull, carry with it a financial benefit for the clerks. By 1517 the practice of granting papal lands to the special administration of the chamber clerks had been extended, so that in effect the college of the chamber diverted the government revenue in these areas to its own use. The chamber continued to control Cesi and the Terra Arnulphorum, and in addition the neighbouring districts of San Gemini and Acquasparta, the important Tyrrhenian port of Civitavecchia, and the alum-producing town of La Tolfa.[25] The 1517 bull makes it clear that the chamber clerks not only administered these areas, but were authorized to collect the subsidies and taxes, and to divide them among themselves as part of the normal revenues of their college. They were allowed to graze and stable their horses in the places granted them, and to collect the proceeds of the licences for low-grade grain export (*tritellorum tractae*). There was also a concession by the government to the chamber of the alum produced in the rich mines at Tolfa. By 1517 the college of the chamber was owed by the pope the proceeds of the sale of 700 loads (*cantaria*) from the alum mines, a residue remaining from an earlier papal grant of 1,200 *cantaria*.[26]

That a group of bureaucrats should be allowed to usurp state rights and to take a profit on the operations of central government in this way is typical of the organization of the papal state at this time. The chamber appointed commissioners to collect their revenues in the subject areas; the arrangement had been terminated by 1530. Other arrangements of a comparable nature were made later in the century, though these did not extend to actually giving direct administration of papal lands to the chamber on its own account. However, the chamber continued to enjoy special grants: for example, in the form of a permanent percentage levy on the revenues of the provincial treasurers, which was paid directly by them as an annual Christmas present (*regalo di Natale*) to the college of the apostolic chamber, or the special assignments on some

---

[25] 12 June 1517, *Magnum Bullarium Romanum*, i. 586-7.
[26] *Magnum Bullarium Romanum*, i. 587. For the alum mines see J. Delumeau, *L'Alun de Rome XVᵉ-XIXᵉ siècle* (Paris, 1962).

provincial treasuries made to swell collegiate revenues so as to finance the increase in the number of chamber clerks decreed in 1571.[27]

An example of one college of officials being apparently indemnified from the revenues earlier attributed to another occurred in 1509 with the establishment by Julius II of the 141 *praesidentes annonae*, whose theoretical duties were the policing of the Roman grain supply. Included in the financial arrangements made for this new college was the stipulation (apparently unconnected in a direct way with the presidents of the annona) that the customs officials of the Roman salaria should thenceforth make an annual payment of 10,000 gold cameral florins to the college of the chamber clerks.[28]

It is possible that some of these assignments to the college of the chamber were made to repay loans which that body had made to the pope. In 1517, for example, the college lent the pope 12,000 ducats, to be repaid from a 7 per cent charge levied in their favour on the papal annates.[29]

VII

Both chamber clerks and papal secretaries were senior officials who enjoyed considerable help in the execution of their duties. There were four scriptors in the apostolic chamber to engross the documents: this was not a dead-end post, as it was at one time occupied by the future chamber clerk Juan de Gerona.[30] The use of substitutes was far more important to the secretaries: in the earlier period there were subordinates in the employ of each secretary to engross the briefs: these secretaries of secretaries were eventually replaced in 1503 by the new papal college of *scriptores brevium*.[31] Some future

---

[27] e.g. the papal budget for 1572 in Arch. Segr. Vat., Miscellanea Arm. XI, 85A, fos. 42b, 48a. See Partner, 'Papal Financial Policy', p. 39 n.

[28] Reg. Vat. 990, fo. 144. See also Von Hofmann, *Forschungen*, ii. 54.

[29] Von Hofmann, *Forschungen*, i. 274–5 in n.; M. M. Bullard, *Filippo Strozzi and the Medici*, p. 105; H. Hoberg, 'Die Einnahmen der apostolischen Kammer am Vorabend der Glaubenspaltung', *Röm.Quart.*, 35 Supplementheft (1976), 69–85, at p. 72. A loan of 1,000 florins made to Pope Nicholas V by the papal treasurer and six named chamber clerks (11 May 1446) is recorded, Div. Cam. 21, fo. 61.

[30] *CPL* xi. 407; also, xiii. 235, 269, 283, 295, 316, 331. For Juan de Gerona as a 'scriptor in registro camere', Kraus, 'Die Sekretäre', pp. 40, 49; Müntz and Fabre, *Bibliothèque*, p. 127.

[31] Von Hofmann, *Forschungen*, ii. 51.

secretaries began their careers as subordinate scriptors of briefs: an example is Sigismondo de' Conti, who in 1482 said that he had been employed for almost twelve years 'dictandis scribendisque epistolis pontificis', but was appointed apostolic secretary only at the end of the preceding year, in 1481. It is, indeed, remarkable that Sigismondo Conti wrote his oration in defence of the secretaries in 1473, eight years before he became one. Eventually, in the early sixteenth century the secretaries, apart from the domestic secretary or secretaries, needed no great help, since the duties even of the four secretaries designated as *mensarii* to sign the briefs were purely formal, and in the ten or so months of the year that the secretaries were not *mensarii* they had no duties at all; what little there was to do as *mensarius* could be performed by deputies.

The notaries of the chamber were no menial subordinates to the clerks, but important and well-remunerated officials who enjoyed a lot of administrative discretion in dealing with petitioners. They executed cameral documents, but also, for example, were responsible for dealing with petitions arising from the resignation and cession of benefices: it was their duty to register these resignations in the cameral proceedings, and their practice of failing to do so, and merely scribbling a note on the back of the petition that they had seen it, was condemned by the chamberlain. Like the chamber clerks, the chamber notaries shared the total fees gained by their members.[32] There was also a *custos* or *magister registri camere*, whose duty to supervise the work of the notaries gave rise to many disputes before his office was suppressed in 1479.[33]

From the mid fifteenth century the chamber clerks were assisted by a professional *computista* or calculator whose duty it was to do the sums for the audits of treasury and papal state officials, and to calculate the monthly remuneration of each clerk; since these audits were among the main duties of the chamber clerks the appearance of the calculator is likely to have been welcome. Calculators were appointed occasionally from 1438 onwards, and from Paul II's time there was a regular, stipendiary calculator. Responsibility for the audit remained with the chamber clerk concerned, as was emphasized in Leo X's bull of 1518.[34]

---

[32] See *Magnum Bullarium Romanum*, i. 591.

[33] Von Hofmann, *Forschungen*, i. 133; ii. 26, 30, 38. Gerardo Maffei held this office.

[34] *Magnum Bullarium Romanum*, i. 589–90. For the *computista*, see P. Cherubini, in Pastura Reggiero, *La reverenda Camera Apostolica*, pp. 179–85. Jacopo

The most onerous duties of the chamber fell upon the clerk who was for the time being the *mensarius*. The *mensarius* enjoyed special discretionary powers in fixing the assessment and payment of the annate charges, the taxes imposed on benefices not conferred in the papal consistory, whose revenues in theory amounted to between 25 and 100 gold florins or ducats of the chamber annually. The *mensarius* is adjured in Leo X's bull to attend the chamber daily on working days, to check all the bulls which are due to be dispatched to petitioners, and to check also that this does not occur until the appropriate payments have been made. He is also to attend the chancery daily, and in particular the office of the *piombo* (where the leaden bulla was applied to the papal document), to make certain that the annates percentage and the *jocalia* due to the college of the chamber have been noted for payment. The bull stipulates a penalty of 6 ducats, to be deducted from the monthly earnings of the *mensarius* who fails to attend as stipulated or to send a substitute. The *mensarius* is, finally, obliged to bring up the cases of all outstanding bulls concerning which there is a legal doubt, at the first formal sitting of the chamber, so the case can be discussed and a legal decision taken.

VIII

Of the disciplinary problems to which the chamber clerks and secretaries gave rise, the most important was absenteeism. The most common reason for the absence of a chamber clerk or secretary from his post was that he had been sent outside Rome on a papal mission or commission of some kind. In this case a question arose whether he should still receive his dues from the common fund as a secretary or clerk, and for how long, and rules were introduced at various times to decide this. But the problem of voluntary absenteeism without papal leave also arose. That these were general problems in the Roman court is made clear from the action reported by Johannes Burckhardt

Olmerii was mentioned as calculator of the chamber, 19 Apr. 1438, Arch. Cam. I, vol. 1468 (the *computa* of Francesco dal Legname: see Partner, 'F. dal L.'), fo. 1b. Paolo Fastelli of Florence and Nicola Masi of Florence are both mentioned as 'computatores' in 1440. See Arch. Cam. I, vol. 1713, fo. 111, and Mandati Camerali 829, fo. 225b (Masi); Müntz, *Les Arts*, i. 60-1, 65; Von Hofmann, *Forschungen*, i. 133; Von Ottenthal, 'Bullenregister', pp. 442, 488 (Fastelli). Francesco de Burgo was *computista*, 1457-60, Peverada, 'Il vescovo Francesco de Lignamine', p. 199 n. (25 n. of offprint).

in 1497 on the occasion of the procession of Corpus Christi,
when all the papal bureaux were sent for to give nominal lists
of their officials, and to include information about whether any
of them were sick, or absent from Rome.[35]

In the first half of the fifteenth century it was common to
issue a papal faculty to a specified chamber clerk, so he could
continue to draw his share of the collegiate revenues in spite of
his absence from Rome. Under Martin V, while the number of
chamber clerks was still abnormally high, an attempt was
made to systematize this practice, and to name all the privileged
clerks.[36] Later, under Nicholas V and Calixtus III, the issue of
absent clerks gave rise to some controversy, as has been discussed above, about whether supernumerary clerks should
perform the duties of absent participating clerks and draw
their revenues. From the pontificate of Pius II onwards no more
is heard of these disputes, although long absences from Rome
of chamber clerks continued to occur, and drew down papal
disapproval when they were without official leave: Paul II
threatened chamber clerks with deprivation for absence of this
sort which exceeded five months.[37] However, the popes continued to send chamber clerks on long missions outside Rome:
in particular, Émile Brouette has noted the absence of Andrea
de' Spiriti from his chamber clerk's post in Rome for a con-
tinuous period of eight years, from 1476 to 1483.[38]

By the end of the century the chamber clerks seem to have
closed their ranks, abandoning the practice of using substitutes, and to have drastically cut down the number of
occasions on which they were sent away from Rome. There
was no better way to defend their corporate identity against
the threat posed by the papal sale of their offices. However,
Hadrian VI felt it necessary to insist that the chamber clerks,
among other officials, should attend the papal chapel, and
should forfeit income if they failed to return to their place of
duty within a month, or two months if they were absent outside
Italy.[39]

Once most of the curial offices were venal, it was in the
interests of the pope to extend the practice of substitution and
to allow an absent office-holder to draw income from the office,

---

[35] *Liber Notarum* (RRIISS xxxii/1), ii. 24 ff. See also Von Hofmann,
Forschungen, ii. 49, for the earlier disposition of 24 July 1494.

[36] Partner, *Papal State*, pp. 217–18.

[37] Von Hofmann, *Forschungen*, ii. 29.

[38] Brouette, 'Les Clercs "mensiers"' (1962), pp. 414–15.

[39] Von Hofmann, *Forschungen*, ii. 66.

since this made it a more attractive proposition to the purchaser, and also encouraged a situation in which the number
of official places could be multiplied. It is not, therefore,
surprising, that the creation of the college of secretaries in
1487 was accompanied by a new rule that a secretary absent
on papal business was empowered to draw the emoluments of
office for a year.

Cases of deprivation for absenteeism are few and far
between. The Milanese humanist Pier Candido Decembrio was
appointed secretary by Nicholas V in 1450, and his name is
found on papal correspondence from 1450-4. He is mentioned
in the first year of Calixtus III, but he evidently found no favour
with the Spanish pope, and in May 1456 he was deprived of the
secretarial office, 'being absent, and having for a long time
intentionally given up the exercise of the office'. In 1458 he
was restored to the office by Pius II, but this time without
participating rights, and evidently only as an honorific gesture.

The most notable instance of the deprivation of a chamber
clerk for absenteeism was that of the Sienese clerk Filippo
Sergardi. Dean of the chamber clerks at the time, he was
deprived of all curial offices, including the clerkship and
secretaryship, in 1526. One of his offices was acquired by no
less a person than the datarius himself, Gian Matteo Giberti.
Filippo Sergardi had been of some political importance under
Leo X, but had evidently seriously offended Clement VII in some
way. However, his position in Rome remained strong enough
for him to act as executor and guardian for Agostino Chigi, and
to sign the contract for the Sebastiano del Piombo altar-piece in
S. Maria della Pace in Rome in 1530. He had probably been
reinstated in his position as dean of the chamber by this time,
and had certainly been so before his death in 1536.

There were cases of deprivation for serious misbehaviour.
Pietro Ramponi was deprived of his chamber clerkship by
Martin V on his being implicated in the rebellion of Bologna in
1428. Ramponi was fully restored to favour under Eugenius IV,
became a protonotary, and governed several papal provinces,
but he was not regranted his clerkship of the chamber. Jacopo
Caetani was removed from his secretary's post for rebellion in
1500, and Ventura Benassai was deprived of both a chamber
clerkship and a secretary's post on being convicted of fraud in
1504. Bartolomé Flores lost all his posts, including the domestic
secretaryship, on being disgraced for corruption in 1497.
George of Trebizond left Rome for three years after coming to
blows with Poggio Bracciolini in 1452, but was immediately

restored to office when Calixtus III became pope. Andrea de' Spiriti did not lose his place as chamber clerk on the occasion of his arrest and disgrace in 1503, but remained dean of the chamber clerks until his death in the following year.

IX

Other attempts to discipline the way the chamber clerks carried out their duties were few. One will arouse the sympathy of most modern civil servants; in 1507 Julius ordered the chamber clerks to return to the chamber any cameral documents in their possession, and strictly forbade any others to be taken out of the chamber.

A far more serious matter was the prohibition issued by Julius II in 1506 against corruption in the apostolic chamber in the contracts for the sale of the alum from papal mines, and for the farm of customs and salt tax and provincial treasuries. The particular charge was that some chamber clerks (the accusation was specific) had interfered ('ad partem facere, ut vulgariter dicitur') in the negotiations for these contracts, to the detriment of papal interests. The prohibition was repeated by Leo X, though it is hard to see how its reissue can have been under that pope more than a formal gesture, since under Leo corruption in these matters was shameless.

At all periods the family connections of chamber clerks with merchants who followed the Roman court was important. Under Eugenius IV, for example, Leonardo Salutati of Pescia was the brother of Antonio Salutati, the then manager of the Roman court branch of the Medici bank, which acted as depositary. Under Julius II the particular clerk of the chamber whom the pope had in mind may have been Ventura Benassai,

TABLE 7. *Merchant and banking connections, for known cases* (% given in parentheses)

	Chamber clerks	Secretaries
From merchant or banking families	34 (24.1)	46 (19.0)
Family with bank in Roman court	14 (10.0)	23 (9.5)
Family bank acting as papal depositary	3 (2.1)	3 (1.2)

the former manager of the Roman Spanocchi bank branch, who had been condemned for corruption in 1504. However, Julius II himself, also in 1504, had appointed as chamber clerk a member or close connection of a papal tax farming family, Francesco Armellini, who was later to become famous for unscrupulous peculation. Under Leo X Niccolò Gaddi was appointed as chamber clerk when his family were important Roman court bankers, and when another relative, Aloisio Gaddi, was papal treasurer of the March of Ancona. In 1525 under Clement VII the treasury of the March of Ancona was held by Luigi Gaddi, and the same firm held a right to a share of 3 per cent of the revenues of papal annates.[40] Niccolò Gaddi had resigned his clerkship of the chamber in 1521, on promotion to a bishopric, but had resumed another post of chamber clerk in 1523. It is hard to imagine that he took no part in these bargains with his relatives.

The proportion of secretaries closely related to Roman court bankers was not much smaller than that of chamber clerks. Behind this was the more general phenomenon, which is further discussed below, of a class of Italian bankers and merchants settled in Rome which expected as a matter of course to place its members into the papal curial bureaucracy, and which gradually, as the sixteenth century progressed, became in some ways fused with the Roman clerical class to form a sort of clerical plutocracy.

40 Partner, 'The "Budget" of the Roman Church', pp. 277, 278; Von Hofmann, Forschungen, i. 274–5, in n.; Bullard, Filippo Strozzi, p. 122.

5

The Curial Point of View

I

During the Middle Ages the Roman Church had made extreme efforts to integrate its members into a single system of ideas and practices, and to ground the cultural and social identity of the western Latin world on a Roman base. Despite external challenges, the Roman Church still powerfully asserted its authority during the Renaissance period. Its priestly power belonged to the charismatic dimension of human experience, and not merely to secular politics. The papal monarchy was exercised through judicial decisions and theological pronouncements, but also through the mystical powers of a holy leader. The popes were chief judges of the highest spiritual court, and worked for peace among Christian princes and war against the infidel. The tradition which assured people about their power also spoke for their holiness: they were the guardians of the pilgrimage, and custodians of the places sanctified by the blood of the martyrs.

The symbolism of Roman primacy was present all over Rome and the other cities of the papal state; for example, it was evident in the papal coat of arms displayed in papal cities and at every seat of local government. The coat of arms was, *par excellence*, the symbol of worldly rule. In the ceremonies of the Roman court, either in strictly religious functions or in the elaborate protocol of the papal consistory, the power and dignity of the Roman See were made public to the pilgrims, supplicants, and envoys of every rank who attended from all over Italy and from every part of the Catholic world. The buildings of the city of Rome, its great churches and basilicas, besides the apostolic palace itself, had for centuries been constructed and reconstructed so as to declare papal authority as well as divine glory. The same function was served by the liturgy of the Roman churches and basilicas, by the processions of church dignitaries, the elaborate protocol of meeting and escorting ambassadors and visiting princes, by the reception of the huge concourses of pilgrims, especially those attending the Jubilees of 1450 and 1475. The great ceremonies of imperial visits and coronations were repeated for the last time in 1433 (though in the war conditions of the time this was a muted feast) and 1452; there was a further imperial state visit in 1468. In 1512, for the last occasion until 1870, Rome witnessed the solemn opening of an ecumenical council. Familiarity may in some people have bred a casual way of treating such splendours, but it seldom bred contempt. Quite apart from the strict social and legal discipline that the pope and his officers exercised over subordinates, papal symbolism weighed heavily on the minds and imaginations of members of the Roman court. It is no accident that two of the most important texts on Renaissance Rome were written by papal masters of ceremonies.

Papal officials were not mere onlookers at this great Roman show: they had to take an active part. Chamber clerks were obliged to attend mass in their chapel in proper clerical garb before any sitting of their chamber; they were to wear pontifical vestments at the solemn papal consistory. In the same way the apostolic scriptors (without distinction between laymen and clerks among them) and abbreviators were supposed to attend a daily mass before beginning work in the chancery. Abstention was not always treated lightly; one of the charges against the suspected academic conspirators against Paul II was their failure to attend mass.

There were important solemnities and feast days, such as Corpus Christi, on which the whole Roman court turned out in a single liturgical body. The various groups of papal officials were organized as religious confraternities as well as professional bodies. There were also occasions when the popes themselves gave a lead in pious practices, and persuaded droves of their clerks to follow them into joining a specific confraternity: this happened in 1478 when Sixtus IV led the cardinals and many clerks of the Roman court to join the confraternity of the Hospital of the Holy Spirit as individuals, and on another occasion when Julius II led a similar group to join the Blessed Sacrament fraternity.

The pressures on papal clerks to obey and conform were therefore intense. This did not make them into faceless men who had lost their individuality within a well-organized machine. On the contrary, the Roman court, rather than being a disciplined body of obedient bureaucrats, in practice consisted of a number of more or less competing groups, of which the most important were not the corporations of officials but the clienteles which formed round each cardinal or other rich curialist leader. The core of each clientele was the *familia* of the cardinal concerned, but beyond the visible group of dependants which actually lived with a cardinal in his palace and followed him in procession, there was an invisible group bound to him by ties of service and patronage. It was likely that a papal clerk would belong to one or more of these interest groups, which would often protect him in a conflict with a senior official.

II

This was a less rigidly centralized society than it appeared, but still an intensely conformist one. However, from the late fourteenth century, some papal officers began to come under the influence of a new literary movement which changed their moral and social attitudes, and made them take up positions which could be somewhat subversive of the established clerical order. In particular, they tended to magnify the active life as opposed to the contemplative one. In doing so, the humanists who were also members of the Roman court were not departing from its spirit, for it was above all a community of busy men of affairs. But they were implicitly challenging some of the Catholic theory which lay behind the earlier history of the papacy, antedating the great movement of centralization which had taken place in the twelfth and thirteenth centuries. For example, most curial humanists would have known that St Bernard's *De Contemplatione* had been written with the specific purpose of encouraging the pope to defend the contemplative values which, Bernard thought, the papacy existed to promote, though the life of the Roman court tended to undermine them.

Humanism was never the unified block of ideas and attitudes that some people have thought it. However, certain humanists offered not only a literary but in some respects an ethical challenge to established clerical values. The challenge was sometimes implicit, but often explicit and polemic. The humanists offered new oratorical forms, new genres of critical essays and dialogues, new ways of writing history. Their inspiration often came from classical writers like Seneca and Quintilian (or later, for example, from Tacitus) who had hitherto played only a minor role, if any, in learned cultural orientations. They defined their outlook as that of the humane studies, the *studia humanitatis*, conceived by them as a body of knowledge based on superior philological method.

114   The Curial Point of View

Such non-conformity as existed among the humanists, although discreetly expressed, had its price. All princely courts exacted subservience. Life in the papal court could be difficult for a self-evaluated élite with an anti-traditionalist programme, even if the humanists were careful to identify the tradition they attacked as literary and not as religious. It is notable what a small part the first generation of humanists in the Roman court played as papal publicists, compared with the much more active role played by papal humanists later in the fifteenth century.

One of the by-products of curial humanism was a literature which looked at the Roman court and at the clergy in general wryly, ironically, and often in a sharply critical spirit. Examples are Poggio Bracciolini's tract on *Hypocrisy* (1447–8) and Valla's *Dialogue on the Religious Orders* (c.1440). It is true that Valla wrote his dialogue while still at the Aragonese court in Naples. But it is striking that a very prominent papal secretary, and another who died as a Lateran canon, should have kept themselves at such a distance from conventional clericalism.

The younger Lapo da Castiglionchio was a writer in this tradition who was by many years Poggio's junior, but died before his own career in the Roman court had seriously begun; he may, in fact, have already abandoned it before his death. Partly because his career never had time to develop, Lapo is a difficult author to evaluate. The interest of his *Dialogue on the Excellence and Dignity of the Roman Court*, written in 1438, is its extraordinarily detached and ironic position.[1] It resembles works like the *Facetiae* and *De Varietate Fortunae* of Poggio in moral standpoint, but differs in literary method. Poggio, following a tradition which goes back to Boccaccio and earlier, makes his moral points by little satirical examples and pen portraits. Lapo offers us what purports to be a connected and eulogistic account of the Roman court, but which turns out when read attentively to be wry and ironic, and much more like a satire than a eulogy.

Lapo da Castiglionchio's *Dialogue* was written at the time of the Council of Ferrara, at a difficult point for the papal court. Eugenius IV had been chased out of Rome, was threatened out-

---

[1] Scholz, 'Eine humanistische Schilderung' (1914); there is an Italian tr. of the first part of the Dialogue in E. Garin, *Prosatori latini del Quattrocento* (Naples, 1952), 169–214. For its author see *DBI* (Fubini), and also his 'Intendimenti umanistici e riferimenti patristici dal Petrarca al Valla', *GSLI*, 151 (1974), 520–78, at p. 564. See also D'Amico, *Renaissance Humanism*, pp. 117–18; Singer, *Renaissance in Rome*, p. 293.

side Italy by the Council of Basle, inside by a host of enemies, and was seeking reconciliation with the Greek Church to support his threatened prestige. The absence of the court from Rome at the time of its composition is important to the moral background of the *Dialogue*, because the moral status of the Roman court has to be justified on ethical grounds, and not propped up because of its location in the holy city of the apostles and martyrs.

Lapo had held no official position in the Roman court (though he professed to hope for one in the future), but when he wrote he was in the entourage of Cardinal Francesco Condulmer, having been earlier the tutor of the nephews of the chamber clerk Jacopo Venieri. His interlocutor in the *Dialogue* is Angelo da Recanati, a connection of the Venieri family. The ostensible aim of the work is to disculpate the Roman court from the common charges of corruption, summed up in the proverbial saying that 'a good curialist is a thorough scoundrel' ('curialis bonus, homo sceleratissimus et omnibus viciis coopertus'). There is a lot of anticlerical sarcasm in the tract, on the lines of that used by Poggio Bracciolini. Whether the whole Dialogue is the defiant parting shot of a humanist who has tried to get preferment in the Roman court and failed (as Riccardo Fubini has suggested it may be), or whether it can be seen as the ironic commentary of a man who has had his disappointments and been denied preferment, but who still hopes for advancement from the rich papal clergy, is hard to decide. The *Dialogue* is dedicated to Cardinal Condulmer, and it ends with its author leaving to join the cardinal in the papal palace—though Angelo da Recanati has just remarked that, although he wishes Lapo well in his search for preferment, he does not envy him! Fubini has shown that soon after he wrote it Lapo da Castiglionchio finally abandoned the Roman court, dying in Venice within the year.

Lapo da Castiglionchio's *Dialogue* can be read as something lying between the traditional tracts *On the Miseries of Courtiers*, which go back to the twelfth century, and to which Aeneas Sylvius Piccolomini contributed a little later in the fifteenth century, and the new genre of satirical tracts on contemporary morals which had been brought in by the generation of Poggio and Alberti. At the end of the *Dialogue* Lapo bitterly comments on the arrogance, ignorance, meanness, and rudeness of some of the princes of the church to be found in the Roman court, and on the contempt with which they treated their suitors, keeping them waiting in ante-rooms until a bell was sounded to summon them to audience, and then cutting them off (after they had at last been admitted to address the great man) in the middle of a sentence to dismiss them.

The satirical aims of Lapo's tract are achieved by playing on the moral overtones of the Latin term *officium*, which has the sense not only of the execution of a public employment, but of the fulfilment of a moral obligation of duty. The pope, his cardinals, the curial bishops, the ambassadors, and distinguished men who throng the court, are by definition officers, who must therefore tend towards probity. That some curialists are corrupt is conceded. But the place where religious worship is carried out by most ordained priests, and by the most eminent clerics from all parts of the world, in a magnificent and fitting manner, must be the most acceptable to God. It is objected against this argument that the motives which draw people to the Roman court are only partly religious. The multitude of priests throng the Roman court either because they wish for religious reasons to see the pope, or because they covet some promotion or other, or because they are pursuing a lawsuit. The objection implied in the last two cases is thrust aside on the grounds that, among such a great concourse of religious men, more must be good than bad!

To the religious arguments in favour of the Roman court, which are the multitude of eminent clerics there, and the coming of the Greek and other eastern princes and bishops to the Council, Lapo adds a cultural argument. The Roman court is held up as a place where the liberal arts, in particular, may be best studied and discussed. Other learned men are present in the court, such as the professors of theology, 'whose studies, however, have nothing to do with us'. There are also scientists, astronomers, musicians, men learned in canon and civil law. But above all Lapo vaunts the presence in the court of 'our people', the curial humanists. He cites, at the summit of eminence in humane studies, the religious Ambrogio Traversari; then Garatone, Poggio, Flavio Biondo, Aurispa, Andrea Fiocchi, Rinuccio Aretino (all, of course, papal secretaries), and Leon Battista Alberti. He laments the absence from the Roman court of Leonardo Bruni and of his own teacher, Filelfo. There is no doubt that this part of the *Dialogue*, at least, is meant to be taken at face value.

However, the praise of famous men far from exhausts Lapo's interests. He goes on to purport to justify the Roman court by a sort of entrepreneurial materialism of his own, though the defence is two-faced, and its argument is almost certainly meant to be sarcastic and satirical. Some corruption may, he concedes, be inevitable in the Roman court, but he insists on the high level of professional skill which the court demands and gets, especially from its secretaries, judges, advocates, proctors. Such men have to be sharp operators, astute, hard-working, capable of flattery and persuasion, and, if necessary, of discreetly bribing the right man. They are not, indeed, absolutely upright men ('non probi illi quidem'), but shrewd, active people who are not going to be done out of the credit due to them for their efforts, and who pursue their attempts to catch up in status with their superiors.[2] There must be some doubt how Lapo intended the passage to be taken, but his description of the psychology and behaviour of the curialists is sharp and convincing. Such men would not look out of place today on Wall Street or in the City of London.

Lapo goes on to condemn the 'stupid people' (presumably those at the Council of Basle and elsewhere) who say that riches are inappropriate to the court of the chief bishop, vicar of a Christ who in life was poor and lacking. The papal court, Lapo has already argued, can offer many pleasures, such as the pomp and circumstance of its state receptions, the pleasures of the tables of its rich members, the stimulation of court scandal-mongering and gossip, and even the arts and charms of the Roman prostitutes, which he does not scruple to set forth in detail, provoking the interlocutor to remark that such descriptions are 'unworthy for the discourse of the learned'. He refuses to condemn the riches which make this agreeable life possible.

Lapo's argument against the duty of evangelical religious poverty for the church of his day is historical and relativist, and also written with tongue in cheek.[3] Sacred prostitution, he remarks, in ancient times was once the rule, but times and customs change! The argument would look familiar in an eighteenth-century context, but is striking in a Renaissance one. Christ's religion, he continues, since the time of its early difficulties has secured universal acceptance: it is now backed up by overwhelming state power and by the testimony of the

[2] Scholz, p. 134.
[3] Scholz, pp. 145–51. There is a good discussion by Fubini in *DBI*. There is a learned bibliography on Lapo da Castiglionchio in Singer, *Renaissance in Rome*, p. 342, but his citations from Lapo's text (28–9, 293) make no reference to the possibility of not taking it literally. Nor does V. de Caprio in his treatment of Lapo in *Letteratura italiana: Storia e geografia*, ii/1 (Turin, 1988), 342–3, which deals only with the part of the text published by Garin. D'Amico, loc. cit., shows awareness of the problem.

holy, as well as confirmed by the literary evidence of the wise and learned ('fortissimorum virorum et sanctissimorum testimonis corroborata, eruditissimorum et sapientissimorum literis monumentisque confirmata'). Religion has abandoned the austere and harsh conditions of early Christianity, and is now adorned by treasures and refined by riches. The drift of the argument is utilitarian. Riches remove the temptation to steal and cheat. Papal riches are necessary to finance splendid buildings and decorous worship, to dispatch some embassies to treat for peace among Christian powers, and other envoys to maintain relations with other bishops. So long as the popes treat their riches as having been given for the proper purpose of the generous execution of the duties of their office, their possessions are held in the spirit of Christ's injunctions (although, he tellingly adds, perhaps against the letter).

Its ambiguity makes it hard to be sure of the right interpretation of Lapo's *Dialogue*, but it remains one of the best and most realistic accounts of life in the Roman court. It spells out in a connected form a critical view of the court, aspects of which can be found in the scattered writings of scores of other curial humanists. The *Dialogue* contradicts the idea that humanists in the Roman court either complacently acted as propagandists and public relations officers for the popes, or retreated to a private world of classical learning and literature. It is characteristic of an earlier generation of humanists in its resolutely non-theological standpoint, and in its remark that professors of theology have 'nothing to do with us'.

III

Though there was, and is, some uncertainty about the nature of the effect of the new humane studies on the collective Catholic point of view, there was none about their importance: at the end of the fifteenth century the curial humanist Paolo Cortesi talked about Lorenzo Valla as having been one of the creators of a 'new Italy'.

The humanist group may now seem to have been a small, closed proto-modern élite which lacked hooking-on points among the late medieval ruling class of Latin Catholic Europe. But they were not as isolated as that. Their point of view appealed strongly to important and widely spread elements in both urban and courtly societies, even if their message was only partly understood. When Poggio Bracciolini sought (vainly, as it turned out) patronage in the English court, when English clerks from that court travelled to Italy to reinforce their knowledge of the new humane studies, confidence was exhibited that those studies were appreciated by the rich and powerful outside Italy.

The humanist programme was not 'pagan', as some nineteenth-century scholars thought. But Catholic scholars of that time were right in stressing the dissident implications of much that the early humanists were trying to do. Their way of thinking did not threaten Catholic doctrine directly, but it threatened to change the commonly accepted manner in which moral issues were discussed. Moreover, their intellectual methods could not with impunity be brushed aside, if only for the reason that their value as publicists swiftly became clear to governments, including the papal government.

The penalties imposed by the church for dissent were well known to the papal curialists. Poggio Bracciolini appreciated the meaning of the execution of the Czech reformer, Jeremy of Prague, at the Council of Constance. Lapo da Castiglionchio, during his brief two years on the fringe of the Roman court, brought down on himself enough suspicion for an examination by the inquisitors to be hinted at as a possibility. Poggio, towards the end of his life, suggested in the course of his controversy with Valla that the latter's religious radicalism ought to attract a heresy prosecution, and Valla himself had for long been aware of the danger.

Attacks on papal symbolism were no less seriously regarded than attacks on orthodox doctrine. When dissident *fraticelli* were scandalized by the way in which Paul II used his extra-vagantly bejewelled papal tiara to assert his power, they drew down on themselves a fierce revenge. Even the suspicion of subversive behaviour among officials led to examination under torture, as happened to the supposed humanist conspirators against Paul II in 1468.

There were no humanist martyrs, unless Stefano Porcari, executed for rebellion by Pope Nicholas V, is counted as such, and he should not be as his rebellion had far more to do with traditional Roman ruling-class privilege than with humanism.[4] In the hands of most of their practitioners, the new humane studies were an evasive technique, not an attacking strategy. Discovering and following classical literary models tended, in

---

[4] See M. Miglio, ' "Viva la libertà et populo de Roma": Oratoria e politica a Roma: Stefano Porcari', *ASR* 97 (1974), 5–38.

the early years of humanist endeavour, to be an individualist affair. Its pursuit was subsidized by the rich, but at the beginning most of its professors belonged either to the bottom side of court life, or to minority groups among university teachers.

The humanist-secretaries of the first half of the century were not prominent papal publicists. One is rather impressed when a writer as little given to hyperbole as Emil von Ottenthal terms the secretarial group 'the press bureau of the Holy See',[5] but it is hard to accept the description. The secretaries can only be considered papal publicists at this time if their activity in actually drafting and giving their stylistic stamp to papal briefs is styled a publicist function. But they wrote very little in the way of pro-papal tracts or pamphlets; Poggio's thin *Invective* against the anti-pope of the Council of Basle, Felix V, is practically the only example.

In this period one or two people who could be perhaps called curial humanists, like Piero del Monte, were acting as papal controversialists, but they were not secretaries. The former chamber clerk Francesco Pizzolpasso, who may be counted as a humanist, attended the Council of Basle as a Milanese envoy, but he avoided publicist activity on either side. The apparent indifference of humanists to the theological issues raised at Basle has often been remarked on: only the religious Ambrogio Traversari took any real part in the disputes.[6] Aeneas Sylvius Piccolomini and Piero da Noceto, also at Basle, at that time had not had anything much to do with the papal court.

The most conspicuous example of the non-conformist curial humanist is Lorenzo Valla. His family connections must have made the young Valla look like a typical curialist in embryo. His family owed most of its resources and prominence to activity in the Roman court, and on the death of his uncle, Melchior de Scribanis, Valla tried in 1428, when still a young man, to obtain his uncle's curial offices, which included that of papal secretary. However, this attempt failed, as did a second attempt made while staying with his curialist brother-in-law, Ambrogio Dardoni, in 1434. For a long time Valla had to give up the idea of a post in the Roman court, and to make his way elsewhere, first in northern Italy, and then in the service of Alfonso of Aragon, for whom he worked not only as a publicist and humanist-courtier, but by accompanying the royal army.

---

[5] Ottenthal, 'Die Bullenregister', p. 462. The opposite stance is taken (rightly, in my view) by Frenz, 'Das Eindringen', p. 299.

[6] See J. Helmrath, *Das Basler Konzil 1431–1449: Forschungstand und Probleme* (Cologne and Vienna, 1987), 166–72.

Only at the end of a long career in Aragonese service, and after he had written his most important works, did Valla in 1448 return to Rome to accept the minor office of a papal scriptorship, and a none too well remunerated job of professor in rhetoric at Rome University, which he at first had to share with George of Trebizond. Valla's religious orthodoxy had been impugned and he had been hauled before inquisitors while he was in Naples, which may have contributed to his wanting to leave the southern city for Rome. A career in Rome for an Aragonese courtier became practical after the reconciliation between the Roman and Aragonese courts in 1443.

While in Aragonese service the hardships of court life and the strain of pursuing controversial studies had made their mark on him; by the time he had settled in Rome, although still in his mid-40s, he seemed to the young Pontano like an old man. He came to Rome with the support of the learned cardinals, Bessarion and Nicholas of Cusa, and not merely with the hope of influencing a pope with humanist sympathies with whom he had old Neapolitan links.

Valla owed his papal secretaryship not to the humanist pope, Nicholas V, who gave him only limited support, but to Nicholas's successor, the Catalan Calixtus III, the former President of the Council of Alfonso of Aragon, and Valla's former colleague. Valla was a papal secretary for the last two years of his life, and he also owed to Calixtus the grant of a canonry at S. Giovanni in Laterano (the Catholic historian Pastor was shocked by this patronage, which he found 'inexplicable'). The nine years of Valla's Roman career were too brief a period for him to be treated by us as though he was a long-serving papal official of the same stamp as Poggio and Biondo. Had he lived there might have been further strain between him and the papal government; his discourse on St Thomas Aquinas, given under Calixtus, suggests a man who was no more willing than he ever had been to conform with conventional ideas. The influential and worldly Cardinal D'Estouteville described the discourse as 'crazy'.

Even when his exceptional early career and origins have been taken into account, the acceptance in papal service of a man with Valla's known opinions is remarkable; this, indeed, was the view taken by Poggio, who by the time Valla came to Rome cordially loathed him. Quite apart from the 'evangelical' character of his religious opinions, Valla had during his stay in Naples written powerful attacks on the ideas and policies of the popes. His tract denouncing the forged Donation of

Constantine is not an academic exercise but a passionate piece
of rhetoric, which condemns bitterly the fraud by which he
says the popes have robbed the liberties of the people they
govern, and asserts the right of that people to seize back what
has been taken from them. The popes are charged with responsibility for violent attacks on churches, and for larceny,
rape, and bloodshed. It was immoral as well as unseemly that
the pope should fight the Perugini or the Bolognesi, whose
bishop he was. That the man who published this pamphlet
should have peacefully lived in Rome as a papal official
through the 1453 conspiracy of Stefano Porcari tells us something both about Valla and about the papal government which
protected him.

Valla was not the only clerk to live quietly in papal Rome
after publishing violent attacks on papal temporal power.
Leonardo Teronda, a Veronese humanist and papal chancery
scriptor, wrote two strongly worded theological-political tracts,
one addressed in 1435 as a petition to Eugenius delivered
through Cardinal Albergati, and the other made to the Council
of Basle through Cardinal Cesarini. Teronda's writings rejected
the papal temporal power for the same kind of historical
reasons as those alleged by Valla, and also used the same kind
of trenchant language about papal misuse of worldly power.
There is no more trace of papal action being taken against
Teronda on this account, than there is of its being taken
against Valla. Teronda, like Valla, seems to have worked
tranquilly in the papal offices through the period of Porcari's
rebellion in 1453, and to have died in papal service not long
afterwards at a ripe old age.[7]

However, Lorenzo Valla did one important service to the
papal idea. It has recently been said that, however unorthodox
his philosophy and moral speculation may have been, he in-
sisted on the priority of Latin culture and the permanence of
the Catholic Latin realm in which the church was a sort of
guardian for Graeco-Roman culture. He thus attributed to the
Roman Church a permanent cultural empire of a new sort. He
stated these ideas most clearly in his inaugural lecture of
rhetoric at Rome University, but he put them out most persuas-
ively in the *Elegantiae*, which acquired great literary authority

[7] Gaeta, *Lorenzo Valla*, pp. 203-52; G. Billanovich, 'Leonardo Teronda
umanista e curiale', *Ital.Med.Uman.* 1 (1958), 379-81; Helmrath, *Das Basler
Konzil*, p. 245; C. Piana, 'Nuovi documenti sull' Università di Bologna e sul
Collegio di Spagna', *Studia Albornotiana*, 25 (1976), 878.

during the Renaissance period.[8] It is probable that the way in which Valla lent his name to this doctrine, which became one of the supporting myths of Counter-Reformation culture and was not seriously challenged—and then, perhaps, only inconclusively challenged—until the Enlightenment, was of much greater importance than his unorthodox philosophical and religious views, which have never been known to more than a few.

<h2 style="text-align:center">IV</h2>

The writing of history in the Renaissance period according to the supposed norms of the classical historians created a new genre, which Flavio Biondo announced in the title and organization of his history of western Christendom from the decline of the Roman Empire, the *Decades*, whose title he borrowed from Livy. Biondo's book was an extraordinarily bold undertaking in that, unlike most of the humanist histories, it was not the story of a single town, region, or dynasty, which might attract patronage and support. He himself made this comment in a resigned way, and he was aware how unusual his book was; indeed, in his view the humanists of his time had not really started to write history at all.

The *Decades* were not a history of the papacy, nor even a history of Europe from the papal point of view; in the early medieval parts of the book the popes are hardly mentioned, nor is the Donation of Constantine even referred to. However, the temporal power is not criticized either, and although the book is not 'Guelph' in the sense that it explicitly apologizes for papal policy, it can be held papalist in its avoidance of discussion of the principles on which papal policy had been based, and in its occasional deference to the idea of providential intervention in history on behalf of the Roman See. In the last books, which are in effect a history of Italy in his own times, the papacy is more or less centre-stage, because Biondo's own experience of statecraft had been in papal service. But the popes are not its heroes; and in so far as they are its main subjects, Martin V's Italian policies get rather kinder treatment than those of Eugenius IV who was alive when Biondo wrote. The oriental church politics of Eugenius are dealt with respectfully, but there is the same detached quality about Biondo's

---

[8] See D'Amico, *Renaissance Humanism*, pp. 118–19; Singer, *Renaissance in Rome*, pp. 289–90.

contemporary history as there is about his accounts of earlier times. His writing is even, sober, somewhat pedestrian; Biondo would have made a fine twentieth-century history professor of the pre-*Annales* period. Livy was a main, but not the only model for the *Decades*, whose style is very different from the ornate, panegyric form which was later to be so fashionable.

Biondo's historical work was much appreciated by another former papal secretary, albeit an honorary one. After Aeneas Sylvius Piccolomini had become Pope Pius II, he went to the trouble (in leisure hours) of epitomizing the earlier *Decades* of Flavio Biondo, at the same time (in his own view) somewhat improving their style. This work was done by Pope Pius II and not by Aeneas Sylvius before his pontificate. That the pope himself should have made the epitome shows that the historical point of view of the *Decades* was acceptable to papal policy of the time.

The growth of papal historiography in the fifteenth century was rather slow and haphazard. The papal secretaries who had to do with it were, after Biondo, none of them the working secretaries who supported the main burden of political correspondence; they were, on the whole, humanists who had been granted secretarial posts on an honorary or short-term basis. Of these, one of the most important for the establishment of new historical genres was the Florentine Giannozzo Manetti.

Manetti was originally granted a papal secretaryship by Nicholas V in 1453 at a time when he was in political disgrace in Florence. He subsequently faced trial there, and was acquitted, but in the following year went into voluntary exile, first at the papal court, and then to Naples. He never took an active part in the work of the papal secretaries, but he was none the less classified as a participating secretary, and so he continued under Calixtus III, being listed as such in November 1458, the year preceding his death. In fact, Manetti's great contribution to papal historiography, his 'Life' of Nicholas V, was written under and perhaps for Calixtus III. His confirmation as secretary under Calixtus is unlikely to have been a purely formal affair, and probably reflected the literary work he continued to perform at the behest of the Holy See.

Manetti's life of Nicholas V is the first papal life to make a pope into a heroic figure of the tradition of the *studia humanitatis*, on the lines of the literary personalities like Cicero made by Plutarch into heroes of public life. Manetti had been trained under the clerical influence of the Camaldolese monk Ambrogio Traversari, and had qualified himself in Hebrew as well as in

Latin and Greek. He became the teacher of literary figures like Jacopo Ammannati, who subsequently became prominent in the Roman court. Under Nicholas V he had begun (but did not finish) a long theological work against the Jews and the Gentiles on behalf of the Catholic faith. He was not, therefore, anticlerical in spirit, even if he had criticized some aspects of the medieval point of view such as the *de contemptu mundi* of Innocent III. He put into his life of Nicholas one or two features common to both the classical and the medieval tradition, such as the dreams which prophesy critical events of the hero's career.

The Manetti 'Life' is not only a skilful piece of publicity, but a statement of the importance of using public buildings and public acts to broadcast the word of God and to emphasize the dignity and divinely decreed role of the Roman bishop. Manetti distinguished between the spiritual and secular duties of the pope, treating the former as principally concerned with ceremonies and with the splendour of religious ornaments and vestments, and the latter (*de saecularibus pompis*) as having to do with building and construction works, either in Rome or elsewhere in the papal state. His account of Nicholas's pontificate contains only the briefest recital of diplomatic and political activity, and quite a long account of Nicholas's interest in learning and libraries, but spreads itself furthest on the pope's ceremonial role in its widest sense. The two events which get the fullest treatment are the Jubilee of 1450 and the coronation of the Emperor Frederick III. The strong emphasis is on the execution of the duties of the papacy as a sort of public performance; in fact, when he comes to Nicholas's death, he speaks of it as a performance which completed the whole play (*comoedia*) in a fitting manner.

The supposed 'will' of Nicholas V, which is almost certainly a literary continuation written by Manetti to adorn the 'Life', contains a list of no less than twenty-one popes who had been 'persecuted', beginning in a somewhat confused way with the revolutions in Rome after the death of Paul I in the eighth century, and continuing with a long catalogue of medieval popes who had suffered from usurpation and violence in the temporal power, including Gregory VII, John XXIII, Eugenius IV, and, in respect of the rebellion of Porcari in Rome, Nicholas V. The list is a pointer towards the way in which the medieval history of the papacy would be drawn on subsequently by other official apologists, from Platina in the same century to the Counter-Reformation historians and writers of later times, in order to illustrate the righteous struggle of the popes to rule the papal state.

Manetti's life of Nicholas V was exceptional, in that either its author showed an out-of-the-way posthumous loyalty to its subject, or Nicholas's successor, Calixtus, decided to support it. The court and intimate entourage of a pope were broken up and dissolved at his death. Many officials, and above all the cardinals, continued to hold their places, but the election of a new pope changed all the main channels of patronage. In normal circumstances it was an unpromising prospect to write a long eulogistic biography of a dead ruler whose faction could no longer dispense great rewards, and, unless the new pope belonged to the same family or faction as the dead one, the latter was lucky to get commemorative attention from the court *litterati* of the following pontificate.

Gaspar of Verona, an elderly but struggling intellectual at the court of Paul II, thought to break into the papal biography market by composing the life of the reigning pope during the lifetime of his subject. There was good precedent for this in the much earlier papal historiography of the *Liber Pontificalis*; in the eighth century Bede had read part of the biography of Gregory II, for example, while its subject was still alive. Gaspar of Verona had earlier in his career enjoyed rather mixed fortune in the papal court: he had been the tutor of Rodrigo Borgia, and had been appointed papal secretary by Borgia's uncle, Calixtus III, in spite of his earlier close association with the disgraced Roman family of Porcari. But under Pius II Gaspar's star waned, or failed to wax, and his office of secretary, in which he had been active only for a short period, apparently lapsed. He secured only a poorly paid appointment as professor of rhetoric in the Roman University.

Seeking favour to get preferment after Paul II came to the papal throne in 1464, Gaspar began to compose a 'Life' of Pope Paul, of which he finished five books. However, this attempt at capturing papal approval seems to have won its author little more than some extra teaching hours at the new school in the papal palace. Gaspar lacked the literary distinction and, even more, the political vision of a Manetti, and his papal biography failed to display the confidence needed to assess the political and ecclesiastical meaning of the pontificate. Much of it took the form of a list of Paul's prominent curialists, most of them treated in a laudatory style which must have been designed to obtain their patronage.

V

In the first half of the fifteenth century the curial humanists professed orthodoxy, but smelt somewhat of anticlerical dissent. In the second half of the century they became better integrated into their clerical environment. The lay humanist-secretaries continued, but dwindled to a small minority. As humanist bishops and cardinals multiplied, the humanist literary method and point of view began to have an ever more pervasive influence on the style of papal official pronouncements. At the same time, from the 1460s onwards, the fierce, quarrelsome individualism of men like Filelfo, Poggio, Valla, and Trebizond, began to give place to a more polished, subservient tradition in which the curial humanist was on the way to becoming a new kind of papal courtier.

No court humanists had been involved in the Roman civic plot of 1453 against Nicholas V, which was headed by a cultivated Roman notable, Stefano Porcari. Guarino of Verona was one of Porcari's family tutors, but he kept his head well down during the abortive rising. Fifteen years later the supposed plot of the Roman Academy against Paul II in 1468 brought the loyalty of a group of Roman humanists into serious question.[9] In so far as the disgrace of this group was preceded by the discontent of one or two of their number who had bought curial posts from one pope, and thought that they were being shabbily treated by another, the incident is directly relevant to the main theme of this book. But its importance is more general because of Paul II's charges in 1468 that the academicians were guilty of some sort of anti-Christian beliefs. The denial of the humanists concerned that this was so, and the relative severity with which they were treated, meant that 1468 was an important stage in the integration of Roman humanists into official, clerical culture.

It may be added that no senior officials of the rank of secretary or chamber clerk were involved, or even suspected, either in the dispute about the curial posts, or in the supposed conspiracy. There are one or two indications of tension between Paul II and his chancery officials, notably the annoyance

---

[9] The most recent works on these events, many aspects of which remain obscure, are P. Medioli Masotti, 'L' Accademia Romana e la congiura del 1468', *Ital.Med.Uman.* 25 (1982), 189–202, and R. J. Palermino, 'The Roman Academy, the Catacombs and the Conspiracy of 1468', *AHP* 18 (1980), 117–55. Also, D'Amico, *Renaissance Humanism*, pp. 91–7; Singer, *Renaissance in Rome*, pp. 8–9; de Caprio, *Letteratura italiana*, pp. 351–2.

exhibited by some papal secretaries when Paul declined to receive them in audience until some weeks after his accession. But no secretary was accused of conspiracy. Indeed, although the three or four main suspects in 1468 were well-known humanists, the majority of those examined by papal police, the men thought actually to have been entrusted with the execution of the projected coup, were not curial officials but young men living in the cardinals' households. Such young men were likely to be involved in court intrigue and disorder; throughout the Renaissance period some of these households became nests of rowdies, or strongpoints of anti-government opposition, or both.

The fullest account we have of the investigation of the supposed academicians' plot is from the pen of Bartolomeo Sacchi (Platina), who was one of the main suspects, and whose account cannot be unbiased, although if it misleads it is probably by omission. Platina's arrest for conspiracy in 1468 was not the first but the second time he had been examined by Paul II's security forces for suspected seditious tendencies.

Five years earlier, Platina had during the preceding pontificate become a member of the new college of abbreviators set up by Pius II in 1463–4. The purchase price due to the pope from Platina and the other new abbreviators for their offices had been assigned to the finances of the Crusade. Paul II after becoming pope in 1464 decided to suspend the financial arrangements then in force for the Crusade, and in connection with this had also dissolved the college of abbreviators, cancelled their tenure of the office, and divided their income between the pope, the major abbreviators, and the vice-chancellor. Besides reflecting changed policy about the Crusade, the action was also meant to restore control over an important section of the papal chancery to the vice-chancellor, and, perhaps, to reverse the policy of Pius II which had sought to make curial offices more widely saleable.

This papal action occasioned an outspoken protest by Platina, including a threat of appeal against the pope's alleged act of administrative abuse to a subsequent church council. The appeal to a future church council was a device often used by princes to try to blackmail the popes, and was a danger signal to any papal government. It was a vain and foolish threat for a subject to make, and led inevitably to Platina's imprisonment, from which he was lucky to be released quite quickly.[10] It is

[10] Platina, *Liber de Vita Christi ac Omnium Pontificum* (RRIISS iii/1), 368–70. For the question of the abbreviators, see Von Hofmann, i. 123–5, ii. 27–8; Tangl, *Kanzleiordnungen*, pp. 183–8; T. Frenz, 'Die Gründung des Abbreviatorenkollegs

hard to know why Platina had reacted so violently, since Paul had promised to indemnify the abbreviators for the purchase price paid for their office, and did in fact do so; the only material damage they suffered was some loss of interest on the principal.

Three years after Platina's release, in February 1468, Paul II received information about a threatened plot against his government in Rome. Whether a serious plot ever existed, and, if it had, what its true aims and motives were, are both questions that have never been satisfactorily answered. The original fear seems to have been that Filippo Buonaccorsi (nicknamed 'Callimachus Experiens' in the Roman Academy), a Tuscan humanist formerly in Rome, had conspired with a Roman exile in Naples and 'certain young men' to execute a coup against the papal government.

Suspicion fell upon a number of curialists, most of whom were members of the humanist Roman Academy whose presiding spirit was Pomponio Leto. Most of the supposed conspirators were members of the Roman court in so far as they were employed in the households of cardinals, but only one or two were in a narrow sense papal officials. The suspects seized by the papal police belonged to unpopular factions: it has been remarked that most of the humanists who fell under suspicion were clients of cardinals and other great men who owed their fortune to Pius II. The ruling clique of Paul II treated curialists promoted during the preceding pontificate with distaste and suspicion, and the suspicion no doubt extended to their dependants. And, vice versa, Paul II was sharply criticized by old courtiers of Pius II like Cardinal Ammanati.

The supposed main conspirator, Buonaccorsi, was never found; he escaped to Poland and the east, and returned to Rome only for a short time, at a much later period, while covered by diplomatic immunity. Pomponio Leto, the leading figure of the Academy, was extradited from Venice and examined in Rome, though never tried, and later released. Platina was also examined over a long period, but, in his case as in those of the others detained in Castel Sant'Angelo, no substantial admissions of guilt were made, and no definite evidence obtained. Some examinations were made under torture. No evidence has remained that points to advanced plans for a coup against the papal government, but the suspicions of serious discontent, and of some kind of organized sedition, were slow to lift.

durch Pius II. und Sixtus IV.', *Miscellanea M. Giusti*, i (Vatican City, 1978), i. 297–329.

One side-effect of the affair was the conviction, entertained by the pope himself, that the supposedly 'pagan' sympathies of the humanist academicians had been nourished in secretive meetings which were on the way to constituting an irreligious fraternity. In later times there was a comparison to be made with Freemasonry, which may have had some effect on the way that historians have treated the affair. Misgivings about the morals of the Roman academicians were entertained by the great Catholic historian, Ludwig von Pastor, as late as the end of the last century. And although Pastor's contemporary, the Anglican Bishop of London, did not go so far, he thought that Paul II's suspicions of the Academy as 'a centre of unseemly buffoonery and sedition, as well as of irreligious talk' were not entirely unreasonable, and that 'the Humanists needed a reminder that they were required to observe the same rules as ordinary citizens, and that no ruler could permit their follies to pass beyond a certain limit'.[11] Presumably the good bishop thought a few hoists on the torturer's rope a permissible 'reminder'.

Papal agents may have feared that some academicians had been corrupted by the pope's political enemies, notably Sigismondo Malatesta and Ferrante of Naples. Platina, a main suspect, had been in contact with Malatesta, and had in the past been foolish enough to threaten the pope with a church council. A yet more potent bogey to the popes was the Turk himself. George of Trebizond, a papal secretary, had in 1468 only recently been released from Castel Sant'Angelo: he had been committed to prison there after he had broadcast his prophetic (though politically only too rational) conviction that Muhammad the Conqueror was the destined ruler of the world, and that previous popes had erred in refusing to recognize it. To a suspicious papal government it was not beyond the bounds of possibility that Turkish agents, planning the invasion of Italy at a later date, had found and corrupted other papal servants.

Gradually, the suspects emerged from the papal prisons, and the 1468 conspiracy joined the long list of conspiracies unproven. Probably its most important result was to convince men of letters that cultural conformity would be enforced in Rome, in the last resort, by prison and the rope. The general drift was, in any case, towards a more conventional, courtly approach to literature and learned leisure.

---

[11] M. Creighton, *A History of the Papacy from the Great Schism to the Sack of Rome*, iv (London, 1897), 55; Pastor's view, *History* iv. 43–6.

Among curial humanists the doubts expressed by intellectuals like Leon Battista Alberti, earlier in the century, that the *otium* of rich ecclesiastics was misused by the idle and ignorant majority, had disappeared. From the pontificate of Sixtus IV onwards (1471–84), papal civil servants were much more likely to have had a humanistic cultural formation, and were more likely to use their leisure either as patrons of humanistic studies, or as participants. For example, the list of historical works composed in the Roman court becomes long. The most important for papal historiography were the papal lives of Bartolomeo Sacchi (Platina). Among the papal secretaries, Sigismondo de' Conti and Jacopo Gherardi of Volterra both spent some of their country retirement in composing well-written accounts of long periods of their time in the Roman court. These were not the literary products of humanists hungry for patronage or promotion; they were the well-bred memoirs of senior civil servants, written at the end of their careers.

VII

Yet independence of mind is not to be controlled so easily. One of the most original figures of the Renaissance papal court was a humanist secretary, George of Trebizond (1395–1472/3), whose committal to prison has been mentioned, and whose quirkiness was subdued by no one, least of all by the popes. George was a Cretan who first obtained favour at the court of Eugenius IV at the time of the Council of Florence, getting from the pope or his nephew, Pietro Barbo, a chancery scriptor's post for which he was allowed to pay 'a small sum'. Under the same pope he became a papal secretary (1444), and worked with the other secretaries until 1452; he was not an easy colleague, and he had a famous public quarrel in which he came to blows with Poggio Bracciolini. He was imprisoned for a time as a result, and fled to Naples, abandoning his house and his substantial capital assets in Rome. Although he was allowed to return to his secretarial post under Calixtus III, his career never entirely recovered from this contretemps, according to his modern biographer. He had married into a prominent Roman family, and was involved in a second violent quarrel, on this occasion with a powerful Roman neighbour, in 1459. He again fled, returning once more when his former pupil and patron became pope as Paul II in 1464.

John Monfasani has depicted George of Trebizond as a prolific and original lay theologian, who thought of himself as such, and considered himself quite capable of instructing priests, bishops, and even popes in their ecclesiastical duties. His theological vision was apocalyptic. It took over his life in an alarming manner after he had been sent by Paul II on a mission to Constantinople in 1465. The employment of this elderly eccentric as a secret agent turned out to be a mistake. George had from the time of the fall of Constantinople in 1453 been sure that Muhammad the Conqueror was predicted in Christian prophecy to be the destined ruler of the world. Fortunately for him, George never obtained the interview by which he had hoped to convert Muhammad to Christianity, and he returned from Constantinople empty-handed. However, a time when Turkish invasion of Italy was imminently feared, and Turkish agents among Christian powers were thought to be active, was not a good one for George to write a tract *On the Eternal Glory of the Autocrat and His World Empire* in which he forecast final victory for Ottoman power. Paul II's tolerance for his old tutor was sorely tried, and he had him imprisoned for a time in Castel Sant'Angelo, though in the care of a humanist castellan who spent his leisure writing elegant Latin epistles to his prisoners.

It is tempting to see George of Trebizond as a half-crazy, though brilliant, religious enthusiast, but his views on Ottoman power were based on first-hand knowledge of the Levant, and were in many respects far more realistic than those of his Italian contemporaries. It is striking that another Greek papal secretary, Alexis Celadoni of Sparta (1451–1517), had a very similar appreciation of the terrifying nature of the Ottoman threat, and of the feebleness of the Christian response. Celadoni's pamphlet about the need for a Turkish war, dedicated in 1500 to his patron Cardinal Olivero Carafa, made many points already put forward by George of Trebizond, though in a much more political way, without the vestment of prophecy. Celadoni was also a sufficiently independent character to introduce some sharp criticism of Alexander VI into his oration after the pope's death, in spite of Alexander's spasmodic involvement with the Crusade, and in spite of the possibility of the election of another pope of the Borgia faction.

These were the writings of men with their own intimate experience of the eastern Mediterranean, and of the realities of life for Christians under the Turk and of war with the Muslims. There was another, far more frequent genre of crusading writing, which drew on the Latin literature of the Crusade, but represented a rather westernized, conventional view. To this genre belongs Flavio Biondo's exhortation to Alfonso of Aragon to lead a crusade, probably penned within a few weeks of the fall of Constantinople in 1453. This was a time when Biondo's own position in the papal court was insecure, and when he may still have been contemplating a jump to the patronage of Alfonso. It also can be viewed as an auxiliary to papal diplomacy, as a papal legation under Domenico Capranica was just leaving Rome at this time (July 1453) to discuss the eastern question with Alfonso in Naples.

A comparable, more elaborate, but incomplete literary production belongs to the next generation of humanists. Leodrisio Crivelli was never an active secretary in Pius II's chancery; he had accepted an honorary appointment as papal secretary at the beginning of Pius's pontificate in 1458, and had been grateful in 1463 to take up residence for a time in the papal court after he had temporarily lost the favour of the Milanese court, in which he had spent most of his career up to that point. He had been interested in Pius's project for the Crusade much earlier, at the time in 1458 when he had appeared in the papal consistory as a Milanese orator, and had been awarded an honorary secretaryship.

Crivelli undertook a work which he called *Pius II's Expedition against the Turks*, and probably wrote it during his stay in the Roman court in 1463–4. He completed the first book, which discusses the medieval origins of the Crusade and the political sequel to the fall of Constantinople in 1453. He wrote a substantial part of the second book, which after a brief excursion on Hungarian politics opens the account of Pius's crusading plans. But the work was broken off abruptly by Crivelli for unknown reasons, so that the narrative stops without explanation at a point which cannot have been intended as a literary break. Crivelli's account ceases at the beginning of Pius's conference at Mantua held in 1459 to consider the Crusade; the narrative does not even reach the official opening of the conference. The book was begun during Pius's lifetime, and perhaps was written during the preparation of Pius's own military expedition at Ancona, that is, during the spring and summer of 1464; though it may have been written at some earlier date when the expedition was being actively contemplated. The most probable explanation for the abandonment of the work is the death of the pope and the collapse of the expedition, in August 1464.

It would be unfair to Crivelli to say that he stopped work on the *Expedition against the Turks* because the pope had died and could no longer reward him, because he showed posthumous loyalty to Pius II in defending him against Filelfo. But politically it would have made no sense to continue the work after the pope's death and the entire abandonment of his crusading project. In the year following Pius's death Crivelli returned to Milan and was reconciled with Sforza, whose courtier he had never really ceased to be. The political drift of Crivelli's *Expedition against the Turks*, like that of much crusading literature, concerns the disabling effects of Christian disunity on crusading plans. But once that disunity had killed the expedition, and the pope with it, the book became a pathetic and politically useless torso. It was, however, much more than a formal rhetorical exercise. In particular, Crivelli's unfinished work showed a great deal of original knowledge of the Hungarian court and its Turkish policies, and also of the papal diplomacy which preceded the Conference of Mantua.

Both Crivelli's posts of secretary and abbreviator were sinecures, and he cannot be treated as a typical papal curialist. But he did typify a type of humanist who accepted honours and financial support from the papal court, in return for his publicist activity. Such men were especially likely to seek the refuge of the papal court when, like Manetti or Crivelli, they had temporarily lost the favour of another Italian government.

VIII

Few chamber clerks or secretaries were theologians. But the majority were priests or in other holy orders, serving the chief bishop of Christendom at a time of uncertainty and dispute about church order, and of widespread concern about the moral condition of the church. These church officials may in some respects have been worldly, but they were articulate and on the whole able, and as well informed as any body of clerks in Europe about church affairs. One therefore looks for evidence of their willingness to involve themselves in religious doctrine or controversy, especially about the reform and government of the church. George of Trebizond and Lorenzo Valla—both laymen—were rare birds in the movement of ideas of their time, though there were equally independent thinkers at an even higher level of the Roman court, such as, for example, Cardinal Nicholas of Cusa. But what of the other papal civil servants with whom we are dealing, the clerks of a more orthodox stamp?

A civil service is not the best place to which to look for spiritual leadership, even if it is a spiritual civil service. The secretaries and chamber clerks were either men of business or men of letters; they were not, as a rule, church thinkers or reformers. As bishops and as canons of cathedral churches they were most frequently absentees, and their understanding of their clerical duties tended to be narrow. But there were exceptions to the reluctance of this group of papal officials to speak out in religious matters.

In the first half of the fifteenth century we may search in vain for secretaries or chamber clerks who had much to say about religion. Religious messages were implied in some of the moralizing of a Poggio Bracciolini about religious hypocrisy, but the silence of the humanists, lay and clerical, about the matters of church order raised by the Council of Basle, has already been noted. The absence of a strong theological content even from the work of Francesco Pizzolpasso, who ended his career as Archbishop of Milan, and whose library was rich in the works of early church fathers, is noticeable. Similar things could be said of his Roman contemporary, the elder Domenico Capranica, who left an important cultural heritage in the college he founded and the books he left with it, but whose own literary remains were mostly orations or legal opinions.

In mid-century, among other protégés of Eugenius IV, Francesco dal Legname and Scipio Mainente were conscientious bishops, strong in the new learning, but neither in any sense a theologian. There were some humanistic religious writers of the period with strong links with the papal court, such as Piero del Monte, Antonio Agli, and Maffeo Vegio who held the important administrative post of papal datarius; but none of these served as secretary or in the chamber. In the second half of the century an experienced, worldly chamber clerk, Stefano Nardini, who became Archbishop of Milan, like Domenico Capranica founded a new college in Rome, but left no legacy of his opinions as a man of religion.

Whether it be coincidental or not, the only chamber clerks or secretaries in holy orders during Renaissance times who left serious writings concerned with religion belong to the closing years of the fifteenth century and to the opening years of the sixteenth: with the exception of Gian Matteo Giberti they had all belonged, in fact, to the court of Alexander VI. One was

Adriano Castellesi, who owed his career almost entirely to the personal favour of Alexander VI.

Castellesi's theological work was written when he was a cardinal: it could hardly have been produced during the frenetic administrative activity in which he was involved under Pope Alexander, although he had been the author of a canon-law treatise on the power of the Roman see, which John D'Amico has dated to the opening years of Alexander's pontificate. His only theological work, *Concerning True Philosophy*, must have been written in the early years of the pontificate of Julius II when he was, although a cardinal, politically out of favour because of his earlier connections with the Borgia faction; it was published in Bologna the year after the pope had retaken the city, in 1507.

Castellesi's *de vera philosophia* is a collection of extracts from four Latin fathers of the church, linked by short titles and comments, and is not a work of connected theological discourse. Its main source is St Augustine, its secondary source St Ambrose. The emphasis is scriptural, humanistic, and anti-dialectical; it might be compared at some points with the much earlier polemic of twelfth-century humanists against the Aristotelian dialecticians. Castellesi's linguistic preference was towards Hebrew and not towards Greek, and the results of this choice are evident in the scriptural, fideistic bias of the booklet. Castellesi was out of step with the Platonizing, speculative humanists of his time, even if he shared their distaste for scholastic theology. John D'Amico has pointed out that his attitudes were to some extent those of another, rather later papal secretary with humanist accomplishments and strong theological interests, Jacopo Sadoleto.

Castellesi's approach was quite different from that of his contemporary in the Roman court, senior in years and accomplishments, but much junior in curial dignity, the apostolic scriptor, Raffaele Maffei. Maffei was a Hellenist of some distinction, and had a powerful, encyclopaedic mind. His theological works, ably analysed by D'Amico, show a strong reliance on the Greek fathers, Basil of Caesarea and Clement of Alexandria. Not by accident was he a reader of St Basil; Basil's treatise on the profit of Greek letters to the young, translated by Leonardo Bruni, made him one of the favourite church fathers for the Renaissance humanists.

The independence of mind still possible to papal curialists under Pope Julius II was shown by the remarkable writings of the Bolognese canon lawyer, Giovanni Gozzadini; though it seems that, like many courtiers, he feared to follow his conscience and to turn his silent criticism of the ruler into public action. Gozzadini owed his rise in the papal court, at the end of Alexander VI's pontificate and in the early years of Julius II, mainly to his legal knowledge and ability, and to a reputation for rectitude. Besides being a consistorial advocate, he taught law in the Roman University. He belonged to an old and powerful Bolognese family which had acquired additional wealth from its papal connections at the beginning of the fifteenth century.

Gozzadini may have been thought useful to the papal government, after the break between Julius II and the ruling Bentivoglio family in Bologna, because of the bitter hostility between his own family and the Bentivoglio, who had despoiled and murdered Giovanni's father. A chamber clerk from 1504, Gozzadini held the key office of papal datarius from the end of 1505 until the summer of 1507. He was then removed from the dataria, and for a time imprisoned, on account of the excessive partisanship he had displayed after the papal recovery of Bologna. Like so many returned exiles, he had been unable to restrain his anger and vengefulness; he was also accused of abetting the disgraced papal legate, Ferreri, in malpractices.

Between the summer of 1510 and the spring of 1511 Gozzadini wrote a remarkable canon-law work, *De Electione Romani Pontificis*, whose scope is much wider than the title suggests. It has been analysed by the late Hubert Jedin, and it evidently amounts to a treatise on the relations between the pope and general church councils, handled in a way which revives the conciliar theories of the earlier fifteenth century. Jedin thought that it had been composed during the period when the opposition to Julius II among the college of cardinals was combining with the French government to organize the Council of Pisa, and that it accurately reflects the opposition to Julius II which had grown up within his own court. Its arguments, though careful to avoid naming the reigning pope or the specific political situation of the time, are roughly those of the pro-French party, that a pope who had shown himself deaf to criticism and to requests for church reform could legitimately be overruled by a council which represented the mystic body of the church, and that the council could be summoned either by pious bishops, cardinals, or secular sovereigns.

Gozzadini had himself stood at the centre of the discretionary curial system of justice; and his criticisms of the popes are the more striking for it. He says that 'The successors of Peter,

especially those of our own day, have the spirit of God rarely or
never with them; they are far from him, and are rather possessed by the spirit of the devil, since they obstinately persist
in sin and error, in wars, in shameful acts, in hatred, in mur-
ders, in despoilings . . .'. The satirical pamphlet attributed to
Erasmus, *Julius Exclusus*, could have said it no better.

As a former director of legal and financial forms for the
papal concessions and dispensations granted in the signatura
and the dataria, Gozzadini understood how fatal to the equit-
able working of the system had been the abuse of the dispensing power: 'If only the popes of our time knew how great their
responsibility is for the administrative use of the power of the
keys, they would not be so prone to abuse it, particularly in
order to satisfy their own vain desires, appetites, or dislikes.'
The central message of Gozzadini's book was the need to set
limits to the arbitrary way in which the popes misused their
administrative system.

Gozzadini used an *ad hominem* argument, as well as others,
against the defenders of papal power, claiming that they had
been influenced by toadyism and the desire for advancement in
the papal court. Though perhaps true of some papal apologists
(it may well have been true of Castellesi's tract on the power of
the Roman Church, mentioned above), it was unfair to others. It
also was an unfortunate argument to use, for a man who was
himself to prove only too human, and only too susceptible to the
arguments of power and office. In the event, when the Council
of Pisa was announced in 1511, Gozzadini made absolutely no
move to join it. Perhaps the knowledge that his own irreconcil-
able Bentivoglio foes were with the French court made it impossible for him to do so. He had never actually left the papal
court, nor abandoned his office of chamber clerk, and when
Julius II saw fit to offer him renewed political responsibility, he
did not refuse it. By the summer of 1512 he had been named
papal governor of Piacenza by Julius II: it was an appointment
with political bias against the Council of Pisa, since the Bishop
of Piacenza was committed to the Council and condemned by
the pope.

Gozzadini was by no means alone in caving in to Julius II.
Cardinal Adriano Castellesi, who had also been out of favour
with the pope for some time, and was in self-imposed exile in
Venice at the period of the calling of the Council of Pisa, after a
short hesitation refused to lend it his support. It is not known
whether Gozzadini's manuscript book on the conciliar issue
ever saw the light of day; certainly he ended his days in papal

service, though he ended them rather brutally and sadly, assassinated by the Bebbio faction in Reggio, of which he was then governor, in 1517. But, though written by a man who was unable to escape from the system he served, his book can be seen as a denunciation of the immorality of Renaissance papal administration, and it has been so considered by the great historian of the Council of Trent, Hubert Jedin, who called him the Cassandra of the Renaissance papacy.

The later literary works of the papal secretary Paolo Cortesi (1465–1510) were almost contemporary with those of Gozzadini; Cortesi died in the year in which his own book, *De Cardinalatu*, was published, and at the time when Gozzadini was beginning the *De Electione Romani Pontificis*. Cortesi was a cultivated Tuscan humanist with strong theological interests, whose work presents a diametrically opposed view of the Roman court to that of Gozzadini. It also represents almost a distorted mirror image of the Roman court as described seventy years earlier by Lapo da Castiglionchio, in that much that is said about the court by Lapo either satirically or ironically is resaid by Cortesi in tones of fulsome approval.

Cortesi's earlier work had included a dialogue about learned humanists, *De Hominibus Doctis*, in which one of the interlocutors was Alessandro Farnese, who had been Cortesi's pupil. Cortesi belonged to an established curialist family; he had secured appointment as papal secretary in 1498, but quite shortly afterwards sold the post and used the proceeds to help finance his learned retirement in San Gimignano. Its first product was a theological tract which expressed in current curial Latin the medieval text of Peter Lombard's *Sentences*. D'Amico, who has described Cortesi's life and works, thinks that he planned a further ecclesiastical career, to be based on the literary prestige gained from works he wrote in retirement. This expectation may have been present in Cortesi's mind, although it is doubtful whether it ever had any chance of fulfilment. Like many others who have hoped for advancement from their literary works, Cortesi found that the great men for whom they were intended (notably Julius II himself, in this case) did not bother to read them.

Cortesi's main work, which he did not live to see through the press, was an ambitious tract, *De Cardinalatu*, which is one of the first of the new Renaissance genre of moral and social handbooks for the court, and which can be treated as a sort of clerical anticipation of the idealized picture of the *Cortegiano* given a few years later by the layman, Baldassare Castiglione.

Cortesi's book is much more than a code of social behaviour, and contains an element of pastoral theology, in that it lays down the moral principles which ought to guide a prince of the church. It is not an easy book to interpret; it was once described by Delio Cantimori as having been written 'almost in code' (*in cifra, o quasi*). But it insists, even in the ethical section, upon the political context; for example, the cardinal is obliged to possess knowledge *ratione principatus*.

Many things which in Castiglionchio's treatise are intended ironically are in Cortesi's asserted literally. Wealth, in particular, is essential to Cortesi's ideal churchman. Not only is wealth necessary to the magnanimous man, but it is required by the cardinal to maintain his dignity and what the English Elizabethans would have called his 'state and port'. The cardinal's household, his *familia*, is not an accidental effect of his status in the church, but an essential aspect of his political importance; Cortesi discusses the financing of the cardinals' *familiae* as a duty incumbent on the universal church. The dispensing of patronage by the cardinals is not a result of man's carnality and human frailty, but a moral duty arising from their position as guardians and senators of the church. The luxurious furnishings of a cardinal's palace are not merely tolerated, but asserted as an integral part of his state; and rules and recommendations are made to specify their nature, and the taste which is to govern them. The system of judicial discretion and central fiscality which underpinned the Roman court is accepted without question.

Cortesi's *De Cardinalatu* is a classical statement of the nature and functions of the Renaissance Roman court seen in an idealized light. It would be wise to remember that it was written at the high tide of Julius II's papal propaganda, when other writers were proclaiming his pontificate as one which would fulfil the apocalyptic expectation of a renewed Rome and a renewed Christendom. Cortesi shared with other curial publicists of his day the idea of giving a philosophical basis to Julius II's Rome; for example, he calls the rebuilding of St Peter's an example of 'correcting injustice'. Cortesi saw no warts on the face of the Roman court; perhaps he might have written with a little more realism if the book had been composed in Rome, the city it concerned, instead of in the Tuscan solitude of San Gimignano.

IX

The uncomfortable position of many earlier humanists in the papal court, unwilling as they were to spend their days as servile publicists yet unable wholly to escape the ties of loyalty and patronage, has already been explained. Most of these men wrote exclusively in Latin; this was the language of their leisure as much as it was that of their duties. For the few who wrote also in the vulgar tongue, the division between duty and literary diversion was even sharper. There is no connection between the Italian poems of the chamber clerk Rosello Roselli (1399–1451) and his papal career; in fact their rather teasing, erotic nature is hard to reconcile with his clerical status.

Roselli was a member of a distinguished Arezzo legal family; he carried out several diplomatic and papal state missions besides serving in the chamber under Eugenius IV. The only public duty he undertook for the pope that had a literary undertone was that of bringing back from Avignon some of the papal library that had been stored there since the Schism. As a poet his vocation was entirely non-clerical. He was an enthusiast for Petrarch's verse to the extent that he copied out the whole Petrarchan *canzoniere* as an introduction to his own collection of love poems dedicated to a lady called Oretta; his verses had the none-too-cryptic title, *Or' è tardi*. Roselli's poems have a comic, satirical edge which he shared with the school of Tuscan poets that sometimes met in the shop of the Florentine barber-poet, Burchiello; there is no courtly feeling to them.

The papal secretaries were made judges in Florence in 1441 of the vernacular verse competition of the *Certame Coronario*. But the competition was itself classicizing by its subject, and none of those secretaries have left any literary work written in Italian; their verdict on the poems submitted was, indeed, unfavourable, and the prize was not awarded. One of the more active Florentines in organizing the competition, the future papal secretary, Leonardo Dati, was the author of a tragedy written in Latin, the *Hiensal*; but he wrote no vernacular works of any merit.

Not until the second decade of the sixteenth century was the dignity that could be accorded to writing in the vernacular high enough for a vernacular poet and literary theorist (though also a distinguished Latinist) to be made papal secretary. Pietro Bembo was by origin a Venetian patrician, prominent enough to be considered, though rejected, for ambassadorial office on behalf of his native city, who deliberately decided on a clerical career. He must have calculated that this career would be assisted in the first place by his Della Rovere connections, which were also the occasion for his sojourn in the court of Urbino (1506–12). He came to Rome in 1512 to live, not in the household of a Venetian prelate, but in that of the aristocratic Genoese, Federico Fregoso, nephew of the last Montefeltro Duke of Urbino. Fregoso was Archbishop of Salerno, Bishop of Urbino, and a former papal secretary. With such favour, preferment came quickly, both to Bembo and to his old acquaintance the Ferrarese humanist Jacopo Sadoleto, who also lived in the Fregoso household; in 1513 they were chosen as the two domestic secretaries of Leo X.

In the second book of his *Prose della volgar lingua*, which was written at this period, Bembo began by making the traditional distinction between the active and the contemplative life, and by saying that the priority between the two is a question that remains undecided: 'E in tanto furono l'una e l'altra per sé di queste vie dagli antichi filosofi lodata, che ancora la quistion pende, quale di loro preporre all'altra si debba e sia migliore'. The hesitation is typical of Bembo, and indicates the shape of his later career. Bembo preferred the clerical state because it promised the learned leisure, the *otium*, which the scholar and poet needed; but, because he also wanted rank and wealth, he was to be compelled even in his clerical life to undertake the political labours which gave them.

Bembo was, none the less, a man of letters before he was a church politician. To confer dignity and order upon the vernacular literary tradition was one of the main tasks of Bembo's life; to this he devoted the kind of philological gifts which earlier talented humanists had reserved for the classical languages. In making this choice Bembo contradicted the priority assigned to classical Latin by the earlier humanist tradition, and he was thus in conflict with the conservative, classicizing views of Paolo Cortesi, especially as these had been expressed in Cortesi's *Lives of Illustrious Men*.

However, the difference of opinion between Bembo and Cortesi about the importance to be attached to the vernacular was compensated by their converging views about the importance of the court. Although Bembo rejected the language of the Roman court as a linguistic norm for educated Italians, by implication he asserted the authority of the courtly life as a standard of manners and literary value. His *Prose della volgar lingua* is a dialogue about the authority of literary conventions. It is addressed to Cardinal Giulio de' Medici and takes place between courtiers, in a courtly setting, like Bembo's own earlier *Asolani*, and like Castiglione's *Cortegiano*. It may be remarked that Archbishop Federico Fregoso is an important participant in the dialogues of both Bembo and Castiglione. But the whole tone of Bembo's work in both prose and verse, with its avoidance of popular usage (*uso popolaresco*) and its frequent reference to the games and customs of the court, its preference for what is *vago e gentile*, is an implicit assertion of courtly values.

There was a certain ambiguity in Bembo's attitude to the Roman court, just as there had been in that of many fifteenth-century humanists. Like them, he tended to treat the Roman court as much as a vehicle for the fulfilment of his literary ambitions as an ecclesiastical career; like many of them, he was reluctant to embrace official chastity and to take major church orders. He became domestic secretary at a time when the office was already losing some of its former political importance, and this, together with his lay status, may have weakened his subsequent career. But he may, equally, be counted as a victim of the Roman spoils system, which often sent the domestic secretary of a deceased pope into long-term disfavour with the papal successors.

After the death of Leo X in 1521 Bembo failed (unlike Sadoleto, who had become a bishop) to continue in residence in Rome, or in office in the Roman court, and he left the city, returning only after his nomination as cardinal in 1539. His bureaucratic career there had lasted only eight years, though these had been eight important years, in the course of which he had been able to provide himself with lucrative benefices, and to work at the peak of public life. His prestige had taken no hurt. He was able much later, for example, to collect for publication a considerable part of his official papal correspondence.

Bembo's literary production was both in Italian and in Latin, but predominantly in Italian, and he wrote Italian verse at most points of his life. As a man of letters he was still in a small avant-garde minority. Carlo Dionisotti has remarked that it was a time when other poets in and around the Roman court—Fracastoro, Sannazaro, Vida, Flaminio—most of them younger than Bembo, were putting all their efforts into the composition of Latin verse. In making himself into a vernacular poet, Bembo was pointing towards later curialist poets and men of letters of comparable ability and ambitions, like Giovanni della Casa.

On the other hand, of Bembo's professional life it might be

remarked that his position as secretary of Latin briefs put him on the traditional wing of the curia, and not with the Italianists. Bembo's arrival in Rome had coincided with a revolution in the linguistic practice of the Roman court, especially as it affected the secretaries. Leo X was the first pope to see to it that much of the most important political correspondence of the popes was not carried out in Latin, but in Italian. Some of the papacy's Italian letters were executed by the secretariat of Cardinal Giulio de' Medici, some by Bernardo Dovizi (Bibbiena), the papal treasurer, at the direct behest of the pope. From this point onwards most communications with papal envoys (the *nunzi*) and many of the most important and secret political letters were drafted and dispatched in Italian. In asserting the dignity and authority of the Italian tongue, Bembo was only calling for something that, on utilitarian grounds, the Roman court had already incorporated into its everyday practice.

X

It would be surprising if, among these rich and on the whole cultivated prelates, there had not been men of taste and patrons of the arts. The works of art most frequently associated with Roman curialists are funerary monuments. Most rich curialists either erected these for themselves or provided for their erection in their wills. The earliest was the best: the Michelozzo tomb of the secretary Bartolomeo Francesco Aragazzi (died 1429), now to be seen only in a mutilated state in the cathedral of Montepulciano. Leonardo Bruni came across overladen carts carrying this tomb to its first home in the collegiate church of S. Maria in Montepulciano, with their protesting driver. According to John Pope-Hennesey, this incident was the occasion for Bruni's selection of his own tomb-type, and thus for the development of the 'humanistic' tomb. Poggio Bracciolini, who had died as ex-Chancellor of Florence, wished to be provided in the church of Santa Croce in Florence with a tomb like those of Leonardo Bruni and Carlo Marsuppini, but the money to build it ran out—an incident not untypical of Bracciolini financial affairs.

Aragazzi's contemporary, the humanist Paolo Cencio Rustici, is commemorated in a much later monument in S. Maria sopra Minerva, erected in 1488 by Antonio to the memory of his father, Paolo, and also to that of his uncle, Marcello (died 1481), who had also been a papal secretary. Among other humanists, there is a rather formal monument to Lorenzo Valla, in the Lateran church of which he was a canon, showing him in a costume which is somewhat ambiguous as between layman and cleric, and which belongs to the humanist tomb model. The other tomb—a fine one—belonging to the group of humanist tombs is that of the papal secretary Piero da Noceto in the cathedral of Lucca, by Matteo Civitali. A work of art of comparable merit erected to a former chamber clerk is the Mino da Fiesole monument to Bishop Leonardo Salutati (died 1466) in the cathedral of Fiesole. The Salutati monument, however, is an orthodox clerical one, and not of the humanist type made popular by the Bruni tomb.

Among the monuments of the later period, the best is probably that to the former secretary, later Cardinal Bartolomeo Roverella (died 1476), in S. Clemente in Rome, probably by Giovanni Dalmata and Andrea Bregno. In the same church is the monument of Cardinal Jacopo Venieri (1422-79), of a notable curialist family who came from Recanati. Among tombs to Spaniards, that formerly in the chapel of Saints Andrew and James in the Vatican, to Calixtus III's minister Bartolomé Regas, has disappeared, but that to Pedro Ferriz, the chamber clerk and jurist (1415-78), has survived (it is probably from the workshop of Andrea Bregno). Of better workmanship are the monuments to Cardinal Jacopo Ammanati and his mother Costanza, in the S. Agostino cloister. In the same cloister is the monument to the Genoese Ottaviano Fornari, former chamber clerk (1464-1500). In S. Maria sopra Minerva there is a tomb of the rich Venetian secretary, Benedetto Soranzo, Archbishop of Nicosia, erected by his layman brother, Vettore, who evidently thought the tomb in distant Rome to be a worthwhile expense. That of the Cypriot Cardinal Lodovico Podocataro, the doctor of Innocent VIII and secretary of Alexander VI, is in S. Maria del Popolo. The willingness of families to spend lavishly on clerical tombs is evident from the Geraldini tombs in S. Francesco in Amelia, of which one has been ascribed to Luigi Capponi and another to Agostino di Duccio.

Of the family tombs in Rome, the Bufalini (Manni) tomb in S. Maria in Aracoeli, decorated by Pinturrichio, is especially interesting in that it was built by Niccolò Bufalini of Città di Castello in the church which was *par excellence* that of the Roman urban magnates, although neither Niccolò nor any of his three sons, all of whom also had careers in the Roman court, attained the highest curial honours. Also in S. Maria in Aracoeli, Sigismondo de' Conti of Foligno, a papal secretary of long standing and domestic secretary of Julius II, in 1512 placed Raphael's Madonna on the high altar as an ex-voto offering for his escape from a thunderbolt. It is less surprising that Conti should have been able to decorate this honoured place in the church, since, though not a bishop or cardinal, he was at the peak point of a distinguished curial career. Among other family tombs, the Ponzetti tombs in S. Maria della Pace and the Pucci tombs in S. Maria sopra Minerva (the church of the Florentine community in Rome) should be mentioned.

It is not remarkable that Sebastiano del Piombo (whose soubriquet derived from his curial office) should have been patronized by this group of curialists. One of his greatest paintings, the Pietà of Viterbo, was commissioned by the chamber clerk Giovanni Botonti (who died in 1528, 'un messer non so di Viterbo', said Vasari) for his family chapel in San Francesco at Viterbo. Filippo Sergardi of Siena (1466–1536), for a long time the dean of the apostolic chamber, was the friend and executor for the banker, Agostino Chigi: for Chigi's estate he signed the contract with Sebastiano del Piombo for the Chigi chapel in S. Maria della Pace. The painting, a 'Visitation', was unfinished at the time of Sebastiano's death in 1547.

From the last decade of the fifteenth century onwards, the opportunities to make money in the Roman court multiplied. It is at this period that the cultivated patron of the arts becomes a typical figure of the upper echelons of the Roman court. The Maecenas role was no longer played, in the first decades of the sixteenth century and the last of the fifteenth, by the exceptionally rich and cultivated cardinal almost alone, but by a comparatively large group of curial prelates. Changes in the church law governing the status of money invested in Roman real estate encouraged rich curialists to build and buy property in Rome, and the court ethos encouraged them to decorate their houses with art objects and collections. At this time the style of life emerged which is associated with the idea of a Renaissance prelate, and in Rome the social type became stable, and carried over into the Baroque period and beyond.[12]

The model of the curial prelate whose main vocation was that of scholar-collector was Angelo Colocci (1474–1549). Colocci's role was not that of patron of the arts, but of the prosperous and magnanimous scholar who accumulated

[12] See Partner, Renaissance Rome, and id., 'Finanze e urbanistica a Roma (1420–1623)', Cheiron, 1 (1983), 59–71; id., 'Sisto IV, Giulio II e Roma rinascimentale: La politica sociale di una grande iniziativa urbanistica', in Società Savonese di Storia Patria, Atti e Memorie, NS, 24 (1988), pt. 2, 81–9.

archaeological treasures, the friend and correspondent of the learned in Rome, a good philologist not only in Latin and Italian, but in Provençal.

The typical housing of such men was not the large and showy palace, but the suburban villa. A richer, but less learned, curialist contemporary of Colocci was Baldassare Turini of Pescia (died 1543), the datarius of Leo X and the builder of Villa Lante on the Janiculum. Turini was the friend of Raphael, and the patron of Polidoro da Caravaggio, among others; and he also collected antique objects. His son gave him a fine tomb in the cathedral of Pescia. A third curialist of comparable stamp was the Frenchman, Thomas Le Roy ('Regis', died 1524), the builder of the palace known as the Farnesina ai Baullari.

Such men played an important role in the cultural life of the period, and have no real equivalent in the Rome of a century earlier. They were perhaps rather more independent than curialists of the end of the fifteenth century like the cultivated Ludovico Agnelli, Bishop of Cosenza (died 1499), who to the end of his life remained in many respects a creature of the Gonzaga court. Agnelli was the patron of humanists, and the commissioner of fine manuscripts; but he continued, even as a senior churchman, to buy in the antiques market for his Gonzaga patrons. (Though this may be unfair to Agnelli, for Turini, for example, was a grovelling Medici adherent, who took as his device a dog adoring the Leonine sun.)

It would be unjust, finally, to depict these curialists as entirely rapacious and greedy men who none of them had a thought for the transmission of their culture (where they possessed it) to others. The urge to divulge information was strong in almost all the humanists, and in many of the lawyers. In some instances this was shown by the setting up of educational establishments, which were given good libraries. The two major cases are those of Domenico Capranica and Stefano Nardini, who both testated large sums and supplied the premises for the establishment of colleges in Rome. They were, in this, in the forefront of their times: the foundation of colleges had some fourteenth-century precedents at Oxford, Winchester, and Bologna, and later in Paris, but in Europe their number was still small. It is true that both Capranica and Nardini only created these foundations after they had for some time been rich cardinals: it is doubtful whether the resources of lesser prelates would have sufficed.

On a more modest scale than the foundations of Capranica and Nardini, such donations may be mentioned as the little law library of Ludovico Garsi, given to the Dominicans of Bologna, or the library given and sumptuously housed at Montepulciano (according to a seventeenth-century source) by Fabiano Benci, another chamber clerk. In Rome there were the larger collections of the Venetian Antonio Orsi, given to the convent of San Marcello, and the books of Bishop Jacopo Feo of Savona, given to the basilica of San Paolo fuori le Mura.

There may also be said to be a certain altruism in taking the post of Vatican librarian, which was occupied at different times by the former papal secretaries Giovanni Andrea Bussi and Giovanni Lorenzi. Though spoken of now with reverence, the job did not lead easily to further political influence, and cannot be regarded as a leg up in an aspiring curial career. The backgrounds of these men were dissimilar; Bussi was a Lombard noble who was already a bishop when he became Vatican librarian under Paul II. Like more than one Lombard humanist, he became committed to a career in the papal court partly because he had lost the favour of the rulers of Milan. Bussi was also an innovator and a patron in his encouragement of the printing press in Italy; to be remembered as having been the main stimulus to the early Italian printers is not a small distinction. Lorenzi came of humble origins and was more vulnerable than Bussi; to him the post of Vatican librarian, from which he was eventually dismissed by Alexander VI, was in itself a major distinction. But it may be remarked that the security of tenure of the secretaries operated in Lorenzi's favour: even though thrown out of the Vatican Library, he remained a secretary until his death.

XI

The attempt to describe the mental and social framework of such a disparate group of men, of whom the oldest were born well before the Great Schism and the youngest were deeply involved in the quarrels of the Reformation, is bound to be blurred at the edges. But one or two judgements are possible. One is that the tensions which affected the lives of the more sensitive and learned among these officials were not predominantly tensions between the values of the Gospel and the values of Mammon, but between the active and the contemplative life. Every one of these men, including Antonio Fatati and Gian Matteo Giberti, who became model bishops, accepted the curial machine for the grant of benefice and favour. Even if they left the Roman court, they continued to defend the material gains they had made from it until long after their departure. Whether or not they were concerned with reform of the church in general, or the reform of its central institutions in particular, acceptance of the main legal principles of the Roman court was universal.

There was, however, a clear and painful tension, in the case of many of these clerks, between the life of business, grace and favour, and promotion, and the life of contemplation and study. And on those who thought, there lay a moral obligation to write. 'Ora se alle buone opere e alle belle contemplazioni la penna mancasse, né si trovasse chi le scrivesse, elle così giovevoli non sarebbono di gran lunga, come sono.' Bembo touches on a theme common to many. In the concept of moral nobility which inspired many Renaissance humanists, the need to escape from the life of subservience, duty, and business to the life of *otium*, of learned leisure, was of the first importance. But the attainment of leisure depended upon the attainment of office and influence, and very often men failed to get out of the toils of the official life they had thought to be a means to an end, but which became an end in itself. It is not the problem of a single age: the same inner conflicts affected Humbert Wolfe, Richard Church, and other men of letters in the British Civil Service, during the 1920s.

There was an additional moral conflict, when papal servants accepted the office of bishop. When three well-known, talented bishops escaped from the papal court to their dioceses between 1521 and 1528—Federico Fregoso, Jacopo Sadoleto, and Gian Matteo Giberti—the feeling to inspire all three was not, in the first instance, their evangelical duty to return to their sees, but the desire for learned leisure. Only after they had taken up their pastoral duties did the moral pressures begin to affect each individual bishop, eventually bringing all three to be important participants in the Catholic reform movement. Such returns of curial bishops to their sees had not been unknown in the preceding century, but the public consequences had been quieter, and the feeling of a common purpose among bishops who behaved in this manner had been less evident. In this new atmosphere, in which the responsible clerk trained in humane studies saw his episcopal duty differently, perhaps lies the most important religious change of the period studied in this book.

6

The Italian Notables and Their Church Interests

I

Only in the dioceses directly subject to the Holy See, most of which were in the papal state or Tuscany, was the relationship of Italian clergy with the Roman bishopric different from that of any other Catholic clergy. In Italy the provision of all bishoprics, and of all abbeys and monasteries valued at more than 200 florins annually, was by chancery rules reserved to the pope.[1] The cathedral chapter was only exceptionally allowed to proceed to an election of its bishop, if an agreement with the secular power enabled it to do so. But in most cases in practical terms the appointment of major Italian bishops outside the papal state was negotiated between the secular rulers and the pope, and effected by apostolic provision. Minor bishoprics were sometimes filled by papal provision made without consultation outside the Roman court, though regimes as powerful in church matters as that of Venice discouraged the filling even of minor sees without their previous consent. Another procedure was that sometimes followed by the Florentine government, by which a short list of nominees for a bishopric was presented to the pope by the government concerned. If a more or less formal concordat or indult had been granted at some point by a pope to an Italian government, the agreement was important for these negotiations, but not always decisive. Arbitrary papal power was too large to be

[1] Von Ottenthal, *Päpstlichen Kanzleiregeln*, 186–7, 238–9. For what follows see McClung Hallman, *Italian Cardinals*; Hay, *The Church in Italy*; Bizzocchi, *Chiesa e potere*; C. Mozzarelli and Schiera (eds.), *Patriziati e aristocrazie nobiliari* (Bologna, 1978); C. Mozzarelli, 'Stato, patriziato e organizzazione della società nell'Italia moderna', *Ann.Ist.Stor.Ital.-germ.Tr.* 2 (1976); A. Prosperi, 'La figura del vescovo fra Quattro e Cinquecento: persistenze, disagi e novità', *Annali della Storia d'Italia*, 9 (Turin, 1986), 219–62; id., '"Dominus beneficiorum": La spartizione dei benefici tra prassi curiale ed esigenze politiche negli stati italiani tra '400 e '500', in P. Prodi and P. Johaneck (eds.), *Strutture ecclesiastiche in Italia e in Germania prima della riforma protestante* (Bologna, 1984), 51–86; Clergeac, *La Curie*; Katterbach, *Sussidi*, ii, XII–XVI; Frenz, *Kanzlei*, pp. 68–77; Von Hofmann, *Forschungen*, i. 51.

contained by such concessions, in spite of their undoubted
political importance.

However, in line with the trend to make similar bargains
with ultramontane governments, and in line also with the
separate arrangements made with some nations at the end of
the Council of Constance, fifteenth-century popes made special
agreements with certain Italian powers about nominations to
benefices situated in their territories. Most of these were due
to Nicholas V, particularly the deals struck with Francesco
Sforza's new regime in Milan in 1450, with Venice in 1451,
with the Duke of Savoy in 1452, and with Genoa in 1453. There
was no similar single agreement applicable to Florence, though
a corpus of customary practice emerged during the fifteenth
century; but each appointment took its place in what Bizzocchi
has called 'the vast, endless negotiations between Rome and
Florence for the provision of church benefices'. Nor was there
a single agreement about the benefices of the Regno, though in
this case there was an ancient and complicated legacy of
special church law.

It is probably, in any case, a mistake to think that the various
agreements controlled the practice of nomination to benefices
in a simple legal or administrative code. Something like this
may have obtained for Venetian benefices, which the Venetian
government tried to control (not always successfully) by the
operation of a single committee in Venice. But in other cases,
for example that of Lombardy, it is clear that earlier agreements had only a moderate or persuasive force upon papal
practice. Pius II's provision of his favourite, Jacopo Ammanati,
to the see of Pavia, in spite of the concession made to Sforza by
Nicholas V, is an example of the way in which popes went back
on the promises of their predecessors.

Similar political principles as those applied to bishoprics
and major abbeys informed the nomination to lesser benefices,
though the legal and administrative procedure was very different. Lesser benefices could be petitioned for in the Roman
court even during the lifetime of a titular owner, and at his
death or resignation several competing claims based on prior
papal grant could often be presented. In such cases the
question of temporal priority was of great importance—hence
the many clerical deathbeds over which the contesting
aspirants to a benefice hovered like vultures. In obtaining
expectative graces and similar favours in the Roman court the
help of skilled advisers and brokers was essential. It was
relatively easy to obtain the *concessum* or *concessum in*

praesentia domini nostri papae written on the schedule of
petitions presented in the Signatura. But the attachment of
some sort of legal right was not enough, in most cases, to
produce the desired access to the benefice. What counted most
in making the grant of the papal petition legally effective were
the *clausulae*, or special legal conditions, subsequently
attached to it by the papal referendaries, prior to its engross-
ment as an official papal document.

The variety of rights available to a clerk with the money and
the influence to get them was bewildering. At the top of the
tree, a consistorial benefice could be obtained as a simple
apostolic provision to a bishopric or monastery, but it could
also be granted in administration, *in commendam*, with the
reservation of some of its fruits to a third party in the shape of
a pension, with the right of subsequent regress, as a coadjutor-
ship, or in union with one or more benefices which were
already held by the grantee. The effect of this flexibility was
to make the curial market for consistorial benefices more
important than it had been in the medieval past, and thus to
encourage the curial officials who sold their legal and
brokerage services to important prelates and princes.

Consistorial benefices could not be petitioned for: they were
conferred in the papal consistory on the referral of cardinals.
The negotiations concerning them were expensive, and were
profitable for the curial lawyers and also for the cardinals and
their secretaries and hangers-on. The chance to hold two or
more consistorial benefices simultaneously, by the device of
grants *in commendam*, was normally available only to the most
powerful curialists, in practice to cardinals. However, curial
bishops lower down the hierarchy were often able to exchange
their bishoprics by resignation or translation, or to pass them
on to others by the same legal means.

Among these 'chop-churches' Jacopo Vagnucci, Bishop of
Rimini, was able to get translation to Perugia (a more attractive
proposition than Rimini for someone who hailed from Cortona)
the year after his first promotion to Rimini in 1448, and then
subsequently in old age in 1482 to resign the see of Perugia to
his nephew, Dionisio Vagnucci, accepting the titular see of
Nicaea in its stead. Or we can look at one of the big plums for
Venetian curialists, Nicosia in Cyprus which had a revenue
roughly ten times that of the central Italian sees like Perugia.
Benedetto Soranzo, a scion of a powerful banking family, and
also the close political ally of Girolamo Riario, had Nicosia in
1484. Soranzo was the brother of the Venetian admiral, the

papal ally in the war of Ferrara. The Venetian government were so suspicious of the Riario connection that when he was papally provided to the see he was flung into prison: however, he managed to convince the Venetian committee of his probity. On Benedetto's death in 1495 Nicosia was granted in administration to the Venetian cardinal, Domenico Grimani. When the necessary deals had been done in Venice, Grimani resigned Nicosia in favour of Soranzo's and Grimani's common relative by marriage, the curialist Sebastiano Priuli.

The numerous clashes between the rival claims of powerful patrons were often compromised by the device of reserving a pension on a rich benefice to one party, while granting it in consistory to another. The keeping back of a pension on a bishopric was also widely used when an uncle resigned it in favour of a nephew: he thus ensured the continuance of the bishopric in family control, while financing a pension for his own retirement. This expedient was used, for example, by Jacopo Vagnucci, who retained a pension amounting to a third of the revenues of Perugia, on resigning it in favour of his nephew. Or a pension could be used to help buy off the opposition; in this way Benedetto Soranzo allowed a pension of 500 florins a year (10 per cent of the gross revenues of the see) from the archbishopric of Nicosia to be granted to Lorenzo Gabrielli. Gabrielli accepted this when, at the same time as Soranzo was appointed to Cyprus, he was appointed to the much poorer see of Bergamo. In this way the Italian bishoprics and abbeys were encumbered with pensions until few were worth anything approaching their nominal value to the titular bishop or abbot. Since the Italian sees were already, on the whole, poorer than those elsewhere in Europe, the effect of the pensions systems was to increase the pressure on Italian bishops to accumulate revenue and benefices from a number of different sources.

It is obvious, and has already been emphasized above, that clerks in the Roman court enjoyed privileged access to papal grants. Chancery rules gave secretaries and chamber clerks special privileges in the way they could petition for benefices. For example, the rule that anyone holding five benefices or more had to resign one of these if he petitioned for a further one, was not applicable to a number of important curial officers, among whom were the secretaries.[2]

[2] Von Ottenthal, *Kanzleiregeln*, pp. 177, 191.

II

The principle governing all these arrangements was that of access to power. Papal centralization could be an instrument of oligarchic ambition, so long as the oligarchs could obtain easy access to the administrative power centres in the papal court. There was often little distinction between the access accorded to governments and that accorded to subjects. For example, in the correspondence between Florence and Rome about benefices, papal negotiations with the Medici were frequently more important than those with the Florentine government proper. On the other hand, there was a sharp distinction between papal negotiation with Milanese and Venetian governments, and negotiation with the subjects of these dominions. In the papal state itself, the policy of according benefices to families like the Baglioni of Perugia, Monaldeschi of Orvieto, or Spiriti of Viterbo, was a branch of political rather than of church management.

The position of senior Italian clerks in the papal court was almost always ambiguous. Their main concern was to use their influence to advance themselves and their families. Their home governments, and the dominating families in those governments, used them as brokers and negotiators, sometimes to obtain things which they themselves were reluctant to ask for. Few papal bureaucrats below the rank of cardinal had a strong independent patronage system of their own; almost all were dependent in some degree on curial patrons who might hail from the same region or city, but might in other cases have nothing to do with their own area of origin. Angelo Geraldini, of Amelia in the papal state, depended either on Milanese or on Aragonese influence. Antonio Jacopo Venieri, another papal state notable, derived his curial power from his Spanish connections. Benedetto Soranzo was, as has just been explained, an object of deep suspicion to the Venetian government. Among the smaller fry, papal state officials like Giannantonio Campano and Niccolò Perotti were the mere tools of powerful patrons; when the Piccolomini faction could no longer support them, their careers collapsed. But for any Italian prince or city, the number of influential clerks to be counted on in Rome was an important factor in church policy.

In Table 8 the high proportion of secretaries and chamber clerks who originated in the papal state is notable. The larger sample of over a thousand chancery officials provided by Frenz (Table 9) shows a lower proportion, but their number still

TABLE 8. Regional origins of Italian chamber clerks and secretaries, 1417-1527

	No.	% of Italians in papal office	% of all in papal office
Piemonte	11	3.9	3.0
Lombardy	23	8.3	6.4
Veneto	31	11.1	8.5
Liguria	31	11.1	8.5
Tuscany	61	21.9	16.8
Papal state	110	39.4	30.3
Regno	12	4.3	3.3
Total Italian origin	279	100.0	76.8
Origin not identified	1		0.3
Non-Italian origin	83		22.9
TOTAL	363		100.0

TABLE 9. Regional origins of chancery officials, 1471-1527 (after Frenz)*

	No.	% of Italians
Papal state	168	26.5
Tuscany	109	17.2
Southern Italy	88	13.9
Sicily and Sardinia	15	2.4
Northern Italy	254	40.0
Total Italian origin	634	100.0
Non-Italian and uncertain origin	460†	
TOTAL	1094	

* T. Frenz, Die Kanzlei der Päpste der Hochrenaissance (1471-1527) (Tübingen, 1986), 241. His figures have been rearranged so as to make the categories as close as possible to those used here.
† i.e. 42% of total.

amounts to over a quarter of the Italian chancery personnel. The proportion of Tuscans is high in this sample, and lower but still very substantial for the chancery as a whole. It may be remarked here that the secretaries form a part of Frenz's data, but the chamber clerks do not; Frenz found rather different proportions among chancery personnel generally than is found here for chamber clerks and secretaries for the regions of Southern Italy and Sicily.

One factor which differentiates Frenz's data from Table 8 is that the venal colleges of papal offices were predominant for roughly half of the period with which he deals. Venality affected papal offices in two ways: first, there were far more of them from the time their sale became standard practice, and second, their conferment was effected on rather different principles than in the case of the earlier non-venal offices. Venality, as has been observed above, affected different offices in different ways. Thus, the number of secretaries was increased by a factor of, perhaps, five, but the number of chamber clerks was sharply reduced by the disappearance of the supernumerary clerk.

The most important factor in all curial advancement is the most difficult to quantify. The only cases in which the patronage which lay behind a clerk's advancement is likely to be clear and unambiguous are those in which it was due to a pope or to a secular prince. Most other cases are doubtful, and the data in Table 10 must be taken as a series of guesses.

It is not at all surprising that most patronage came from inside the Roman court, from popes, cardinals, or curial bishops. The direct route to papal favour was, of course, the most effective. Particularly at the beginning of a pontificate, the popes would give place and favour to their own regional and kinship groups, and also especially to the *familia* which had followed them as a cardinal. Such men frequently became chamberlains (*cubicularii*) of the new pope, and from their number came the personnel of the secret finances. In this way

TABLE 10. *Probable sources of patronage* (% given in parentheses)

	Chamber clerks	Secretaries
Pope	15 (10.7)	59 (23.8)
Cardinal	19 (13.6)	34 (13.8)
Major noble	6 (4.3)	14 (5.6)
Bishop	7 (5.0)	4 (1.6)
King or prince	3 (2.1)	2 (0.8)
Unknown	90 (64.3)	135 (54.4)

unknown men, who had previously enjoyed modest office or none in the Roman court, rose to sudden power and influence. Oddo de' Varri under Martin V, Francesco dal Legname under Eugenius IV, Bartolomé Regas under Calixtus III, and Gianbattista Ferrari under Alexander VI, were examples of obscure clerks who rose to sudden prominence in the financial administration by such a route. Under Calixtus III Regas was simultaneously papal secretary, scriptor, chamber clerk, vice-treasurer, and papal secret chamberlain in charge of the pope's secret household accounts. He survived in office in the Roman court after Calixtus's death, and continued his long career as chamber clerk (though he was no longer secretary or treasurer).

But the chances of keeping gain acquired in such a way were not always good. Oddo de' Varri disappears from history after the revolt of the Colonna in 1433.[3] Bartolomé Regas and Francesco dal Legname retained a certain influence and place in the papal court, though the latter was in deep disgrace for a time, and lost his bishopric, and 'the former lost his major offices after Calixtus's death. Similar examples of sudden power and favour bestowed by a new pope upon the previously obscure can be found among the domestic secretaries: Pietro da Noceto under Nicholas V, Matteu Johan under Calixtus III, and Gregorio Lolli under Pius II are examples. Of these, the first was allowed to keep some offices after his patron's death, but after a time left Rome to seek favour in Milan, and the second retreated into obscurity under Pius II, whereas the third stayed in the Roman court and found some favour under Paul II.

That the relatives and close family connections of popes would gain promotion almost indiscriminately goes without saying. Gaspare Colonna (of the Riofreddo branch, though probably a nephew of Martin V through intermarriage between the Riofreddo and Paliano lines) was made by Martin V into the first known example of a chamber clerk whose tenure of the post was as a sinecure. Tommaso 'de Testa' Piccolomini was one of the secret chamberlains running the confidential accounts of Pius II, and was made chamber clerk and lieutenant of the Chamberlain.

The household or *familia* of a cardinal or other great church dignitary in Rome was one of the basic social units of the Roman court, and its importance has been clearly explained by John D'Amico. The figures given in Table 10 quite certainly

[3] For Oddo Poccia de' Varri (de' Barri), see Partner, *Papal State*, p. 132; id., 'Camera Papae', p. 67; D. A. Perini, *Genazzano e il suo territorio* (Rome, 1924).

understate the frequency of attachment to a cardinal by the place-seekers in the Roman court. They also disregard the extent to which clerks in the Roman court passed from the service of one cardinal to that of another, sometimes because a cardinal's *familia* broke up on his death, but also because a cardinal might leave Rome for a long period and dissolve the household, or because a clerk might quarrel with his master, or think he had found a better one.

As is well known, humanist scholars, whether clerks or laymen, found it very hard to rise in the Roman court without the springboard offered by service to a great churchman. From Poggio Bracciolini, who started as secretary to Cardinal Maramoldo at the beginning of the fifteenth century, to Paolo Bombace, the secretary of Cardinal Lorenzo Pucci a century later, the humanists rose in the court by this route. Some learned cardinals, like Nicholas of Cusa (patron of Gianandrea Bussi), Bessarion (patron of Perotti), and Oliviero Carafa (patron of Alessio Celadoni and Sadoleto), tended to attract more scholarly dependants than others. Few humanists were so distinguished or so fortunate as to by-pass the *familiae* in their pursuit of advancement. Rinuccio d'Arezzo was at one point a follower of Cardinal Gabriele Condulmer, Domizio Calderini of Cardinal Pietro Riario. Leonardo Dati passed to the service of Gabriele Condulmer after the death of his earlier patron, Giordano Orsini.

III

Over a very long period—say, over the two centuries from the mid fifteenth to the mid seventeeth—there were two general trends which applied almost over all Italy, one towards the closure of public office in favour of a restricted number of families, and the other towards the emergence of these and similar families in a new nobility which had only tenuous connections with the people in Italy who called themselves nobles at the end of the Middle Ages. As Stuart Woolf has cautiously said, these phenomena were probably related, but separate.[4] The varied nature of social organization from one part of the Italian peninsula to another makes it hard to

---

[4] In *Patriziati e aristocrazie nobiliari*, p. 82. For what follows, see Partner, 'Lo stato della chiesa nel XV e nel XVI secolo', *Storia della Società Italiana*, 8 (Milan, 1988), 412–17, and also in M. Greengrass (ed.), *Early Modern State Building: Intentions and Reality* (forthcoming).

identify the general factors clearly. It is easy to see, for example, the big differences between the social organization of Venice, of Rome, and of the kingdom of Naples. But it is less obvious that a number of parallels can be made between, say, the Milanese patriciate, the more affluent and established Florentine families, and the ruling groups in other parts of Tuscany and in the cities of the papal state.

The slow, general drift was towards a dominant noble order. In some respects the meaning of nobility in Renaissance Italy was a somewhat fugitive one. In the papal state, for example, nobility arose from repute or common fame, rather than from a legal right based on the fief. Pius II wrote that the Malatesta, whose defeat and depression he desired, were not nobles of ancient date: the family was believed old and noble, but falsely, for they were new possessors 'totally unknown two centuries ago'. In the papal state, few of the 'lords' who exercised authority over papal cities possessed ancient feudal titles. The most ancient nobility of the papal state, the Orsini, Colonna, Savelli of the Roman Campagna, were members of *consorterie*, allodial nobles whose feudal titles derived in the fifteenth century from the Regno and not from the popes.

The 'nobles' of the late medieval and early Renaissance papal towns were notables rather than a legally defined class of nobility. For example, at the beginning of the century two opposed groups of *nobili* and *popolani* faced one another in Rome. The nobles were so termed because rich and powerful, not because they possessed specific titles of nobility, still less because they belonged to any baronage. As late as the end of the century the Lateran Confraternity of the Saviour, the group to which Marcantonio Altieri, the great literary advocate of the idea of nobility in Renaissance Rome, acted as custodian, listed its members. These are in two groups: 'princes and barons' and 'other laymen'. Of nobles not a word is said. Nobility was a term of social distinction in Rome, but not yet a term of social status; a similar situation obtained in England at the same time.

The sluggish transformation of oligarchic into noble groups began to speed up in the early sixteenth century. Its components could assemble even in a specifically communal and mercantile atmosphere. For example, at Bologna certain guilds, such as those of the notaries, moneychangers, drapers, silk manufacturers, came to be termed 'noble'. This was a mere indication of trend to be seen in Bologna long before the senatorial class began to take shape in the sixteenth century.

An important element was the urbanization of noble or gentry landowners who had earlier been excluded from city life. Thus from the early fifteenth century the nobility ceased to be excluded from the Perugian guilds, and the regime governing the city came to be known as that of the gentry (*gentiluomini*). The new nobility formed slowly; for example, the customary right of certain Perugian families to occupy the main civic offices was achieved only at the end of the sixteenth century. But all over the papal state the idea of hereditary right to public office took shape, leading to the closure of the municipal councils in favour of families which in some areas called themselves patrician, in others noble. The beneficiaries of this oligarchic process in the papal state were a composite of merchants, urbanized gentry, judges and notaries, doctors of medicine. They could be compared, perhaps, to a *noblesse de robe*. In the Roman court itself, the automatic appointment of secretaries, papal scriptors, and *sollicitatores* as Palatine counts (admittedly only for their lifetimes) by Leo X was a significant indication of the way things were going. Leo not only made the abbreviators into Palatine counts, but specifically allowed them (although they were clerks) to carry a sword and weapons, even in Rome, and to create new knighthoods.[5]

If in some areas the growth of a new nobility was slow, in others the growth of bastard feudalism, as it has been termed in Britain, was universal by the fifteenth century. In the Ferrarese, for example, the Este rulers by sub-infeudation, treaties of *accomandigia*, recognition of imperial fiefs, and similar actions to win support of the petty nobility, produced a pattern of petty lordships in the countryside which thenceforth excluded any real influence of the urban commune over the inhabitants of the rural districts.[6] Similar developments can be found outside the papal state not only in other parts of Emilia, but also in the Milanese, in Piemonte, in the Riviera di Levante within the Genoese boundaries, and in the Appenine zone between Lunigiana and Parma-Piacenza.

The appointment of members of dominant families as papal officials is an instance of the late medieval tendency of local

[5] For the abbreviators, see *Magnum Bullarium Romanum*, i. 560. For the secretaries, sollicitatores, scriptors, see Von Hofmann, *Forschungen*, ii. 56, 61, 62.

[6] T. Dean, 'Lords, Vassals and Clients in Renaissance Ferrara', *EHR* 100 (1985), 106–19; id., *Land and Power in Late Medieval Ferrara: The Rule of the Este, 1350–1450* (Cambridge, 1988), especially pp. 59–64, 74–178; W. L. Gundesheimer, *Ferrara: The Style of a Renaissance Despotism* (Princeton, 1973).

notables to seek access to the politics of the bureaucracy and the court. Whether access to power was sought primarily for the family to which a clerk belonged, or for the government which controlled it, varied according to times, regions of origin, and people. Where government in the place of origin was powerful, the incentive to act as a Roman agent of the home government was rather reduced, since in normal circumstances the Holy See had to be circumspect in trying to satisfy a strong Italian power. For clerks from less powerful states like Ferrara or Mantua the function of representing local interests at the papal court was more important than it was, for example, for Venetian clerks, who knew that most ecclesiastical questions of importance would be settled by direct negotiation between the papacy and the Venetian republic. On the other hand, there were moments when even a strong government would try to mobilize all the influence it could command in the papal court.

IV

A Renaissance courtier looked first to the ruler, second to his countrymen. In the case of the papal court he might depend on the ruler of the government under which he had originated to get advancement from the pope. Many papal officials through-out their careers stayed attached to the princely faction which had contrived their advancement. This was especially true of the Mantuans. Three Mantuans who made careers in the papal court, Gianpietro Arrivabene (1441–1504), Ludovico Agnelli (died 1499), and Floramonte Brognolo (died after 1513), all remained closely linked to the Gonzaga house throughout their papal service. Arrivabene, who became a papal secretary, was the son of the chancellor of the Marquis, and became Cardinal Gonzaga's longest serving official and closest familiar, giving him twenty-two years of service. He remarked that 'io sono più mantuano che d'altropaese, e non mancho di fede a chi son nato debitore di essa'. Arrivabene was over a long period the author of intelligence reports from the Roman court to Mantua. The correspondence of Giacomo Gherardi makes it clear, how-ever, that Arrivabene was an important man in his own right in the court of Innocent VIII, and that he enjoyed considerable influence over the pope.

Ludovico Agnelli was a clerk of the same stamp as Arriva-bene. Cardinal Gonzaga in the year before the former's appointment as chamber clerk remarked that the 'reverendo protonotaro mio di Agnelli' was not yet provided with benefices adequate to his status ('non anchor bene provisto de beneficii secondo la qualitate sua'), and that he ought to have a benefice in Mantuan territory. Agnelli and his brother Onorato were also extensive buyers in the antique market for Isabella d'Este at Mantua. But, like Arrivabene, Agnelli rose to considerable power and influence in the Roman court, even though he had stood on the shoulders of the Gonzaga. Floramonte Brognolo, who also acted as a fine arts agent for the marchioness, was another long-serving Mantuan agent at Rome who held a secretary's office.

The house of Este was rather less well represented in Rome, though Lorenzo Roverella, who eventually became Bishop of Ferrara, and the papal secretary and master of the registry, Leonello Trotto, were both good servants of Borso d'Este. Trotti, in particular, belonged to a powerful family which owed most of its wealth and influence to the ruling family of Ferrara. It was also a family which put down roots in clerical Rome, while retaining its ties with the Este.

The same story of princely influence in Rome could be repeated for other Italian dynasties. The Visconti, and after them the Sforza, were always very powerful in Rome. Giovanni Alimenti Negri (1439–99), who was a cousin of Duchess Bianca Maria Visconti, had little trouble in getting advancement in the Roman court: he became a chamber clerk at the same time that he became Governor of Rome in 1484. If he failed to obtain the red hat, a great Lombard aristocrat of this stamp was unlikely to spend his whole life in Rome. After a career in the chamber Negri returned to Milan after 1495, and had the misfortune to be murdered there by his black servant. Another such Milanese grandee was Bernardino Lunati (1452–97), who became one of the cardinals and agents of the policies of Alexander VI, and died in Rome while at the height of power and favour.

But Milanese control of papal politicians was not exercised only over clerks who originated in Milan. Angelo Geraldini (1422–86) was a successful careerist who for a large part of his career in papal service was the client of Francesco Sforza: when this ceased he turned to another dynasty, the Aragonese house of Naples. Nor was Milanese influence exerted only from the ducal chancery: Milanese prelates spun their own webs. Half a century after Geraldini, the Neapolitan Marino Caracciolo (1469–1538), who had grown up as a page in the household of Cardinal Ascanio Sforza, divided his career between Milanese and papal service. Under Julius II Caracciolo was papal secretary and Milanese agent: later, under the Medici popes, he embarked on a sparkling career in papal, Milanese, and imperial diplomacy.

The history of Florentine and Medici influence on office-holding in the papal court is a vast subject. It is also one which overlaps with another topic, the influence upon patronage in the Roman court of the bankers who operated there. Twenty-three of the chamber clerks and secretaries of the sample (6.3 per cent) came from families which operated banks in the Roman court; of these, twelve were Florentines. The Florentines with Roman banking connections include (besides Carlo Medici) Cardinal Alberto Alberti (1386–1445), Cardinal Antonio Pucci (1484–1544), Cardinal Lorenzo Pucci (1459–1531), Andrea Buondelmonti, Archbishop of Florence (1465–1542), Cardinal Niccolò Gaddi (1491–1552), Onofrio Bartolini 'de Medici', Archbishop of Pisa (died 1555). At a more modest level of the bureaucracy were Giovanni Boscoli (died 1448), a chamber clerk and Governor of Bologna, Leonardo Salutati, another chamber clerk of Eugenius IV, and Antonio Francesco Torna-buoni. All three were near relations of managers of the Medici branch in Rome.

To assume that all Florentine curialists were Medici clients and nothing else would be an error. Niccolò Pandolfini (1440–1518, cardinal in 1517) was the son and grandson of important Florentine political figures, and an able lawyer. His rise in the Roman court was supported by the Medici, but it also owed a great deal to others; for example, his promotion to the bishopric of Pistoia in 1474 was directly due to Cardinal Giuliano della Rovere and not to Lorenzo de' Medici, although Lorenzo was not displeased. However, Pandolfini remained a Medici client, even after their expulsion from Florence in 1494.

Moreover, like the rulers of Milan, Lorenzo de' Medici could acquire as clients clergy in the Roman court who were by origin quite extraneous to his own region; and such clergy could get themselves accepted as bishops of towns in the Florentine dominions. An example was Cristoforo Bordini (died 1502), a prominent noble of Pratella, who came from the Umbrian area near Città di Castello, just outside the Florentine borders. Bordini was later to become a powerful man in the court of Innocent VIII. He had been the client and former vicar of Cardinal Jacopo Ammanati: he owed his promotion to the see of Cortona in 1477, and his transfer to the clientage circle of the Medici, to a bargain by which Ammanati had supported the candidature of Gentile Becchi (the creature of Lorenzo de' Medici) to the cardinalate.

Naturally, Florentine internal politics were reflected in the

church politics of Florentines in Rome. The Medici could sometimes ruin a clerical career, as Cosimo did for a chamber clerk
in Rome called Antonio Peruzzi, who seemed to be lined up for a
bishopric and high honours in 1433, but who disappeared from
sight after Cosimo came to power in the following year. It is
probable that Cosimo's influence with Pope Eugenius robbed
Peruzzi of further advancement. On the other hand, the distinguished humanist Leonardo Dati (1408–72), who was in the
later stages of his career counted as anti-Medici, and described
by Lorenzo as 'sempre capitale inimico alla caxa Medici',
nevertheless had a very good career in Rome. The Florentine
government asked the pope to give Dati 'qualche dignità o
beneficio splendido' in 1455, at a time when the Medici had
temporarily lost control in Florence. But Dati's career only
really prospered under Paul II in the 1460s, when he was the
pope's confidential secretary, and got a bishopric (albeit a
modest one) as a prize. He did not, however, get a cardinal's
hat, and there is a polite but firm letter from Lorenzo de' Medici
to Dati telling him that he was not going to get Medici support
for one. Like so many humanists, Dati began his curial career
as a clerk in the *familiae* of a cardinal, in his case of Giordano
Orsini; subsequently he served others.

There are some parallels with the career of the Florentine
Dati in that of the Milanese Gian Andrea Bussi of Vigevano
(1417–75), who succeeded Dati as domestic secretary of Sixtus
IV in 1472. Bussi came from a Milanese family notable enough
for its opposition to Sforza rule to have been thought of some
political importance. His career in the Roman court was made
extremely difficult by Milanese disfavour, in spite of his having
got an expectancy to a secretary's post and the provision to an
abbey, under Calixtus. Stories of his having to sell his services
in the street as a scrivener may be exaggerated, but his
economic position was not strong when he entered the service
of Nicholas of Cusa in 1458. Cusa's support got him promotion
to the office of Vicar of the Archdiocese of Genoa, but Sforza
opposition on account of his 'pride and arrogance' stopped the
nomination from taking effect, as it also blocked him from
occupying his abbey of S. Giustina de Sezzadio. The nomination
to one poor Corsican bishopric, and the translation to another,
salvaged his pride rather than his pocket. Nor was the Vatican
librarianship a great financial prize.

There is a long list of clergy who, although they came from
important political families in Florence, and were not the mere
creatures of the Medici as so many of the humanists were, still

owed their curial careers to Medici patronage. Francesco Soderini (1453-1524), at one time the friend of Machiavelli, was one of these, though in his later years his family became the Medicis' sworn enemies. The son of Tommaso Soderini, who had been an important Medici ally in 1469, Francesco got both Sforza and Medici support for his nomination to the see of Volterra in 1478, at the age of 25. In 1503, when Florentine politics were unrecognizably different, and his own brother was in power in opposition to the exiled Medici, he obtained the cardinalate.

Another family of Medici clients which obtained a strong position in the Roman court was the Pucci. Lorenzo (1459-1531) established himself in the Roman court as a relatively young man, but the main stages of his ascent there, including his appointment as coadjutor to Pandolfini, the Medici-appointed Bishop of Pistoia, took place after the Medici expulsion from Florence. His cardinalate was one of the first of those of Leo X. After this the rise of the nephew Antonio Pucci (1484-1544) in the Roman court was unstoppable: he was made Bishop of Pistoia after Pandolfini's death in 1518. All three of these men, Pandolfini and the two Pucci, were chamber clerks at some stage of their careers. They also fully conformed to the Medici fiscal regime: Pandolfini paid 20,000 ducats for promotion to the cardinalate in 1517, and Antonio and Lorenzo Pucci were both involved in the payment of 20,000 ducats for the office of apostolic penitentiary.

V

Family strategies followed a broadly similar pattern, from whatever part of Italy a family came. The practice of resignation in the Roman court by uncle to nephew of both benefices and Roman court offices, often keeping a right of regress, meant that very large numbers of benefices and offices were in effect enfeoffed to particular families. The peak of such practices was reached in the Medici pontificates, and its greatest masters were clerks like the Pucci, just discussed, Andrea Buondelmonti, or the equally notorious Pietro and Benedetto Accolti. But in effect these strategies were employed throughout the whole period, though with increasing frequency from the second half of the fifteenth century. Papal state families, like the de' Spiriti, de' Sinibaldi, Capranica, Cesi, used them with just as much effect as the Tuscans. So did

Genoese curial magnates like Carlo, Agostino, and Francesco Spinola, among whom the key figure was Agostino (died 1537, cardinal chamberlain in 1527).

The bishoprics involved were not necessarily those of the regions from which the clerks came: the dominance of the Tuscan Accolti family over the papal March of Ancona is notorious, and the Spinola for a time established a lien over the papal state bishopric of Perugia. From Paul II's time onwards, but again with increasing frequency under the Medici popes, it was normal practice to put out benefices, particularly bishoprics, to farm for an annual rent.[7]

One of the main building blocks of family clerical influence was the cathedral chapter. Over most of Italy a place in the chapter in the town of origin was expected as a right by clerical members of the dominant course, often at a tender age, to those members of such families who had the requisite influence and advice in the Roman court.

There were other ways of transferring the profits of church revenues from a prelate to his family, besides that of resigning benefices and offices. In theory, on the occasion of the death of a clerk at the Holy See all the property which he left which had arisen from ecclesiastical sources was due to the apostolic chamber as 'spoils'.[8] This liability could be avoided in several ways. A papal licence to testate could be procured, and this licence could be made to include goods deriving from church revenues. After the legislation passed by Sixtus IV between 1475 and 1480, it also became possible for a curialist prelate to escape the consequences of the rule about spoils by investing the proceeds of church revenues in the construction of houses, palaces, or villas in Rome.[9] Such buildings could then be freely testated to his heirs. It was a rule directed to encourage papal courtiers to invest their profits in Rome, instead of exporting

[7] For family strategies see McClung Hallman, Italian Cardinals, ch. 5; P. Stella, 'Strategie familiari e celibato sacro in Italia tra '600 e '700', Salesianum (1979), 73–109; E. Brambilla, 'Per una storia materiale delle istituzioni ecclesiastiche', Società e Storia, n. 24 (1984), 395–450.

[8] Spoils and facilities to testate, see D. Williman, Records of the Papal Right of Spoil 1316–1412 (Paris, 1974); J. Favier, 'Temporels ecclésiastiques et taxation fiscale: Le Poids de la fiscalité pontificale au XIVᵉ siècle', Journal des Savants (1964), 102–27; Reinhard, Papstfinanz und Nepotismus unter Paul V., i. 26; J. Grisar, 'Päpstliche Finanzen, Nepotismus und Kirchenrecht unter Urban VIII.', Xenia piana dno nro Pio Papae XII dicata (Rome, 1943), 205–365, at 217–18, 314.

[9] Partner, 'Finanze e urbanistica a Roma (1420–1623)', Cheiron, 1 (1983), 59–67.

the capital to their place of origin. The history of Roman urban-
ism shows it to have been very effective.

That most curialists managed to escape the legal consequences
of the rule about spoils is shown by the comment aroused when
the papal government decided to apply it. On the death of
Leonardo Griffi, the former domestic secretary, within the
Vatican Palace in 1485, Innocent VIII broke the will and confiscated the estate of about 12,000 ducats, thus frustrating the
expectations of Griffi's brothers, of various churches, and of
charities in Rome and Milan. In 1502 Alexander VI is said to
have set aside the will of Cristoforo Bordini, Bishop of Cortona,
and to have instituted himself (not the apostolic chamber) as
heir. A similar measure was taken after the death of the Viter-
bese Cardinal Fazio Santori in 1510 by Julius II, and the pope
on this occasion remarked, as he confiscated the goods for the
benefit of the apostolic chamber, that the validity of the will
depended on him. Leo X carried out the same sort of confiscation against the goods of the former chamber clerk Giovanni
Gozzadini, in 1517. Hadrian VI carried out a wholesale and
very unpopular application of the spoils rule against dead
curialists in respect of their houses in Rome, and Clement VII
is recorded as having applied it to the detriment of Giulio
Tornabuoni.[10]

There was, thus, no guarantee against falling into disfavour
or dying at a time when the pope was especially hard up or
particularly grasping, and thus exposing a clerk's estate to
confiscation. But such occasions seem to have been the exceptions, as were refusals by the pope to allow a curial clerk the
papal licence to testate.

Investment of their gains in real property was one of the most
obvious courses open to successful curialists. From Sixtus IV's
time onwards there were important legal advantages in con-
structing new property in the Roman city. Even before Sixtus's
time, from Nicholas V's day onwards, rising courtiers like
Gerardo Maffei were investing in property in Rome. But the
old practice of building or buying in the city or region of origin
also remained, perhaps so as to bequeath or transfer the
property to collaterals, but also because showy buildings in
the native area emphasized the power and splendour of the
family. The building of Pienza by Pius II is proof enough of the
existence of this mentality.

[10] Ferrajoli, *Il ruolo della Corte di Leone X*, pp. 168–9; for another case
concerning Raffaele Petrucci, ibid. 123–4.

Instances where the financial gains were made by clerks beneath the rank of cardinal include the Rizzoni family of curialists who built in Quinzano near their native Verona, and the fine palace of Angelo Geraldini in the little Umbrian town of Amelia. Battista Bagarotti, who was richer and more powerful than these, made big real property investments in the areas around Piacenza and Milan, particularly after the sale of most of his curial offices when he transferred from Rome to Lombardy. Bagarotti successfully bequeathed his Milanese properties to his nephew. In Umbria the curial humanist Niccolò Perotti built himself a villa with the appropriate name of 'Curifugia' at Isola near Sassoferrato in the Duchy of Spoleto, though Perotti was always short of money, and the building was probably modest.

The builders and investors in Rome were very numerous; indeed, a large part of the rebuilding of Renaissance and Baroque Rome was due to the activities of clerical courtiers. A conspicuous example was the investment made in Roman real property by the scholarly Angelo Colocci. He took part in the great property boom in Rome under Leo X: buying or building in the area of S. Maria del Popolo (where the Via Leonina appeared), near Trajan's Column, in Campo Marzio, and in Parione. He also owned villas in the Rione Colonna, on the Quirinale (where he sited a Greek printing press), and near the Baths of Constantine (this was the humanist Pomponio Leto's old house). His main villa was in the Orti Coloziani, at the Acqua Vergine. The whole was a very large capital investment indeed and, in addition, Colocci owned Roman vineyards.

Comparable investors of the same period were the French chamber clerk Thomas le Roy (Regis), the builder of the Farnesina ai Baullari, which now stands in the Corso Vittorio Emmanuele, and the Medici client Baldassare Turini, the builder of the beautiful and important Villa Lante on the Janiculum. Le Roy successfully willed the palace to his heirs. Turini also owned a palace in the Rione S. Eustachio, which had formerly belonged to the Roman family of Leni, and a large house in the Rione Colonna near the Piazza S. Macuto. Villa Lante is known to have passed to his nephew, Giulio Turini. As a final example we may take Jacopo Cardelli of Imola (1473–1528), a member of an obscure notarial family which found favour with the Riario dynasty at the time of Girolamo Riario's rule in Imola in 1473–4. Cardelli came to Rome under Riario patronage as a youth, and became papal secretary in 1504. Although in clerk's orders, he had a mistress who bore him nine children, and whom he eventually married. Besides his house in Campo Marzio, he built the palace which is now known as Palazzo Firenze.

There were instances of property in Rome being left by curialists for charitable purposes. Cardinal Stefano Nardini left his palace (the well-known palace in Via del Governatore) to the hospital of S. Salvatore at the Lateran, on condition that the hospital paid an annual rent of 100 ducats to the college which Nardini founded at the same time. The Spanish chamber clerk Pedro Ferriz (1415–78) left the palace which he had bought from the heirs of Vianesio Albergati, the former papal treasurer, to the Augustinian convent of S. Maria del Popolo. This was the palace later bought by Alessandro Farnese to become the site for the present Palazzo Farnese.

VI

The nature of the approach of the Italian magnates to office in the Roman court varied widely from region to region. Papal state notables came from dioceses immediately subject to the Holy See, and were at home in the papal court as temporal subjects of the pope, sometimes even as his feudatories, or the close relations of feudatories. The Roman nobles had held office in the Roman court ever since it can be said to have existed, and they had supplied clerks to staff the Roman bishopric long before that, in the earliest Middle Ages. The Roman merchant and landowning families, though they lacked the aristocratic distinction of the great baronial groups like the Colonna, Orsini, or Caetani, had a long tradition of clerical and temporal service to the Holy See. They relied on the memories of that service to comfort them in the idea that they were entitled to privileged treatment from the popes, as is clear from the resentment expressed by the Roman notable, Marcantonio Altieri, at the end of the fifteenth century, that the service rendered to the temporal power by his immediate ancestors had been ungratefully and unjustly forgotten by later popes.[11]

Outside Rome, in other parts of the papal state, other networks of connections linked scores of families to the Holy See or to families which had controlled or influenced it. The dynastic policies of the popes survived the holders of the papal office, and influenced papal politics for generations. Marriage

[11] *Li nuptiali di Marco Antonio Altieri*, ed. E. Narducci (Rome, 1873), 15.

alliances with a papal family could merely have the effect of strengthening a local magnate group, as the Monaldeschi of Orvieto were strengthened by their alliance with the Colonna in the 1420s. But they could also transform the entire politics of a region of the papal state, as the politics of the March of Ancona were transformed by the marriage alliance of the Montefeltro and Della Rovere.

All these factors influenced the great web of clientage in the Roman court. Belonging to one of the families of *signorotti* which had dominated in one area or another of the papal state could help a clerk towards a good career in the Roman court, even if his family had been ejected from power. This was the case of Francesco Alidosi, descended through his mother from the house of the tyrants of Forlì, who had a very successful career as the financial right hand of Julius II. Alidosi owed his intimacy with the Della Rovere family to having been brought up in the *familia* of Sixtus IV, which made him the friend and intimate of Cardinal Giuliano della Rovere.

The papal state notables had, of course, the best opportunities in Rome and they used them ruthlessly to further their interests in their native cities. To take two examples from the late fifteenth century, a chamber clerk from Viterbo called Andrea de' Spiriti and his contemporary, the Roman chamber clerk (subsequently papal treasurer) called Falco de' Sinibaldi, were both notorious masters of the arts of self-advancement at the Roman court. Both men came from local magnate groups, and their place-hunting was directed not only to their own advancement but to that of the entire clan.

Andrea de' Spiriti belonged to a prominent and disorderly family which followed the Gatteschi faction in Viterbo in the squabbles of the time. His Viterbo clique included his relative, the chamber clerk and later cardinal, Fazio Santori. Falco de' Sinibaldi was a gifted and witty humanist as well as an able (though venal) administrator and a great property speculator in Rome; he belonged to a well-connected Roman family. Andrea de' Spiriti, when arrested for corruption in 1503, threw the keys of his safes into a cesspool. Sinibaldi apparently misused his power as apostolic treasurer; he was charged with having executed a Roman merchant who had asked a servant of de' Sinibaldi who had stolen goods from him to restore their value. Both de' Spiriti and de' Sinibaldi established their respective clans so firmly in the Roman court that each, after the founder's death, was able to establish control of a papal state bishopric and to enjoy it for half a century.

Similar voracious devourers of papal state patronage were the Roman Campagna family of the powerful Cardinal Domenico Capranica (1400–58), whose original influence sprang from the client-relationship between his family and that of the Colonna. Domenico Capranica's power, and that of his elder brother Paolo, the Bishop of Embrun and Archbishop of Benevento (died 1429), a powerful figure in the household administration of Martin V, dated from the early fifteenth century. Later members of the family extended it so that by the end of the century the Capranica family controlled extensive church patronage, not only in Lazio from which they came, but in the March of Ancona. Such examples could be multiplied indefinitely: sixteenth-century ones are legion.

Not only did properly Roman families like the Leni, Cesarini, Foschi de Berta, and Rustici, establish their members in lucrative posts, but other families from various parts of Italy migrated to Rome, made good clerical careers there, and turned themselves into Roman families. Most of these immigrants were lawyers. A striking example is Paolo Planca of Giovinazzo, who was a chamber clerk under Boniface IX in the last decade of the fourteenth century, and is one of the few clerks from the Kingdom of Naples who managed to put down roots in Rome. That he achieved this is partly explained by the fact that, in spite of his clerical status and his many canonries, he had three sons, all of whom also had careers in the Roman court, and two of whom were also clerks. The protonotary Paolo Planca was one of the richest and most prominent figures of the court of Martin V; he was one of the executors of the will of Cardinal Brancaccio in 1427. His middle son, Giustino, was a consistorial advocate who married a lady of the Coronato-Mattei family, thus assuring the Planca a permanent and solid place in Roman society. Cornelio, another of Paolo's sons, the canon of St Peter's, was made a chamber clerk in 1439. His brother, the layman and consistorial advocate Giustino, seems to have succeeded Cornelio as chamber clerk in 1442, and Giustino's son Marcello (1428–85), canon of S. Maria Maggiore, was in turn conceded a clerkship of the chamber when his father died in 1448.

A similar family was the Valla family from the Piacenza area, which entered the Roman court in the early fifteenth century under the powerful patronage of Cardinal Branda da Castiglione. The humanist and philosopher Lorenzo Valla, as already explained, came from this family with deep roots in Rome and the Roman court. His brother-in-law was Ambrogio

Dardoni, a powerful curialist under Eugenius IV. Lorenzo had another curialist cousin, the Roman Giovanni Tartarini, who succeeded to Lorenzo's post of scriptor after the latter's death. Such spider's webs of Roman curial cousins were to be found in every corner of the Roman court.

At the end of the fifteenth century an Umbrian family, the Cesi of Narni, descended on the mother's side from the famous mercenary soldier Gattamelata of Narni, established themselves as a Roman family on a very grand scale. The founder of the family's power in the Roman court was the consistorial advocate Angelo (1450–1528), who in spite of his lay status and his twelve sons also held a papal secretary's post from 1503 to 1511. Angelo was the father of two future cardinals, Paolo (1481–1537, who became a papal secretary in 1502 at the age of 17) and Federico. At least another four members of the family were active in the Roman court in the early sixteenth century. Though their ducal title, when the popes granted it, was attached to the little Umbrian villages of Cesi and Acquasparta, the Cesi had by then become a Roman family. Theirs was the pattern for many other successful 'Roman' families who originated in various parts of the papal state in the early modern period.

In one respect the popes exercised some caution: although papal state curialists were often appointed to papal state bishoprics, it was unusual to appoint them to the bishopric of their own city. However, appointments of local nobles to be local bishops in the papal state were not unknown in the period: there were, for example, two Baglioni bishops of Perugia, three Eroli bishops of Spoleto, one of Todi, and one of Narni, a Malatesta at Cesena and one at Rimini, a Vitelli at Città di Castello, and a Monaldeschi at Orvieto (though the last was translated through a kaleidoscope of bishoprics).

Hardly any of these native bishops were curial officials: an exception was the saintly (or at all events well-behaved) chamber clerk Antonio Fatati, who was translated from the see of Teramo in the southern kingdom to his own city of Ancona. Another local curial bishop was Jacopo Passerella of Cesena, successively bishop of the neighbouring towns of Imola and Rimini. Passerella's local record was not good; on being appointed Governor of Cesena in 1488 he favoured one of the local factions to a degree which made the town ungovernable, and led to his being removed in disgrace. He had had more success with more distant papal appointments: his mission to England in 1485 for the dispensation for the royal marriage had caused Henry VII to appoint him an English royal councillor.

Papal state bishoprics were on the whole poor. They were the bread-and-butter appointments, together with some of the small South Italian sees, for the ambitious curialist who wanted the dignity of a bishop's office but was not powerful enough to aspire to one of the great sees. Papal state sees were accumulated in administration, and resigned to their clients and relatives, by the great corrupt cardinals of the Medici papacy in the first half of the sixteenth century. The sees played an important role in the pattern of curial politics, but the patterns of influence they represented were subtle and indirect. The Spiriti and Santori families of Viterbo were for some time the bishops not of Viterbo but of Cesena. Curialist families which originated in or had migrated to the city of Rome —Rusticci, Capranica, Cesarini, De Cupis, Cesi, Capodiferro, Foschi de Berta, Della Valle—were given bishoprics all over the papal state.

A striking instance of the power of local nobles to exercise a veto over the appointments of papal state bishops occurred in the case of the promotion of the chamber clerk Ventura Bufalini to the see of Città di Castello in 1498. The Bufalini (Manni) family of Città di Castello had been solidly established in the Roman court by the father of Ventura, Niccolò Bufalini. In their native city they were notables, but very far from being the political equals of the powerful Vitelli family which had controlled it since the middle of the century. It was soon after Giannozzo Vitelli had defeated papal troops, and the Vitelli party in Città di Castello refused Ventura Bufalini access to his bishopric. The time for Cesare Borgia's liquidation of the Vitelli was still far off; in 1498 Alexander VI accepted the rebuff, and translated Ventura to the other papal state see of Terni, making Giuliano Vitelli Bishop of Città di Castello in his stead (though Giuliano was deprived in 1503 after the murder of Vitellozzo and the fall of his family).

VII

That some two-thirds of the bishops promoted to sees in the Florentine Tuscan *dominio* were curialists is not surprising, and does not denote weakness in the Florentine position *vis-à-vis* Rome. Because of the economic hegemony of the Tuscans in Rome, and the great influence exerted in Rome by Florentine diplomacy, the relationship between the Roman and Florentine upper clergy came close to being symbiotic, a situation which is undeniable under the Medici popes, but which had been present during the whole preceding century. The advantages in the Roman court did not all go to native Florentines: nobles and notables of the Florentine *dominio* were able to get hold of important patronage. Of the sixty-one chamber clerks and secretaries of the period who originated in Tuscany, only twenty-five were Florentines. Some of this had its roots further back in the history of the Roman court: for example, the family of Dellante of Pisa was represented in Rome in the first half of the fifteenth century by two important curialists, Bartolomeo and Agostino, who had been firmly established there since the time of John XXIII. Another Pisan, Guinforte Buonconti (died 1462), succeeded another Tuscan of the *dominio*, Niccolò Forteguerri of Pistoia, as papal treasurer, when the latter was made cardinal in 1460. Buonconti was an influential man who would probably have achieved further honours had he lived longer.

It is notable that many of the most important brokers in church offices and benefices in the Roman court came not from Florence but from the *dominio*. Examples are Gherardo Maffei of Volterra, Antonio Cortesi and his son Alessandro of San Gimignano, Cardinal Jacopo Ammanati, who could be considered as having come either from Lucca or from Florentine Pescia, Ammanati's secretary Jacopo Gherardi of Volterra, Bartolomeo Turini the datarius under Leo X, also of Pescia, and Jacopo Vagnucci of Cortona. All these were indefatigable managers and chasers of benefices, in ceaseless correspondence with the Medici and the other Florentine bosses.

One of the most striking groups in the Roman court from the *dominio* was that of the lawyer families of Arezzo. They were to be found early in the fifteenth century, for example, in the person of the poet and chamber clerk Rosello Roselli. Pietro Accolti, the later cardinal and founder of the curial dynasty, was an Aretino lawyer whose career began as a teacher in the law school at Pisa. His nephew Benedetto was a worthy follower. Two successful lawyers from Montepulciano in the *dominio* were Bartolomeo Aragazzi, the secretary of Martin V, and the civilized chamber clerk Fabiano Benci. Another noble from this area was the papal secretary Domenico Galletti of Monte San Savino (died 1501), who started curial life as a familiar of Leonardo Dati, and went on to a lucrative career: his son married a lady of the Del Monte family, sister of the future Pope Julius III.

Outside the Florentine *dominio*, the ruling Tuscan nobles were usually able to get respectful treatment from the popes for their members who had curial posts. The Sienese chamber clerk Memmo Agazzaria, the relative of a well-known Augustinian of S. Salvatore in Lecceto, ended his curial course by appointment in 1445 as Bishop of Grosseto; after his death in 1452 the papal court obligingly appointed Giovanni Agazzaria to succeed him. That the Sienese curialists who were on good terms with the Piccolomini got favoured treatment after 1458 needs no emphasis. Two noble brothers from the southern Sienese *contado*, Sinolfo and Bonifacio da Castel Lotario, had lucrative careers in the chamber (one as commissioner of papal armies) in the last two decades of the fifteenth century: one succeeded the other as Bishop of Chiusi.

Two Lucchesi were successful chamber clerks: one was Niccolò Ghinizzano of Ghinizzano, who ended his life in 1470 as papal governor of Cesena. The other was the more aristocratic, learned, and in every way more important, Niccolò Sandonnino (1435–99), who became a papal secretary as well as a chamber clerk, and was one of the most influential servants of Pius II and Paul II, and the agent of several important diplomatic missions for the popes. Sandonnino had been Archpriest of Ferrara, and Paul II made him Bishop of Modena, a see which the hostility of Borso d'Este prevented him from occupying. He was eventually translated by Sixtus IV to be Archbishop of Lucca to succeed the deceased Cardinal Ammanati. Sandonnino was the close relative and patron of a junior pair of successful curialists from Lucca, Giovanni Gigli (the later Bishop of Worcester) and Silvestro Gigli.

VIII

The Venetian republic had the tightest hold over the church in its dominions of any Italian government, and its curialists were the most strictly controlled. Families which supplied clerical curialists to Rome were classified in Venice as *papalisti*, and were automatically excluded from voting in the council on clerical matters.[12] Venetian legislation controlling appointment to clerical benefices extended to all the subject towns, and the limited autonomy of towns in the Florentine *dominio* had no place in the Venetian scheme of things. The same rules about

12 *I diarii di Marino Sanudo* (Venice, 1879–1903), vii. 734–5. Cited by F. Gilbert, *The Pope, His Banker, and Venice* (Cambridge and London, 1980), 129.

approving all concessions of major benefices in the council of church *probae* were extended to the recently acquired Cyprus in 1490. The effect was to place the Venetian nobles in a position of clear superiority over the nobles of the subject towns in the contest for clerical patronage.

This did not mean that nobles of the Venetian subject cities had no share in the curial cake. Such men acquired the patronage of Venetian cardinals and popes, and some rose to eminence in the Roman court. The favour of Eugenius IV launched Franceso dal Legname of Padua on an impressive, if rather uncertain, course in the curia; he became papal treasurer and Bishop of Ferrara, but both dignities in the end slipped from him, and he ended in the more modest Venetian see of Feltre. Daniele da Sansebastiano of Verona (died 1503) made a good middle-rank career as scriptor and secretary: he was helped by his being the nephew of one of the Maffei family, Alessandro. The most successful and powerful of all the Venetian curialists who were not members of the Venetian patriciate was one who was neither chamber clerk nor secretary, but who gained the confidence of Eugenius IV and climbed from obscurity straight to the top of the tree, Cardinal Ludovico of Treviso ('Scarampo').

Able lawyers from the Veneto with strong social positions in their towns of origin, like Sulimano de' Sulimani and Antonio Capodilista of Padua, were able to secure canonries in the cathedral of their native city, and decent careers in the Roman court, without depending overmuch on the Venetian regime. A few nobles from Venetian overseas possessions got favour in Rome: Ludovico Podocataro of Cyprus, however, had left Cyprus and risen to influence in Rome before the island fell under Venetian control. One of the most successful nobles from the Venetian *dominio* in the Roman court was Gerolamo da Schio (died 1533), from Vicenza, who amassed a considerable fortune, some of which he spent on buildings in his native city. Da Schio made his own way in the Roman court in the household of Cardinal Giulio de' Medici, and then as the major-domo of Clement VII. It is significant that he did not get a Venetian bishopric but was made Bishop of Vaison.

There was the exception of Ludovico da Treviso, but virtually all Venetian curialists to get the highest and richest promotions came from the main Venetian families, such as Condulmer, Barbo, Soranzo, Grimani, or Priuli. These men virtually shared out, by the vote of the appropriate Venetian council, all the most valuable benefices under the control of the republic, whether in the terrafirma or in the overseas empire. A middle-ranking noble like Pietro Bembo was unable to exert the sort of political pressure in Venice which could obtain him church promotion at this exalted level. A number of Venetians from minor families, not members of the council, pursued relatively undistinguished careers in the Roman court.

IX

The number of Lombards who made successful careers in the Roman court was modest, when the size and strength of the Lombard church is considered. This was connected with the chronological distribution of Lombard cardinals, who pressed the claims of Lombard clerks in their households. Cardinal Branda da Castiglione (died 1440) introduced many Lombards into the curia, and Ardicino della Porta (died 1434) no doubt introduced others. The troubled relations of the Holy See with the successive rulers of Milan meant that no Lombard cardinals were appointed in mid-century. Only with Giovanni Arcimboldo's appointment by Sixtus IV in 1473 did the line of Lombard cardinals revive, and in the 1480s, with the appearance of Cardinals Ascanio Sforza and Federico di Sanseverino, direct Milanese patronage in the Roman court once more became formidable. But this patronage was not necessarily devoted to Milanese subjects. Cardinal Ascanio Sforza was a potentate of European status, and his household was not merely a Lombard one. It is noticeable that two clerks from the Regno, Francesco Rizardi of Aversa and Marino Caracciolo, owed their curial careers to service in Sforza's household, as did Bartolomeo Saliceto of Bologna, later the joint secretary of the Lateran Council.

The low share of South Italian clergy in curial appointments is noticeable from the thirteenth century onwards. Only so long as the generation of clergy endured which had been appointed by the popes of the Schism period, was there a notable number of Neapolitans in influential curial posts. While the Angevin party had some strength in the Roman court, which it continued to have until 1443, there was fierce opposition to such appointments, and not too much effective pressure from the Aragonese side to have them made. With Calixtus III things changed radically, but preference was accorded to Iberian clergy rather than to clerks originating in the southern kingdom. The only Neapolitan cardinal appointed by Calixtus was short-lived; the first Neapolitan cardinal after the generation of the

Schism to be a real power in the Roman court was Olivero Carafa, who was influential from his promotion in 1467 until his death in 1511. Like Ascanio Sforza, Carafa was a patron to clerks of all sorts, and not only to those of his home region. Not until Alexander VI was an appreciable number of natives of the southern kingdom promoted to the Sacred College.

The smaller South Italian bishoprics were, like the papal state bishoprics, the small change of curial patronage. Numbers of curial officers who had no connection with the southern kingdom were given bishoprics in the Abruzzo and Campania, sometimes even in Puglia and further south. Such bishops seldom or never visited their sees. The practice extended even to major sees: of the Archbishops of Benevento (which was a temporal possession of the popes) between the Schism and the end of the sixteenth century only two were not curialists. There were also curialists like the Geraldini family of Amelia with some political claim on the Aragonese dynasty, who were awarded southern bishoprics; Angelo Geraldini became Bishop of Sessa, and Giovanni and Angelo Geraldini were both bishops of Catanzaro.

In the early sixteenth century the native nobles of Southern Italy perhaps obtained a slightly larger number of Roman court posts than in the past. Malizia Gesualdi (Bishop of Rapolla) had had a nodding acquaintance with the Roman court under Innocent VIII, having been for a few months one of the first venal secretaries after 1487. Camillo Gesualdi, Bishop of Conza, from the same powerful family, was an active curial prelate under Leo X. Gabriele Tolosa, of the family of Neapolitan nobles and bankers, was a papal secretary under Julius II. But the indications of any real participation by southern clergy in Roman curial life at this period are slight.

X

A few Genoese clergy are to be found in the Roman court in the first half of the fifteenth century, but they arrived in numbers, as did the Genoese bankers, with Sixtus IV in 1471. From this time onwards the great Genoese *alberghi* were strongly represented in Rome. Only one member of the Spinola family was a papal secretary before 1471; between that time and 1527 there were four. A few clerks from Liguria were active in the Roman court in mid-century. One was the hard-working Jacopo Feo of Savona, a client of Nicholas V's half-brother,

Filippo Calandrini, for whom he was vicar-general in the diocese of Bologna. Feo was a chamber clerk and also the governor of various papal state towns and provinces, of which the most important was Perugia, and Bishop of Ventimiglia. A relative of his worked as Governor of Imola for Girolamo Riario in 1487–9. But the Feo were a comparatively modest family.

From Sixtus IV's time the pretensions of the Genoese nobles in Rome were no longer modest. The connections of the popes themselves, such as Innocent VIII's close relation, Lorenzo de' Mari Cibo, obtained instant promotion: Lorenzo was an investor in the first venal secretary offices in 1487, and a cardinal in 1489. The Cibo were powerful for many years: Giuliano, for example, was a domestic prelate of Julius II, and a substantial figure in Rome until his death in 1536. The chamber clerk, Ottaviano Fornari, was a canon lawyer who was capable of working for his living, and was for a time, under Alexander VI, also the clerk of the chamber of college of cardinals. Ottaviano Fornari followed his brother as Bishop of Mariana in Corsica. Four other brothers, of whom at least one is likely to have been resident in Rome, placed his funeral monument.

But other Genoese clerks were perhaps less deserving. Giovanni Battista Usumari (1480–1512), of the banking family, followed Ottaviano Fornari as Bishop of Mariana in 1500. Usumari had been an apostolic protonotary since his appointment in 1490, at the age of 10. He was 15 years old when appointed apostolic secretary. Giovanni Battista Pallavicini, later cardinal (1480–1524), Bishop of Cavaillon, was another typical representative of this gilded generation.

One of the most active of the Genoese prelates was the close associate of Julius II, Lorenzo Fieschi (1465–1519). Fieschi came from a family whose days of Roman grandeur dated from the thirteenth century, and his own relative, Niccolò, was a prominent cardinal. But Lorenzo Fieschi was one of the workhorses of Julius II: he was, for example, appointed as vice-legate to clear up the mess in Bologna, after the failure and disgrace there of the papal legate Antonio Ferreri, in 1507. Fieschi made his career in the temporal power; he was subsequently Legate of Perugia and Governor of Rome. He was also Bishop, in succession, of Brugnato, Ascoli, and Mondovi, all places which he can have rarely seen. Antonio Ferreri of Savona, the former major-domo of Julius II, whom Fieschi replaced in Bologna, was another Ligurian to achieve greatness (and in his case, the cardinalate) in Rome, although he died in 1508 in disgrace.

XI

The participation of the Italian possessing classes in the distribution and exchange of benefices and offices which took place in the Roman court was a complex phenomenon. Individual, family, factional, and governmental interests were involved. The government interests involved were not always Italian, although the clerks who represented them were. Movements of capital, both into and out of Rome, took place on a very large scale. The common supposition that the Roman court was a sort of basin of gold into which huge quantities of money flowed, to be retained indefinitely in Rome, was wrong. Very large sums of money did indeed flow into the Roman court from 'spiritual' sources; this transfer represented, in the last analysis, the value paid to satisfy the supply of a Europe-wide demand for spiritual services. Other considerable sums were paid by supplicants to the Roman court for services which it supplied to them directly. Large sums were spent on conspicuous consumption in Rome, and other large sums invested in Roman real property, by clergy and bankers who profited or hoped to profit from the Roman markets in money, benefices, and offices. But there were also important flows of money out of Rome, either to pay to satisfy the huge demand for imported goods and skilled labour which the weak local economy had no capacity to supply, or in the form of profits which successful clerical or banking entrepreneurs sent back to their places of origin.

Participation in the struggle and bargaining for place and office in the Roman court was not free. Life in the Roman court—as in any other court—could be a costly gamble, and the examples of Italian clerks withdrawing from Rome to their native regions show that there were losers as well as winners. It could be necessary to invest considerable sums in offices or benefices in Rome before a career there could be begun. The career of an exceptionally successful curialist who ended as papal datarius and cardinal, Giovanni Battista Ferrari of Modena, was given a decisive push by his lay brother lending him 1,200 gold ducats in 1479, 'so that he could buy offices in the Roman court, and subsist and live there honourably'. It is impossible to know how much capital was brought into Rome by speculators like Ferrari and Angelo Colocci, in order to finance the launch of their clerical careers. But it is likely that these sums from outside Rome were restricted to the early transactions of gaining access to the Roman clerical market, and that subsequent major loans in the curia were financed by the curial bankers.

Rome was a privileged market in which an enterprising clerk could trade in offices and benefices for himself and others. The activities of some clerks were directed to getting office and benefices for themselves and their families; others worked largely as brokers. The effect, especially in the latter part of the period when very many benefices were put out to farm, was to create an Italian market in church rents—not in the restricted sense of *censi* but in the general one of church property assessed or rented at an annual value. Such a market was very much to the advantage of those families—Tuscan, Ligurian, Lombard, Venetian—which had a banking arm, especially when the bank was represented in Rome. It is possible that the weakness of Neapolitan banking was one factor in the low representation of South Italian families in the Roman court.

That the eventual result of the Roman clerical market was to transfer clerical property to lay hands is by no means certain.[13] The curial banks certainly made large profits, and there were indeed numerous occasions on which transfers of money or real property were made either by donation or will by clergy to lay relatives. Huge *fideicommissi* began to be set up in the sixteenth century. And there were other procedures of the same nature. It is hard to know, for example, how often the financing of dowries was assisted in this way. The resignation or legacy of church property from clerical uncle to clerical nephew was also very frequent. Roman prelates benefited their families, but also very frequently used their funds to endow religious houses of various kinds. They also rationalized and improved the management of church property.

That many families were enriched by their clerical relatives is beyond dispute. Some families, especially in the papal state, owed their very existence as magnate groups to clerical money. But it has not yet been proved that the process led to a wholesale transfer of church property to lay ownership. The continuing worries of the Venetian and other governments about a serious mortmain problem point in a different direction. In the papal state it is unlikely that the balance between clerical and

[13] See R. Bizzocchi, *Chiesa e potere*; G. Chittolini, 'Un problema aperto: La crisi della proprietà ecclesiastica fra Quattrocento e Cinquecento', *RSI* 85 (1973), 353–93; E. Stumpo, 'Problemi di ricerca: Per la storia della crisi della proprietà ecclesiastica fra Quattrocento e Cinquecento', *Critica Storica*, 13 (1976), 62–80.

lay property was seriously shifted during the late Renaissance period. In other parts of Italy the question whether church property was alienated to lay hands, on a vast scale in the same period, is likely to remain contentious.

7

The Struggle For Place in the Roman Court

I

The long conflict over the control of the papacy ended in 1417 with the victory of the Italians. For centuries the different ruling groups of the former Frankish Empire had sought to dominate its most revered bishopric. Saxons, Lorrainers, Salians, Burgundians, the South German Hohenstaufen, the French, and, at the time of the Great Schism, the Iberians, had tried at various times to influence or direct the Roman clergy. At some points after 1266 the French royal house seemed to have won, especially during the papal sojourn at Avignon from 1307 until 1376. The Great Schism of the West, which began in 1378, saw French ascendancy over the papacy challenged and defeated. The French monarchy became divided and weak, and at the church council which began in Constance in 1414 its policies were obstructed by the Luxemburgers, by the English Lancastrians, by the upstart Burgundians, and by the obstinate Iberians.

Pope Martin V (Oddo Colonna), a member of the most ancient of the Roman magnate families, was elected at Constance in 1417 as a result of the diplomatic manœuvres of the nations hostile to the French royal house. He represented the wealthy Romans who had influenced the choice of the Roman bishop since the early Middle Ages. But although the Roman notables had always tried to use their voice in the election of their bishop to serve their own interests, after 1417 there was no question of a return to the early medieval situation of a papacy controlled by the Roman nobility. Among the Roman clergy, which had for long in effect meant the college of cardinals, power was widely distributed both among the ultramontane nations and among the Italian regions. All future questions of patronage in Rome were to depend on a new balance of power, which was linked with an emerging European state system and with a changing system of relations between the various Italian civic republics and principates. The first two pontificates of the restored Roman regime, those of Martin V (1417–31) and

Eugenius IV (1431–47), together set up the pattern of patronage and influence peculiar to the early modern papal court. Subsequent pontificates, from that of Nicholas V (1447–55) to that of Paul II (1464–71), modified the pattern of group interests slightly, without making any basic change. At the half-way point of our period, Sixtus IV (1471–84) and Innocent VIII (1484–92) introduced a new system of borrowing money through the creation of new colleges of papal officers, which radically and, as Thomas Frenz has remarked, irreversibly altered the way in which the Roman patronage system worked.[1]

The 'Roman' papal obedience of John XXIII, from which Martin V (as Cardinal Oddo Colonna) came, had been run by a clique of Neapolitan clergy and Tuscan bankers. Some powerful Neapolitan clerks who had enjoyed John XXIII's favour, such as Cardinal Filippo Brancaccio and the Romanized Paolo Planca of Giovinazzo, remained important under Martin; and another Neapolitan chamber clerk, Paolo Capograssi of Sulmona, was also close to the new pope.[2] But a group of Colonna princes and cousins, and trusted Colonna servants, formed the core of the new regime. The Colonna grandees and their henchmen dominated the patronage of the new papal court. Several clerks who had originated in Colonna-owned villages were used to control the pope's finances; of these the most important were the papal treasurer, Oddo Poccia de Varris or de Barris, and Paolo Capranica the Archbishop of Benevento.[3] Paolo's brother, Domenico Capranica, chamber clerk and papal secretary, was destined for a long and important career which extended far beyond Martin's pontificate. A minor Colonna (Gaspare) was given, along with other church patronage, a sinecure appointment as chamber clerk.

Martin V's court was neither an exclusively Roman nor an exclusively Italian affair. There were powerful figures in it from north Italy as well as from south: for example, Cardinal Branda da Castiglione of Piacenza, and Cardinal Ardicino della Porta of Novara. In the second rank there were a few influential Germans, such as Herman Dwerg. French power was far from dead in the papal court. Martin's creation, Cardinal Louis Aleman, vice-chamberlain, and then legate in Bologna after the failure of the Venetian Condulmer, was no cypher. In theory

---

[1] Frenz, *Kanzlei*, pp. 39–40.

[2] See Esch, 'Das Papsttum', in *Heimpel Festschrift* (1972); Lightbown, *Donatello and Michelozzo* (1980).

[3] For Oddo de Varri, see above, p. 157. For Paolo Capranica, Partner, *Papal State*, pp. 88 n., 138; and see also Reg. Vat. 352, fos. 143b, 156b.

one or two big French officers of state remained, although the nominal apostolic chamberlain, François de Conzié, remained outside Italy in the Comtat Venaissin for most of the pontificate. At lower levels, Martin sought to accommodate the existing office-holders from the obedience of John XXIII, while making some concession to those who had come over from Gregory XII and (to a lesser extent) from Benedict XIII. Martin also exercised his own powers of appointment for patronage and profit: the result of having to find office for four different streams of claimants was to push up curial numbers substantially.[4]

II

The first test of the Italianized curial system came with the death of Martin V in 1431, and the accession of the Venetian Cardinal Condulmer, on whom Martin had never looked with favour, as Eugenius IV. The purge of the curial power structure was sharp, swift, and instructive. Eugenius IV feared a Colonna revolt from the moment of his accession. Within weeks he had the vice-treasurer, Oddo Poccia de Varris, arrested on suspicion of corruption, and shortly after this the expected Colonna rebellion occurred. Some other trusted Colonna servants who had become curial officers were dismissed and disgraced. The long and enfeebling civil disorders of Eugenius's pontificate stem from this point.

Eugenius IV brought in a new Venetian clientele from the city and the subject cities of the Veneto region, permanently modifying the patronage map of Rome. Round the pope gathered the usual small knot of trusted countrymen and other confidential agents who were to manage the secret monies and the inner policies. Among these were two from the Venetian dominions: the future chamber clerk Francesco dal Legname of Padua and the agile, able Ludovico da Treviso ('Scarampo'), who was made Archbishop of Florence in 1437, Patriarch of Aquileja in 1439, and cardinal in 1440. The papal nephew, Daniele Scoti, was made papal treasurer. But just as Martin's entourage had been far from exclusively Roman, so Eugenius's was far from being entirely Venetian. One of the key new men under Eugenius was Cardinal Giovanni Vitelleschi, who came from the papal state. Eugenius's familiars included a relative of Lorenzo de Valla, Ambrose de Dardanonibus, the Florentine papal secretary Andrea Fiocchi, the Spanish jurist (later,

4 Frenz, 'Problem'.

under Calixtus III, cardinal) Juan de Mella, and one or two Germans. Among his backstairs financial agents was the monk, Arsène of Liège.[5]

In so far as they influenced the stable patronage system, the key promotions to the cardinalate made by Eugenius IV were those of his two nephews, Francesco Condulmer (1431) and Pietro Barbo (1440), and that of Ludovico da Treviso. Francesco Condulmer became apostolic chamberlain in 1432, vice-chancellor in 1437. He was succeeded as chamberlain in 1440 by Ludovico da Treviso, who retained the office for a generation, to be succeeded in it in 1465 by the Venetian, Marco Barbo. The longevity of the cardinals at the head of affairs in the Roman court in this period is notable. Having directed the financial administration from 1431, Francesco Condulmer was vice-chancellor from 1437 until 1457. On his death Rodrigo Borgia succeeded him, and remained in office until his own election as pope in 1492. Thus men emanating from the Venetian group controlled the chamber from 1432 until 1471, and the chancery from 1437 to 1457. There was Spanish control of the chancery from 1457 until 1492.

On the other hand, the disgrace of the Colonna under Eugenius did not mean the disgrace of all former Colonna favourites and agents. The Roman, Angelotto Foschi de Berta, had been a papal secretary, a councillor of the chamber, and an important agent of the secret financial machine under Martin, but this did not stop his prospering under Eugenius; he was, on the contrary, elevated to cardinal by the new pope within a few months. At a much lower level, an administrative dogsbody like Bartolomeo Bertini da Vinci of Pistoia, who had served Martin V in various financial and administrative capacities, was adopted by his successor for the key post of registrar of apostolic letters, and made Bishop of Valva-Sulmona. There was no immediate influx of Venetians into the staff of the chamber or among the secretaries after the accession of Eugenius; in fact, for a long time the only secretary who came from the Venetian dominions was Antonio Loschi, who had entered the Roman court in 1409, and been Martin V's secretary throughout the pontificate.

---

[5] For the familiars of Eugenius IV, see Cod. Vat. lat. 4988, fo. 45; Von Ottenthal, Die päpstliche Kanzleiregeln, pp. xxxvii–xxxviii, 455, 476; G. Mercati, Ultimi contributi, p. 101. Schuchard (Die Deutschen) misses the significance of Henricus Erkel de Cassel as a papal familiar (p. 49 n.), and does not mention another papal familiar of Eugenius IV with an apparently German name, 'magister H. Gidastaff'.

The first Venetian to enter the chamber as a clerk under
Eugenius (Pietro Conti) did so in 1439, and there is doubt
whether he ever quit his supernumerary status; the second,
Giacomo Turlono, who later became Bishop of Trau, joined the
chamber at about the same time, and was a regular working
official (*mensarius*) from 1442 until his promotion to a bishopric
in 1452.

Nor, as has been already mentioned, were the households of
great cardinals necessarily dominated by the region from
which the cardinal came. The household of Cardinal Gabriel
Condulmer, for example, had harboured the humanist, Rinuccio
d'Arezzo; that of Cardinal Francesco Condulmer contained
Tommaso Parentucelli, Lapo da Castiglionchio, Leonardo Dati,
and Jacopo Vagnucci. None of these dependants were Venetians.
The household of Cardinal Francesco Condulmer also contained, over a twenty-two-year period, no less than fifty-six
German familiars.[6]

The position of cardinals was strong, even if they were the
creations of a pope to whose faction the following pope was
hostile, as occurred with Martin V and Eugenius. But if a doubt
existed about the legal status of such a cardinal, the new pope
would exploit it. Domenico Capranica had been named cardinal
by Martin only *in petto*, and the nomination had not been
published, nor had he been received and 'opened his mouth' in
consistory. Eugenius refused for a long time to recognize him as
a cardinal, and only after the implied threat that Capranica
might appeal to the authority of the Council of Basle (which he
attended) did the pope give in.

In one respect Eugenius much reinforced an existing tendency in the Roman court. Florentine merchants had been
among the main backers of Pope John XXIII, and the Florentine
merchant community had become the most important immigrant
community of Rome. Martin V had retained the Tuscan bankers,
on whom he relied almost as much as his predecessor. But
Martin's political relations with Florence were fluctuating and
distrustful. Under Martin the future Eugenius IV, as Cardinal
Gabriel Condulmer, had had the reputation of being favourable
to Florence to a degree not at all approved by the pope. When
Eugenius ran almost immediately into grave political difficulties
after his election in 1431, he played the Florentine card for all
it was worth. The flight of Eugenius IV to Florence in 1434, and
the support given by the pope at the same time to the political

6 Schuchard, *Die Deutschen an der päpstlichen Kurie*, p. 55.

coup of Cosimo de' Medici, had important effects on the political, financial, and cultural policies of the papacy. Until Eugenius's return to Rome in 1443, and the peace which he shortly afterwards concluded with Alfonso of Aragon, papal policy was heavily influenced by Florence—one or two papal towns like Borgo San Sepolcro were literally in pawn to the Florentines. With the definitive return to Rome, the popes recovered the freedom of action which for almost a decade Eugenius had partially lost. Tuscan influence and patronage in the Roman court, however, remained almost as important as before.

The patronage of cardinals, particularly of cardinals who enjoyed the highest office or had papal favour, was all important to supplicants. Special influence was exercised over apostolic chamber patronage by Cardinal Ludovico da Treviso; for example, the Paduan jurist Antonio Capodilista swore for the office of chamber clerk in the chamberlain's personal residence and not in the chamber itself, and the witnesses were three familiars of the cardinal. Capodilista was himself the cardinal's legal auditor, and a member of his household. Similarly, the Piedmontese noble, Giovanni Giliaco, swore as chamber clerk in the cardinal's titular church of S. Lorenzo in Damaso. But the chamberlain's control over appointments was far from absolute, as his failure to stop the pope appointing Juan Margarit as chamber clerk showed.

The vital importance to an ambitious clerk of finding a place in the household of a cardinal may be illustrated from the career of the Florentine humanist Leonardo Dati. After Dati had quarrelled with Cardinal Francesco Condulmer and left his household in 1442, he began a desperate search for another patron in the Sacred College. At this earlier stage of his career Dati was evidently more acceptable to the Medici than he later became, and recourse was had to Giovanni di Cosimo de' Medici, who told Martelli, the Medici factor in Rome, to assist Dati. After almost two years, a place was found for him in the household of the newly appointed Cardinal Alfonso Borgia, and it was from this somewhat unlikely springboard that Leonardo's curial career took off, after Borgia's election as pope in 1455.

At the end of Eugenius IV's pontificate the regional and national distribution of patronage in the Roman court still reflected the situation at the end of the Schism. The German element was substantial, although there was no resident fifteenth-century German cardinal in Rome before Nicholas of Cusa (1448–64), and none after him for the rest of the century.

Christiane Schuchard has shown that the Germans present in Rome in the papal court proper were numerous as a grand total, some 362 during the pontificate of Martin V, and some 304 during that of Eugenius IV.[7] If we exclude subordinate personnel, couriers, and personal staff of the household, and allow also for those abbreviators who were also scriptors, the number of 'new' German officers (i.e. appointed during those pontificates) would seem to total about 390 in the thirty-year period.

If we allow a standard turnover of 7.5 years for tenure of a curial office (which may be too long for Germans with stronger reasons for returning home), the number of German curialists present at any one point during the thirty-year period may have been rather less than a hundred, which amounts to rather less than 20 per cent of the total curial employees in the 'narrow' sense. This is a very high proportion, perhaps too high, but it corresponds very roughly with the number of appropriate 'old' offices which Schuchard reckoned to have been left with Germans manning them at the end of the Schism and the end of Martin's pontificate. It is impossible to compare it with other gross national totals, since the archival work for computing the total numbers of French and Spanish curialists in the Roman court has not been done.

The high proportion of Germans during the early fifteenth century does not apply to the chamber, nor to the secretaries. Three or four German chamber clerks were active under Martin V and Eugenius IV, out of a total of some forty-five persons. Two German secretaries were active in the same period, out of a total of twenty-nine or thirty.

The French presence at the Roman court cannot be calculated in the same way. The French cardinal D'Estouteville was a very important patron, especially because of his longevity as a cardinal. He was promoted in 1439, and lived in the Roman court almost continuously, apart from his legations, until his death in 1483. It is noticeable, however, that very little French influence can be traced at this period in the apostolic chamber, and none among the secretaries. A Burgundian, Nicholas De Lavelle of Térouanne, was made chamber clerk early in Martin's pontificate, and died under Calixtus. After his appointment the next French-speaking chamber clerk was another Burgundian, Robert Cambrin, who was appointed in 1449 and resigned in 1468.

---

[7] Schuchard, *Die Deutschen*, pp. 35–41.

Figures for other nations in the Roman court at this period are not available: it would be especially interesting to know the number of Spaniards. The number of Englishmen in Rome was certainly negligible. One well-known English clerk, Adam Moleyns, was made a chamber clerk under Eugenius, but it is doubtful whether he spent long in Rome.

III

Before Nicholas V became pope in 1447 he had been a poor cardinal of only a few months' standing, without powerful connections. As pope his power base continued, outside the bare powers of his office, to be frail. He had a special interest in the chamber, since his last curial appointment before becoming cardinal (16 December 1446) had been as papal vice-chamberlain, and as pope most of his appointments in the chamber were of clerks who enjoyed his personal favour. He placed two favoured courtiers in the chamber in spite of opposition: the Spanish lawyer Juan Margarit, and Jacopo Vagnucci of Cortona. Vagnucci had been in the *familia* of Cardinal Francesco Condulmer, perhaps at the same time as the future pope, Tommaso Parentucelli, and was the nephew of the Prior of the Florentine Certosa, who also enjoyed the confidence of the pope. Jacopo Vagnucci was made vice-chamberlain in 1449, and in 1452 became Nicholas V's papal treasurer. The pope allowed two former holders of the latter office (Dal Legname and Cavazza) to retain their claims, a negligence which stored up disputes for the future.

There was an almost complete turnround of the chamber clerks under Nicholas. The new clerks were all Italian, with the exception of Cambrin and Margarit. Their provenance was distributed according to a pattern which had already become typical of the Roman court. One was a Bolognese lawyer (Jacopo Mucciarelli): Nicholas V had before his pontificate been Bishop of Bologna, and had earlier been the protégé of the Bolognese cardinal, Niccolò Albergati. Another was a Paduan lawyer (Suliman de' Sulimannis). Another, who evidently enjoyed papal favour as his first bull of appointment gave him special participating rights, was Jacopo Feo of Savona, the region contiguous to Parentucelli's place of origin, Sarzana. The other three came from the papal state. One, the future Blessed Antonio Fatati of Ancona, had won Nicholas's favour and had been made vicar-general and canon of St Peter's.

Another was a notable of Forlì, Antonio Laziosi, whose patronage is unknown. The last also came from Forlì: this was Stefano Nardini, the future Archbishop of Milan and cardinal, who was to prove one of the most skilful political operators of the Roman court.

Nicholas V was the first pope to use a 'domestic' or secret secretary: this was Pietro da Noceto, who in the 1430s had been a secretary to Niccolò Albergati when Parentucelli had been the major-domo of the cardinal's household. Pietro da Noceto was one of the familiars most in the confidence of Nicholas V, and was perhaps one of the few secretaries in papal service as likely to have had a hand in formulating policy as in executing it. A bull addressed to him mentions both his work in writing papal letters and his being given special papal commissions.

The fall of Pietro da Noceto in 1455 at the end of Nicholas's pontificate was dramatic only at its earliest stage. As Nicholas lay dying, Pietro da Noceto threw himself into Castel Sant' Angelo, seeking protection from his enemies. He was imprisoned briefly by the new pope, Calixtus III, but subsequently freed. Although Pietro lost his office of papal secretary, Calixtus on the day of his coronation pardoned him and reinstated him in the lucrative office of *custos* of the papal chancery, saying that the supposition that the office of *custos cancellarie* was automatically vacated upon the death of the reigning pope was false.[8] Pietro da Noceto did not finally resign this office until 1458, three years after he had lost his domestic secretarial office. He then appears to have left the papal court to go to Milan. Closely related members of his family were in papal service until late in the century; one relative was Francesco da Noceto, a secretary and chamber clerk under Sixtus IV.

The financial official disgraced by Calixtus was one who owed his career to Eugenius IV and not to Nicholas V. Francesco

---

[8] See Von Hofmann, *Forschungen*, i. 150, where he says that the 'bitter pill' of having to leave the domestic secretaryship was sweetened by confirmation in another of his offices, in this case that of 'custos cancellarie' (see also Von Hofmann, *Forschungen*, ii. 79, 112, 123-4). If he was reinstated as secretary by Calixtus III and Paul II, as Von Hofmann says (ii. 112), this was an inactive post; there is no sign of his working as papal secretary in Rome after the death of Nicholas V. For the family, see J. Bicchierai, 'Antonio di Noceto', *ASI*, 5th ser., 4 (1891), 34-49, and *Le vite di Paolo II*, p. 211. Antonio da Noceto had a distinguished career in the curia, starting under Nicholas V and continuing under Calixtus and Paul II, and ending with retirement in 1472. Francesco, secretary and chamber clerk (d. 1484) was of the same family. They came from Val di Nure, in the Piacentino.

dal Legname, who had been a household financial official, and subsequently the treasurer of Eugenius IV, had been continued for a short time in the treasurer's office by Nicholas V. Calixtus charged Dal Legname with peculation, and ordered his arrest in his own bishopric of Ferrara; the arrest was executed by Borso d'Este, who demanded Dal Legname's deprivation of his bishopric.[9]

IV

The close advisers of Calixtus III were all Catalan: this had inevitable effects on curial appointments, although perhaps less drastic ones than contemporaries thought. Calixtus's Catalan appointments were important for their strategic location in the power structure rather than for their number. In the financial administration Calixtus had little option but to retain Ludovico da Treviso as chamberlain, since the appointment endured beyond a pope's death, and cancelling it might have meant a damaging conflict with the cardinals. The vice-chancellor's office had been occupied only by regents since the death of Francesco Condulmer in 1453: this enabled Calixtus in 1457 to name his nephew Cardinal Rodrigo Borgia to the post; this turned out to be one of the decisive papal administrative appointments of the century.[10]

Calixtus seems to have had three confidential personal secretaries, of whom one (Matteu Joan) was a former secretary of the Aragonese King of Naples, Alfonso. Beneath the level of chamberlain he made big changes in the financial administration. His main agent here was Bartolomé Regas, a priest from Gerona who had been formerly a member of Cardinal Alfonso Borgia's household. Regas became controller of the secret papal household account: he was given a number of other curial posts, including those of secretary and chamber clerk, and was also named Archbishop of Barcelona (though the promotion to bishop never took effect). Calixtus left the treasury in the hands of Nicholas V's last treasurer, Jacopo Vagnucci, for just over a year; he then replaced Vagnucci, first by Pedro d'Altello of Barcelona, who proved unsatisfactory and was removed, and eventually by Bartolomé Regas (September 1456). The Spanish clique was completed by the papal con-

---

9 Partner, 'Francesco dal Legname'.
10 For the sequence of appointments, see H. Bresslau, *Handbuch*, i. 265-6.

fessor and datarius, Cosmo of Monserrat, who had financial as well as spiritual responsibilities.

Thus, although the chamber remained under Cardinal Ludovico da Treviso, and under a new vice-chamberlain, Giorgio da Saluzzo (appointed in 1456), the main treasury and secretarial administration were placed in the hands of trusted Spanish clerks. Another such clerk, Pedro Climent, was granted the rank of chamber clerk and made depositary of the apostolic chamber; he was also given a number of posts concerned with the provisioning and security of Rome, such as control of the Dogane di Ripa and Ripetta and of the city grain supply, *soldano* of the prison, Governor of Frascati, and so on. Thus Calixtus placed in the hands of specially trusted Spanish familiars all the main financial, military, and civic logistic control points. It was a distrustful policy which occasioned much resentment.

Outside these areas of special control, the main patronage machine proceeded much as it had done before. Calixtus's numerous appointments to secretaryships were complained of, but no new secretaries (apart from the three domestic secretaries and Bartolomé Regas) were Spanish. Two Spanish chamber clerks have been mentioned; a third, Garcia Mota, was supranumerary. The other two chamber clerks appointed by Calixtus were Italian, Niccolò Sandonnino and Antonio Jacopo Venieri. Some Spaniards were appointed elsewhere in the chancery (for example, two masters of the registry of petitions), but the deluge of Catalans which was so murmured against does not show up clearly in the lists of senior officials.

V

Pius II resembled Nicholas V in that before his pontificate he had not worked for long years in the Roman court, either as a junior curial official or as a cardinal. His office of secretary, which he had held since 1446, had been a sinecure, and he had been a cardinal for only a year and a half before his election as pope in 1458.

The inner circle of Pope Pius II was composed, as was more or less the rule, of a nucleus of his own countrymen and family, with some other trusted helpers and advisers whom Pius had known as a cardinal or earlier. The two domestic secretaries, of whom the first was certainly a political adviser as well as a secretary, were Jacopo Ammanati of Lucca, who had served with Piccolomini in the household of Cardinal Capranica, and Gregorio Lollio, the pope's cousin and friend from earliest days. Ammanati, though by no means the first former secretary to become a cardinal, was the first papal secretary to be promoted bishop and cardinal while actually working for the pope in the office of secretary. Pius II said in his autobiographical *Commentaries* that he denied access to the pope to the other secretaries, receiving only these two.[11]

So far as the top curial offices were concerned, Pius II did not love Cardinal Ludovico da Treviso but he was obliged to leave him in office, as his predecessor had done; and the same considerations applied to Cardinal Rodrigo Borgia, the vice-chancellor. The treasury was secured for his own preferred nominee by Pius in 1459, when he compelled three claimants to the office (Francesco dal Legname, Jacopo Vagnucci, and Bartolomé Regas) to resign their claims, and appointed as vice-treasurer his own relative by marriage, Niccolò Fortiguerra of Pistoia. This did not mean that Pius obstructed the career administrators in the chamber; on the contrary, when he made Fortiguerra a cardinal in 1460 he gave the treasury first to the Pisan chamber clerk Gilforte Buonconti, and then, after Buonconti's death in 1462, to Antonio Laziosi of Forlì, the senior chamber clerk. The only appointments of new chamber clerks made by Pius were of his own relative, Tommaso Piccolomini, who had been managing his secret finances, and of another Pisan clerk (Niccolò da Ghinizzano) to succeed to the place of Buonconti.

Pius deliberately abandoned Calixtus's policy of distributing a large number of expectancies for the post of apostolic secretary, and confined himself to a handful of appointments, one of which was the transfer of Flavio Biondo's post to his son, Gaspare. The well-known dissatisfaction of career humanists with Pius is indirectly connected with this reluctance to hand out new secretarial offices to them; the only instance of his having done so seems to be the sinecure secretaryship given to Leodrisio Crivelli.

The pontificate of Pius II may be taken as the point at which the system of curial patronage reinstated by Martin V after 1417 had settled into a permanent, informal organism for the bargaining and distribution of power and privilege. The spine of the system was the relationship between the pope and the

[11] See Kraus, 'Die Sekretäre', especially pp. 27–9. For the inexact affirmation of Campano (*Le Vite de Pio II*, ed. G. C. Zimolo, p. 63) that Pius II reduced the number of secretaries to two, see Kraus, loc. cit.

college of cardinals, and this had not changed much during the post-Schism period. Attempts to convert the relationship into a more formal constitutional one, in which the oligarchic claims of the college were strengthened, had failed. The cardinals had during the conclaves produced various electoral capitulations which future popes had been obliged to sign. But all attempts to bind popes by this means failed. The promises made by popes in the electoral capitulations of 1471 and 1484 to share papal state patronage with the cardinals were not honoured. The patronage system would later be much modified by the advent of the colleges of venal offices, but these had just made their first timid appearance under Pius, and were then (in the instance of the college of abbreviators) to be cancelled by his successor.

The regional and national composition of the Roman court had been most influenced, after the final return to Rome in 1442, by the pontificate of Calixtus. The Spanish presence in Rome remained strong throughout the Renaissance period and into the Counter-Reformation. On the other hand, the words 'Iberian' and 'Spanish' cannot be taken as always indicating people who had had no roots in Italy before they came to Rome. Calixtus was himself a former senior chancery official of Alfonso of Aragon in Naples. One of Calixtus's confidential secretaries, Matteu Joan, was a former secretary of Alfonso. The Spanish element in the Roman court can in many instances be treated as a South Italian one.

VI

The court historian Gaspar of Verona drew a sharp distinction between the households of Pius II and Paul II.[12] He implied the moral superiority of the latter over the former: there is no means of knowing whether this was so. But the change of personnel is clear, and so is the break of policy. Few of the familiars of Pius II turned up in the household of his successor —an exception was Antonio, the brother of Pietro da Noceto, who came from a family with exceptional powers of survival, and another was the jurist bishop Agapito Cenci dei Rustici, a relative of the Roman secretary and humanist, Cencio Paolo dei Rustici. The Piccolomini in the Roman court were treated coldly but correctly. Pius II's former domestic secretary, Gregorio

---

[12] *Le vite di Paolo II*, p. 50.

Lolli, retired to Siena. Tommaso Piccolomini, made chamber clerk by Pius, was regent of the chamber from soon after Paul II's coronation until the following summer; and in the spring of 1463 he was working normally in the chamber as *mensarius*. Not until 1467 was he promoted out of the Roman court to be Bishop of Pienza. Important courtiers like Cardinal Ammanati were out of favour with the new pope, and complained bitterly about it. But those who had a legal entitlement to court office were either not disturbed or else were offered compensation, as happened in the case of the displaced abbreviators.

Paul II's domestic secretary was the veteran Florentine, Leonardo Dati, an accomplished humanist and an adroit politician, who had made a career in Rome in spite of a long period of Medici coldness towards him. Paul was, at the beginning of his pontificate, reluctant to receive the existing papal secretaries in audience, which may have proceeded from distrust of the servants of his predecessor's regime. But this reluctance to give access to secretaries other than the domestic secretary was the same as that earlier displayed by Pius II. It was a logical consequence of the introduction of the confidential domestic secretary. The only secretaries appointed by Paul II were the learned lay jurist, Guillelmo Paghelli of Vicenza (whose advancement was probably due to one of the Barbo family), and the Bolognese humanist, Lianoro de' Lianori: the latter was a member of Paul II's household.

There is very little to suggest that Paul II went out of his way to disrupt curial seniority and precedent, in spite of the lamentations of Platina and his fellows. The evidence is that he followed a conservative policy. Paul appointed his own relative, Lorenzo Zane, as papal treasurer in 1464; but Zane was an able man, and an archbishop of twelve years standing, when he was appointed. Of Paul's five appointments to the post of chamber clerk, one, already a papal secretary, the Roman Falco Sinibaldi, was a coming man in the court, well known for his humanist gifts and administrative ability. The other appointments as chamber clerk were in every way orthodox. Two were Tuscan and two Roman; of the latter, one was the son of the humanist Poggio Bracciolini. This is in line with Paul's other curial appointments.

That Venetian patronage grew hugely under Paul II, especially through his own nephews and family, there is no doubt. But he continued to use men who had served the popes under other pontificates. Examples are, among the cardinals, Lorenzo

Roverella and (his own appointment as cardinal) the ex-chamber clerk Stefano Nardini. As executants at a lower level he used whatever suitable instrument came to his hand: for example, the Bolognese Vianesio Albergati, vice-chamberlain and Governor of Rome, the agent for the suppression of the supposed conspiracy of the Academicians.

VII

The pontificates which followed that of Paul II, those of Sixtus IV (1471–84) and Innocent VIII (1484–92), marked a turning point in the history of patronage in the papal court. The sale of the office of papal scriptor had been going on since the beginning of the century, and had been bringing a thousand or so florins a year to the pope's confidential account. But the scriptors were a very restricted class of official; in fact, as they took no oath to the pope, were often laymen, and could be considered as monopoly contractors for the work, they were perhaps not papal officials at all. The extension by Pius II of venality to the abbreviators was a radically new departure. It was a practice very unwelcome to the vice-chancellor, who lost jurisdiction and patronage by it. As we know from the Platina incident, its abolition was fiercely resented by those who had bought offices: the setting up of a new venal college at once created a new class of privileged office-holders.

From the beginning, the pope's powers to create new office-holders had been feared and obstructed by the existing officials, and also by the heads of the papal departments, whose powers of patronage were threatened. Restrictions on the pope's powers, such as the bull issued by Eugenius IV restricting the number of chamber clerks, or the similar but weaker guarantees which were put out to place a limit on the number of secretaries, had never been fully effective, although the popes did not entirely disregard them.

The setting up of new colleges of venal offices by Sixtus IV, reversing the decision of Paul II to abolish the college of abbreviators, and massively extending the policy to many other offices, some of which were new, was the biggest single change ever made to the rights of office-holders in the Roman court. Its effects on papal internal policy were far-reaching, although they have not been much noticed by historians.[13] The earlier

---

[13] Paolo Prodi is well aware of the problem (see e.g. *Il sovrano pontefice*, pp. 103–7). But two recent, lengthy surveys of the Della Rovere pontificates fail

policy had been to restrict office-holding so as to maximize the value of the offices, and thus to make existing patronage more valuable. This policy was now reversed, with obvious short-term results for existing patronage-holders. But the papal government also lost a great deal of freedom to choose its own officers, except for the small group of confidential courtiers which immediately surrounded the pope. Outside this, and with the exception of another small group on whom the pope graciously conferred office without payment, the papacy's choice of servants became in effect restricted to men with the capital and the expertise to invest in papal offices.

The new policy was accompanied, inevitably, by decisions to increase the fees paid by some supplicants, and to raise the incomes of offices, so as to support the price at which they could be sold. Radical reform of the Roman court in the sense of reducing the total fees paid by supplicants, or of abolishing the sale of offices, became impossible, and remained so for the rest of the early modern period. The fees could be to some extent rationalised, but they could not be reduced, since a main part of their function was to support the payments on an ever-increasing burden of papal debt. The colleges of offices were, once the policy had been launched, multiplied in order to float what were in effect new loans.

The change of policy affected different offices in different ways. As has been explained above, the effects on the college of chamber clerks were very different from the effects on the new college of secretaries set up in 1487. Late fifteenth-century popes froze the number of chamber clerks at the level set by Eugenius IV in 1438 and 1444, and the supernumerary chamber clerk appointments so common in the mid fifteenth century were abandoned. The theoretical limit of six on the number of secretaries was, on the other hand, quintupled in 1487, and major changes were made to the duties and privileges of the new college. Thus the rights of chamber clerks were in some respects improved; those of the secretaries depreciated both from a financial point of view, and with regard to their political functions.

The clique surrounding the current pope stood to gain enormously from the creation of new classes of venal office,

even to mention the matter. See G. Pistarino, 'Elogio di Sisto IV', and R. Belvederi, 'Il papato dell'età dei Della Rovere', in 'V Convegno Storico Savonese, L'Età dei Della Rovere', pt. 1, Società Savonese di Storia Patria, *Atti e Memorie*, NS, 24 (1988), pp. 21–79 and 81–128 respectively. Pastor, to do him justice, noticed the importance of the venal offices (*History*, iv. 418–21).

and its greed was limitless. When Sixtus IV created a new college of seventy-two notaries of the Roman court in 1483, it was reported to the Este that the 20,000 ducats which came to the pope from the operation would immediately be paid over to Count Girolamo Riario.[14] But these were single windfall operations, which could not be repeated for any one class of office. Once a new class of office-holders had been created, a new market in the office came into existence. An office could be vacated by the death of the office-holder, by his promotion to a rank incompatible with the office concerned, or *per resignationem*, which meant by sale or gift to a third party. The number of offices vacated by death was much smaller than those vacated by gift or sale (for the chancery in the period 1471–1527 Frenz lists 224 vacancies *per obitum* and 358 *per resignationem*).[15] The pope, now represented in the matter by the new organization of the dataria, took a fee on the sale of an office; if the office-holder died without having transferred it to a third party under strict conditions laid down by papal rules, the office was resold by the dataria for the whole purchase price.

The introduction of the colleges of venal offices did not create a completely free market. Certain categories of office, later called the 'third category', had no duties or minimal ones, and these were freely transferable without papal consent; women or minors, for example, could be *porzionari di Ripa*. But other offices continued to require specific consent by the pope or datarius before they could be conferred. This was particularly the case for offices of so-called prelatial rank (*officia prelatitia*), and the procedure has been explained above for the cases of the chamber clerks and secretaries, who both fell into this prelatial class.

The colleges of venal offices were prejudicial to the patronage of great papal officers of state like the vice-chancellor and chamberlain.[16] They may have upset the patronage of the cardinals and the other curial bigwigs when they were first introduced; on the other hand, they opened up the market in

---

[14] Quoted by Partner, 'Papal Financial Policy', p. 29. For the greed of the men round the pope to sell further offices, see Verde, *Studio fiorentino*, ii. 442, where a letter of Lorenzo Pucci to Lorenzo de' Medici is quoted which refers to Count Ieronimo Riario's wish to make the pope promote Giovanni Priore, the then auditor of the apostolic chamber, to some dignity which would require him to vacate the office, which could then be sold (7 Apr. 1484). But the initiative must have failed, as Priore died in office a year later (Von Hofmann, *Forschungen*, ii. 91).

[15] *Kanzlei*, p. 195.

[16] See Von Hofmann, *Forschungen*, i. 22–3, ii. 43; Frenz, *Kanzlei*, pp. 202–3.

offices, and encouraged the investment of capital in the Roman court in a way that must, in the long run, have served the interests of all the great courtiers. There is no record of any curial disquiet at their introduction.

Large amounts of capital were attracted to the Roman court by the new venal colleges. If Frenz is correct in supposing that about two-thirds of those purchasing in the new colleges had not held office in the Roman court before,[17] then the total flow of capital into the Roman court from external sources must have been well over one and a half million florins on the occasion of the first investments, and more, when subsequent investments are taken into account—though Frenz may be right in saying that, once an investor had established himself in the Roman court, most of his subsequent investments in offices were financed from the original capital. However, we cannot assume that new investors were genuinely from outside the Roman court, even though they had held no previously recorded office within it. For example, the 'new' *sollicitatores* must have been previously resident in the Roman court, since their occupation made no sense if they had not already been intimately acquainted with its workings.

VIII

As has been repeatedly emphasized in this book, a social consequence of the new venal colleges was the increased importance of possessing a substantial sum of disposable capital, for anyone who wanted a career in the Roman court. Fifteenth-century governments had always tended to require their richer officials to lend them money; this requirement now became, in Rome, formal and almost insurmountable. It was, of course, always open to a ruler to make a gracious gift of office to someone he chose to honour, instead of requiring payment. This had always been a part of court practice, and it continued to be so. But the ordinary clerk who wished to make his way in Rome, and who was not a papal favourite, had no choice but to invest large sums in the purchase of office.

In the period 1471–1527 the average investment in offices of each of the 64 major abbreviators was 8,774 ducats; that of each of the 369 minor abbreviators was 4,649 ducats; that

17 *Kanzlei*, p. 247.

of each of the 158 secretaries was 8,056 ducats.[18] Although the three offices overlapped (for example, 26 per cent of major abbreviators and 13.8 per cent of minor abbreviators were also secretaries), there were clearly different investment patterns at work in each case. The main office represented only 30 per cent of the total investment in the case of the minor abbreviators, 38 per cent in the case of the secretaries, and 44 per cent in the case of the major abbreviators. The investments made in other offices by the chamber clerks cannot be so exactly calculated, but we know that most were pluralists in offices, so they must have been appreciably larger, since the value of their main office alone was in excess of 8,000 ducats, more than double the value of a major abbreviatorship.

It is true that the total value of the offices held by a clerk in the course of his curial career represents his total investment activity over a period of years, and that he must therefore have come to the Roman court with a much smaller capital sum, probably far less than the eventual total investment. Direct evidence is scarce, but we have the instance of Gianbattista Ferrari (later datarius and cardinal) who in 1479, when he had already been a minor abbreviator for eight years, was lent 1,200 ducats by his brother to buy offices; this must have been the basis for his purchase of a major abbreviatorship (for perhaps, at that time, 900 ducats) in 1482. It is noticeable that it took him three years to negotiate the purchase. The importance of the sums involved may be gathered from referring them to the average annual income of a cardinal of the period, which was in the region of 8,000 ducats.

The launch of the new colleges of venal offices was undertaken not from a position of papal strength, but from one of declared financial weakness. These fresh borrowings were used to shore up the political and military position of the

---

[18] This is based on a long and necessarily rather approximate calculation, from the figures for prices paid for offices in calculation, Frenz's table, 'Cumulationes officiorum' (*Kanzlei*, pp. 242–5), and in Von Hofmann, *Forschungen*. In order to get a price for the various offices which was not too distorted by the greatly increased prices paid in the latter part of the period, the available figures for the prices paid for each office have been broken down into three series, one for the period 1464–86, one for 1487–1506, and one for 1507–26. The arithmetic mean was taken for each of the three series, and then combined into a single mean for the whole period. Using this system values were obtained for the mean value of a major abbreviatorship of 3,882 ducats, of a minor one of 1,405 ducats, and of a secretaryship of 3,121 ducats. No attempt was made to calculate the figures for the other offices held by chamber clerks, as these are not all given by Frenz, and it was thought best to restrict the figures to the single matrix supplied by his 'cumulationes officiorum'.

papacy, and to help maintain the brilliant court and the extraordinary architectural and cultural enterprises of the great Renaissance popes. But the financial need which underlay the sales of offices is written into many of the texts of the bulls which set up the new sales. Sixtus IV mentioned the urgent need to raise troops to repel the assault of the Duke of Calabria on the papal state in 1482, when he raised 30,000 ducats from the *sollicitatores* to set up their college. Innocent VIII cited the indebtedness of the Holy See and the pledging of the papal mitre in the bull establishing the college of secretaries in 1487. Alexander VI in 1503 referred to the urgent need for money to fight the Turkish peril, when he raised 60,000 ducats from setting up the college of scriptors of briefs. Julius II raised 60,000 ducats from the *scriptores archivii curiae Romanae* in 1507, as he said, to help pay for the costs of war in the papal state and for the rebuilding of St Peter's.[19]

The achievements of these and subsequent popes need not blind us to the fact that for most of their time the Holy See was on the brink of bankruptcy, and was searching desperately for new ways to finance the deficit. The last attempt to reorganize the old borrowing methods had been that of Innocent VIII, when he unsuccessfully attempted to farm the spiritual revenues to a consortium of bankers.[20] After this, no way of borrowing new funds except the sale of more classes of offices was found until the first papal 'Monte' was launched in 1526. The practice of attaching the name of some new emergency which required the fresh borrowing went on throughout the sixteenth century, and occasioned the titles given to the 'Monti' of the later period, such as 'Monte della Liga', 'Monte delle Galere', and so on.

IX

Like Nicholas V and Pius II, when he came to the papacy in 1471 Sixtus had not been in the Roman court as a cardinal for long enough to have acquired an influential clientele, and this fact has often been urged in his defence when he has been accused of excessive nepotism and favouritism. His pontificate certainly witnessed the shameless aggrandizement and enrich-

---

[19] *Sollicitatores*, Frenz, *Kanzlei*, pp. 458–60; secretaries, *Magnum Bullarium Romanum*, i. 440 ff.; *scriptores brevium*, Frenz, pp. 461–5; *scriptores archivii*, Von Hofmann, *Forschungen*, ii. 53.
[20] M. M. Bullard, 'Farming Spiritual Revenues'.

ment of a small clique of courtiers, most of them the pope's close relations, but also including some other arrivistes who enjoyed the pope's confidence, such as the brothers Gabriele and Gian Giacomo Sclafenati, two Milanese clerks in the papal household. Gabriele, who occupied several responsible curial posts, was made Bishop of Gap; Gian Giacomo, who apparently had nothing but his charm to recommend him, was not only made Bishop of Parma but was promoted cardinal.[21]

The patronage map of Rome was redrawn under Sixtus. The violent manner in which he used the resources of the church in order to make his hitherto extremely modest family into a rich and powerful dynasty recalls the policies of Boniface VIII, almost two centuries earlier. Sixtus's creations of Riario and Della Rovere cardinals and great Riario and Della Rovere nobles were on a grand scale: six family cardinals, of whom four survived into the next pontificate, was a record unequalled in earlier papal history. Cardinal Raffaele Riario was rendered yet more powerful through his long tenure of the office of papal chamberlain, which he held actively from 1483 until his disgrace in 1517.

But the advancement of his own family was not the only result of Sixtus IV's policy for the Sacred College. His promotion of Cardinal Ascanio Sforza brought direct Milanese patronage back to Rome in a more powerful manner than any similar creation of that century. Sforza became yet more powerful by his advancement to papal vice-chancellor in 1492, an office he held until his death in 1505. The advancement of the young Cardinal Francesco Gonzaga to cardinal by Pius II had been a comparable promotion of a member of a princely house, but the power and wealth of the two houses were not commensurate. Ascanio Sforza, the brother of the Milanese ruler, was one of the richest and most powerful men in Italy.

Sixtus, by making no less than four members of the great Roman families into cardinals (Colonna, Orsini, Savelli, Conti), also inflated Roman influence as no earlier pope of the century had done since Martin V, and brought the quarrels of the great Roman families into the heart of the Sacred College. This was not the policy of an enlightened absolute ruler who brought the great families into court to domesticate and control them, but something more akin to the divide-and-rule policies of a feudal monarch.

[21] Gian Giacomo Sclafenati was 33 when made a cardinal in 1482, and not 23, as is said by Pastor and copied by others. See the photograph of his tomb in S. Agostino in Davies, *Renascence*, facing p. 194.

The question of Ligurian influence in Rome should be looked at not only in the context of Sixtus IV but also in that of his compatriot and successor, Innocent VIII (1484–92). Between them these two pontiffs appointed (if Gian Battista Cibo's own appointment is counted) ten Ligurian cardinals. These were mostly members of their own families, but there were also a couple of representatives of the great families of the region: Campofregoso and Pallavicini. But Ligurian influence was not only a matter of red hats: there was also the massive employment of Genoese bankers in the service of the Holy See. Under Sixtus the earlier stranglehold of Tuscan bankers on the Roman court was broken. The new generation of Ligurian curial bankers, the Spannocchi, Centurioni, Sauli, and their like, brought to the Roman court a further influx of capital; in Rome they gained a lot of political influence, and the power to advance the careers of their clerical relatives, employees, and protégés. Two members of the Sauli family, one of whom was the future cardinal, Bandinello Sauli, were papal secretaries under Julius II. The brilliant career in the apostolic chamber of the flawed Sienese man of affairs, Ventura Benassai, was due to his having worked as factor in Rome for the Spannocchi, and even though Ventura was eventually disgraced and broken under Julius II, his brother Latino rose to the position of datarius under Leo X.

Julius II continued the series of Ligurian appointments to the Sacred College, as might have been expected, although his general policy for the creation of cardinals was conservative, and at the end of his pontificate the college was much smaller than at its beginning. Nevertheless, the Ligurians Clemente Grosso della Rovere, Antonio Ferreri of Savona (a former secretary), Leonardo Grosso della Rovere, Sesto Franciotto della Rovere, and Bandinello Sauli, all owed their red hats to Julius. There were four Ligurian cardinals out of thirty-one in the college at the time of Julius II's death in 1513.

The secretariat of Julius II was the last conservative one before the great transformations of the Medici popes. The domestic secretary of Julius, Sigismondo de' Conti, had been a secretary since 1481 and had worked with the secretaries long before that. Conti was the first domestic secretary since Andrea di Trebisonda under Sixtus IV to have had a conventional career as secretary before his appointment as secret or confidential secretary. He was also the last domestic secretary of the sort which had become customary since Nicholas V in the mid-fifteenth century.

X

The policy of expanding the numbers of curial officers so as to bring money and influence to the hands of the popes who named them was applied by the late fifteenth-century and early sixteenth-century popes not only to the lower offices of the Roman court, but to the college of cardinals itself. It is true that the college of cardinals was not made into a venal class of papal officers of the same sort as the other colleges of papal offices, and that a taint of illegality attached to the sale of cardinal's places, but such sales did occur, even if they were infrequent.

The trend to increase their number was resisted by the cardinals, not only because it tended to weaken the oligarchic pretensions of the college, but—the same reason for resistance to expansion of the lower offices—because 'you wish to add others to take the bread out of our mouths', as Cardinal Ludovico da Treviso ('Scarampo') objected to Pope Pius II. As late as 1464 the electoral capitulations of the conclave required the new pope to observe a maximum of twenty-four places in the college of cardinals. It is noticeable that Paul II, who was the last pope to follow a conservative policy in the creation of new offices, made no vigorous attempt to exceed this limit: at his death in 1471 there were still only twenty-five cardinals; this exceeded the set number by only one cardinal.

Eighty-five cardinals were created between 1417 and 1468 over a space of fifty-two years, but in the fifty years from 1471 to 1520 the number of creations was 155, or approaching double the number made in the preceding half-century. Of these creations, Sixtus made 34 cardinals in a pontificate lasting thirteen years; Innocent VIII made 8 in eight years; Alexander VI made 43 in eleven years; Julius II made 27 in ten years; and Leo X made 43 in a space of eight years. As a result, the college of cardinals, which numbered 26 at the death of Eugenius IV in 1447, numbered 45 at the death of Pius III in 1503, and 48 cardinals at the death of Leo X in 1521. The upward trend continued through the first half of the sixteenth century, and there were 66 cardinals in the fifth year of Paul III (1539), and over sixty cardinals when the last session of the Council of Trent began.[22]

---

[22] Calculations are from Eubel, and also from R. Gregoire, 'Il sacro collegio', and J. F. Broderick, 'The Sacred College of Cardinals: Size and Geographical Composition (1099-1986)', *AHP* 25 (1987), 7-71.

The increase in the number of cardinals seems to have been accompanied by a decrease in the proportion of cardinals resident in Rome, though estimates differ. In the period 1417–84 the proportion of non-curial cardinals is said to have been 15.4 per cent. According to calculations based on the cardinals said to have been present and absent at the various conclaves (the calculations allow for those who were normally resident in Rome but absent on mission), in the period 1484–1523 the proportion of non-curial cardinals was 23.6 per cent.[23]

Even though the doubling of the number of cardinals was slightly offset by the increase in non-curial absentees, the number of curial cardinals was greatly increased after 1484, and this must have had profound results on the patronage system. An increase in the number of cardinals meant an increase in the number of privileged patrons, since the cardinals all enjoyed the most extraordinary legal and social privileges in their ability to influence the conferment of benefices and offices. Overall there was a big rise in the demand for benefices and offices which could be had against payment. Many of the cardinals themselves acted as brokers in this market, besides the established *sollicitatores*. The result was to drive up the prices of offices and benefices, and also to stimulate the popes into taking measures to increase the income of the papal offices, and thus to support the rising market.

From 1471 onwards the trend of income of the papal offices was inexorably upwards. The income of a chamber clerk from fees was estimated at 150 ducats in 1470, at 300 ducats in 1500, at 500 ducats under Julius II, and at 700 or 800 ducats in 1514. After this date there were further increases in the incomes of chamber clerks, such as that which arose from the grant of a percentage charge on the annates received in the chamber. Similar increases are likely to have occurred in the fees income of the secretaries, although they are less easy to document, but the increase in price for a secretary's place from 2,275 ducats in 1488 to over 5,000 ducats under Leo X tells its own story.[24] Von Hofmann's estimate of a doubling of the value of the income deriving from curial offices between

23 The earlier figure is given by Broderick, at p. 20 (see n. 22), from the work of B. Arle. I cannot agree with the calculation of D. S. Chambers, in his important article, 'The Economic Predicament of Renaissance Cardinals', p. 290, that little more than a tenth of cardinals of the period 1471–1527 were non-resident.

24 Von Hofmann, *Forschungen*, i. 282–7; for 1500 see Burckardi, *Liber Notarum*, ii. 228.

1500 and 1514 is almost certainly correct, and a further increase of about 25 per cent on the 1514 value is likely for the later years of the pontificate of Leo X. The period between 1513 and the Sack of Rome in 1527, before the spiritual revenues had been touched by the Protestant schisms, and before papal income had been burdened by the issue of a new funded debt in the 'Monti', was looked back to in Rome, at a later date, as the golden age of papal officialdom.[25]

XI

The strongly Hispanic nature of the Roman court under Alexander VI is an historical commonplace. Under Alexander, Catalan became in effect a third court language to Italian and Latin: Roman culture was strongly Hispanicized, and Spanish plays and entertainments became as common as Italian. Whether this change was more drastic than the increase in Genoese influence under Sixtus and Innocent, or the increase in Sienese influence under Pius, is uncertain. It is likely that the effect of Spanish influence was different at the various levels of the court hierarchy, and that it was particularly strong in the household offices which contained an element of personal service to the ruler, less strong in the upper administrative offices.

The private secretaries of Alexander VI do not seem to have been clearly designated as domestic secretaries, and it is likely that the confidential business was dispatched by a small group, some of whom, like the secret chamberlain Gaspar Pou, did the business of a secretary without possessing the formal title. Of the four officials who at various times during the pontificate probably did the business of the domestic secretary, two (Bartolomé Flores and Francesco Troche) were Spanish, and one, Adriano Castellesi, who was appointed to succeed Flores, was Italian. The first domestic secretary of the pontificate was Ludovico Podocataro, a Cypriot, the former doctor of Innocent VIII, who had subsequently been Cardinal Borgia's secretary. Bartolomé Flores was disgraced in 1497 for corruption in the execution of his office, and died in prison.

Some forty-five secretaries were appointed under Alexander VI, which meant much more than a complete turnover of the college of thirty members (supposed to have declined to twenty-nine with the death of Gaspare Biondo in 1493). Of Alexander's

[25] See Partner, 'The "Budget" of the Roman Church', p. 272.

appointments, seven (15.6 per cent) were Spanish, three were French, and the rest Italian except for the Greek Celadoni. There was no German appointment. Seven chamber clerks were appointed under Alexander, which amounted to a rotation of all seven members of the college. Of those appointed by Alexander, only one (Juan Gualbes) was Spanish: the rest were Italian.

There is a striking difference between the figures for the geographic origins of all chancery officials, and those for the origins of chamber clerks and papal secretaries alone. This must mean that the forces influencing patronage in other parts of the papal organization must have differed from those that influenced the chamber clerks and secretaries. The tight oligarchic conditions which obtained for the appointment of chamber clerks and secretaries, and the high prices which were charged for the offices, must have favoured Italians over all others. The close correspondence between the geography of cardinals (Table 12) and that of chancery officials (Table 11) suggests a consistent geographical pattern for papal officers as a whole. The much more Italianate pattern for chamber clerks and secretaries suggests that these were particularly attractive posts for the Italians with the means to bid for them.

The situation had not been dissimilar (though for different reasons) in the earlier fifteenth century, when chamber clerks and secretaries were already predominantly Italian. However, there were big changes in the general factors governing the national origins of papal clerks, between the earlier and later parts of the fifteenth century. Under Martin V and Eugenius IV German chancery personnel had numbered almost a fifth of the

TABLE 11. *Geographical origins of chamber clerks and secretaries* (% given in parentheses)

	1417–1470	1471–1527	1417–1527
Empire	10 (5.7)	8 (4.2)	18 (5.0)
Spain	18 (10.3)	24 (12.6)	42 (11.6)
France	11 (6.3)	7 (3.7)	18 (5.0)
England	2 (1.1)	0	2 (0.6)
Other	2 (1.1)	1 (0.5)	3 (0.8)
Total non-Italian	43 (24.7)	40 (21.2)	83 (22.9)
Italy	131 (75.3)	149 (78.8)	280 (77.1)
TOTAL	174 (100.0)	189 (100.0)	363 (100.0)

TABLE 12. Geography of chancery personnel and cardinals
1471-1527 (% given in parentheses)

	Chancery personnel*	Cardinals†
Empire	61 (5.8)	8 (4.4)
Spain	202 (19.3)	31 (17.1)
France	129 (12.3)	26 (14.4)
England	2 (0.2)	4 (2.2)
Other	19 (1.8)	4 (2.2)
Total non-Italian	413 (39.4)	73 (40.3)
Italy	634 (60.6)	108 (59.7)
TOTAL	1047 (100.0)	181 (100.0)

* T. Frenz, *Die Kanzlei der Päpste der Hochrenaissance (1471-1527)*
(Tübingen, 1986), 241.

† Calculated from the data in C. Eubel and others, *Hierarchia Catholica
Medii Aevi* (Münster, 1898-1923).

Roman court. In the period 1471–1527 the proportion of
German clerks in the chancery had sunk to about 6 per cent,
and in the later period the nation contributing almost 20 per
cent of papal clerks was not Germany, but Spain.

XII

In 1513, with the election of Giovanni de' Medici as Leo X, the
economic and administrative hold of Florence on Rome, which
had been substantial for over a century, became almost absolute. This persisted for over twenty years, enduring beyond the
Sack of Rome in 1527. The pontificate of the Netherlander
Adrian VI (January 1522–September 1523) was a brief episode
which had no real effect on administrative practice, nor on the
patronage system. Giulio de' Medici (Clement VII, 1523-34),
probably the illegitimate cousin of Leo X, conserved as far as
possible the curial system he had inherited.

The nature of Florentine financial involvement in the Roman
court had changed in the course of this long period. For the
first half-century after the papal return to Rome in 1420, the
Florentine banks, particularly the Medici bank, had had vast
direct responsibilities in the management of papal finance. The
depositary (*depositarius*) of the apostolic chamber, an official
who formed part of the college of the chamber, had normally

been a Tuscan banker, often the Medici factor in Rome. The change in papal credit status and methods after 1471 had transformed this, as had the partial substitution of Ligurian for Tuscan bankers. The last was due to the great quarrel of the Medici with Sixtus IV, and to covert papal participation in the Pazzi plot against the Medici in 1478.

The manager of the Medici bank branch in Rome, Giovanni Tornabuoni, whose relative Antonio Francesco Tornabuoni had been a chamber clerk for a short time, wrote under Sixtus IV that the office of papal depositary now involved more risk and worry than it did profit. The depositary had had to handle a papal deficit of some 70,000 ducats in mid-century; under Sixtus IV this had risen to 100,000 ducats, or over a third of current revenue. The policy followed by the Medici bank earlier in the fifteenth century, based on the frequent appointment of the Medici manager as depositary, and on the cash investments made by papal courtiers in the Roman branch, had broken down. Courtiers had changed their investment policies, which were now as frequently in Roman real estate as in cash deposits. From 1464 onwards the profits of the Roman Medici branch from banking declined and eventually disappeared; the only remaining source of Medici profit in Rome came from participation in the papal alum industry. The branch achieved profitability for a short time after its return to Rome in 1483, and then relapsed into deficit. In 1486 the winding-up document of the 'old' Medici Roman branch showed a loss of almost 19,000 ducats. Medici participation in the farm of the spiritual revenues under Innocent VIII led to further losses. By 1495 the bad debts shown in the company accounts included 30,000 ducats owed by the apostolic chamber. By this date the branch had virtually failed.[26] Papal favour, in fact, was as necessary for a bank as it was for any other courtier. Not until 1513 was this favour fully available again to the Florentines.

Leo X's pontificate in 1513 inaugurated, from a Florentine point of view, a very different situation from that of the fifteenth century. The underlying position of the Florentine banking and export industry in Rome perhaps did not change as quickly as might have been expected. The number of Florentine banks attached to the Roman court, already substantial under Julius II, did not vary much as a result of Leo's pontificate. The Florentine export industry had already been sending about

---

[26] A. Sapori, 'Il "bilancio" della filiale di Roma del Banco Medici del 1495', *ASI* 131 (1973), 163–224; R. de Roover, *Il banco Medici dalle origini al declino* (Florence, 1970).

10 per cent of its products to Rome: there must have been some increase under Leo, especially as from the War of Urbino onwards (1517), the Florentine government was in effect subsidizing the papal government, and the Roman credit balance must to some extent have been spent on Florentine goods. The Medici were no longer bankers, but rulers: there was an ironic commentary on this when it was queried whether Filippo Strozzi, the brother-in-law of Lorenzo de' Medici, would not be dishonouring the name of the Medici family (now proposing a marriage with the royal house of Naples) by accepting the low (*vile*) occupation of papal banker. This was, in Strozzi's case, the office of depositary of the apostolic chamber, many times occupied by the Medici in the preceding century.

Papal Rome had always been run by small cliques of papal relatives and favourites, but the Medici hegemony, which built a new principate in Rome and Florence simultaneously, was a more radical departure from ecclesiastical precedent than that of the Borgia had been, twenty years earlier. The Borgia, though they had dreamt of an alternative power base in the kingdom of Naples, never succeeded in creating it. Cesare Borgia had been an orthodox bishop's 'nephew' (though, in his case, an acknowledged son) seeking permanent dynastic gains from the fleeting political power of a family cleric. Leo X, on the other hand, brought to the Holy See the dowry of his own family rule in Florence. As Melissa Meriam Bullard has shown, Florence and Rome were run as a pair of linked, partly integrated governments, both geared to the single dynastic interest. No such connection had been known in papal politics since the abortive plan of Innocent III, at the beginning of the thirteenth century, to marry his nephew to Philip of Swabia's daughter, and to secure for him the grant of the Duchy of Tuscany. It would be necessary to go back to Marozia's marriages with Guy of Tuscany and Hugh of Provence, at the time of the 'pornocracy' in Rome in the early tenth century, to find a close analogy.

The great men of Leo X's court were, above all, the cardinals related by blood or marriage to the Medici line: Cardinals Giulio de' Medici, Lorenzo Pucci, Giovanni Salviati, Niccolò Ridolfi, Francesco Soderini, Innocenzo Cibo, Ludovico de' Rossi. These men, with a few other cardinals who were Medici tools and great curial financiers (Francesco Armellini the later chamberlain, Pietro Accolti, Silvio Passerini the datarius), stood at the very top of the queue for benefices, offices, and privileges. In the shoal of Roman sharks, they had the biggest mouths and the strongest teeth. The fact that even some of those closest to the pope had been made to pay huge sums for their elevation to the cardinalate, or to one of the great curial offices, meant that they had to be the more ruthless in the subsequent chase for favours, in order to recoup their expenses.

Below the greatest men was an almost equally formidable group of Medici agents and intimate dependants, some of whose names are forgotten, but whose benefices, such as those of the musically inclined Spanish prelate Stefan Gabriel Merino, were numerous. One, in spite of his holding a cardinal's dignity, was never a very important political figure in his own right: this was the intimate secretary, Bernardo Dovizi of Bibbiena. There were also trusted and important Medici servants who moved from papal to Florentine service and back without a break in their careers. One such was the papal protonotary Gregorio Gheri, bishop of the papal state see of Fano from 1518, who had been an early governor of the papal state acquisition of Piacenza, then the effective governor of Florence from 1516–20. He finished his career by returning to the rule of Piacenza, subsequently becoming vice-legate of the papal state city of Bologna (1521–4, 1525–8).[27] Both Gheri and Baldassare Turini, the later papal datarius, before they came to Rome had been the secretaries of Lorenzo de' Medici in Florence. Nor can another distinguished Florentine papal servant, the layman Francesco Guicciardini, who succeeded the murdered chamber clerk Giovanni Gozzadini as Governor of Reggio and went on to occupy a string of key posts in the papal temporal power, be omitted from such a list.

Men of the Florentine *dominio*, such as Accolti, Passerini, Bibbiena, Gheri, and at the next level Turini, were important at the very top of the Medici court. There was also an important branch of Medici policy aimed at the domination of non-Florentine Tuscany, and, in particular, of Siena: this involved the two mutually hostile Petrucci cardinals (Alfonso and Raffaele), the Petrucci castellan of Sant'Angelo, the Piccolomini cardinal, Giovanni, besides many minor figures such as the chamber clerk, Filippo Sergardi.

The Roman rebellion of 1512 meant that for the last year of the pontificate of Julius and the first four of that of Leo it was

27 K. J. P. Lowe, 'Towards an Understanding of Goro Gheri's Views on *amicizia* in Early Sixteenth-Century Medicean Florence', *Florence and Italy* (Rubinstein Studies, 1988), 91–105; J. N. Stephens, 'Machiavelli's "Prince" and the Florentine Revolution of 1512', *Italian Studies*, 41 (1986), 45–61, at 48–9.

rare for a Roman clerk to get preferment in the Roman court. This exclusion disappeared after the Petrucci plot of 1517 and the subsequent great promotion of thirty-one cardinals of the same year. This promotion included not only the great Roman baronial families (Colonna, Orsini, Conti) and representatives of the city magnate families (Della Valle, Jacobazzi, Cesarini, De Cupis), but members of successful curialist families who had emigrated from other parts of the papal state to Rome during the preceding half-century, such as Cesi. It would perhaps not be an exaggeration to say that a large part of the top nobility of the early modern papal state owed their distinction to the cardinals' promotion of 1517. Round them, their relatives burrowed like ants to pile up the pickings of the papal court: for example, three clerical brothers of Cardinal Paolo Cesi became abbot or bishop, and one, Federico, also became a cardinal in 1544.

The central place of the banks in the Medici system needs no emphasis. Many papal secretaries, for example Sebastiano and Bandinello Sauli, or another secretary who became auditor of the chamber, Ieronimo Ghinucci, or a chamber clerk (Niccolò Gaddi), were members of banking families intimately connected with the chamber. Unsurprisingly, Sebastiano Sauli joined with the bankers Filippo Strozzi and Pietro del Bene in 1521 in a loan of 30,000 ducats to pay the dead Leo X's funeral expenses. However, one peculiarity of the Medici arrangements was to allow lay bankers not only to receive curial offices in pledge, but actually to assume them in their own names, so that the great German banker, Anton Fugger, occupied two *loci* of secretaries in 1521, and another banker, Tommaso Salvago, took up two secretarial places in 1521 and another in 1523. The same policies continued under Clement VII: it is not surprising to learn that the Florentine banker, Filippo Strozzi, had title at various times to at least 258 venal offices, of which one was a secretary's post.[28]

XIII

The accession of another Medici pope in 1523 did not restore to

[28] M. M. Bullard, *Filippo Strozzi*, p. 151. Id., ' "Mercatores Florentini Romanam Curiam Sequentes" in the Early Sixteenth Century', *Journal of Medieval and Renaissance Studies*, 6 (1976), 51–71 has also been drawn on in this paragraph.

power all the former members of the inner circle of Leo X. Some of the key men of Clement VII's pontificate, like Cardinal Giovanni Salviati and his father Jacopo, the banker Filippo Strozzi, and Cardinals Innocenzo Cibo and Niccolò Ridolfi, were Medici relatives and figures from the earlier Medici pontificate. Others, like Pietro Lippomanno and Gian Matteo Giberti, were favourites of the new regime. It is typical of the way things went that one former secretary of Leo X, Sadoleto, found advancement in the new Medici order, while the other, Pietro Bembo, did not.

The four years between the accession of Clement VII and the Sack of Rome in 1527 gave little time for a new pattern to develop. They were years of political and economic crisis, in which the balance of European power which had developed in the 1520s, to some extent to the advantage of the papacy, collapsed, while the Luther quarrel became a Lutheran schism. The Battle of Pavia in 1525 left the papacy isolated and exposed as it had not been since the Battle of Ravenna in 1512. In Rome the external crisis was mirrored in 1526 by the damaging revolt of the Roman baronial families. A new system of papal loans was floated in the same year, but without rescuing the tottering papal credit.

Inevitably, the policy of getting the maximum possible profit from the venal offices continued under Clement. Perhaps the most critical drift in this field was towards making the whole college of cardinals venal. Clement VII consciously resisted this trend, but was compelled to give in to it at the height of the military crisis of 1527, when a promotion of cardinals took place whose main aim was to get money from the successful aspirants to the red hat. But, as has been already mentioned, this final, logical extension of the principle of the venal offices, was not, in the end, allowed to prevail. That it was not, illustrates the power of the historic claims of the cardinalate, which prevented the office from being treated merely as another part of the papal bureaucracy.

By 1527 a system was in place which determined the way in which offices other than that of cardinal were distributed in the papal court. In essentials the arrangements scarcely changed for the rest of the early modern period. During the Counter-Reformation some important changes in the organization of papal government were effected, but the offices were hardly touched. The relationship between the Italian ruling classes and the papal civil service had been established by 1527, and subsequent variations in church policy only modified it. Recent work on the social composition of the papal bureaucracy in the early eighteenth century has revealed a situation not unlike the one described in this book.[29] Not until the Napoleonic period and the papal Restoration of 1815 was the way in which the Roman court recruited its members substantially changed.

---

[29] See R. Ago, 'Burocrazia "nazione" e parentela nella Roma del Settecento', *Quaderni Storici*, NS, 67 (1988), 73–98; P. Schmidtbauer, 'Prolegomena zu einer Sozialgeschichte des Kapitels von St. Peter im Vatikan', *Röm.Hist.Mitt.* 28 (1986), 243–301.

Appendix

aud. cam.	auditor of the court of the apostolic chamber
cl. cam.	chamber clerk
consil. cam.	councillor of chamber
expect.	expectancy
particip.	participating
sec.	secretary
sec. dom.	domestic secretary
supranum.	supranumerary

CHAMBER CLERKS AND SECRETARIES 1417-1527

ACCIAIOLO, GIOVANNI (d. 1450). Cl. cam. (?supranum.). 12 Feb. 1448, decretorum doctor, Reg. Vat. 435, fo. 3. See also M. Cosenza, *Biographical Dictionary*, i. 32; L. Martines, *Social World of the Florentine Humanists* (Princeton, 1963), 335-6, 348-9; Litta, *Famiglie celebri*, vii, tav. V.

ACCOLTI, BENEDETTO (1497-1549). Sec. dom. 1523. *DBI* (E. Massa); Frenz, *Kanzlei*, p. 301; McClung Hallman, *Italian Cardinals*, pp. 9, 28, 70-1.

ACCOLTI, PIETRO (1455-1532). Sec. 2 June 1504, resigned Mar. 1511. Von Hofmann, *Forschungen*, ii. 119; Frenz, *Kanzlei*, p. 423; *DBI* (B. Ulianich); Katterbach, *Sussidi*, ii. 55; McClung Hallman, *Italian Cardinals*, p. 25; G. B. Picotti, 'Lo studio di Pisa dalle origini a Cosimo Duca', *Boll.Stor.Pis.* 11-13 (1942-4), 48; Verde, *Lo studio fiorentino*, ii (1975), 538-40.

ACRE, ALFONSO (d. ?1516). Sec. 10 Sept. 1507. Von Hofmann, *Forschungen*, ii. 62, 120; Frenz, *Kanzlei*, p. 275; see also J. Burckardi, *Liber Notarum*, i. 430; ii. 29, 33, 103, 145, 149.

AGAZZARIA, MEMMO (d. 1452). Cl. cam. on 3 Dec. 1425. Partner, *Papal State*, p. 218. Commissioner in temporals in Rieti, ibid. 134 n., cancelled [?]Reg. Vat. 351, fo. 160 (5 Oct. 1430). And Eubel, *Hierarchia*, ii. 179; Ughelli, *Italia Sacra* (2nd edn.), iii. 680.

AGNELLI, LUDOVICO (d. 1499). Cl. cam. 19 Jan. 1478, Sec. 1487, resigned 1488. *DBI* (unsigned); Von Hofmann, *Forschungen*, ii. 93, 117; Frenz, *Kanzlei*, p. 399; Brouette, 'Les Clercs "mensiers"' (1962), 413; id., 'Les Clercs "mensiers"' (1973), 583; Cosenza, *Biographical Dictionary*, i. 72; C. M. Brown, '"Lo insaciabile desiderio nostro de cose antique": New Documents for Isabella d'Este's Collection of Antiquities', in C. H. Clough (ed.), *Cultural Aspects of the Italian Renaissance: Essays in honour of Paul Kristeller* (Manchester, 1976), 324-53, at pp. 331-2,

Appendix   217

348-9, and see also p. 491; D. S. Chambers, 'A Defence of Non-Residence in the Later Fifteenth Century: Cardinal Francesco Gonzaga and the Mantuan Clergy', *JEH*, 36 (1985), 605-33, at pp. 616-17, 628-31; J. Burckardi, *Liber Notarum*, ii. 57. Alleged cruelty as Governor of the Marches, Ubaldini, *Vita di Mons. A. Colocci*, p. 11; V. Fanelli, *Ricerche su Angelo Colocci e sulla Roma Cinquecentesca* (Vatican City, 1979), 19-29.

AJELLO, GENTILE (d. 1430). Consil. cam. 20 Sept. 1417. Baix, *La Chambre apostolique*, pp. CCCXXXIX-CCCXL. See also Göller, *Päpstliche Pönitentiarie*, i/2. 111; Lightbown, *Donatello and Michelozzo*, i. 65, ii. 265, 297.

ALBERINI, LUCA (1393-1452). Cl. cam. 1 Dec. 1429. Uginet, *Le Liber officialium de Martin V*, p. 52; Baix, *La Chambre apostolique*, pp. CDIII, CCLXXXII; Eubel, *Hierarchia*, ii. 103; Arnold, *Repertorium Germanicum*, p. XLII; Forcella, *Iscrizioni*, ii. 76; appointed lieutenant of Bishop of Lucca as vicar in spirituals in Rome, Div. Cam. 13, fo. 99; Ughelli, *Italia Sacra*, i. 398.

ALBERTI, ALBERTO (1386-1445). Cl. cam. 1 Oct. 1431. Arch. Cam. I, vol. 1712, fo. 17. Legum doctor. *DBI* (A. D'Addario). Papal treasurer in Bologna and collector in Romagna 21 May 1425. Introitus et Exitus 383, fo. 4. Envoy to Queen of Naples 20 May 1432. Reg. Vat. 370, fo. 70b, and see fo. 131a. Governor of Perugia 8 Mar. 1434. Reg. Vat. 373, fo. 140b. Still Governor of Perugia on promotion to cardinal 9 Jan. 1440. Reg. Vat. 367, fo. 141b. Eubel, *Hierarchia*, ii. 8, 30, 129.

ALDERIGHI, GIOVANNI (dates unknown). Sec. 1487-91. Frenz, *Kanzlei*, p. 361.

ALIDOSI, FRANCESCO (1455-1511). Sec. 1500-5. Von Hofmann, *Forschungen*, ii. 89; Frenz, *Kanzlei*, pp. 324-5; *DBI* (G. de Caro).

ALTELL, PEDRO (d. before 12 Apr. 1457). Cl. cam. 28 Apr. 1455, Reg. Vat. 467, fo. 2b; Von Hofmann, *Forschungen*, ii. 110, 114, 186. See also Rius Serra, 'Catalanes y Aragones', pp. 248-9; id., *Regesto iberico*, iii. 156 n., 361, 364; Pitz, *Supplikensignatur*, p. 280; Célier, *Les Dataires*, p. 32. Papal chamberlain, 30 May 1446, Arch. Cam. I, vol. 1713, fo. 23.

ALTISSEN, PETER (d. 1491). Sec. 1487. Von Hofmann, *Forschungen*, i. 239, ii. 82, 117, 185; Frenz, 'Problem', p. 269; id., *Kanzlei*, p. 424; Egidi, *Necrologi*, i. 515, 539; *CPL* xiii/2. 844; J. Burckardi, *Liber Notarum*, i. 313, 314, 315; Tangl, *Päpstl. Kanzleiordnungen*, pp. 393, 398-400.

ALTOAMORE, THEODOR (d. 1428). Sworn as sec. Jan. 1419. Von Hofmann, *Forschungen*, ii. 110; Schuchard, *Deutschen Kurie*, p. 86.

AMI, MICHEL ROGER (d. after 1464). Sec. 1 May 1457. Von Hofmann, *Forschungen*, ii. 115; see also Rius Serra, *Regesto iberico*, i. 58; Pitz, *Supplikensignatur*, pp. 109, 170; Tangl, *Päpstl. Kanzleiordnungen*, pp. 183-8; *CPL* viii. 272 n., x. 190, xi. 59; Frenz, 'Gründung', p. 302.

AMMANATI, JACOPO CRISTOFORO (1422-79). Sec. sworn 12 Apr. 1455, appointed 10 May 1457; sec. dom. under Pius II. Von Hofmann, *Forschungen*, ii. 113, 123; *DBI* (E. Pásztor); Hausmann, 'Armarium 39

Tomus 10'; Pitz, Supplikensignatur, p. 111; Frenz, 'Eindringen', pp. 459-61; Bernardo, Campano, pp. 206-8; G. S. Davies, Renascence: The Sculptured Tombs of the Fifteenth Century in Rome (1910), 192-4; W. R. Valentiner, Studies in Italian Renaissance Sculpture (1950), 95-6; Cherubini, in Scrittura, biblioteche e stampa, ii. 175-256; Un pontificato e una città, p. 477.

ANCONA, LANZELOTTO (dates unknown). Sworn as cl. cam., 30 July 1455. 'Et post die XXII novembris 1455 fuit admissus ad osculum et iuravit observare statuta', Reg. Vat. 467, fo. 3.

ANGEROLI, GIOVANNI (dates unknown). Cl. cam. supranum. under Pius II. Von Hofmann, Forschungen, ii. 180-1.

ARAGAZZI, BARTOLOMEO FRANCESCO (c.1385-1429). Sec. 1414 and 1421-2. Von Hofmann, Forschungen, ii. 109; Frenz, 'Problem', p. 259. DBI (unsigned); Lightbown, Donatello and Michelozzo, passim.

ARANDA, ALFONSO (dates unknown). Sec. 5 Nov. 1495, resigned 1498; Von Hofmann, Forschungen, ii. 118; Frenz, Kanzlei, p. 276; Burckardi, Liber Notarum, ii. 90, 116-17, 200-1.

ARANDA, PEDRO (d. 1500). Cl. cam. 5 Dec. 1470, resigned 1477. See Von Hofmann, Forschungen, ii. 92, 152, 192; Brouette, 'Les Clercs "mensiers"' (1962), p. 412; Frenz, Kanzlei, p. 424; Rius Serra, Regesto iberico, i. 12, 198, 231; Egidi, Necrologi, ii. 154-5; Burckardi, Liber Notarum, ii. 116-17; J. Fernandez-Alonso, 'Pedro de Aranda, obispo de Calahorra († 1500), un legado de Alejandro VI ante la Senoria de Venecia (1494)', in Miscellanea M. Giusti (Vatican City, 1978), 255-95, at pp. 283-5.

Arce, Alfonso, see Acre, Alfonso.

ARGENTINI, FRANCESCO (d. 1511). Sec. 1510. Von Hofmann, Forschungen, ii. 102, 120, 134-5; Frenz, Kanzlei, p. 325; Ughelli, Italia Sacra, v. 365; Ciacconius, Vitae, iii. 197; Burckardi, Liber Notarum, ii. 500.

ARMELLINI, FRANCESCO (1470-1527). Cl. cam. 1505-17; Sec. 7 Feb. 1497. Von Hofmann, Forschungen, ii. 88, 93; Frenz, Kanzlei, p. 325; DBI (G. De Caro); K. J. P. Lowe, 'Questions of Income and Expenditure in Renaissance Rome', Studies in Church History, 24 (1987), 175-88.

ARRIANI, AFRICA LUCE (dates unknown). Sec. 1488- , 1492-1506, 1506, resigned 1508. Von Hofmann, Forschungen, ii. 117; Frenz, Kanzlei, p. 271; J. Burckardi, Liber Notarum, ii. 484.

ARRIVABENE, GIOVANNI PIETRO (1439-1504). Sec. 1483, resigned 1491. Von Hofmann, Forschungen, ii. 116; Frenz, Kanzlei, p. 362; D. S. Chambers, 'Giovanni Pietro Arrivabene 1439-1504: Humanistic Secretary and Bishop', Aevum, 1 (anno LVIII, 1984), 397-438; Frasso, Ital.Med.Uman. 20 (1977), 395-6; Gherardi, Dispacci, p. 191 and passim; Pélissier, 'Catalogue des documents de la collection Podo-cataro' (1901), 582-3.

ASCOLI, ENOCH DE (d. 1457). Sec. sworn 19 Sept. 1455. Von Hofmann, Forschungen, ii. 102. No trace of activity as secretary. See also R. Sabbadini, Storia e critica di testi latini (Catania, 1914), 263-87.

ATZEL, JOHANNES (d. 1472). Cl. cam. honoris 1423, particip. 1425. Uginet, *Le Liber officialium*, pp. 48, 50; M. C. Miller, 'Participation', p. 400; Eubel, *Hierarchia*, i. 522, ii. 291; K. A. Fink, *Repertorium Germanicum*, iv/2 n. 1610; Schuchard, *Deutschen Kurie*, pp. 79, 81. Atzel was not only supernumerary as a chamber clerk, as Schuchard claims, according to the list issued by the vice-chamberlain on 3 Dec. 1425; see Partner, *Papal State*, p. 217.

AURISPA, GIOVANNI (1376–1459). Sec. 1437 and active again 1450–1, 1458. Von Hofmann, *Forschungen*, ii. 111; Frenz, 'Eindringen', p. 454; *CPL* x. 481; R. Cessi, 'La contesa fra Giorgio da Trebisonda, Poggio Bracciolini e Giovanni Aurispa durante il pontificato di Niccolò V', *Archivio Storico per la Sicilia orientale*, 9 (1912), 211–32. E. Bigi, article in *DBI*, takes no account of his office in the Roman court.

AVVOGARI, NICCOLÒ (dates unknown). Sec. dom. 1503. Von Hofmann, *Forschungen*, ii. 124.

AVVOGARI, PARIS (dates unknown). Sec. 1480. Frenz, *Kanzlei*, p. 420.

BAGAROTTI, BATTISTA (1437–1522). Sec. 1479, resigned 1486. Von Hofmann, *Forschungen*, ii. 83; Frenz, *Kanzlei*, p. 295; *CPL* xvi, civ; *DBI* (N. Raponi).

BALBANI, IERONIMO. Sec., Sec. dom. 1487. Von Hofmann, *Forschungen*, ii. 117, 123; Frenz, *Kanzlei*, p. 346; *CPL* xvi, civ; Gherardi, *Dispacci*, pp. 78–80; Burckardi, *Liber Notarum*, i. 160, 167, 168, 391; Giusti, 'I registri Vaticani', p. 434; Paschini, *Carteggio Barbo-Lorenzi*, p. 156.

BANDINI, MELCHIOR (dates unknown). Sec. 27 Apr. 1444. Von Hofmann, *Forschungen*, ii. 112; see also p. 96; Kraus, 'Die Sekretäre', p. 34; *CPL* x. 261–4.

BAROCCI, CRISTOFORO (dates unknown). Cl. cam. 3 Aug. 1517. Von Hofmann, *Forschungen*, ii. 94; Frenz, *Kanzlei*, p. 312. Von Hofmann, *Forschungen*, ii. 83, 248; Hergenroether, *Regesta*, nos. 4378, 5040, 16121; Burckardi, *Liber Notarum*, ii. 33, 196, 488.

BARONCI, FILIPPO. Sec. 1414, 1418, resigned 1427. Von Hofmann, *Forschungen*, ii. 109; Frenz, 'Problem', p. 264; Schuchard, *Deutschen Kurie*, p. 130.

BARTOLINI DE' MEDICI, ONOFRIO DI LIONARDO (d. 1555). Appointed sec. 22 Feb. 1516. Von Hofmann, *Forschungen*, ii. 62, 191; Frenz, *Kanzlei*, p. 351, seems mistaken in saying that the grant of secretarial office did not take effect, since he was sec. on promotion to archbishopric of Pisa in 1518; see also Eubel, *Hierarchia*, iii. 274. See also Stephens, *Fall*, p. 250. For family see Bullard, *Filippo Strozzi*, pp. 16, 35; Stephens, *Fall*, p. 13 n.; Ferrajoli, *Ruolo*, p. 440 n.

BARZIZZA, GASPERINO (c.1360–1431). Sec. 1414, swears 29 Nov. 1417. Von Hofmann, *Forschungen*, ii. 109. See *DBI* (Martellotti) and G. W. Pigman, 'Notes on Barzizza's Correspondence', *Ital.Med.Uman.* 25 (1982), 390–9; R. G. G. Mercer, *The Teaching of Gasparino Barzizza with Special Reference to His Place in Paduan Humanism* (London, 1979).

BEMBO, PIETRO (1470–1547). Sec. dom. 1513. Von Hofmann, *Forschungen*, ii. 124; Frenz, *Kanzlei*, p. 425; *DBI* (C. Dionisotti); C. Dionisotti, 'Appunti sul Bembo', *Ital.Med.Uman.* 8 (1965), 269–91; N. Borsellino and M. Aurigemma, *La letteratura italiana: Storia e testi*, iv/1 (Bari, 1973), 329–58.

BENASSAI, LATINO (d. 1518). Sec. 1 July 1517. Von Hofmann, *Forschungen*, ii. 102–3, 121; Frenz, *Kanzlei*, p. 393; Ferrajoli, *Ruolo*, p. 14.

BENASSAI, VENTURA (d. 1511). Cl. cam. Nov. 1499. *DBI* (De Caro); Von Hofmann, *Forschungen*, i. 232–3, ii. 84; Frenz, *Kanzlei*, p. 452; Brouette, 'Les Clercs "mensiers"' (1973), p. 586; Gottlob, *Aus der Camera apostolica*, p. 276; Clergeac, *La Curie*, p. 270. De Caro missed the main entry for the disgrace of V.B. in J. Burckardi, *Liber Notarum*, ii. 441, 463. He managed the secret accounts of Alexander VI after 1501, Introitus et Exitus 532, fos. 141–53, quoted by Gottlob.

BENCI, FABIANO (1423–81). Cl. cam. 11 Dec. 1465. Patrizi's 'Life' in J. Mabillon, *Iter Italicum*, i. 254. For the correspondence with Tornabuoni and the Medici see Bizzocchi, *Chiesa e potere*, pp. 142–3, where Benci is not identified by name, except as 'il chierico della Camera Apostolica originario di Montepulciano'. For Benci see also *DBI* (Z. Zafarana); S. Benci, *Storia di Montepulciano* (1968 edn.), 79–82. See also Brouette, 'Les Clercs "mensiers"' (1962), 412–13; Reg. Vat. 545, fo. 5 (nomination as chamber clerk, 11 Dec. 1465); *Le vite di Paolo II*, p. 133; Gherardi, *Diario romano*, pp. 81–2; Lightbown, *Donatello and Michelozzo*, pp. 145, 166, 179, 274; Theiner, *Codex Diplomaticus*, iii. 493. Palermino, 'The Roman Academy', p. 148, wonders whether he is the 'Fabianus' of the Roman Academy of that time, but see Bernardo, *Campano*, pp. 88, 168.

BERNARDI, LUDOVICO, of Narni (dates unknown). Sec. 6 May 1455. Von Hofmann, *Forschungen*, ii. 113, and see also ii. 79. See Frenz, 'Eindringen', p. 457; Pitz, *Supplikensignatur*, pp. 170, 173, 245; Sciambra and others, *Il 'liber brevium'*, p. 152; *CPL* x, *passim*; Egidi, *Necrologi*, i. 432.

BERTINI, BARTOLOMEO (d. 1442/3). Sec. 1427. Von Hofmann, *Forschungen*, ii. 81, 111; Frenz, 'Problem', p. 259; Finke, *Acta*, iii. 184–93; Ughelli, *Italia Sacra*, i. 1381. Papal scriptor and familiar, to rule castle of Sassoferrato following disputes among the Atti family 16 Jan. 1421. Reg. Vat. 353, fo. 107. 'Commissarius super reparatione et fabrica basilicarum et ecclesiarum urbis', 1 Apr. 1423. Von Hofmann, *Forschungen*, i. 88 n.

BERTINI, DOMENICO (1417–1506). Sec. under Sixtus IV and Innocent VIII. Frenz, 'Gründung', p. 313; *DBI* (D. Corsi); Frenz, *Kanzlei*, p. 318.

BIONDO, FLAVIO ANTONIO (1392–1463). Sec. 13 Apr. 1436 until death. Von Hofmann, *Forschungen*, ii. 111; *DBI* (R. Fubini); N. Nogara, *Scritti inediti e rari di Biondo Flavio* (Vatican City, 1927); Frenz, 'Eindringen', pp. 441–4; for the treaty of Calcarella see Partner, 'Florence and the Papacy', p. 394.

BIONDO, GASPARE (d. 1493). Sec. 9 June 1463 until death, cl. cam. 12

Dec. 1481 until death. *DBI* (V. Fanelli); Brouette, 'Les Clercs "mensiers"' (1962), 413; id., 'Les Clercs "mensiers"' (1973), 583; Frenz, *Kanzlei*, pp. 220, 338; Lee, *Sixtus IV*, pp. 67–9; D'Amico, *Renaissance Humanism*, p. 71; Setton, *The Papacy and the Levant*, ii. 260.

BIONDO, PAOLO FRANCESCO (1486–1530). Sec. 16 May 1503, resigned under special conditions 1521. Frenz, *Kanzlei*, p. 420; Arch. Cam. I, 1719, fos. 7–12. Also Giusti, *Miscellanea Archivistica*, p. 441 n.; Pastor, *History*, vii. 478; Dorez, *La Cour du Pape Paul III* (Paris, 1932), i. 45, ii. 91.

BOMBACE, PAOLO (1476–1527). Sec. 1526. Frenz, *Kanzlei*, p. 420; *DBI* (E. Mioni).

BONAPARTE, NICCOLÒ, of San Miniato (d. by June 1475). Cl. cam. Jan.-Feb. 1468. Von Hofmann, *Forschungen*, ii. 82, 92; Brouette, 'Les Clercs "mensiers"' (1962), 412; Frenz, *Kanzlei*, p. 411; Reg. Vat. 545, fo. 6 (19 Feb. 1468). He had been papal treasurer of Perugia 1 Oct. 1458–31 July 1464. Fumi, *Inventario e Spoglio*, pp. 71–8. He resigned as clerk of Sacred College on 18 Feb. 1468. Eubel, *Hierarchia*, ii. 39 n. See also Göller, 'Untersuchungen über das Inventar' (1924), 258; Clergeac, *La Curie*, p. 142 n.; Müntz, *Les Arts*, ii. 46–7, 106, ii. 47–8 (dead by 15 June 1475).

BONGNIER, GUILLERMUS (d. 1504). Sec. from 1500. Von Hofmann, *Forschungen*, ii. 118; Frenz, *Kanzlei*, p. 341.

BONIZI, BARTOLOMEO (d. 1445). Cl. cam. 1413, 1417. See Baix, *La Chambre apostolique*, pp. CCCLXXII–CCCLXXIII; Von Hofmann, *Forschungen*, ii. 95–6; Partner, *Papal State*, pp. 105, 141 n.; Cerchiari, *Capellani Papae*, ii. 42, 45; Frenz, 'Problem', p. 259. Master of the hospital of S. Giacomo of Altopascio; see F. Muciaccia, 'I cavalieri dell' Altopascio', *Studi Storici*, 8 (1899), 364, 384–5. Rector of the Patrimony 17 Mar. 1431. Reg. Vat. 381, fo. 5; Guiraud, *L'État pontifical*, p. 88; A. Anzilotti, 'Cenni sulle finanze'. Aud. cam. 3 July 1435. Von Hofmann, *Forschungen*, ii. 95–6; Reg. Vat. 366, fo. 54^v.

BORDINI, CRISTOFORO (d. 1502). Sec. 1487. Von Hofmann, *Forschungen*, ii. 116; Frenz, *Kanzlei*, p. 312; Katterbach, *Sussidi*, ii. 56. See *DBI* xii. 506; Hausmann, 'Armarium 39 Tomus 10', pp. 136, 155, 156, 178; Bizzocchi, *Chiesa e potere*, pp. 231–2; Ughelli, *Italia Sacra*, i. 628; J. Burckardi, *Liber Notarum*, i. 344 (death and will); Gherardi, *Dispacci*, no. CXXXV, 208–9, 261, 323–4, 372, 373–4, 381–3, 386 and *passim*.

BORGHERINI, GIOVANNI (c.1498–after 1528). Sec. 28 Feb. 1520. Von Hofmann, *Forschungen*, ii. 121; Frenz, *Kanzlei*, p. 366; see also Bullard, 'Mercatores Florentini', p. 66.

BOSCOLI, GIOVANNI (d. 1448). Date of appointment as chamber clerk (?supernumerary) unknown. See *DBI* (O. Amore); Piana, 'Nuovi documenti', pp. 561 n., 755; Baix, *La Chambre apostolique*, p. CCCXLVIII, 'n'a fait que passer, puis, vient Antonius de Peruzzis'. For the family see R. de Roover, *Il banco Medici dalle origini al declino* (Florence, 1970), 57, 197; Bizzocchi, *ASI* (1984), 264.

BOTONTI, GIOVANNI (d. 1528). Cl. cam. 14 Dec. 1505. Von Hofmann, *Forschungen*, ii. 93–4; Frenz, *Kanzlei*, p. 365. The clerkship was vacated on Fazio Santori's promotion to cardinal. Reg. Vat. 989, fo. 97. Santori was another clerk from Viterbo. Botonti was formerly the sec. of Card. Antoniotto Pallavicini. See also J. Burckardi, *Liber Notarum*, ii. 10–11; L. Guasco, *L'Archivio storico del comune di Roma* (Rome, 1919), document of 23 Mar. 1519 mentioning G.B. as 'prefetto dell'Annona di Roma'; Signorelli, *Viterbo nella storia della Chiesa*, ii/2 (Viterbo, 1940), 388; Hirst, *Sebastiano del Piombo*, pp. 43–4.

BRACCIOLINI, GIOVANNI BATTISTA (1440–70). Cl. cam. 27 Jan. 1468, Reg. Vat. 545, fo. 5; Von Hofmann, *Forschungen*, ii. 92, 96; Frenz, 'Gründung', p. 313; *DBI* (G. Schizzerotto); Cosenza, *Biographical Dictionary*, iv. 2872.

BRACCIOLINI, POGGIO (1380–1459). Sec. 1415, 1423. Von Hofmann, *Forschungen*, ii. 110; *DBI* (Petrucci); Frenz, 'Problem', p. 262; Frenz, 'Eindringen', pp. 434–8. He was active up to the time he left the Roman court in 1453; see C.-M. de Witte, 'Notes sur les plus anciens régistres de brefs', *BIHBR* 31 (1958), 153–68, at p. 167. See also F. Kranz, 'Between Bruni and Machiavelli: History, Law and Historicism in Poggio Bracciolini', in P. Mack and M. C. Jacob (eds.), *Politics and Culture in Early Modern Europe: Essays in honour of H. G. Koenigsberger* (Cambridge, 1987), 119–51; R. Ristori, 'Contratti di compre di bene' di Poggio Bracciolini: Il Ms. Horne n. 2805 (Florence, 1983); A. Field, *The Origins of the Platonic Academy of Florence* (Princetown, 1988), 38–43, 91–7.

BREDIS, PANTALEONE DE (dates unknown). Cl. cam., 1423. Baix, *La Chambre apostolique*, pp. CCCXCIV–CCCXCV; Von Hofmann, *Forschungen*, i. 112, ii. 91; Partner, *Papal State*, p. 218; F.-C. Uginet, *Le Liber Officialium*, p. 47; Cherubini, *Mandati*, p. 76.

BREUCQUET, JACQUES (d. 1498). Sec. 7 Jan. 1493, resigned 1496. Von Hofmann, *Forschungen*, ii. 83, 117; Frenz, *Kanzlei*, p. 353; *CPL* xvi, xxi, civ. See also J. Burckardi, *Liber Notarum*, ii. 99, 100.

BRIE, GÉRARD (alias du Règne), canon of Narbonne (d. 1426). Cl. cam. 31 Dec. 1417. Baix, *La Chambre apostolique*, p. CCLXXXVI; Fink, 'Die politische Korrespondenz', p. 212; Valois, *La France et le Grand Schisme d'Occident*, pp. 444, 445, 447–9, 458.

BRUGNOLI, FLORAMONTE (d. after 1513). Sec. 25 Feb. 1503, resigned 1505. Von Hofmann, *Forschungen*, ii. 119; Frenz, *Kanzlei*, p. 324. See also Pastor, *History*, v. 541–2, 549, vi. 634–5; N. H. Minnich, 'The Participants at the Fifth Lateran Council', *AHP* 12 (1974), 157–206, at p. 183.

BRUNI, ENRICO (d. 1509). Sec. 1487. Von Hofmann, *Forschungen*, ii. 89–90, 116; Frenz, *Kanzlei*, p. 345; Eubel, *Hierarchia*, ii. 57, 184; J. Burckardi, *Liber Notarum*, i. 244 n., ii. 515; *DBI* (L. Bertoni) where, however, his place of origin is said to be Asti and not Acqui. The congratulatory letter of Giacomo Gherardi (*Dispacci*, pp. 76–7) refers to Bruni's career as clerk of the college. 'Candidatus es iam, et pileatus cum magnis dominis sedes et iudicas' (11 Feb. 1488).

BUFALINI, VENTURA (d. 1504). Cl. cam. 27 Jan. 1495. Von Hofmann, *Forschungen*, ii. 93, where the reference to his being Bishop of Civita Castellana should be amended to Bishop of Città di Castello (see Eubel, *Hierarchia*, ii. 145, 186); Brouette, 'Les Clercs "mensiers"' (1973), 587; Frenz, *Kanzlei*, p. 452. See also the biography of the father, Niccolò Bufalini, in *DBI* (C. Gennaro). The family were also called 'Manni': Frenz, *Kanzlei*, p. 412, no. 1710, misses the identity of Manni with Bufalini.

BUONCONTI, GUINIFORTE (GIULIO FORTE) (d. 21 Aug. 1462). Cl. cam. 28 Sept. 1446; taking the place of Ludovico de Garsiis, Arch. Cam. I, vol. 1713, fo. 22b. See also Kraus, 'Die Sekretäre', pp. 44, 80; Hausmann, 'Campano', p. 466; E. Meuthen, *Die letzten Jahre des Nikolaus von Kues: Biographische Untersuchungen nach neuen Quellen* (Cologne and Opladen, 1958), 37, 162, 163, 242; Frenz, 'Eindringen', p. 395; Rius Serra, *Regesto iberico*, i. 445; Cherubini, *Mandati*, p. 79. He was made treasurer, Siena 5 Mar. 1460 (on appointment of Niccolò Forteguerri as cardinal). Reg. Vat. 515, fos. 211b, 228b–229. Died at Pienza 21 Aug. 1462. Div. Cam. 29, fos. 312b–314b. Member of a well-known Pisan family, brother of Bartolomeo.

BUONDELMONTE, ANDREA (1465–1542). Sec. 10 Dec. 1519, resigned 1532. Von Hofmann, *Forschungen*, ii. 121, 190, 191; Frenz, *Kanzlei*, p. 279; *DBI* (De Caro).

BUSSETTO, GIOVANNI ANTONIO (dates and provenance unknown). Cl. cam. (supranum.?), 24 Mar. 1477, resigned Jan. 1478. Von Hofmann, *Forschungen*, ii. 92.

BUSSI, GIOVANNI ANDREA (1417–75). Sec. 1 Jan. 1456 (supranum.) and 1472. Frenz, *Kanzlei*, p. 366. See E. Meuthen, 'Briefe des Aleriensis an die Sforza', *Röm.Quart.* 59 (1964), 88–99; *DBI* (M. Miglio); D'Amico, *Renaissance Humanism*, p. 14; Lee, *Sixtus IV*, pp. 105–10; Stinger, *Renaissance in Rome*, p. 284; *Prefazioni alle edizioni di Swenheym e Pannartz prototipografi romani*, ed. M. Miglio (Milan, 1978).

CAETANI, JACOPO (d. 1500). Sec. 1487, removed 1500. Von Hofmann, *Forschungen*, ii. 117; Frenz, *Kanzlei*, p. 354; see also J. Burckardi, *Liber Notarum*, i. 399.

CALCAGNI, ALESSANDRO (dates unknown). Sec. 31 Jan. 1515, resigned after 1528. Von Hofmann, *Forschungen*, ii. 121; Frenz, *Kanzlei*, p. 273.

CALDERINI, DOMIZIO (1446–78). Sec. 1471, particip. 17 June 1474. Von Hofmann, *Forschungen*, ii. 116; Frenz, *Kanzlei*, p. 316; *DBI* (Perosa); D. Coppini, 'Il commento a Properzio di Domizio Calderini', *Annali della Scuola Normale Superiore di Pisa* (Classe di lettere e filosofia, 3rd ser. 9/3; 1979), 1119–73; R. Weiss, 'In memoriam Domitii Calderini', *Ital.Med.Uman.* 3 (1960), 309–21; D'Amico, *Renaissance Humanism*, p. 255.

CALVI, JACOPO (d. after ?1450). Cl. cam. by 1413, and 27 Nov. 1417. Baix, *La Chambre apostolique*, pp. CCCLXXVI–CCCLXXVII; Partner, *Papal State*, p. 218. See *DBI* (G. Bartolini) which says that Calvi 'nacque presumilbilmente a Roma'; but Guasti, 'Gli avanzi', p. 41, says he came from Prato. See also Frenz, 'Problem', p. 272.

CAMBRIN, ROBERT (dates unknown). Cl. cam. 7 Apr. 1449, resigned 3 Jan. 1468. Reg. Vat. 435, fo. 3b; Von Hofmann, *Forschungen*, ii. 92; Pitz, *Supplikensignatur*, p. 263; Bååth, *Diplomatarium Svecanum*, ii. 391–3; *CPL* ix. 391–2.

CANDIDI, GIOVANNI (dates and provenance unknown). Mentioned as sec. 20 Mar. 1477. Von Hofmann, *Forschungen*, ii. 116; Frenz, *Kanzlei*, p. 367.

CAOURSON, GUILLAUME, of Arras (dates unknown). Sec. (supranum.?) 1485. Frenz, *Kanzlei*, p. 341.

CAPODIFERRO, BATTISTA EVANGELISTA (d. 1527). Cl. cam. 12 July 1477 (supranum.). See article on his brother, Evangelista, *DBI* (Ballistreri); Von Hofmann, *Forschungen*, ii. 92–3.

CAPODILISTA, ANTONIO (1420–89). Cl. cam. (supranum.) 26 Nov. 1450 and 29 Dec. 1450. Reg. Vat. 435, fo. 11^v. He swore the oath in the house of the chamberlain, Ludovico of Treviso, whose dependant he was, as is emphasized in *DBI* (O. Ruffino).

CAPOGRASSI, PAOLO, of Sulmona (dates unknown). Cl. cam. by 1419. Baix, *La Chambre apostolique*, pp. CCCLXXV–CCCLXXVI; Von Hofmann, *Forschungen*, ii. 180; *CPL* vi. 171, 182, 186; Partner, *Papal State*, pp. 67 n., 177 n., 213–14, 217; Piana, 'Nuovi documenti', index. Vice-regent of March of Ancona 11 Sept. 1410. Reg. Vat. 342, fos. 44b–45b. Commission to reform Subiaco 23 Nov. 1419. Reg. Vat. 348, fo. 188b. Treasurer of Bologna 25 Aug. 1420, Reg. Vat. 349, fo. 79b; sworn 25 Aug. 1419, Arm. 34, vol. 4, fo. 156; revoked 3 Dec. 1420, Reg. Vat. 353, fo. 73b. Treasurer of Perugia, Duchy of Spoleto, etc. 25 July 1424. Reg. Vat. 350, fo. 41. Agreement with castrum of Bascita 1 Dec. 1424. Reg. Vat. 355, fo. 101.

CAPRANICA, DOMENICO (1) (1400–58). Cl. cam. 3 Feb. 1423, Sec. 1424. *DBI* (A. A. Strnad). See also Partner, *Papal State*, p. 88 n.; Frenz, 'Eindringen', pp. 433–4; student in Bologna, Piana, 'Nuovi documenti', pp. 580–1. For the family's church patronage in the March, U. Camelli, 'Il monastero'. Tomb, Davies, *Renascence*, pp. 267–9.

CAPRANICA, DOMENICO (2) (d. 1500). Cl. cam. 19 Nov. 1493. Von Hofmann, *Forschungen*, ii. 93; Brouette, 'Les Clercs "mensiers"' (1973), 585. See also Burckardi, *Liber Notarum*, ii. 10.

CAPRANICA, NICCOLÒ (d. before 1517). Sec. 1 Nov. 1495. Von Hofmann, *Forschungen*, ii. 118; Frenz, *Kanzlei*, p. 412. See also Burckardi, *Liber Notarum*, ii. 358; Egidi, *Necrologi*, ii. 506.

CAPRANICA, PAOLO (d. 1429). Sec. by Jan. 1418. Von Hofmann, *Forschungen*, ii. 81, 110; Frenz, 'Eindringen', p. 430 (quoting impossible death date from Von Ottenthal); id., 'Problem', p. 262; Partner, *Papal State*, p. 88 n.; id., 'Camera Papae', pp. 66–7 (gives death as 1428); Lombardo, *Camera Urbis*, p. 115. Tomb, Davies, *Renascence*, p. 239 (with inaccuracies about career and date of death).

Caracciolo, Corrado, see Stagna, Corrado.

CARACCIOLO, MARINO (1469–1538). Sec. 9 Dec. 1496, resigned 1531. Von Hofmann, *Forschungen*, ii. 118; Frenz, *Kanzlei*, p. 404; see *DBI* (De Caro).

CARDELLI, JACOPO (1473–1528/30). Sec. 24 Apr. 1504 to death. Von Hofmann, *Forschungen*, ii. 119; Frenz, *Kanzlei*, p. 354. See also I. Robertson, 'The *Signoria* of Girolamo Riario in Imola', *Historical Studies*, 15 (1971), 88–117, at p. 106; Burckardi, *Liber Notarum*, ii. 36–7; D. Tesoroni, *Il Palazzo di Firenze e l'eredità di Balduino del Monte, fratello del papa Giulio III* (Rome, 1889).

CARDONI, ZACHARIAS (dates and provenance unknown). Sec. 1519. Von Hofmann, *Forschungen*, ii. 121; Frenz, *Kanzlei*, p. 455.

CARROZ, JUAN (dates unknown). Sec. 1504–18. Frenz, *Kanzlei*, p. 368.

CASALI, CATALANO (1453–1501). Sec. 25 Oct. 1493, resigned 1495. Von Hofmann, *Forschungen*, ii. 117; Frenz, *Kanzlei*, p. 310; Frenz, 'Gründung', p. 326; Burckardi, *Liber Notarum*, ii. 11.

CASTELLESI, ADRIANO (1461–1521). Cl. cam. 2 Dec. 1494; sec. 1 Sept. 1495. Von Hofmann, *Forschungen*, ii. 89, 124; Brouette, 'Les Clercs "mensiers"' (1973), 586; Frenz, *Kanzlei*, p. 344; *CPL* xiv. 54, 55. See *DBI* (G. Fragnito), and D'Amico, *Renaissance Humanism*, *passim*.

CASTEL LOTARIO, BONIFACIO (d. 1504). Cl. cam. 7 June 1503, sec. 23 June 1494. Von Hofmann, *Forschungen*, ii. 78, 93, 117, 173; Frenz, *Kanzlei*, p. 307; see also Burckardi, *Liber Notarum*, ii. 454.

CASTEL LOTARIO, SINOLFO (d. 1503). Cl. cam. 18 Sept. 1483, sec. 1487–1503. Von Hofmann, *Forschungen*, ii. 93, 117, 215; Eubel, *Hierarchia*, ii. 54, 147; Brouette, 'Les Clercs "mensiers"' (1962), 413, and (1973), 582; Frenz, *Kanzlei*, p. 445; id., 'Gründung', p. 310; Tangl, *Kanzleiordnungen*, pp. 183–8; *CPL* xii. 257 ff. See also Burckardi, *Liber Notarum*, i. 28; Pontani, *Diario romano*, pp. 32–3; Infessura, *Diario*, pp. 125–6; Gherardi, *Diario*, p. 510; id., *Dispacci*, *passim*.

CASTIGLIONE, FRANCESCO (d. 1517). Sec. 1503 to death. Frenz, *Kanzlei*, p. 327; Burckardi, *Liber Notarum*, ii. 36; Von Hofmann, *Forschungen*, ii. 119.

CASTIGLIONE, RINUCCIO (D'AREZZO) (1395–1457). Sec. Aug. 1455. Sabbadini's entry in *Enciclopedia Italiana*; id., 'Bricciole umanistiche', *GSLI* 47 (1906), 25–40; D. P. Lockwood, 'De R. Aretino Graecarum Litterarum Interprete', *Harvard Studies in Classical Philology*, 24 (1913), 51–109; Cosenza, *Biographical Dictionary*, pp. 3056–60; Von Hofmann, *Forschungen*, ii. 79, 114; Pitz, *Supplikensignatur*, pp. 76, 112, 357; *CPL* x. 215 f., 481, and *passim* in vol. xi.

CATALAN, JUAN (dates unknown). Sec. 7 July 1456, sworn 26 Sept. 1457. Von Hofmann, *Forschungen*, ii. 114; Pitz, *Supplikensignatur*, pp. 73, 173, 242; Sciambra, *Il 'liber brevium'*, pp. 74, 78, 105.

CATTANEO, BERNARDO (d. 1517). Cl. cam. 1517, but the appointment was declared invalid. Von Hofmann, *Forschungen*, ii. 94; Frenz, *Kanzlei*, p. 302.

CATTANEO, BONIFACIO (d. 1523). Cl. cam. 8 Aug. 1517. Von Hofmann, *Forschungen*, ii. 94; Frenz, *Kanzlei*, p. 306; see also Von Hofmann, *Forschungen*, ii. 97.

CAUDIACO, JACQUES, of Uzès (dates unknown). Cl. cam. 8 July 1431. Arch. Cam. I, vol. 1712, fo. 16b.

CELADONI, ALESSIO (1451–1517). Sec. 4 Oct. 1500. Von Hofmann, *Forschungen*, ii. 118; Frenz, *Kanzlei*, p. 275. *DBI* (H. J. Kissling); A. A. Strnad, 'Francesco Todeschini-Piccolomini: Politik und Mäzenatentum im Quattrocento', *Röm.Hist.Mitt.* 8–9 (1964/6), 387; Setton, *The Papacy and the Levant*, ii. 522–3 n.; Stinger, *Renaissance in Rome*, pp. 92–3; J. M. McManamon, 'The Ideal Renaissance Pope: Funeral Oratory at the Papal Court', *AHP* 14 (1976), 9–70, at pp. 61–70.

Celidonio, Alessio, see Celadoni, Alessio.

CENTELLES, GUILLELMO RAIMONDO (dates unknown). Sec. 8 Sept. 1495, resigned 1499. Von Hofmann, *Forschungen*, ii. 118; Frenz, *Kanzlei*, p. 342; Burckardi, *Liber Notarum*, ii. 100–1; Marini, i. 230–1. See also Pastor, *History*, vi. 56; for the family see E. Pontieri, *La Calabria a metà del Sec. XV e la rivolta di A. Centelles* (Naples, 1963), esp. pp. 170–3.

CENTORI, GIOVANNI ANTONIO (dates unknown). Sec. 1508–11, renewed 1512, resigned 1529. Von Hofmann, *Forschungen*, ii. 121; Frenz, *Kanzlei*, p. 368.

CESARINI, ALESSANDRO (d. 1542). Sec. 6 Sept. 1512, cardinal 1517. Von Hofmann, *Forschungen*, ii. 121; Frenz, *Kanzlei*, p. 273. See also *DBI* (F. Petrucci), and McClung Hallman, *Italian Cardinals*, pp. 56–7, 121.

CESARINI, GIULIANO (1465–1510). Sec. 1487, promoted to cardinal 1493. Von Hofmann, *Forschungen*, ii. 117, 195; Frenz, *Kanzlei*, p. 391; Burckardi, *Liber Notarum*, i. 462; Ciacconius, *Vitae*, iii. 181.

CESI, ANGELO (1450–1528). Sec. 1503, resigned 1511. McClung Hallman, *Italian Cardinals*, pp. 133, 135; Von Hofmann, *Forschungen*, ii. 119; Frenz, *Kanzlei*, p. 282; Burckardi, *Liber Notarum*, i. 329 n.; Ferrajoli, *Ruolo*, pp. 469, 471; Pastor, *History*, viii. 479; Ubaldini, *Vita di Colocci*, p. 23. He came from Narni, and was married to the niece of the well-known mercenary, Gattamelata of Narni.

CESI, CLEMENTE (d. after 1521). Sec. 30 Jan. 1511, resigned 1521. Von Hofmann, *Forschungen*, ii. 120; Frenz, *Kanzlei*, p. 311.

CESI, OTTAVIO (d. c.1534). Cl. cam. 26 Oct. 1524. Lunt, *Papal Revenues*, ii. 537. See also Frenz, *Kanzlei*, p. 417; Eubel, *Hierarchia*, iii. 163.

CESI, PAOLO EMILIO (1481–1537). Sec. 25 Mar. 1501, resigned 1517. Von

Hofmann, *Forschungen*, ii. 75, 111–19; Frenz, *Kanzlei*, p. 421; Katterbach, *Sussidi*, ii. 67, 77; Ciacconius, *Vitae*, iii. 301–2.

CEVA, RAFFAELO (d. 1518). Sec. 1 Sept. 1495, resigned 1501, reappointed 1502, resigned 1506. Von Hofmann, *Forschungen*, ii. 117–18; Frenz, *Kanzlei*, p. 437; CPL xvi, p. ciii. See also Burckardi, *Liber Notarum*, i. 360.

CHIGI, AGOSTINO (1516–21). Sec. 17 July 1521. Von Hofmann, *Forschungen*, ii. 65, 122; Frenz, *Kanzlei*, p. 273.

CHIGI, ANGELO (d. 1504). Sec. 1503. Von Hofmann, *Forschungen*, ii. 119; Frenz, *Kanzlei*, p. 282.

CHIGI, ALESSANDRO (1516–21). Sec. 1521. Von Hofmann, *Forschungen*, ii. 65, 122; Frenz, *Kanzlei*, p. 273.

CIBO, GIULIANO (d. 1536). Sec. 1504, 1510–28. Von Hofmann, *Forschungen*, ii. 120; Frenz, *Kanzlei*, p. 391; Eubel, *Hierarchia*, iii. 98.

CIBO, LORENZO DE'MARI (d. 1503). Sec. 1487, resigned 1489 on promotion to cardinal. Von Hofmann, *Forschungen*, ii. 116; Frenz, *Kanzlei*, p. 394. See also *DBI* (F. Petrucci).

CIGALA, BATTISTA (dates unknown). Sec. 1418, sworn 13 Jan. 1419. Von Hofmann, *Forschungen*, ii. 110.

CLAMANGES, NICHOLAS (1355–1437). Sec. Apr. 1418. Von Hofmann, *Forschungen*, ii. 110. See also *Dictionnaire de biographie française*, viii. 1347; P. Santoni, 'Les Lettres de Nicolas de Clamanges à Gérard Machet', *Mélanges*, 99 (1987), pt. 2, 793–823; M. Harvey, 'Martin V and Henry V', *AHP* 24 (1986), 49–70, at p. 56 n. Cedes scriptor's office to Johannes de Templis, 30 Dec. 1418, Baix, *La Chambre apostolique*, p. CCCXCV.

Clementi, Petrus, see *Climent, Pedro*.

CLERC, PIERRE, of Cambrai (dates unknown). Cl. cam. (supranum.) 6 May 1447. Reg. Vat. 435, fo. 2.

CLIMENT, PEDRO (d. before 18 Dec. 1455). Cl. cam. sworn 4 July 1455 and admitted 12 July 1455. Reg. Vat. 467, fo. 3; Rius Serra, *Regesto iberico*, pp. 189, 219, 279, 316, 422, 483; Pitz, *Supplikensignatur*, pp. 75–6, 213; Gottlob, *Aus der Camera apostolica*, p. 111; E. Göller, 'Inventar des Finanzarchivs der Renaissancepäpste', *Miscellanea E. Ehrle* (Vatican City, 1924), v. 255. Magister artium et medicine. Rius Serra, 'Catalanes y Aragones', p. 243.

COLLI, AGOSTINO (d. 1495). Sec. 8 Aug. 1489. Von Hofmann, *Forschungen*, ii. 117; Frenz, *Kanzlei*, p. 291. See also Piana, *Il 'liber secretus'*, 400 n.

COLOCCI, ANGELO (1474–1549). Sec. 1511, resigned 1521. Ubaldini, *Vita di Mons. A. Colocci* (1969); Fanelli, *Ricerche su Angelo Colocci* (1979); *Atti del Convegno di Studi su Angelo Colocci. Jesi, 13–14 sett. 1969* (Iesi, 1972); *DBI* (unsigned); Frenz, *Kanzlei*, p. 282. Frenz rightly puts a question mark against the appointment of Colocci as master of the registry in the papal chancery in 1492, when he was 18. This was one of the main chancery posts, and a very technical one; it is most unlikely that Colocci held such a post at that age, and if he had his biographer, Ubaldini, would have noted it. See Fuller, in *CPL* xvi, p. civ.

COLONNA, GASPARE (d. 1435). Cl. cam. 6 Sept. 1425. See *DBI* (Partner).

CONTI, ANDREA, of Venice (d. 1465). Cl. cam. 14 Apr. 1455. Reg. Vat. 467, fo. 2; Von Hofmann, *Forschungen*, ii. 96.

CONTI, GIOVANNI FRANCESCO (1477–1534). Sec. 1 Mar. 1511. Von Hofmann, *Forschungen*, ii. 120, 195; Frenz, *Kanzlei*, p. 370. See also biography of father, Sigismondo, in *DBI*.

CONTI, IERONIMO (d. 1501). Sec. 1487, resigned 1489. Von Hofmann, *Forschungen*, ii. 116; Frenz, *Kanzlei*, p. 347. See also Burckardi, *Liber Notarum*, i. 20, 21, 215; Eubel, *Hierarchia*, ii. 206.

CONTI, NICCOLÒ (1462–95). Sec. 23 Dec. 1490. Von Hofmann, *Forschungen*, ii. 117; Frenz, *Kanzlei*, p. 413; Katterbach, *Sussidi*, ii. 56; Eubel, *Hierarchia*, ii. 149.

CONTI, PIETRO (dates unknown). Arch. Cam. I, vol. 1713, fo. 13. Nomination of Pietro Conti as cl. cam. 30 Apr. 1439. Reg. Vat. 467, fo. 2a. Reception of Andrea Conti as cl. cam.: 'prefati domini clerici acceptaverunt eum ad osculum pacis et ad sedem seu stallum', 14 Apr. 1455. Von Hofmann, *Forschungen*, ii. 96.

CONTI, SIGISMONDO (1432–1512). Sec. 1481. *DBI* (R. Ricciardi); D'Amico, *Renaissance Humanism*, pp. 31–3; Frenz, *Kanzlei*, p. 443; *CPL* xvi, p. ciii; Von Hofmann, *Forschungen*, ii. 116, 124. Resigned his *locus* in 1502. When he attempted to take up the *locus* of Daniele San Sebastiano in 1504, at the same time as becoming domestic secretary of Julius II, there was a legal wrangle. For Conti's son (1477–1534), see *DBI* and also Von Hofmann, *Forschungen*, ii. 120, 195; Frenz, *Kanzlei*, p. 370.

COPIS, JOHANNES (1438–1527). Cl. cam. 6 Aug. 1526. Von Hofmann, *Forschungen*, ii. 78; Frenz, *Kanzlei*, p. 370; Lunt, *Papal Revenues*, ii. 537; Frenz, 'Gründung', p. 328; Katterbach, *Sussidi*, i. 30, 89; Pastor, *History*, ix. 406; Ferrajoli, *Ruolo*, p. 550.

COPPINI, FRANCESCO (d. 1463). Cl. cam. (supranum.) 3 Aug. 1448. Reg. Vat. 435, fo. 3; Von Hofmann, *Forschungen*, ii. 177. See *DBI* (A. I. Galletti); Cosenza, *Biographical Dictionary*, v. 144; Katterbach, *Sussidi*, ii. 33–4; E. Peverada, 'Appunti di Storia Ferrarese del Quattrocento', *Quaderni del Giornale Filologico Ferrarese*, 3 (1982), 5–27, at p. 12 (includes note of his ordination as deacon, 1446); Pitz, *Supplikensignatur*, p. 262. Influence on Gilforte de Buonconti, I. Aliotti, *Epistolae et Opuscula* (Arezzo, 1769), i. 225–6, 'apud Julium Fortem Pisanum clericum c.a. sciote te id posse, quod velis' (7 May 1448). See also A. Gottlob, 'Der Nuntius Franz Coppini', *Deutsche Zeitschrift für Geschichtswissenschaft*, 4 (1890), 75–111; C. Head, 'Pope Pius II and the Wars of the Roses', *AHP* 8 (1970), 149–73; I. Schuster, *La basilica e il monastero di S. Paolo fuori le mura* (Turin, 1934), 210.

CORNO, GALEAZZO (dates unknown). Cl. cam. (supranum.) 3 Nov. 1468. Von Hofmann, *Forschungen*, ii. 92. See also Zonta and Brotto, *Acta Graduum*, p. 226.

CORRER, GIOVANNI (dates unknown). Sec. 8 June 1503. Von Hofmann, *Forschungen*, ii. 118; Frenz, *Kanzlei*, p. 370.

CORTESI, PAOLO (1465–1510). Sec. 7 Apr. 1498. Von Hofmann, *Forschungen*, ii. 118. Resigned 8 July 1503. Frenz, *Kanzlei*, p. 421; D'Amico, *Renaissance Humanism*, pp. 76–81 and *passim*; K. Weill-Garris and J. D'Amico, 'The Renaissance Cardinal's Ideal Palace: A Chapter from Cortesi's *De Cardinalatu*', in H. A. Milton (ed.), *Studies in Italian Art and Architecture 15th through 18th Centuries* (Rome, 1980), 45–123; *DBI* (R. Ricciardi); D. Cantimori, 'Questioncine sulle opere progettate di Paolo Cortesi', *Studi in onore di Tammaro de Marinis*, i (Verona and Vatican City, 1964), 273–80; C. Dionisotti, 'Chierici e laici nella letteratura italiana del primo Cinquecento', *Atti del convegno di storia della chiesa in Italia: Bologna 2-6 sett. 1958* (Padua, 1960), 178–81.

COSIDA, GIOVANNI (dates unknown). Sec. sworn 20 Sept. 1455 (sec. dom.?). Von Hofmann, *Forschungen*, ii. 114, and see ii. 20, 123; also Rius Serra, *Regesto iberico*, p. 334. See also Pitz, *Supplikensignatur*, pp. 111, 163, 293-7; Frenz, 'Eindringen', p. 456; *CPL* xi. 186 n.

COSTA, GEORGES (d. 1501). Sec. 5 May 1501. Von Hofmann, *Forschungen*, ii. 118; Frenz, *Kanzlei*, p. 339; Burckardi, *Liber Notarum*, ii. 299; Eubel, *Hierarchia*, ii. 123.

COTIN, PIERRE, dean of St. Pierre d'Avignon (d. 1445). Cl. cam. 1417–25. Baix, *La Chambre apostolique*, pp. CCCLXXIII–CCCLXXIV; Eubel, *Hierarchia*, ii. 215.

CRIVELLI, LEODRISIO (1413–c.1488). Sec. 17 Oct. 1458. Von Hofmann, *Forschungen*, ii. 115. *DBI* (F. Petrucci); Kraus, 'Die Sekretäre', p. 34; Tangl, *Kanzleiordnungen*, p. 185; *De Expeditione Pii Papae II adversus Turcos*, ed. G. C. Zimolo (Muratori, RRIISS xxiii/5); L. F. Smith, 'Lodrisio Crivelli and Aeneas Sylvius'; G. Ianziti, *Humanistic Historiography under the Sforzas: Politics and Propaganda in Fifteenth-Century Milan* (Oxford, 1988), 103–26; Frenz, 'Gründung', p. 308.

CUGNA, ANTONIO (CUNNA, ACHUNA) (d. ?1527). Sec. 27 July 1499. Von Hofmann, *Forschungen*, ii. 118; Frenz, *Kanzlei*, p. 285; Eubel, *Hierarchia*, iii. 339; Burckardi, *Liber Notarum*, i. 436, ii. 150.

DATI, LEONARDO (1408–72). Expect. of sec. place 10 Apr. 1455 and again 7 May 1456, sec. dom. 1464. Von Hofmann, *Forschungen*, ii. 113, 123; *DBI* (R. Ristori); Flamini, 'Leonardo di Pietro Dati'; Frenz, *Kanzlei*, p. 397; id., 'Eindringen', pp. 466-7; Pitz, *Supplikensignatur*, p. 111; Kraus, 'Die Sekretäre', pp. 30 (where he is called 'Lorenzo'), 31; G. Gualdo, 'Il "liber brevium"', pp. 311 ff. Tacchi Venturi, 'La pietra tombale di Leonardo Dati'; Lefèvre, 'Fiorentini a Roma'; Berrigan, 'Leonardo Dati'; Gorni, 'Storia del Certame Coronario'; D'Amico, *Renaissance Humanism*, p. 33; Martines, *Lawyers and Statecraft*, pp. 340-1 (with some errors). On 21 Nov. 1470 Lorenzo de' Medici described Dati as 'sempre capitale inimico a la caxa di Medici', *Lettere*, i. 227-9. He had, however, had Giovanni di Cosimo's patronage in 1445 (Ristori). See also *CPL* xi, *passim*; Gaspare da Verona, *Vita di Paolo II*, in *Vite di Paolo II*, p. 23. Dati served in the households, first of Card. Giordano Orsini (1433-9), then of Card. Francesco Condulmer (1439-42), then of Card. Alfonso Borgia (1444-55).

DE ARCHIDIACONIS, GIOVANNI BATTISTA (dates unknown). Sec. sworn 4 Oct. 1455. Von Hofmann, *Forschungen*, ii. 114; Pitz, *Supplikensignatur*, p. 173; Kraus, 'Die Sekretäre', p. 32; *CPL* xi. 122 and *passim*.

DECEMBRIO, PIETRO CANDIDO (1390-1467). Sec. 13 Oct. 1458. *DBI* (P. Viti); Von Hofmann, *Forschungen*, ii. 113; Pitz, *Supplikensignatur*, p. 112; Kraus, 'Die Sekretäre', p. 34; *CPL* x, p. xi.

DE CUPIS, GIOVANNI DOMENICO (1493-1553). Sec. 1503, 2nd sec. place 1517, resigned 1517 on promotion to cardinal. *DBI* (F. Petrucci); Von Hofmann, *Forschungen*, ii. 119-20; Frenz, *Kanzlei*, p. 371; Ferrajoli, *Ruolo*, p. 226 n.; McClung Hallman, *Italian Cardinals*, pp. 25, 125-6.

DELLANTE, BARTOLOMEO (d. 1436?). Cl. cam. 1414, and from Nov. 1417. Baix, *La Chambre apostolique*, pp. CCCLXXVII-CCCLXXVIII; Von Hofmann, *Forschungen*, ii. 91; Partner, *Papal State*, pp. 67, 69, 148, 217; Kühne, *Repertorium Germanicum*, iii. 28*-29*. Regent of aud. cam. 31 July 1424. Div. Cam. 8, fo. 198. Commissioned to hear lawsuit against dom. de Carraria 6 Mar. 1426. Div. Cam. 3, fo. 180. Treasurer of Patrimony 8 July 1426. Reg. Vat. 350, fo. 258b. Doganerius, Partner, 119 n., and see also J. C. Maire Vigeur, *Les Pâturages de l'église*, p. 11. Rector of Patrimony 6 Mar. 1427. Div. Cam. 11, fo. 61b.

DELLA VALLE, ANDREA (1464-1534). Sec. 1506. Von Hofmann, *Forschungen*, ii. 74-5, 120; Frenz, *Kanzlei*, p. 281. See Eubel, *Hierarchia*, ii. 155; Burckardi, *Liber Notarum*, ii. 358, 485.

De Valle, Nicholas, see *Lavelle, Nicholas*.

DE MAGISTRIS, GIOVANNI LAZARO (dates unknown). Sec. 10 Apr. 1520. Von Hofmann, *Forschungen*, ii. 121-2; Frenz, *Kanzlei*, p. 378; Pastor, *History*, viii. 92-4 n.

Du Règne, Gérard, see *Brie, Gérard*.

DUT, JOHANNES (dates unknown). Sec. 1508. Frenz, *Kanzlei*, p. 372.

EBU, (MARIANO) GIOVANNI (d. 1496). Sec. 1487. Von Hofmann, *Forschungen*, ii. 116; Frenz, *Kanzlei*, p. 389; Eubel, *Hierarchia*, ii. 155, 254; Burckardi, *Liber Notarum*, i. 361, 649.

ENCKENVOIRT, WILHELM (1464-1534). Cl. cam. 17 Aug. 1523. Von Hofmann, *Forschungen*, ii. 97, 123; Frenz, *Kanzlei*, p. 454; Pastor, *History*, ix. 79-80 and *passim*.

Errici, Gian Battista, see *Henricis, Gian Battista de*.

FARA, GASPARE (dates unknown). Sec. 1457. Von Hofmann, *Forschungen*, ii. 115.

FARNESE, ALESSANDRO (1468–1549). Sec. 16 Aug. 1490. Von Hofmann, *Forschungen*, ii. 88–9; Frenz, *Kanzlei*, p. 274.

FARNESE, PAOLO PIETRO (d. 1500). Sec. 1487. Von Hofmann, *Forschungen*, ii. 117; Frenz, *Kanzlei*, p. 420.

FATATI, ANTONIO (d. 1463). Cl. cam. 21 Apr. 1449. Reg. Vat. 435, fo. 9. M. Natalucci, 'Mostra di documenti e cimeli riguardante il papa Pio II e il vescovo Fatati', *AMSM*, 8th ser. 4 (1964/5), 177–84. He was treasurer-general of the March of Ancona, 1449–53. Further, E. Lodolini, 'I libri di conti', article in *Dictionnaire d'histoire et de géographie ecclésiastiques*, iii (Paris, 1924), 770–2.

FAYDIT, GÉRARD (d. in 1433–9). Cl. cam. 20 Dec. 1417. Baix, *La Chambre apostolique*, pp. CCCLXXXVII–CCCLXXXVIII; Von Hofmann, *Forschungen*, ii. 72; Katterbach, *Sussidi*, ii. 1; Fink, 'Politische Korrespondenz', p. 229; H. Bresslau, *Handbuch*, pp. 264–5; Miller, 'Participation', p. 402. Lends 100 florins to chamber, 11 July 1421, Introitus et Exitus 379, fo. 44.

FEO, JACOPO (d. 1467). Cl. cam. (supranum.) 14 Aug. 1450, (particip., in the absence of another cl. cam. particip.) 27 Oct. 1451. Reg. Vat. 435, fo. 10ᵛ; Div. Cam. 26, fo. 209. Piana, *Il 'liber secretus'*, p. 66; id., *Nuove ricerche*, p. 288; id., 'Nuovi documenti', pp. 920, 922. See also Frenz, 'Eindringen', p. 395 and plate V (for his 'humanist' script). He was Governor-General of the Patrimony, 13 Apr.–13 Sept. 1460, Arch. Cam. I, busta 9, vol. 32, fo. 175ᵛ; Governor of Perugia, 1463–4, Fumi, *Inventario e spoglio*, p. 77; Governor of Todi 1466, *Vite di Paolo II*, p. 135 n. and see p. 162 n.; and finally Governor of Cesena, Robertson, 'Return of Cesena', p. 160 and id. in *Storia di Cesena*, ii/2 (Rimini, 1985), 91.

FERRARI, GIOVANNI BATTISTA (1445–1502). Sec. 26 Nov. 1496, Von Hofmann, *Forschungen*, ii. 74, 101, 118. Ferrari paid 2,500 ducats for the office. See also Célier, *Les Dataires*, pp. 59–66, 139–40; Frenz, *Kanzlei*, p. 372; CPL xiii 2. 845; Schulte, *Die Fugger*, i. 262; Katterbach, *Sussidi*, ii. 62; Ferrari Moreni, 'Vita'; CPL xvi, pp. ci–cii. For his death see Burckardi, *Liber Notarum*, ii. 332.

FERRER, MICHAEL (dates unknown). Sec. 20 Apr. 1455. Von Hofmann, *Forschungen*, ii. 20, 70, 113–14, 123; Vespasiano da Bisticci, *Vite di uomini illustri*, pp. 360–1; Pitz, *Supplikensignatur*, pp. 74–5, 111, 173, 205; CPL xi. 8, 152, 165; Frenz, 'Eindringen', pp. 457–9; Kraus, 'Die Sekretäre', p. 32.

FERRERI, ANTONIO (d. 1508). Sec. 4 Jan. 1502 until promoted to cardinal in 1505. Von Hofmann, *Forschungen*, ii. 118; Frenz, *Kanzlei*, p. 285. See also Pastor, *History*, v. 304, 644; Burckardi, *Liber Notarum*, ii. 444.

FERRIZ, PEDRO (1415–78). Cl. cam. 20 Apr. 1455. Von Hofmann, *Forschungen*, i. 95–6, ii. 28, 100, 132, 180, 189; Rius Serra, *Regesto iberico*, i. 53; Eubel, *Hierarchia*, ii. 18, 276; Ciacconius, *Vitae*, iii. 57; Katterbach, *Sussidi*, ii. 38; Göller, 'Untersuchungen' (1924), 246, 267; *Vite di Paolo II*, pp. 52, 213; *Acta Pontifica Danica*, iii. 2324; K. Walsh, 'Päpstliche Kurie und Reformideologie', *AHP* 20 (1982), 145–6; J. W.

O'Malley, *Praise and Blame in Renaissance Rome* (Durham, NC, 1979), 169; Davies, *Renascence*, pp. 283–4; Forcella, *Iscrizioni*, i. 421.

FIESCHI, LORENZO (1465–1519). Sec. 1 May 1511, resigned 1512. Von Hofmann, *Forschungen*, ii. 121; Frenz, *Kanzlei*, p. 394. See also Re, Mons. *Governatore*, p. 73; Pastor, *History*, vi. 304.

FILELFO, FRANCESCO (1398–1481). Sec. 1 Sept. 1453. G. Gualdo, 'Francesco Filelfo'; Kraus, 'Die Sekretäre', p. 35 n.; R. G. Adam, *Francesco Filelfo at the Court of Milan (1439–1481)* (Tübingen, 1987).

FIOCCHI, ANDREA (1401–52). Sec. 1431. Von Hofmann, *Forschungen*, ii. 111; Mercati, *Ultimi contributi*, i. 97–131; Frenz, 'Problem', p. 263; id., 'Eindringen', pp. 438–9. Payment to the pope for the office of apostolic scriptor 20 June 1433. Arch. Cam. I, vol. 1468, fo. 2b.

FLORES, ANTONIO (d. 1512). Sec. 1494. Frenz, *Kanzlei*, p. 286. See also Von Hofmann, *Forschungen*, ii. 134; Katterbach, *Sussidi*, ii. 56, 66; Burckardi, *Liber Notarum*, i. 462–3; Pastor, *History*, v. 293, 297–8.

FLORES, BARTOLOMÉ (d. 1498). Secret sec. 1492. Von Hofmann, *Forschungen*, ii. 124; see also i. 232–3, ii. 159. Burckardi, *Liber Notarum*, i. 384, ii. 54–6, 114; Frenz, *Kanzlei*, p. 298; Paschini, *Carteggio Barbo-Lorenzi*, p. 191; Eubel, *Hierarchia*, ii. 158.

FORNARI, OTTAVIANO (1464–1500). Cl. cam. 11 Dec. 1493. Von Hofmann, *Forschungen*, ii. 83, 93; Brouette, 'Les Clercs "mensiers"' (1973), 585; Frenz, *Kanzlei*, p. 417; Eubel, *Hierarchia*, ii. 57, 204; Célier, *Les Dataires*, p. 70 (shows him not to have been datarius); Katterbach, *Sussidi*, ii. 62; Davies, *Renascence*, p. 195 (with wrong first name); Forcella, *Iscrizioni*, v. 27.

FOSCHI, MATTEO (d. 1450). Cl. cam. 1431. Arnold, *Repertorium Germanicum*, pp. XXXVII, XL, XLV–XLVI, XLV; Bååth, *Diplomatarium Svecanum*, ii. 301; Eubel, *Hierarchia*, ii. 244, 262.

FOSCHI DE BERTA, ANGELOTTO (1378–1444). Cl. cam. 1414, mensarius until 1425, consil. cam. Baix, *La Chambre apostolique*, pp. CCCLXXXII–CCCLXXXIII; Partner, *Papal State*, pp. 61, 96, 133; Von Hofmann, *Forschungen*, i. 88, 212, ii. 188; Guasti, 'Gli avanzi', pp. 203, 337; Göller, *Päpstliche Pönitentiarie*, i. 2, 111; Cosenza, *Biographical Dictionary*, ii. 1508, v. 199; Puncuh, 'Carteggio', pp. 130, 136, 195, 196, 198, 204–6. For his character see Poggio Bracciolini, *Les Facéties de Pogge*, ii. 138–9 and 148, 'fuit enim rapax et violentus, ut cui nulla esset conscientia'; Piccolomini, *Aeneas Sylvii Epistolae*, p. 199; for his family see Esch, *Bonifaz IX*, p. 612; Lombardo, *La Camera Urbis*, pp. 126–7.

FRANCHOMME, PIERRE (dates unknown). Sec. sworn 7 June 1420. Von Hofmann, *Forschungen*, ii. 108–9.

FREGOSO, FEDERICO (1470[?]–1541). Sec. 7 July 1506, resigned 1507. Von Hofmann, *Forschungen*, ii. 120; Frenz, *Kanzlei*, p. 322; Eubel, *Hierarchia*, iii. 193, 289. See also V. Cian (ed.), *Libro del Cortegiano* (Florence, 1947), 513–14; McClung Hallman, *Italian Cardinals*, p. 39, and see pp. 26, 28, 83; Musso, 'Cultura genovese', pp. 121–87.

FUGGER, ANTON (1493–1560). Sec. (two *loci*) 10 Sept. 1521. Von Hofmann, *Forschungen*, ii. 122; Frenz, *Kanzlei*, p. 286.

GABRIELI, GABRIELI (1440[?]–1511). Sec. 1504–5. Frenz, *Kanzlei*, p. 336; Von Hofmann, *Forschungen*, ii. 85; Reg. Vat. 885, 898, 901, 985 ('Urbinas': information kindly supplied by Dr Michael Haren); Marchesi Buonaccorsi, *Antichità*, pp. 256–7; Portenari, *Della felicità di Padova* (1623), 283–4.

GABRIELI, LORENZO (d. 1512). Sec. 31 Oct. 1495 to death. Von Hofmann, *Forschungen*, ii. 118; Frenz, *Kanzlei*, p. 394. See Paschini, *Carteggio*, pp. 86, 108; G. dalla Santa, 'Benedetto Soranzo' (1914), 372; Burckardi, *Liber Notarum*, i. 163.

GADDI, NICCOLÒ (1491–1552). Cl. cam. 15 July 1517, resigned Oct. 1521. Von Hofmann, *Forschungen*, ii. 94, 97; Frenz, *Kanzlei*, p. 414; Pastor, *History*, ix. 384–5; Ferrajoli, *Ruolo*, p. 15; Cosenza, *Biographical Dictionary*, ii. 1515.

GALLETII, DOMENICO (d. 1501). Sec. expect. 1486, appointed 25 Aug. 1491, resigned 1492, and reappointed 13 Jan. 1496. Von Hofmann, *Forschungen*, ii. 116, 117; Frenz, *Kanzlei*, p. 317; *CPL* xvi, p. ciii. See also Egidi, *Necrologi*, ii. 217; Burckardi, *Liber Notarum*, ii. 304–5; *Vite di Paolo II*, p. 64.

GARATONE, CRISTOFORO (d. 1448). Sec. 1434. Pesce, 'Cristoforo Garatone'; Von Hofmann, *Forschungen*, ii. 82, 111; Blet, *Histoire*, pp. 172–3; Setton, *The Papacy and the Levant*, ii. 65; Frenz, 'Problem', p. 272.

GARIGLIATI, NICCOLÒ (dates unknown). Sec. 1485, resigned 1500. Von Hofmann, *Forschungen*, ii. 82, 117; Frenz, *Kanzlei*, p. 414; Frenz, 'Gründung', p. 237; *CPL* xii, *passim*; Eubel, *Hierarchia*, ii. 187; *CPL* xii, *passim*; *CPL* xiii/1. 354, xiii/2. 607, 618; *CPL* xvi, pp. xx–xxi, civ; Tangl, *Kanzleiordnungen*, pp. 183–8; Gherardi, *Dispacci*, i. 246; Burckardi, *Liber Notarum*, i. 438, ii. 38, 112. Appointed to the bishopric of Ivrea in 1485 against the wishes of the Duke of Savoy. Resigned the bishopric to Bonifacio Ferrer in 1500. See Paschini, *Carteggio*, p. 128. No more is heard of Garigliati after 1500.

GARSI, LUDOVICO (d. 1450). Cl. cam. Feb. 1427. Baix, *La Chambre apostolique*, pp. CCCXCVIII–CCCXCIX; Von Hofmann, *Forschungen*, ii. 91; Frenz, 'Problem', p. 264; A. Sorbelli, *Storia dell'Università di Bologna*, i (Bologna, 1944), 244; U. Dallari, *I rotuli dei lettori e legisti dello studio bolognese dal 1384 al 1799*, i (Bologna, 1888), 14, 16, 19; id., *Il 'liber secretus'*, ii. (Bologna, 1942), 211–12; Piana, *Il 'liber secretus'*, pp. 79*–80*; id., 'Nuovi documenti', pp. 887–9 (list of books in legacy). Bååth, *Diplomatarium Svecanum*, ii. 340, 344; Cosenza, *Biographical Dictionary*, ii. 1552, v. 206; Eubel, *Hierarchia*, ii. 107. Resigned chamber clerkship on appointment as aud. cam. 6 Aug. 1446, Von Hofmann, *Forschungen*, ii. 91; Arch. Cam. I, vol. 1713, fo. 22ᵛ.

GAVIONI, BATTISTA (d. 1494). Sec. 1487. Von Hofmann, *Forschungen*, ii. 83, 117; Frenz, *Kanzlei*, p. 296; Burckardi, *Liber Notarum*, i. 434, 438.

GERALDINI, ANGELO (1422–86). Sworn sec. 31 July 1455. Von Hofmann, *Forschungen*, ii. 114; Frenz, *Kanzlei*, p. 283. See J. Petersohn, *Ein Diplomat des Quattrocento: Angelo Geraldini (1422–1486)* (Tübingen, 1985); Partner, review of Petersohn, *EHR* 102 (1988), 725–6.

GERONA, JUAN (d. before 2 Dec. 1494). Cl. cam. 8 Jan. 1486. Von Hofmann, *Forschungen*, i. 93. Sec. 1487. Ibid. and also ii. 82, 117, 185, 211; Brouette, 'Les Clercs "mensiers"' (1973), 583; Frenz, 'Problem', p. 270; id., *Kanzlei*, pp. 253, 374; id., 'Gründung', p. 311; Pitz, *Supplikensignatur*, p. 199; Rius Serra, 'Catalanes y Aragones', p. 259; Kraus, 'Die Sekretäre', pp. 40, 49, 51; E. Müntz and P. Fabre, *La Bibliothèque du Vatican au XVe siècle* (Paris, 1887), 127; Cherubini, *Mandati*, p. 41; Egidi, *Necrologi*, ii. 300. Brouette, 'Les Clercs "mensiers"' (1962), 416 n.; id., 'Les Clercs "mensiers"' (1973), 583; Theiner, *Codex Diplomaticus*, iii, no. 398, at p. 467; Clergeac, *La Curie*, pp. 265, 267, 271; Egidi, *Necrologi*, i. 523 (*pace* Cherubini, Mandati, p. 41 n.). His long service to the King of England and English churchmen (as proctor he solicited the bulls for Westminster Abbey in 1463, Von Hofmann, *Forschungen*, ii. 211) is mentioned in *CPL* xiii/1. 242; see also *CPL* xi. 491, xii. 391; *Calendar of the Patent Rolls 1467–1477* (London, 1901), 510.

GESUALDI, CAMILLO (dates unknown). Sec. 1513. Von Hofmann, *Forschungen*, ii. 121; Frenz, *Kanzlei*, p. 308; Eubel, *Hierarchia*, iii. 175; Burckardi, *Liber Notarum*, i. 378; Ughelli, *Italia Sacra*, vi. 820.

GESUALDI, MALIZIA (1448–88). Sec. 1487, resigned 1488. Von Hofmann, *Forschungen*, ii. 116–17; Eubel, *Hierarchia*, ii. 243; Ughelli, *Italia Sacra*, vii. 882.

GHERARDI, GIACOMO (1434–1516). Sec. 1479, resigned 1506. Von Hofmann, *Forschungen*, ii. 116; D'Amico, *Renaissance Humanism*, pp. 31–4; Frenz, *Kanzlei*, p. 360; id., 'Gründung', p. 310; *CPL* xvi, p. ciii; Gherardi, *Diario*; id., *Dispacci*; Hausmann, 'Armarium 39 Tomus 10', p. 128. He owed his nomination to the office of papal chamberlain in 1479 not to Ammanati (who was dead by then) but to Card. Antonio Basso della Rovere (*Il diario romano*, pp. 9–10).

GHINIZZANO, NICCOLÒ (d. May 1470). Cl. cam. by Mar. 1462. Bååth, *Diplomatarium Svecanum*, pp. 468, 474, and see also p. 487. To be distinguished from Niccolò Sandonnino 'de Luca' (*pace* Von Hofmann, ii. 92, and see ii. 96, 213). N.G. and N. Sandonnino de Luca were both present simultaneously in the chamber as chamber clerks on 23 Apr. 1463, Div. Cam. 29, fo. 331, and again on 12 Dec. 1464, Reg. Vat. 545, fo. 4. Protonotary, Governor of Cesena from 5 Sept. 1468 until death. Robertson, 'Return of Cesena', p. 160; for *locus* going to Andrea Spiriti on N.G.'s death, see Reg. Vat. 543, fo. 35.

GHINUCCI, IERONIMO (d. 1541). Sec. 18 Dec. 1505, cl. cam. 6 Aug. 1507, aud. cam. 1511–35. Von Hofmann, *Forschungen*, ii. 91, 94, 120; Frenz, *Kanzlei*, pp. 347–8; Katterbach, *Sussidi*, ii. 84; Pastor, *History*, vii. 363, xi. 141; Burckardi, *Liber Notarum*, ii. 418 n.; McClung Hallman, *Italian*

Cardinals, pp. 83, 136-7. Brought up as a child in the Roman court, Ciacconius, *Vitae* iii. 569.

GIBERTI, FRANCO (dates unknown). Cl. cam. 30 Apr. 1511, resigned June 1517. Von Hofmann, *Forschungen*, ii. 94. Sec. 24 Feb. 1508, resigned before 1 May 1511. Von Hofmann, *Forschungen*, ii. 120. Prosperi, *Tra evangelismo e controriforma*, pp. 5-7; Frenz, *Kanzlei*, p. 330; Hergenroether, *Regesta*, p. 346.

GIBERTI, GIAN MATTEO (1495-1543). Sec. 1523. Prosperi, *Tra evangelismo e controriforma*; Frenz, *Kanzlei*, p. 374; Arch. Cam. I, vol. 1719, fo. 24.

GILIACO, GIOVANNI MICHELE (d. 1456). Cl. cam. 31 Oct. 1450, supranum. Reg. Vat. 435, fo. 10b; numerarius 30 Dec. 1452, admitted and sworn 28 Feb. 1452. Reg. Vat. 435, fo. 13. See also Ughelli, *Italia Sacra*, iv. 808; Eubel, *Hierarchia*, ii. 290; Forcella, *Iscrizioni*, v. 9.

GOCH, JOHANNES (dates unknown, but last mentioned in 1422). Cl. cam. under Gregory XI and Martin V. Baix, *La Chambre apostolique*, p. CCCLXXI: *Repertorium Germanicum*, iv. 1934; Schuchard, *Deutschen Kurie*, p. 81.

GOMEZ, GUNDISALVO (dates unknown). Cl. cam. sworn 2 Aug. 1419. Uginet, *Le Liber Officialium*, pp. 46, 47; Baix, *La Chambre apostolique*, p. CCCXCII.

Gori Piccolomini, Gregorio Lollio, see *Lollio, Gregorio*.

GOZZADINI, GIOVANNI (1477-1517). Cl. cam. 8 Nov. 1504. Frenz, *Kanzlei*, p. 375; Von Hofmann, *Forschungen*, ii. 93, 102; Katterbach, *Sussidi*, ii. 67; G. Gozzadini, *Delle torri gentilizie di Bologna* (Bologna, 1875), 303-14; Piana, *Il 'liber secretus'*, pp. 390-1; Burckardi, *Liber Notarum*, ii. 375-6 n.; Hergenröther, *Regesta*, nos. 118, 227, 1673, 3430, 3922, 5686; E. Göller, 'Untersuchungen über das Inventar des Finanzarchivs der Renaissancepäpste, 1447-1521', *Miscellanea Francesco Ehrle*, v (Vatican City, 1924), 268; L. Beliardi, *Cronaca della città di Modena (1512-1518)*, ed. A. Biondi and M. Oppi (Modena, 1981), 133. Pastor, *History*, vii. 468; H. Jedin, 'Giovanni Gozzadini, ein Konziliarist am Hofe Julius II.', *Kirche des Glaubens Kirche der Geschichte*, ii (Freiburg, Basle, and Vienna, 1966), 17-74.

GRACIADEI, ANTON (d. ?1538). Sec. 1 Oct. 1509, resigned 1528. Von Hofmann, *Forschungen*, ii. 120; Frenz, *Kanzlei*, p. 286. See also Gherardi, *Diario*, p. 35; Paschini, *Carteggio*, p. 72; A. Strnad, 'Francesco Todeschini-Piccolomini: Politik und Mäzenatentum im Quattrocento', *Röm.Hist.Mitt.*, 8-9 (1964/6), 255-6; Petersohn, *Ein Diplomat*, pp. 155 and 183-211.

Grassi, Ludovico, see *Garsi, Ludovico*.

GRIFO, LEONARDO (1437-85). Sec. dom. 12 Mar. 1472. Von Hofmann, *Forschungen*, ii. 123; Frenz, 'Eindringen', p. 467; id., *Kanzlei*, p. 397; D'Amico, *Renaissance Humanism*, p. 33; Lee, *Sixtus IV*, pp. 225-31; Egidi, *Necrologi*, i. 499; M. Borsa, 'Pier Candido Decembrio e l'umanesimo lombardo', *ASL* 20 (1893), 415; L. Grifo, *Conflictus Aquilani*

quo Braccius Perusinus Profligatus est (Muratori, RRIISS, 25). M. M.
Bullard, 'Farming Spiritual Revenues: Innocent VIII's "appalto" of
1486', *Renaissance Studies in honor of Craig Hugh Smyth* (Florence,
1985), i. 29–42, at p. 30, calls him Grisi. See Burckardi, *Liber Notarum*,
i. 133, and see also i. 20, 108, 109–10.

GRIMANI, DOMENICO (1461-1523). Sec. 1 Oct. 1491 until promoted to
cardinal 1493. Von Hofmann, *Forschungen*, ii. 117; Frenz, *Kanzlei*,
p. 317; P. Paschini, *Domenico Grimani Cardinale di San Marco (died
1523)* (Rome, 1943); id., *Il cardinale Marino Grimani ed i prelati della
sua famiglia* (Rome, 1960); T. Gasparini Leporace, 'Il Cardinale
Domenico Grimani (1461–1523)', *Almanacco dei Bibliotecari Italiani*
(1961), 193–204.

GUALBES, JUAN (d. 1507). Cl. cam. 16 Jan. 1503. Von Hofmann,
Forschungen, ii. 93 and ii. 83; Frenz, *Kanzlei*, p. 374. For career see
Burckardi, *Liber Notarum*, i. 26, ii. 54, 364; Eubel, *Hierarchia*, ii. 272.

GUIDALOTTI, BENEDETTO (d. 1429). Cl. cam. 1417. Baix, *La Chambre
apostolique*, pp. CCCLXXXIV–CCCLXXXV; Partner, *Papal State*, pp. 132,
217; Von Hofmann, *Forschungen*, ii. 96; Giusti, 'I registri Vaticani',
p. 419 n. Treasurer of Patrimony and Spoleto 1422. Reg. Vat. 354,
fo. 141; Reg. Vat. 349, fo. 224^v; Fink, 'Die politische Korrespondenz',
p. 232. He was also vice-treasurer (1417) and vice-chamberlain (1420,
1424–9). Cherubini, *Mandati*, pp. 74–5. He had taken his doctorate in
civil law at Padua 27 Sept. 1414. Zonta and Brotto, *Acta Graduum*,
p. 92.

GUISCARDO, EUSEBIO DE BLANZATE (dates unknown). Sec. (not particip.?)
6 Jan. 1459. Von Hofmann, *Forschungen*, ii. 115; Kraus, 'Die
Sekretäre', pp. 33–4.

HEEZE, DIETRICH (1470–1555). Sec. dom. 1523. Von Hofmann,
Forschungen, ii. 124; Frenz, *Kanzlei*, p. 448. See also Dury, 'Curialistes
Belges', pp. 152, 159; Pastor, *History*, ix. 80–1.

HENRICIS (ERRICI TUZIO), GIOVANNI BATTISTA DE (d. 1449). Cl. cam.
1431–3. Arnold, *Repertorium Germanicum*, pp. XXXVII, XL, XLV–XLVI. See
also Eubel, *Hierarchia*, ii. 129; Frenz, 'Eindringen', p. 393 and table V;
Egidi, *Necrologi*, i. 394, 412; *CPL* x. 316, 404; Katterbach, *Sussidi*, ii. 23.

HEREDIA, JUAN FEMAN (dates unknown). Sec. 9 Dec. 1509. Von Hofmann,
Forschungen, ii. 120; Frenz, *Kanzlei*, p. 376.

HOSPITAL OF S. GIOVANNI IN LATERANO. Pays 600 ducats for *locus* of
Fernando Ponzetti as sec. 1 Oct. 1502. Von Hofmann, *Forschungen*, ii.
119.

Ilperini, Luca, see Alberini, Luca.

JAMES, THOMAS (d. 1504). Sec. 1487, resigned 1491. Von Hofmann,
Forschungen, ii. 116; Frenz, *Kanzlei*, p. 449; Eubel, *Hierarchia*, ii. 175.
See also R. Fubini, 'Federico da Montefeltro e la congiura dei Pazzi:
politica e propaganda alla luce di nuovi documenti', in C. B. Baiardi,
G. Chittolini, and P. Floriani (eds.), *Federico di Montefeltro: Lo stato le
arti la cultura* (Rome, 1986), i. 357–470, at pp. 433–5, 440.

JOAN, MATTEU (dates unknown). Sec. 20 Apr. 1455, sec. dom. Von Hofmann, *Forschungen*, ii. 113, 123. Rius Serra, 'Catalanes y Aragones', pp. 72–3; Frenz, 'Eindringen', pp. 455–6; Pitz, *Supplikensignatur*, p. 111; Kraus, 'Die Sekretäre', p. 34; *CPL* xi. 79 n.; Pastor, *History*, ii. 538; Ryder, *Kingdom of Naples*, p. 234.

JUX, JOHANNES (d. after 1421). Sec. sworn 1421. Von Hofmann, *Forschungen*, ii. 111; Schuchard, *Deutschen Kurie*, p. 86.

Kerazred, Alain, see *Rue, Alain de la*.

LACERTIS, ANGELO (d. 1508). Sec. 1504. Frenz, *Kanzlei*, pp. 269, 283; Eubel, *Hierarchia*, ii. 209, iii. 241.

LANGUSCO, JACOPO (d. after 1452). Sec. sworn 30 Sept. 1428. Von Hofmann, *Forschungen*, ii. 111. See also Frenz, 'Eindringen', pp. 439–40 and table IV.

LATINI, GUILLELMO (d. after 1441). Cl. cam. 1412, 1418 onwards. Baix, *La Chambre apostolique*, pp. CCCLII, CCCLXXVI; Partner, *Papal State*, p. 218; Bååth, *Diplomatarium Svecanum*, ii. 306–7; Frenz, 'Eindringen', p. 393.

Laudi, Alessandro, see *Leccani, Alessandro*.

LAVELLE, NICHOLAS (d. 1456). Cl. cam. from Mar. 1422. Baix, *La Chambre apostolique*, pp. CCCXII–CCCXIV; Partner, *Papal State*, p. 217; Von Hofmann, *Forschungen*, ii. 96; Frenz, 'Problem', p. 261. Appointed treasurer of Perugia 20 Dec. 1428. Reg. Vat. 351, fo. 80; see also Fumi, *Inventario e Spoglio*, pp. 31–9. Commissioned to hear lawsuit 6 Mar. 1426. Div. Cam. 3, fo. 180.

LAX, JOHN (d. by 1466). Sec. 20 Dec. 1455. Von Hofmann, *Forschungen*, ii. 114; *CPL* xi. 99; Kraus, 'Die Sekretäre', p. 34; *CPL* x. 160, 615, xi. 134–7, 597–9; Emden, *Biographical Register*, ii. 1113–14.

LAZIOSI, ANTONIO (d. 1484). Cl. cam. supranum. 10 Aug. 1448. Reg. Vat. 435, fo. 3; particip. 1452. Von Hofmann, *Forschungen*, ii. 92; Brouette, 'Les Clercs "mensiers"' (1962), 411, with an error in dating. Mensarius by 1455. Gottlob, *Aus der Camera apostolica*, p. 139; Pitz, *Supplikensignatur*, p. 262; Frenz, *Kanzlei*, p. 286. He was 'decanus' of the chamber, 1471–84; see Bååth, 'L'Inventaire', p. 146, and Göller, 'Untersuchungen', pp. 231–3, 233–6. Also Theiner, *Codex Diplomaticus*, iii. 424, 428; Müntz, *Les Arts*, iii. 140–7; Hausmann, 'Die Benefizien', p. 173; Egidi, *Necrologi*, i. 494; Cherubini, *Mandati*, p. 79. Laziosi came of a prominent family of Forlì: see B. Nogara, *Scritti inediti e rari di Biondo Flavio* (Vatican City, 1927), XL; P. Bonoli, *Istorie della città di Forlì* (Forlì, 1661), 150; Giovanni di Mº Pedrino, *Cronica*, ed. G. Borghezio and M. Vattasso (Vatican City, 1929–34), i. 67, 94, 447, 489.

LECCANI (DI LAUDI), ALESSANDRO (dates unknown). Sec. 4 Nov. 1517 (resigned 1521) and 18 Jan. 1524. Von Hofmann, *Forschungen*, ii. 121; Frenz, *Kanzlei*, p. 274. See also Ferrajoli, *Ruolo*, pp. 12, 477.

LEGNAME, FRANCESCO DAL (d. 1462). Cl. cam. 26 Jan. 1443. Peverada, 'Il vescovo Francesco de Lignamine'; id., *La visita pastorale del vescovo Francesco del Legname a Ferrara (1447–1450)* (Deputazione Provinciale

Ferrarese di Storia Patria, ser. monumenti, 8; 1982); Partner, 'Francesco dal Legname'; *DBI* (A. Strnad).

LEIS, NICCOLÒ (dates unknown). Cl. cam. sworn 1 Dec. 1433. Rome, Arch. Cam. I, vol. 1712, fo. 22. Active until 1450. See also Bååth, 'L'Inventaire', 151, 157; Hofmann, *Concilium Florentinum*, iii. 111; Bååth, *Diplomatarium Svecanum*, ii. 357, 361; Göller, *Päpstliche Poenitentiarie*, i/2. 116–18, 122; *CPL* x. 273–4; C. Burroughs, 'Below the Angel', *JWCI* 45 (1982), 117 n.

LELIIS, LELIO DI TERAMO (dates unknown). Sec. 1487–91. Frenz, *Kanzlei*, p. 396.

LENI, BATTISTA (d. 1498). Sec. 13 Nov. 1493. Von Hofmann, *Forschungen*, ii. 117; Frenz, *Kanzlei*, p. 296. See also Burckardi, *Liber Notarum*, ii. 119.

LENI, LUCA (d. 1486). Cl. cam. 11 Dec. 1465. Von Hofmann, *Forschungen*, ii. 92, 93; Brouette, 'Les Clercs "mensiers"' (1962), 411; id., 'Les Clercs "mensiers"' (1973), 584; Reg. Vat. 545, fo. 5^v, for nomination of L.L. to the *locus* formerly held by Tomasso Piccolomini, 11 Dec. 1465. For L.L.'s death and funeral see Burckardi, *Liber Notarum*, i. 166–7. See also Frenz, 'Gründung', p. 324; Salimei, 'Note di topografia romana'; J. Garms, R. Juffinger, and B. Ward Perkins, *Die mittelalterliche Grabmäler in Rom und Latium bis zum 15. Jahrh.*, i (Österreichischen Kulturinstituts in Rom, 2/5; Rome and Vienna, 1981), 297. Luca is mentioned as clerk of the chamber in 1459, *CPL* xii. 26 n. So he must have had a supernumerary post by that date.

LENI, PIETRO (d. 1493). Cl. cam. in place of brother, 8 Nov. 1486. Von Hofmann, *Forschungen*, ii. 93; Brouette, 'Les Clercs "mensiers"' (1973), 584; Clergeac, *La Curie*, pp. 267, 271; *Diario Romano di Antonio de Vascho*, ed. G. Chiesa (RRIISS xxiii/3), 531, 533; Infessura, *Diario*, p. 124.

LERMA, JUAN (d. 1523). Cl. cam. 1519, resigned 1521, reappointed 18 Oct. 1521. Von Hofmann, *Forschungen*, ii. 94, 122; Frenz, *Kanzlei*, p. 377.

Le Roy, Thomas, see Regis, Thomas.

LIANORI, LIANORO (1425–?1477/8). Sec. 1470. Mercati, *Ultimi contributi*, p. 92; *Vite di Paolo II*, pp. 21–2, 211; Cosenza, *Biographical Dictionary*, p. 1983; Blet, *Histoire*, p. 185; Piana, *Nuove ricerche*, p. 475; L. Frati, 'Lainoro de' Lianori ellenista bolognese', *Studi e memorie per la storia dell'Università di Bologna*, 10 (1930), 163–77.

LOLLIO, GREGORIO (d. 1474). Sec. 1459, sec. dom. Von Hofmann, *Forschungen*, ii. 115, 123; Kraus, 'Die Sekretäre', pp. 28–9; Frenz, 'Eindringen', pp. 464–5; Hausmann, 'Armarium 39 Tomus 10', p. 124; N. Mengozzi, 'Il pontefice Paolo II e i Senesi', *Bull.Sen. SP* 21 (1914), pp. 160–1; Gualdo, 'Il "liber brevium"', p. 311; *Vite di Paolo II*, p. 50.

LOMELLINI, NICCOLÒ (dates unknown). Cl. cam. 10 Aug. 1503. Von Hofmann, *Forschungen*, ii. 119; Frenz, *Kanzlei*, p. 415.

LOPEZ, JUAN (d. 1501). Sec. 23 Dec. 1493. Von Hofmann, *Forschungen*, ii. 117, and see ii. 101; Frenz, *Kanzlei*, p. 378. See also Célier, *Les Dataires*, pp. 56–9; Burckardi, *Liber Notarum*, i. 135, ii. 295; Eubel, *Hierarchia*, ii. 65, 132, 237.

LORENZI, GIOVANNI DE DIONISIIS (1440–1501). Sec. 12 Sept. 1484. Von Hofmann, *Forschungen*, ii. 116; Frenz, *Kanzlei*, p. 377. See also D'Amico, *Renaissance Humanism*, p. 103; J. Bignami-Odier, *La Bibliothèque Vaticane de Sixte IV à Pie X* (Vatican City, 1973); Paschini, *Carteggio*; Célier, *Les Dataires*, p. 151.

LORIZ, FRANCESCO BORGIA (d. 1506). Sec. 10 Mar. 1500. Von Hofmann, *Forschungen*, ii. 118; Frenz, *Kanzlei*, p. 331. See also Burckardi, *Liber Notarum*, ii. 57.

LOSCHI, ANTONIO (1368–1441). Sec. sworn 12 Dec. 1418 (renewal). Von Hofmann, *Forschungen*, ii. 107; Frenz, 'Problem', p. 266; *Commissioni di Rinaldo degli Albizzi*, ed. C. Guasti (Florence, 1867–73), ii. 279; P. Herde, 'Politik und Rhetorik in Florenz am Vorabend der Renaissance', *Archiv für Kulturgeschichte*, 47 (1965), 141–220, at p. 192; E. Garin, in *Storia di Milano*, vii. 550–6; V. Zaccaria, 'Le epistole e i carmi di Antonio Loschi durante il cancellierato visconteo', *Atti Acc.Naz.Linc.*, Memorie, Classe di scienze morali, storiche e filologiche, ser. 8, 18 (1975), 367–443, and review by Fubini in *RSI* 88 (1976), 865–71.

LOSCHI, FRANCESCO (dates unknown). Sec. 30 July 1460. Von Hofmann, *Forschungen*, ii. 115. See also D'Amico, *Renaissance Humanism*, p. 254 n. 136.

Lucca, Niccolò di, see Ghinizzano, N., and Sandonnini, N.

LUDOVICO DI PERUGIA (dates unknown). Cl. cam. supranum. 18 Apr. 1455. Reg. Vat. 467, fo. 2b.

LUNATI, BERNARDINO (1452–97). Sec. 1492 until promoted to cardinal 1493. Von Hofmann, *Forschungen*, ii. 117; Frenz, *Kanzlei*, p. 305. See also Pastor, *History*, v. 445, 452, 458, 459, 488, 503.

LUNI, PIETRO DI (d. by 1459). Sec. 1448. Von Hofmann, *Forschungen*, ii. 112. See also Frenz, 'Eindringen', pp. 451–3; *CPL* x. 42–3.

MAFFEI, GERARDO (1408–66). Sec. 1457. D'Amico, *Renaissance Humanism*, p. 81; Von Hofmann, *Forschungen*, ii. 115; D. Brosius, 'Das Itinerar Papst Pius II.', *Quellen*, 55–6 (1976), 421–32; Kraus, 'Die Sekretäre', p. 29; Burroughs, 'Below the Angel', pp. 110–11; Forcella, *Iscrizioni*, i. 143.

MAINENTI, SCIPIONE (d. 8 Oct. 1444). Cl. cam. Oct. 1436. Eubel, *Hierarchia*, ii. 218 (but see below); Clergeac, *La Curie*, pp. 254–5. Rector of Patrimony of St Peter in Tuscia 26 Dec. 1443, Reg. Vat. 382, fo. 199b; and 15 Mar. 1444, Reg. Vat. 367, fo. 165b. Death: Arch. Cam. I, Patrimonio, busta 3, vol. 11, fo. 99b. See also Frenz, 'Eindringen', p. 394 and table v; Cosenza, *Biographical Dictionary*, iii. 2077; Piana, 'Nuovi documenti', pp. 200–1; G. Mercati, 'Dell'anno in cui Scipione Mainenti divenne vescovo di Modena', *Opere minori*, i (Vatican City, 1937), 117–21. He was at Basle, R. Sabbadini, *Le scoperte dei codici latini e greci* (Florence, 1905), 118.

MANCINI, STEFANO (dates unknown). Cl. cam. (supranum.?) 31 May 1451. Reg. Vat. 435, fo. 12b.

MANETTI, ZANOTTO (1396–1459). Sec. 29 July 1451, confirmed 27 Nov. 1458. Von Hofmann, *Forschungen*, p. 113. See Miglio, *Storiografia pontificia*; J. Pagnotti, 'La "Vita" di Niccolò V scritta da Giannozzo Manetti', *ASR* 14 (1891), 411–36; L. Onofri, 'Sacralità, immaginazione e proposte politiche: La "Vita" di Niccolò V di Giannozzo Manetti', *Human.Lovan.* 28 (1979), 27–77; Martines, *Social World*, pp. 131–8, 176–91; Stinger, *Renaissance in Rome*, pp. 46–7, 84–5, 264; C. F. Westfall, *In This Most Perfect Paradise: Alberti, Nicholas V, and the Invention of Conscious Urban Planning in Rome, 1447-55* (University Park, 1974); A. Field, *The Origins of the Platonic Academy of Florence* (Princeton, 1988), 79.

MARADES, JUAN (d. 1499). Sec. 1 July 1494. Von Hofmann, *Forschungen*, ii. 117; Frenz, *Kanzlei*, p. 378. See also Burckardi, *Liber Notarum*, i. 54, 662; Eubel, *Hierarchia*, ii. 258, 283 n.

MARGANI, ANTONIO (dates unknown). Cl. cam. (supranum.?) 21 May 1455. Reg. Vat. 467, fo. 2b.

MARGARIT, JUAN MOLES (1404[?]–84). Cl. cam. supranum. 3 Jan. 1450. Sworn 16 Jan. 1450 and received with kiss of peace by other clerks. Reg. Vat. 435, fo. 9b; Von Hofmann, *Forschungen*, ii. 92, 188; and see Frenz, 'Eindringen', p. 396; Rius Serra, 'Catalanes y Aragones', p. 270; Vespasiano da Bisticci, *Vite*, p. 98; Div. Cam. 26, fo. 178, which records both the chamber session of 2 Oct. at which the Card. of S. Crisogono made the pope's nomination known (and at which, it may be presumed, the chamberlain tore the habit from the candidate), and the session of 5 Oct. at which J.M.M. was finally installed as a participating chamber clerk. Only the session of 5 Oct. is recorded in Reg. Vat. 435, fo. 10. See also Ciacconius, *Vitae*, ii. 83–4. The latter's claim that J.M.M. was 80 when he died is made very doubtful by Vespasiano's statement that he was 'molto giovane e riputato' under Nicholas V.

MARINONI, ASTOLFINO (dates unknown). Sec. sworn 10 July 1422. Von Hofmann, *Forschungen*, ii. 111. See also Partner, *Papal State*, p. 135; Frenz, 'Problem', p. 265.

MARLIANO, MICHELE (dates unknown). Cl. cam. supranum. 9 Sept. 1454. Admitted as participating 3 Jan. 1455, in absence of Jacopo Mucciarelli. Reg. Vat. 435, fo. 15b. See also Von Hofmann, *Forschungen*, ii. 180; Mercati, *Ultimi contributi*, p. 103 n.

MARNA, BERTRAND (dates unknown). Sec. 7 May 1451. Von Hofmann, *Forschungen*, ii. 113.

Mattheus Johannis, see *Joan, Mateo*.

MAZANCOLI, GIOVANNI (dates unknown). Sec. before 1450(?). Von

Hofmann, *Forschungen*, ii. 91. See also Fumi, *Inventario e spoglio di Città di Castello*, p. 23; F. Angeloni, *Storia di Terni* (2nd edn., Pisa, 1878), 216; Partner, *Papal State*, pp. 105–6 n.; O. Besomi and M. Regoliosi, 'Valla e Tortelli III', *Ital.Med.Uman.* 12 (1969), 147–8.

MEDICI, CARLO (c.1430–92). Cl. cam. 15 Mar. 1452. Appointment, Reg. Vat. 435, fo. 13ᵛ (C.M., 'decret. doctor, canonicus florentin.'). He was admitted only as a non-participating clerk ('cum protestationibus de non participantibus'). See also Pieraccini, *La stirpe de' Medici*, pp. 90–2; Cosenza, *Biographical Dictionary*, iii. 2264; Paschini, *Carteggio*, p. 102. C.M. was present as a chamber clerk at the admission of Michele de Marliano as chamber clerk 3 Jan. 1455. Reg. Vat. 435, fo. 15ᵛ.

MEDICI DE' CAIMI, FRANCESCHINO (d. 1529). Sec. 22 Oct. 1526. Von Hofmann, *Forschungen*, ii. 122; Frenz, *Kanzlei*, p. 331; Arch. Cam. I, vol. 1719, fo. 18.

MEDICI D'ORVIETO, NICCOLÒ (dates unknown). Cl. cam. 1417–18. Baix, *La Chambre apostolique*, p. CCCLXXI; Von Hofmann, *Forschungen*, ii. 180.

MERCATELLO, NICCOLÒ (dates unknown). Cl. cam. 17 Aug. 1418. Baix, *La Chambre apostolique*, pp. CCCLXXXVIII–CCCXC; Von Hofmann, *Forschungen*, ii. 180; Partner, *Papal State*, p. 165 n., 217; Frenz, 'Problem', p. 265; Uginet, *Le Liber Officialium*, p. 40. Lends 600 gold florins to chamber 19 Feb. 1420. Div. Cam. 6, fo. 42.

MINUTOLO, FLAMENGO (d. 1442). Cl. cam. 24 Nov. 1418 (but did not exercise office, or not for long?). Baix, *La Chambre apostolique*, p. CCCXCII.

MOLEYNS, ADAM (d. 1450). Cl. cam. (supranum.?), date of appointment unknown. *DNB* article and also *CPL* viii. 285–6, 317, 318.

MONTAGNA, LEONARDO (dates unknown). Sec. 20 Apr. 1455. Von Hofmann, *Forschungen*, ii. 113.

MORRONI (MOIRONI), GIOVANNI BATTISTA (d. 1475). Sec. 26 Oct. 1455. Von Hofmann, *Forschungen*, ii. 114. See also Frenz, *Kanzlei*, p. 296; Kraus, 'Die Sekretäre', p. 32; *Vite di Paolo II*, xxxi. 61; *CPL*, xii, *passim*.

MOTA, GARCIA (dates unknown). Cl. cam. supranum. 6 Apr. 1458. Reg. Vat. 467, fo. 4; Von Hofmann, *Forschungen*, ii. 85, 255, 257.

MUALDI, ANSALDO (dates unknown). Sec. 1523. Frenz, *Kanzlei*, p. 283.

MUCCIARELLI, JACOPO (d. 1476). Cl. cam. (supranum.) 9 Feb. 1448, particip. in *locus* of Rosello Roselli 9 Feb. 1451. Reg. Vat. 435, fo. 2b. Frenz, *Kanzlei*, p. 356; Pitz, *Supplikensignatur*, p. 252; Von Hofmann, *Forschungen*, ii. 91; Pastor, *History*, ii. 561; Cherubini, *Mandati*, p. 79. Treasurer of Perugia 1 Aug. 1451–1 June 1454. Fumi, *Inventario e spoglio*, pp. 64–6. Treasurer of the March of Ancona 1455. Reg. Vat. 435, fo. 15ᵛ. He resigned from chamber clerkship on appointment as aud. cam. 1458.

MULTEDO, ANTONIO (dates unknown). Cl. cam. supranum. 2 Dec. 1455. Reg. Vat. 467, fo. 3.

Muzzarelli, Jacopo, see Mucciarelli, Jacopo.

NARDINI, STEFANO (d. 1484). Cl. cam. 22 Dec. 1449 (supranum.) 4 Apr.
1453 (particip.). Reg. Vat. 435, fo. 9b and see also Von Hofmann,
Forschungen, ii. 92, 177; Frenz, Kanzlei, p. 446. Rector and reader in
Bologna 1444-5. U. Dallari, I rotuli, i (Bologna, 1888), 19; Piana, Il 'liber
secretus', pp. 47*, 102*; Cherubini, Mandati, p. 79. Governor of
Campagna and Marittima May 1453-Jan. 1454. Arch. Cam. I, busta 1,
vol. 3, fo. 692, and vol. 4, fo. 3. Governor of Patrimony May 1455-29 Jan.
1456. Arch. Cam. I, busta 6, vol. 22, fo. 111^v. By 15 Mar. 1459 lieutenant
in the apostolic treasury ('prothonot., referend., cler.cam., thesauriatus
locumtenens'). Div. Cam. 29, fo. 73. Resigned chamber clerkship 19 July
1461. Archbishop of Milan 13 Nov. 1461 ('Can. Ferrarien., referend.
s.p., utr. juris doctor insignis'). He was Governor of Rome 30 Apr. 1462.
See Re, Mons. Governatore, p. 63. Cardinal 7 May 1473. Governor of
Patrimony again, July 1483-19 Oct. 1483. Arch. Cam. I, busta 21,
vol. 72, fo. 124b. See also Vite di Paolo II, p. 51. For the vicissitudes in
Soriano of his nephew Pierpaolo, see Burckardi, Liber Notarum, i. 282,
and Infessura, Diario, p. 253.

NARNI, FABIANO MATTEO DI (dates unknown). Sec. 24 Nov. 1457. Von
Hofmann, Forschungen, ii. 115; see also Kraus, 'Die Sekretäre', p. 34.

NASI, GIOVANNI BATTISTA (dates unknown). Sec. 6 Apr. 1513.
Von Hofmann, Forschungen, ii. 121; Frenz, Kanzlei, p. 381. See also
Ferrajoli, Ruolo, p. 15.

NEGRI, GIOVANNI ALIMENTI (1439-99). Cl. cam. 12 Sept. 1484, sec. 31 Dec.
1487-7 Apr. 1488, and again 1488-92. Von Hofmann, Forschungen, ii.
92, 117; Frenz, Kanzlei, pp. 381-2. See also Re, Mons. Governatore,
p. 68; Gherardi, Dispacci, nos. CXIX-CXX; Brouette, 'Les Clercs
"mensiers"' (1973), 583; Egidi, Necrologi, ii. 309; Clergeac, La Curie,
p. 267.

NOCETO, FRANCESCO DE (d. 1484). Sec. 22 June 1478, cl. cam. 23 May
1483. Von Hofmann, Forschungen, ii. 93, 116; Frenz, Kanzlei, p. 332;
Brouette, 'Les Clercs "mensiers"' (1962), 412. See also Lee, Sixtus IV,
pp. 57-8.

NOCETO, PIETRO DA (1397-1467). Papal sec. by Aug. 1440, see Göller,
Päpstliche Poenitentiarie, i/1. 276-7. For the rest of his curial career
see Von Hofmann, Forschungen, ii. 112, 122. Further, Nasalli Rocca,
'La famiglia di Lorenzo Valla'; Bicchierai, 'Antonio da Noceto'. He was
Domenico Capranica's chancellor in Perugia in the legation of 1430.
Div. Cam. 12, fo. 15, '[Ego] Petrus filius Ser Johannis de Noxeto dioc.
Placentin.'. See also Partner, Papal State, pp. 174-5; Fink, 'Dominicus
Capranica', pp. 275-7. For his time in Basle see Dephoff, Urkunden,
pp. 80-1. He was brother-in-law of Pietro da Luni, the sec. of Cardinal
Vitelleschi. M. L. Madonna, Il Quattrocento a Viterbo (Rome, 1983), 49.
See Von Hofmann, Forschungen, ii. 79, 122; Pitz, Supplikensignatur,
p. 171; Frenz, 'Problem', pp. 270, 273; Ryder, Kingdom of Naples,
p. 222. For P. da N. under Nicholas V and at his death, see Pastor,
History, ii. 196, 311, 532, iii. 139. Von Hofmann, however, confuses him

with the scriptor, Pietro de Spinosis de Luculo, who clashed with P. da N. in 1455 over the office of custos of the chancery, which they both claimed. See Pitz, *Supplikensignatur*, pp. 31, 165–6 n., 171. See also Frenz, 'Eindringen', pp. 448–53; Giusti, 'I registri Vaticani', pp. 422–3. After leaving Rome P. da N. became a councillor of Francesco Sforza. Tomb, J. Pope-Hennesey, *Italian Renaissance Sculpture* (London, 1958).

ORLANDINI, PAOLO (dates unknown). Sec. 24 Nov. 1418. Von Hofmann, *Forschungen*, ii. 109.

ORSINI, GIOVANNI BATTISTA (d. 1503). Cl. cam. 1473–83. Brouette, 'Les Clercs "mensiers"' (1962), 413; D. S. Chambers, 'Studium Urbis and Gabella Studii: The University of Rome in the Fifteenth Century', *Cultural Aspects of the Italian Renaissance: Essays in honour of Paul Oskar Kristeller* (Manchester, 1976), 86, 110; Katterbach, *Sussidi*, ii. 53.

ORSINI, ONOFRIO GIOVANNI (dates unknown). Sec. 11 Oct. 1498, resigned 1529. Von Hofmann, *Forschungen*, ii. 118; Frenz, *Kanzlei*, p. 351.

ORSO, ANTONIO (d. 1511). Sec. Nov. 1502. Von Hofmann, *Forschungen*, ii. 119; Frenz, *Kanzlei*, p. 289. See also Baumgarten, *Aus Kanzlei und Kammer*, pp. 357–8; Burckardi, *Liber Notarum*, ii. 518; Katterbach, *Sussidi*, ii. 43, 66; ASR 6 (1883), 488.

ORTEGA DE GOMIEL, JUAN (1462–1503). Sec. 1499. Von Hofmann, *Forschungen*, ii. 101; Frenz, *Kanzlei*, p. 375; CPL xvi, cii; Célier, *Les Dataires*, pp. 66–9; Burckardi, *Liber Notarum*, i. 204; Ughelli, *Italia Sacra*, vii. 141; Eubel, *Hierarchia*, ii. 127, 138, 145, 241.

PAGELLI, GUILLELMO (dates unknown). Sec. 8 Sept. 1464. Von Hofmann, *Forschungen*, ii. 116; *Vite di Paolo II*, pp. 4 n., 164 n.

PALLAVICINI, ANTONIOTTO (d. 1525). Sec. 1517. Von Hofmann, *Forschungen*, ii. 121. Cf. Frenz, *Kanzlei*, p. 287, who equates him with the long-dead cardinal; McClung Hallman, *Italian Cardinals*, p. 132; Litta, *Famiglie celebri*, iv.

PALLAVICINI, GIOVANNI BATTISTA (1480–1524). Sec. 24 Oct. 1513. Von Hofmann, *Forschungen*, ii. 121; Frenz, *Kanzlei*, p. 382; Eubel, *Hierarchia*, iii. 161; McClung Hallman, *Italian Cardinals*, p. 89.

PALMIERI, MATTEO GIOVANNI (1423–83). Sec. 1457, particip. 19 Dec. 1470. Von Hofmann, *Forschungen*, ii. 115; Frenz, *Kanzlei*, p. 407; CPL xi. 164, 177, and xii. 257; Pitz, *Supplikensignatur*, p. 173; Giusti, 'I registri Vaticani', p. 424 ('Mattheus Johannis'); Frenz, 'Problem', p. 269; Kraus, 'Die Sekretäre', p. 31. His 'De captivitate Pisarum' (RRIISS xix/2).

PANDOLFINI, NICCOLÒ (1440–1518). Cl. cam. 14 Oct. 1462 (probably supranum. and certainly not mensarius 1471–4) until 13 Oct. 1474, sec. 4 Dec. 1501 until promoted to cardinal 1517. Von Hofmann, *Forschungen*, ii. 76, 118; Frenz, *Kanzlei*, p. 415; Baumgarten, *Aus Kanzlei und Kammer*, pp. 357–8. See also Bizzocchi, *Chiesa e potere*, pp. 224, 230,

231, 240; Pastor, *History*, v. 280. Paid 20,000 ducats for promotion to cardinal. Bullard, *Filippo Strozzi*, p. 125. Opinions on him vary: see Bizzocchi, *Chiesa e potere*, p. 240; Pastor, *History*, vii. 204; McClung Hallman, *Italian Cardinals*, p. 24.

PASSERELLA, JACOPO (d. 1495). Sec. 30 Apr. 1478 and 1487. Von Hofmann, *Forschungen*, ii. 116 (nos. 130, 143); Frenz, *Kanzlei*, pp. 356–7. See also Eubel, *Hierarchia*, ii. 107; Paschini, *Carteggio*, pp. 58, 103, 106, 121, 146; Ughelli, *Italia Sacra*, ii. 436; I. Robertson, in *Storia di Cesena*, ii/2 (Rimini, 1985), 72–3; *CPL* xiv. 14–28, 56–7.

PEROTTI, NICCOLÒ (c.1430–80). Sec. 1455. Mercati, *Per la cronologia*; Prete, *L'umanista Niccolò Perotti*; Greco, 'Vecchi e nuovi elementi'; Piana, 'Nuovi documenti', pp. 216–19.

PERUZZI, ANTONIO RIDOLFO (dates unknown). Cl. cam. 30 June 1433. Arch. Cam. I, vol. 1712, fo. 20b. See also Bizzocchi, *Chiesa e potere*, pp. 237–8; Arnold, *Repertorium Germanicum*, p. XL; Piana, 'Nuove Ricerche', pp. 155–6.

Pescia, Leonardo di, see *Salutati, Leonardo*.

PICCOLOMINI, AENEAS SYLVIUS (1405–64). Sec. 8 July 1446. Von Hofmann, *Forschungen*, ii. 112.

PICCOLOMINI, TOMMASO (DE TESTA) (d. 1483 or 1484). Cl. cam. 9 Dec. 1460. Von Hofmann, *Forschungen*, ii. 92; Reg. Vat. 515, fo. 291b–292, and also fos. 293–4 where he is referred to as 'cubicularius secretus', and the appointment as chamber clerk is made 'non obstantibus felicis recordationis Nicolai pape V predecessoris nostri atque aliis constitutionibus'. See E. Casanova, 'Un anno della vita privata di Pio II', *Bull.Sen. SP*, NS, 2 (1931), 19–34, at p. 19; Partner, 'Camera Papae', pp. 66, 68 (where the no. of the 2nd vol. of Pius II's accounts is to be amended to '1289'); Clergeac, *La Curie*, p. 261. 'Locumten. Camerar.' Sept. 1462. Div. Cam. 29, fo. 316; Cherubini, *Mandati*, p. 80. Mensarius in Mar. 1463. Bååth, *Diplomatarium Svecanum*, ii. 482, 485. Eubel, *Hierarchia*, ii. 238, 267.

PICHERIER, JACQUES (d. 1500). Sec. 1487. Von Hofmann, *Forschungen*, ii. 117; Frenz, *Kanzlei*, p. 357. See also Burckardi, *Liber Notarum*, ii. 241; Baumgarten, *Aus Kanzlei und Kammer*, p. 351; L. Schmitz-Kallenberg, *Practica cancellariae apostolicae saec. XV exeuntis* (Münster, 1904), 71.

PILI, ANDREA (d. 1476). Cl. cam. (supranum.) 12 May 1451. Reg. Vat. 435, fo. 12. Castellan S. Angelo, 1470–1, Pagliucchi, *I castellani*, ii. 10–13. Treasurer in Perugia and Spoleto under Eugenius. Fumi, *Inventario e spoglio di Perugia*, pp. 50–7. Scriptor of penitentiary 1455. Von Hofmann, *Forschungen*, ii. 180. Governor of Patrimony 1463–4. Arch. Cam. I, busta 11, vol. 39, fo. 120^v, vol. 38, fo. 159^v. See also *Vite di Paolo II*, pp. 119, 223.

PISA, MICHELE DE (d. 1436). Sec. 12 Jan. 1419. Von Hofmann, *Forschungen*, ii. 110. See also Miller, 'Participation', p. 405.

PIZZOLPASSI, FRANCESCO (d. 1443). Cl. cam. by 1413, and 1418. Baix, *La*

Chambre apostolique, p. CCCLXXIII; Kühne, *Repertorium Germanicum*, iii. 28*–29*; Arnold, *Repertorium Germanicum*, p. XXV; Foffano, 'La costruzione'; Cosenza, *Biographical Dictionary*, iv. 2832–4; Frenz, 'Problem', p. 265; Paredi, *Biblioteca*; Fubini, 'Tra umanesimo e concilio'; Piana, *Nuove ricerche*, pp. 465–6; id., 'Nuovi documenti', pp. 194–5 and index. Cl. cam., to receive composition payment due to chamber from Todi and to pay it out to Braccio da Montone, 1 Apr. 1413. Reg. Vat. 345, fos. 49b–50. He was vice-rector of Viterbo 1419, and vice-rector of Narni, Orte, and a number of adjacent villages in 1420 (Partner, *Papal State*, pp. 63 n., 183 n.).

PLANCA, CORNELIO (dates unknown). Cl. cam. 30 Apr. 1439. Arch. Cam. I, vol. 1713, fo. 15. See also Von Hofmann, *Forschungen*, ii. 181.

PLANCA, MARCELLO (1428–85). Cl. cam. 5 June 1458, citing bull of 25 Mar. 1458. Reg. Vat. 467, fo. 4; Forcella, *Iscrizioni*, xi. 33; *Un pontificato e una citta*, pp. 97, 100.

PLANCA, PAOLO (d. after 27 Mar. 1427). Cl. cam. under Boniface IX and so also under Martin V. Baix, *La Chambre apostolique*, pp. CCCLXVIII–CCCLXIX. See also Katterbach, *Sussidi*, ii, no. XXXII; Partner, *Papal State*, p. 217; Esch, *Bonifaz IX*, index; Tellenbach, *Repertorium Germanicum*, ii (Berlin, 1933–8), 76*, 962; Burckardi, *Liber Notarum*, ii. 515–16.

PODOCATARO, LUDOVICO (1429–1504). Sec. to Pope Alex. VI ('die Bezeichnung secr. domesticus habe ich nie gefunden'). Von Hofmann, *Forschungen*, ii. 123–4; C.-M. de Witte, 'Notes sur les plus anciens registres de brefs', *BIHBR* 31 (1958), 153–68, at p. 166; Frenz, *Kanzlei*, p. 401; id., 'Gründung', p. 301; D. Brosius, 'Breven und Briefe Papst Pius II.', *Röm.Quart.* 70 (1975), 180–224; L. G. Pélissier, 'Catalogue des documents de la collection Podocataro à la Bibliothèque Marciana à Venise', *Centralblatt für Bibliothekswesen*, 18 (1901), 473–93, 521–41, 576–98; Davies, *Renascence*, pp. 302–3.

PONTECORVO, FILIPPO (d. 1499). Sec. 24 Nov. 1498. Von Hofmann, *Forschungen*, ii. 118; Frenz, *Kanzlei*, p. 435. See also Gherardi, *Dispacci*, nos. XXV, CXIX, pp. 27, 109; Egidi, *Necrologi*, i. 536; Giusti, 'I registri Vaticani', p. 430; Burckardi, *Liber Notarum*, i. 157, ii. 155.

PONZETTI, FERNANDO (1444–1527). Cl. cam. 23 Sept. 1503. Von Hofmann, *Forschungen*, ii. 90; Ferrajoli, *Ruolo*, pp. 215–46; Cosenza, *Biographical Dictionary*, iv. 2931; Frenz, *Kanzlei*, p. 323; CPL xvi, p. civ. Secret treasurer of Leo X in 1514–15. Div. Cam. 65, fos. 92^r–103^v.

PONZETTI, JACOPO (dates unknown). Cl. cam. 24 Apr. 1517. Von Hofmann, *Forschungen*, ii. 90; Frenz, *Kanzlei*, p. 357.

Pratella, Cristoforo de' Marchioni di, see Bordini, Cristoforo.

PRIULI, SEBASTIANO (d. 1502). Sec. 20 Oct. 1489, resigned 1496. Von Hofmann, *Forschungen*, ii. 117; Frenz, *Kanzlei*, p. 442; Burckardi, *Liber Notarum*, ii. 339; Eubel, *Hierarchia*, ii. 224; Katterbach, *Sussidi*, ii. 57; Sanudo, *Diarii*, i. 748, iv. 336, 344; C. Cenci, in Piana and Cenci, 'Promozioni', pp. 425 n., 427, 431 n., 432.

PUCCI, ANTONIO (1484–1544). Cl. cam. Sept. 1513, Dec. 1523. Von Hofmann, *Forschungen*, ii. 94; Frenz, *Kanzlei*, p. 288; Ciacconius, *Vitae*, iii. 522–3. See also Pastor, *History*, vii. 158, viii. 50, 108, 391; K. Setton, 'Pope Leo X and the Turkish Peril', *Proceedings of the American Philosophical Society*, 113 (1969), 367–424, at pp. 399–400; Hergenroether, *Regesta*, p. 286 (no. 4675); Erasmus, *Opus Epistolarum*, ed. P. S. Allen, iii (Oxford, 1913), 347, 379–82, and iv. 447; J. Fraikin, *Les Nonciatures de France*, i (Paris, 1906), xxxix. For the family see Martines, *Lawyers and Statecraft*, p. 495; Stephens, *Fall*, pp. 88, 145, 169; Forcella, *Iscrizioni*, i. 445.

PUCCI, LORENZO (1459–1531). Cl. cam. June 1504, resigned Sept. 1513 on promotion to cardinal. Von Hofmann, *Forschungen*, ii. 97–8, 102; Frenz, *Kanzlei*, p. 395 (listing 13 posts in the Roman court which L.P. held at one time or another); Burckardi, *Liber Notarum*, ii. 233 n., 454–5; Ciacconius, *Vitae*, iii. 337–8; *CPL* xvi, p. cii; Katterbach, *Sussidi*, ii. 69; Göller, *Päpstliche Pönitentiarie*, ii, pt. 1, 11, pt. 2, 91–3; McClung Hallman, *Italian Cardinals*, pp. 123, 138; Pastor, *History*, vii. 82 and *passim*; Verde, *Studio fiorentino*, ii. 438–43. He was a patron of Erasmus (who dedicated his edn. of Cyprian to him in 1520) and Bombace.

PUCCINI, BATTISTA. Sec. 1521. Von Hofmann, *Forschungen*, ii. 122; Frenz, *Kanzlei*, p. 296. Resigned 1524.

QUESTENBERG, JACOB AURELIUS (1465–1524). Sec. 1506, resigned 1512. Frenz, *Kanzlei*, p. 358; D'Amico, *Renaissance Humanism*, pp. 7–8; F. Güldner, 'Jacob Questenberg, ein deutscher Humanist in Rom', *Zeitschrift der Harzvereins für Geschichte und Altertumskunde*, 38 (1905), 213–76; G. Mercati, 'Questenbergiana', in *Opere minori*, iv (Vatican City, 1937), 437–61.

RAM, BLASIUS, archdeacon of Tarragona (dates unknown). Cl. cam. (?supranum.) 31 Oct. 1450. Reg. Vat. 435, fo. 11.

RAMPONI, PIETRO (d. 1443). Cl. cam. 16 Sept. 1425. Partner, *Papal State*, p. 134. Sworn 11 Feb. 1426. Uginet, *Le Liber officialium*, p. 51. Deprived 31 Aug. 1426. Partner, *Papal State*, p. 134. See also Guiraud, *L'État pontifical*, p. 97. Governor of Campania and Marittima 1 May 1432. Reg. Vat. 381, fo. 119b. Appointed Governor of Patrimony 27 Nov. 1434; still, or again, Governor of Patrimony 19 Jan. 1439–11 June 1439, and 16 Oct. 1442–23 Dec. 1443. Arch. Cam. I, Patrimonio, busta 2, vols. 6 and 7. And see G. Gozzadini, *Delle torre gentilizie di Bologna* (Bologna, 1875), 443–9; Piana, *Nuove ricerche*, p. 117; id., 'Nuovi documenti', pp. 392–4, 466–7, 517, 820, and index; P. Scarcia Piacentini, 'Controfigure della storia: Bartolomeo Aragazzi da Montepulciano, Pietro de' Ramponi da Bologna', in *Roma humanistica: Studia in honorem Rev. i adm. Dni. Iosaci Ruysschaert* (Human.Lovan. Journal of Neo-Latin Studies, 34A; 1985), 236–55.

RASI, BENEDETTO (dates unknown). Sec. 17 Apr. 1484. Frenz, *Kanzlei*, p. 302.

REGAS, BARTOLOMÉ (1418–75). Sec. sworn 6 Sept. 1456, particip. 27 Mar.
1457, cl. cam. particip. 13 Sept. 1456. Von Hofmann, *Forschungen*, ii.
92, 114; Frenz, *Kanzlei*, p. 299; Brouette, 'Les Clercs "mensiers"'
(1962), 411; Pitz, *Supplikensignatur*, pp. 71, 76, 132 n., 209 n., 280; Rius
Serra, 'Catalanes y Aragones', pp. 286–8; id., *Regesto iberico*,
pp. 107–8, 348–52; *Vite di Paolo II*, p. 215; for other later activities see
CPL xii. 517 n.; Bååth, *Diplomatarium Svecanum*, ii. 447, 508, 535; for
tomb, Forcella, *Iscrizioni*, vi. 43.

REGIS, THOMAS (d. 1524). Cl. cam. 12 Sept. 1521. Von Hofmann,
Forschungen, ii. 94; Frenz, *Kanzlei*, p. 449; Clergeac, *La Curie*,
pp. 59–60; Eubel, *Hierarchia*, iii. 186; Burckardi, *Liber Notarum*, i. 612;
Pastor, *History*, viii. 115; G. Mollat, 'Thomas le Roy (dit Régis) et le
palazzeto de la Farnèsine à Rome (via de' Baullari)', *Annales de Saint
Louis des Français*, 6 (1902), 159–200.

RIETI, ANGELO DE (dates unknown). Sec. sworn 27 Dec. 1417. Von
Hofmann, *Forschungen*, ii. 108. See also Partner, *Papal State*, p. 237.

RIZARDI, FRANCESCO (1471–1508). Sec. 25 Dec. 1495. Von Hofmann,
Forschungen, ii. 118; Frenz, *Kanzlei*, p. 332; Eubel, *Hierarchia*, ii. 230,
iii. 274. See also Burckardi, *Liber Notarum*, ii. 442.

ROBERT, BERTOLDUS (BERTRAND) (d. 1433?). Cl. cam. by Sept. 1426. Baix,
La Chambre apostolique, pp. CCCXCVII-CCCXCVIII. See also Katterbach,
Sussidi, ii. 20; Eubel, *Hierarchia*, ii. 202; Introitus et Exitus 385,
fo. 140b (autograph 6 Aug. 1427).

RODRIGUE DE MALVENDA, ALFONSO (d. after 1447). Cl. cam. 1427. Baix,
La Chambre apostolique, pp. CCCXCIX-CDI. See also Arnold, *Repertorium
Germanicum*, no. XLII; Clergeac, *La Curie*, p. 107; Eubel, *Hierarchia*,
ii. 250.

ROMA, GIOVANNI FILIPPO DE (dates unknown). Sec. 1 Dec. 1517, resigned
1519. Von Hofmann, *Forschungen*, ii. 121; Frenz, *Kanzlei*, p. 385.

ROMA, GIOVANNI MARIA DE (d. 1525). Sec. 1517 (two *loci*). Von Hofmann,
Forschungen, ii. 121; Frenz, *Kanzlei*, p. 385; Arch. Cam. I, vol. 1719,
fo. 55.

Rondoni Passerella, Jacopo, see Passerella, Jacopo.

ROSELLI, ROSELLO (1399–1451). Cl. cam. 7 Dec. 1429. Uginet, *Le Liber
officialium*, p. 57; see also Baix, *La Chambre apostolique*, pp. CDII-CDIII;
Frenz, 'Eindringen', pp. 392–3 and taf. V. Official posts in papal state
under Eugenius IV, E. Presutti, 'I Colonna di Riofreddo', *ASR* 35 (1912),
127–8; Fumi, *Inventario e spoglio in Perugia*, pp. 40–3. Div. Cam. 16,
fo. 128; Div. Cam. 22, fo. 15b; Reg. Vat. 373, fo. 302b. Family: Martines,
Lawyers and Statecraft, pp. 498, 500. See also R. Cessi, 'Rosello Roselli
studente', *Nuovo Archivio Veneto*, NS, 25 (1913), 489; E. Bruti, *Il
canzoniere di Rosello Roselli* (Rovereto, 1925); D. de Robertis, *Storia
della letteratura italiana*, iii (Milan, 1965), 424–5; A. Tartaro and
F. Tateo, *La letteratura italiana: Storia e testi*, iii/1 (Bari, 1971), 241–2.
Other documents: Theiner, *Codex Diplomaticus*, iii. 349; E. Müntz and
P. Fabre, *La Bibliothèque du Vatican au XVe siècle* (Paris, 1887), 9. His

'exemption' is mentioned in a lawsuit 5 Feb. 1450. Div. Cam. 26, fo. 139.

ROVERE, ANTONIO DELLA (dates unknown). Sec. 5 Apr. 1518. Von Hofmann, Forschungen, ii. 121; Frenz, Kanzlei, p. 288.

ROVERE, ORLANDO DELLA (CARETTO) (d. 1527). Sec. 1512. Von Hofmann, Forschungen, ii. 90; Frenz, Kanzlei, p. 417. See also Chambers, Cardinal Bainbridge, pp. 110–11.

ROVERELLA, BARTOLOMEO (1406–76). Sec. c.1442. Enciclopedia cattolica, x (Giuntella); Von Hofmann, Forschungen, ii. 112, 188; Frenz, 'Eindringen', pp. 445–8; Frenz, 'Gründung', p. 301; J. Monfrin, 'A propos de la bibliothèque d'Eugène IV', Mélanges, 119 (1987), 101–21, at p. 119; Cosenza, Biographical Dictionary, iv. 3100; Vespasiano da Bisticci, Vite, p. 98; Vite di Paolo II, pp. 161–2; Davies, Renascence, pp. 212–14; Un pontificato e una città, pp. 441, 447.

RUE, ALAIN DE LA, (DE KERAZRED) (d. 1424). Cl. cam. 1418. Baix, La Chambre apostolique, p. CCCXCI.

RUSTICI, CENCIO PAOLO (d. ?1445). Sec. 28 Nov. 1417. Von Hofmann, Forschungen, ii. 110. See Frenz, 'Problem', p. 259; id., 'Eindringen', p. 430; L. Bertalot, 'Cincius Romanus und seine Briefe', Quellen, 21 (1929/30), 209–55; R. Sabbadini, Le scoperte dei codici Latini e Greci (Florence, 1905), 78. Tomb, Davies, Renascence, pp. 272–3.

RUSTICI, MARCELLO CINCIO (d. 1481), son of Cencio Paolo Rustici. Sec. 9 Aug. 1449. Von Hofmann, Forschungen, ii. 112; Frenz, 'Problem', p. 269; id., Kanzlei, p. 403; id., 'Eindringen', p. 459; id., 'Gründung', p. 322; Gualdo, 'Il "liber brevium"', p. 311; Pitz, Supplikensignatur, p. 111; Kraus, 'Die Sekretäre', p. 31; Schwarz, 'Die Abbreviatoren unter Eugen IV.'; Vite di Paolo II, p. 84 n.; Davies, Renascence, pp. 272–3.

SACCEN, BERNARDO, archpriest of Padua (dates unknown). Cl. cam. (supranum.?) 22 Apr. 1449. Reg. Vat. 435, fo. 3b.

SADOLETO, JACOPO (1477–1547). Sec. and sec. dom. 1513–18. Von Hofmann, Forschungen, ii. 124; Frenz, Kanzlei, p. 358; R. M. Douglas, Jacopo Sadoleto (1477–1547): Humanist and Reformer (Cambridge, Mass., 1959).

SAGUNDINO DI SINIPONTO. Sec. 1 Aug. 1439. Von Hofmann, Forschungen, ii. 111–12.

SALICETO, BARTOLOMEO (1449–1524). Sec. 26 Nov. 1503, resigned 1505. Von Hofmann, Forschungen, ii. 119; Frenz, Kanzlei, p. 300; Burckardi, Liber Notarum, ii. 406; Minnich, 'Participants', p. 193 n.

SALUTATI, LEONARDO (LEONARDO DI PESCIA) (d. 1466). Cl. cam. by 1436. Audits as commissioner of chamber 1 Sept. 1436. Arch. Cam. I, Tes. Prov., Patrimonio, busta 2, vol. 2. At Council of Ferrara as chamber clerk 10 May 1438. Hofmann, Concilium Florentinum, iii. 37. Witness as chamber clerk 26 Jan. 1440. Bååth, 'L'Inventaire', pp. 138, 156. Also Gottlob, Aus der Camera apostolica, p. 162. 'Monitorium contra

R. de Rosellis et Leonardum de Piscia', 25 Aug. 1446. Div. Cam. 21, fos. 74b-75a. See also M. Cecchi and E. Coturri, *Pescia e il suo territorio* (Pistoja, 1961), 307-8; Bizzocchi, *Chiesa e potere*, pp. 223, 236; id., 'Chiesa e aristocrazia', p. 264; Eubel, *Hierarchia*, ii. 170. Tomb, W. R. Valentiner, *Studies in Italian Renaissance Sculpture* (London, 1950), 93-4.

SALVAGO, TOMMASO (dates unknown). Sec. 1521 (two places, one resigned by Angelo Colocci and the other by Paolo Francesco Biondo), another 1523. Von Hofmann, *Forschungen*, ii. 122; Frenz, *Kanzlei*, p. 450.

SALZMANN, WITTEKIND (d. 1418). Cl. cam. 17 Dec. 1417. Baix, *La Chambre apostolique*, pp. CCCLXXX-CCCLXXXI; Schuchard, *Deutschen Kurie*, pp. 81, 82.

SAMINO, SEBASTIANO (dates unknown). Sec. 1487-9. Frenz, *Kanzlei*, p. 442.

SANCTOLARIA, PIETRO (d. 1450). Cl. cam. supranum. by 14 Aug. 1444. Arch. Cam. I, vol. 1713, fos. 20b, 16b. Admitted as cl. cam. particip. 19 Sept. 1446. Div. Cam. 21, fo. 83, and see also Div. Cam. 6, fo. 78b; Gottlob, *Aus der Camera apostolica*, p. 162; Cherubini, *Mandati*, p. 78. Perhaps identical with 'P. de Scanlaria' in Bourgin, 'La "familia" pontificia sotto Eugenio IV', *ASR* 27 (1904), 224, but see also p. 215.

SANDONNINI, NICCOLÒ (1435-99). Cl. cam. (supranum.) 14 Mar. 1455. Reg. Vat. 435, fo. 15ᵛ. Sec. (supranum.) 1456. Pitz, *Supplikensignatur*, p. 173. Cl. cam. (particip.) 13 Dec. 1458. Resigned chamber clerkship 14 June 1465 on promotion to bishopric of Modena. Reg. Vat. 545, fo. 4ᵛ. See also Von Hofmann, *Forschungen*, ii. 92 (he is not, however, the same official as Niccolò Ghinizzano of Lucca, q.v.); Pitz, *Supplikensignatur*, p. 262; Ughelli, *Italia Sacra*, i. 826-7, ii. 132-3; Eubel, *Hierarchia*, ii. 199, 218; Gaspare da Verona, *Vita di Paolo II*, pp. 103, 134, 211; L. Vedriani, *Historia dell'antichissima città di Modena*, pt. 2 (Modena, 1667), 413; Burckardi, *Liber Notarum*, i. 85; G. Calamari, *Il confidente di Pio II, card. Iacopo Ammanati Piccolomini (1422-1479)* (Rome, 1932), ii. 482, 570; Hausmann, 'Campano', p. 491; Bernardo, *Campano*, p. 378.

SAN GIOVANNI, FERNAN (d. 1527). Sec. 31 Oct. 1521. Von Hofmann, *Forschungen*, ii. 122; Frenz, *Kanzlei*, p. 324.

SAN SEBASTIANO, DANIELE (d. 1504). Sec. 24 Nov. 1498. Von Hofmann, *Forschungen*, ii. 118; Frenz, *Kanzlei*, p. 314. See also Egidi, *Necrologi*, ii. 506; Burckardi, *Liber Notarum*, ii. 27, 36, 111, 117, 151, 654.

SANTA MARIA, ANTONIO (d. by 1498). Sec. 5 Jan. 1492. Von Hofmann, *Forschungen*, ii. 117; Frenz, *Kanzlei*, p. 288. See also Fumi, *Inventario e spoglio di Città di Castello*, pp. 51-6; C. F. Black, 'Politics and Society in Perugia, 1488-1540' (B.Litt. Oxford, 1966), 218; Baumgarten, *Aus Kanzlei und Kammer*, p. 351.

SANTORI, FAZIO (1447-1510). Cl. cam. 12 Aug. 1500. Von Hofmann, *Forschungen*, ii. 93, 82, 101-2, 105; Frenz, *Kanzlei*, p. 322. On his death

250　*Appendix*

see A. Schulte, *Die Fugger in Rom*, i. 51, ii. 21. The confiscation was presumably made as 'spoils'. See also Pastor, *History*, vi. 221; Burckardi, *Liber Notarum*, ii. 26, 373; Cosenza, *Biographical Dictionary*, iv. 3169; Ciacconius, *Vitae*, iii. 259–60.

SANTUCCI, IERONIMO (d. 1494). Cl. cam. supranum. 20 Feb. 1458, Reg. Vat. 467, fo. 3b. See also Von Hofmann, *Forschungen*, ii. 188; Frenz, *Kanzlei*, p. 350 (if Hieronimus de Urbino is I.S.); Eubel, *Hierarchia*, ii. 172.

SARZANA, GOTTARDO DI (dates unknown). Sec. 1447. Von Hofmann, *Forschungen*, ii. 112.

SARZANA, PAOLO DI (dates unknown). Sec. 20 June 1455. Von Hofmann, *Forschungen*, ii. 114; Egidi, *Necrologi*, i. 480; *Vite di Paolo II*, p. 6.

SAULI, BANDINELLO (d. 1518). Sec. 1505. Frenz, *Kanzlei*, p. 301. See also Von Hofmann, *Forschungen*, ii. 83, 120; Burckardi, *Liber Notarum*, ii. 499; Pastor, *History*, vii. 182 ff.; Hirst, *Sebastiano del Piombo*, pp. 99–100. There is a forthcoming article on B.S. by J. Jungić.

SAULI, SEBASTIANO (dates unknown). Sec. 1512–13. Von Hofmann, *Forschungen*, ii. 121; Frenz, *Kanzlei*, p. 442. See also Bullard, *Filippo Strozzi*, p. 128.

SAVELLI, FRANCESCO (d. 1503). Sec. 27 Apr. 1500. Von Hofmann, *Forschungen*, ii. 118; Frenz, *Kanzlei*, p. 333.

Schio, Ieronimo, see *Scledo, Ieronimo*.

SCIONI, GIOVANNI TOMMASO (d. Jan. 1452). Cl. cam. 1429. Baix, *La Chambre apostolique*, pp. CDI–CDII; Partner, *Papal State*, pp. 105, 184; Maire Vigeur, *Les Pâturages*, pp. 81, 110. Rector of Patrimony 1 Sept. 1431, Reg. Vat. 381, fo. 45ᵛ, and again 16 Dec. 1441, Reg. Vat. 182, fo. 147, until 30 Oct. 1442, Arch. Cam. I, Patrimonio, busta 2, vol. 7c, fo. 67ᵛ. He was also rector of the March of Ancona. Political missions to Rome, Reg. Vat. 352, fo. 251, dated Florence 13 Apr. 1419, and Theiner, *Codex Diplomaticus*, iii (1862), nos. 271, 325, dated Florence, 12 July 1434. Other appointments: Von Hofmann, *Forschungen*, ii. 77, 96; Schwarz, 'Abbreviature officium', p. 821; Baumgarten, *Untersuchungen*, LXVIII. 206, 264–5. Death and funeral, Wasner, 'Tor der Geschichte', pp. 139–40.

SCLEDO, IERONIMO (d. 1533). Sec. 31 Aug. 1524, resigned 1532. Von Hofmann, *Forschungen*, ii. 122; Frenz, *Kanzlei*, p. 350. See also Ferrajoli, *Ruolo*, pp. 199–200 n.; Pastor, *History*, ix. 460; B. Morsolin, *Girolamo da Schio* (Vicenza, 1875).

SCRIBANI, MELCHIOR (d. by 6 Dec. 1429). Sec. 1426–9. Von Hofmann, *Forschungen*, ii. 111. See also Partner, *Papal State*, p. 205 n.; Fink, 'Politische Korrespondenz', p. 218; Nasalli Rocca, 'La famiglia', pp. 239–40.

SCUTARI, EUSEBIO (d. 1532). Sec. 1504. Von Hofmann, *Forschungen*, ii. 121; Frenz, *Kanzlei*, p. 320. See also Cosenza, *Biographical Dictionary*, iv. 3237.

Appendix 251

SENE, PHILIPPE DE (dates unknown). Sec. 1502-34, cl. cam. 1510-25. Frenz, *Kanzlei*, p. 435.

Serapica, see *De Magistris, Giovanni Lazaro*.

SERGARDI, FILIPPO (d. by 1536). Cl. cam. 27 Nov. 1504 (deprived 1526), sec. 26 Sept. 1505. Von Hofmann, *Forschungen*, ii. 83, 93, 120, 198; Frenz, *Kanzlei*, p. 435; Lunt, *Papal Revenues*, ii. 537. See also Egidi, *Necrologi*, ii. 375; Pastor, *History*, ix. 467; Ferrajoli, *Ruolo*, p. 107; M. Hirst, 'The Chigi Chapel in S. Maria della Pace', *JCWI* 24 (1961), 161-85; id., *Sebastiano del Piombo*, p. 126. Reinstated as cl. cam. some time between 1526 and 1535, since Baldassare Turini became cl. cam. 15 Mar. 1536, 'per obitum Phy. de Sergadis', Frenz, *Kanzlei*, p. 295, and on 24 Nov. 1535 F.S. had been listed as dean of chamber, L. Dorez, *La Cour du Pape Paul III*, i (Paris, 1932), 83.

SINIBALDI, FALCONE (d. 1492). Sec. 1455, 1487, cl. cam. 1455. Von Hofmann, *Forschungen*, ii. 113; Brouette, 'Les Clercs "mensiers"', (1962), 411-12; id., 'Les clercs "mensiers"' (1973), 582; Frenz, *Kanzlei*, pp. 321-2, no. 649; Piana, *Il 'liber secretus'*, p. 94; *Vite di Paolo II*, pp. 61-2, 144, 223; *Diario Romano di Sebastiano di Branca Tedallini* (Muratori, RRIISS, xxiii/3), 517, 541, 554; Infessura, *Diario*, pp. 246-9, 282; Kraus, 'Die Sekretäre', pp. 60-1; Pitz, *Supplikensignatur*, p. 111; Schwarz, 'Die Abbreviatoren unter Eugen IV.', p. 269; Pastor, *History*, v. 323; Hausmann, 'Campano', p. 439; Gherardi, *Dispacci*; Cosenza, *Biographical Dictionary*, iv. 3283; Kristeller, *Iter Italicum*, i. 114. For the Sinibaldi family in possession of the bishopric of Osimo from 1498, see Eubel, *Hierarchia*, ii. 112, iii. 125.

SODERINI, FRANCESCO (1453-1524). Sec. 1487 until promoted to cardinal 1503. Von Hofmann, *Forschungen*, ii. 116, 119; Frenz, *Kanzlei*, p. 333. See also Bizzocchi, *Chiesa e potere*, p. 229; Stephens, *Fall*, pp. 27, 118, 120-1, 123; Katterbach, *Sussidi*, ii. 53, 62; Ciacconius, *Vitae*, iii. 203; Pastor, *History*, vii. 186-7, 195; McClung Hallman, *Italian Cardinals*, p. 160.

SOLE, MARCO (dates unknown). Cl. cam. supranum. 12 July 1473. Von Hofmann, *Forschungen*, ii. 92; Frenz, *Kanzlei*, p. 404.

SORANZO, BENEDETTO (1442-95). Sec. 1487. Von Hofmann, *Forschungen*, ii. 116; Frenz, *Kanzlei*, p. 302. See G. Dalla Santa, 'Benedetto Soranzo patrizio veneziano: Arcivescovo di Cipro, e Girolamo Riario', *Nuovo Archivio Veneto*, NS, 25 (1914), 308-87; Cenci, in Cenci and Piana, 'Promozioni', pp. 415, 426; Davies, *Renascence*, p. 277.

SPINOLA, AGOSTINO (d. 1537). Sec. Dec. 1505-Dec. 1509; then again 28 Feb. 1510, and buys 2nd and 3rd secretarial offices in 1532. 'Card. et Camerar. S.R.E.' 1527-8. Von Hofmann, *Forschungen*, ii. 120; Frenz, *Kanzlei*, p. 292. See also Ciacconius, *Vitae*, iii. 479-80; McClung Hallman, *Italian Cardinals*, pp. 42, 117, 138; Bullard, *Filippo Strozzi*, pp. 159-60, 170; Cherubini, *Mandati*, p. 82; A. Schiavo, 'Un personaggio della "Messa di Bolsena": Agostino Spinola', *Studi Romani*, 12 (1964), 289-95.

SPINOLA, FRANCESCO (dates unknown). Sec. 13 Sept. 1498, resigned 1503; again 13 Jan. 1518–July 1530. Von Hofmann, Forschungen, ii. 118; Frenz, Kanzlei, p. 334. See also Pastor, History, vii. 475, 486.

SPINOLA, JACOPO (dates unknown). Sec. under John XXIII and Martin V, sworn 1 July 1422. Uginet, Le Liber officialium (fo. 37).

SPINOLA, LUDOVICO (d. 1498). Sec. 29 Jan. 1490 to death. Von Hofmann, Forschungen, ii. 117; Frenz, Kanzlei, p. 401; Burckardi, Liber Notarum, ii. 23, 30.

SPIRITI, ANDREA DE (d. 1504). Cl. cam. 26 May 1470. Von Hofmann, Forschungen, i. 123, ii. 92, 178; Brouette, 'Les Clercs "mensiers"' (1962), 411–12; id., 'Les Clercs "mensiers"' (1973), 583; Frenz, Kanzlei, p. 281; id., 'Gründung', pp. 309–10; Burckardi, Liber Notarum, ii. 9, 160, 345, 357–8; Cronache e statuti, p. 102; Katterbach, Sussidi, ii. 59; Barbini, 'Fazioni', iv. 17–20; Signorelli, Viterbo, i. 228; Lee, Sixtus IV, pp. 131, 240–1. A relative, Cristoforo de' Spiriti, followed Fazio Santori as Bishop of Cesena in 1516 and was succeeded in the bishopric by Gianbattista de' Spiriti in 1545, Eubel, Hierarchia, iii. 144. Cristoforo was described as the nephew of Santori (ibid.).

STAGNA, CARACCIOLO (d. 1513). Sec. 1511–13. Von Hofmann, Forschungen, ii. 120; Frenz, Kanzlei, p. 311 (sec. 28 Aug. 1511, according to Dr Michael Haren). See also Burckardi, Liber Notarum, ii. 117.

SULIMAN DE' SULIMANNIS, canon of Padua (d. 1468). Cl. cam. supranum. Oct. 1446. Von Hofmann, Forschungen, ii. 92, 96. Mensarius Aug. 1449. Bååth, Diplomatarium Svecanum, ii. 539; see also Pitz, Supplikensignatur, p. 263; A. Portenari, Della felicità di Padova (Padua, 1623), 283–4. Lieutenant of chamberlain 4 June 1455, Clergeac, La Curie, p. 259, and again Sept. 1462, Theiner, Codex Diplomaticus, iii. 424 (and see also iii. 410); Cherubini, Mandati, p. 80; Egidi, Necrologi, ii. 136.

Sulmona, Paulus de, see Capograssi, Paolo.

TARASCONO, EVANGELISTA (d. 1532). Sec. 10 Mar. 1511, sec. dom. 1531. Von Hofmann, Forschungen, ii. 121, 124, and see p. 154. See also Frenz, Kanzlei, p. 320; Ferrajoli, Ruolo, pp. 349, 350; Pastor, History, ix. 115; Piana, Il 'liber secretus', p. 8*; Notizia d'opere di disegno nella prima metà del secolo XVI, pubblicata e illustrata da D. Iacopo Morelli (Bassano, 1800), 67, 203–4.

TEMPLI, JOHANNES (d. 1423). Sec. sworn 28 Nov. 1417. Von Hofmann, Forschungen, ii. 110; see also Baumgarten, Aus Kanzlei und Kammer, pp. 135–6; Baix, La Chambre apostolique, p. CCCXCV.

Testa, Tommaso, see Piccolomini, Tommaso.

TOLOSA, GABRIELE (d. 1512). Sec. 1510. Von Hofmann, Forschungen, ii. 120; Frenz, Kanzlei, p. 336; Ferrajoli, Ruolo, p. 227 (for family).

TORNABUONI, ANTONIO FRANCESCO (dates unknown). Cl. cam. supranum. 30 Mar. 1451, 'eximius decretorum doctor, canonicus florentin. . . . de speciali concessione rev. Ludovici camerarii', Reg. Vat. 435, fo. 11b.

TREBISONDA, ANDREA DI (d. 1496). Sec. 5 Mar. 1457 (expectancy only), appointed particip. 13 July 1466, sec. dom. of Sixtus IV. Von Hofmann, *Forschungen*, ii. 114, 123; Frenz, *Kanzlei*, pp. 280-1; Pitz, *Supplikensignatur*, pp. 167, 173; Monfasani, *George of Trebizond*, pp. 236-7; Egidi, *Necrologi*, i. 503; Tangl, *Kanzleiordnungen*, pp. 213-15; L. Onofri, in *Un pontificato e una città*, pp. 74-5.

TREBISONDA, GIORGIO DI (1395-1473). Sec. 7 Feb. 1444, resigned 13 July 1466 in favour of Andrea di Trebisonda. Von Hofmann, *Forschungen*, ii. 112, 114; Kraus, 'Die Sekretäre', p. 30; Monfasani, *George of Trebizond; Collectanea Trapezuntiana*, ed. J. Monfasani (New York, 1984); D'Amico, *Renaissance Humanism*, p. 69; Setton, *The Papacy and the Levant*, ii. 257-8.

TRILHIA, PETRUS DE (dates unknown). Sec. 1417, active until 1428. Von Hofmann, *Forschungen*, ii. 109; Dykmans, 'D'Avignon à Rome', pp. 220-1; Piana, 'Nuovi documenti', p. 546. He was chamber notary at the Council of Basle 1437-9. Dephoff, *Urkunden*, p. 69.

TROCHE, FRANCISCUS (d. 1503). Sec. 1500, sec. dom. 1502. Von Hofmann, *Forschungen*, ii. 118, 124; Frenz, *Kanzlei*, p. 334. See also Burckardi, *Liber Notarum*, ii. 279-80, 330, 337, 339; P. de Roo, *Materials for a History of Pope Alexander VI* (Bruges, 1924), iv. 556-7.

TROFINO, FELIX (d. 1527). Sec. dom. 1526. Von Hofmann, *Forschungen*, ii. 124; Frenz, *Kanzlei*, p. 322. See also Eubel, *Hierarchia*, iii. 311; Katterbach, *Sussidi*, ii. 82; Prosperi, *Tra evangelismo e controriforma*, pp. 27, 96.

TROTTI, LEONELLO (d. 1494). Sec. 1487. Von Hofmann, *Forschungen*, ii. 83, 117; Frenz, *Kanzlei*, p. 398; *CPL* xvi, p. civ. See also A. Frizzi, *Memorie per la storia di Ferrara*, ed. C. Laderchi, iv (Ferrara, 1848), 96, and also pp. 118, 151; A. Piromalli, *La cultura a Ferrara al tempo di Ludovico Ariosto* (Florence, 1953), 38-43; O. Montenovesi, 'La famiglia ferrarese Trotti e i suoi documenti nell'Archivio di Stato in Roma', *Archivi*, 8 (1941), 21-34, at p. 31; Pastor, *History*, iv. 493.

TUERDUS, BALDASSARE (d. 1519). Sec. 1508-13. Frenz, *Kanzlei*, p. 294. See also Ferrajoli, *Ruolo*, pp. 11, 262-7.

TURINI, BALDASSARE (d. 1543). Sec. 1 July 1517, resigned 1521. Von Hofmann, *Forschungen*, ii. 102-3, 121; Frenz, *Kanzlei*, pp. 294-5; Dorez, *Cour de Paul III*, i. 82, 260; Pastor, *History*, viii. 101, 115-16; A. Marabottini, *Polidoro da Caravaggio* (Rome, 1969), i. 63-8, 257-8; Bullard, *Filippo Strozzi*, pp. 36, 101; D. R. Coffin, *The Villa in the Life of Renaissance Rome* (Princeton, 1979), 157-65; R. Lanciani, *Storia degli scavi di Roma*, i (Rome, 1902), 212-13; C. Conforti, 'Architettura e culto della memoria: La commitenza di Baldassare Turini datario di Leone X', in M. Fagiolo and M. L. Madonna (eds.), *Baldassare Peruzzi: Pittura scena e architettura nel Cinquecento* (Rome, 1987), 603-28.

TURLONO, GIACOMO (d. 1483). Cl. cam. 1446. G. Bourgin, 'La famiglia pontificia sotto Eugenio IV', *ASR* 27 (1904), 203-24, at p. 215. Resigned 1452. Von Hofmann, *Forschungen*, ii. 92. See also Fumi, *Inventario e spoglio di Perugia*, pp. 59–63; Bååth, 'L'Inventaire', p. 150; Eubel, *Hierarchia*, ii. 278; Frenz, 'Eindringen', p. 395; *CPL* x. 272, 274; Gottlob, *Aus der Camera apostolica*, p. 162.

TUSCANIA, ANTONIO MARIA DE (d. 1464). Sec. 11 Sept. 1455. Von Hofmann, *Forschungen*, ii. 114; Kraus, 'Die Sekretäre', p. 34; Schwarz, 'Abbreviature officium', p. 816.

Tuzio, Giovanni Battista, see Henricis, Giovanni Battista de.

USUMARI, GIOVANNI BATTISTA (1480–1512). Sec. 19 July 1495, resigned 10 Oct. 1500. Von Hofmann, *Forschungen*, ii. 17; Frenz, *Kanzlei*, p. 388; Eubel, *Hierarchia*, ii. 204; see also Burckardi, *Liber Notarum*, ii. 11.

VAGNUCCI, JACOPO (1416–87). Cl. cam. 22 Mar. 1447. Reg. Vat. 435, fo. 1. See also Von Hofmann, *Forschungen*, ii. 84; Frenz, *Kanzlei*, pp. 359–60; Katterbach, *Sussidi*, ii. 29. Appointed apostolic treasurer 30 June 1452. Reg. Vat. 433, fo. 244a; Reg. Vat. 435, fo. 13b; Cherubini, *Mandati*, p. 78. See also G. Mancini, *Cortona nel Medio Evo* (Florence, 1897), 336–8; Bizzocchi, *Chiesa e potere*, p. 191. Mancini says he held a doctorate in law. Apostolic collector in Emilia and Lombardy 1445–6. See E. Peverada, 'Appunti di Storia Ferrarese', *Quaderni del Giornale Filologico Ferrarese*, 3 (1982), 6–7 n.; Mancini, loc. cit. Papal cubicularius on appointment as Bishop of Rimini 10 June 1448. Eubel, *Hierarchia*, ii. 107 (see also ii. 237). Governor in Bologna 1450. Piana, 'Nuovi documenti', p. 878. Governor of Fano 16 Aug. 1464. Petersohn, *Ein Diplomat*, p. 107. Governor of Spoleto and Narni 25 Oct. 1466–24 Feb. 1469. Arch. Cam. I, Patrimonio, busta 12, reg. 46; busta 13, reg. 49; busta 14, reg. 51. He resigned the bishopric of Perugia in favour of his nephew, Dionigio, reserving a third of the income, 1482. Among numerous benefices he held the monastery of Farneta; see I. Aliotti, *Epistolae* (Arezzo, 1769), i. 361–4; S. Felice, *L'Abbazia di Farneta in Val di Chiana* (Arezzo, 1972).

VALDES, GARCIA (d. 1511). Sec. 19 Jan. 1508. Von Hofmann, *Forschungen*, ii. 120; Frenz, *Kanzlei*, p. 337; Burckardi, *Liber Notarum*, ii. 111.

VALLA, LORENZO. Sec. 1455. Von Hofmann, *Forschungen*, ii. 114; F. Gaeta, *Lorenzo Valla: Filologia e storia nell'umanesimo italiano* (Naples, 1955); M. Fois, *Il pensiero storico di Lorenzo Valla nel quadro storico-culturale del suo ambiente* (Rome, 1969); Nasalli Rocca, 'La famiglia'; Gualdo, 'Francesco Filelfo'; R. Fubini, 'Ricerche sul "De voluptate" di Lorenzo Valla', *Medioevo e Rinascimento*, 1 (1987), 190–239.

VEGNATE, ANTONIO (dates unknown). Sec. 16 June 1458. Von Hofmann, *Forschungen*, ii. 115.

VENIERI, ANTONIO JACOPO (1422–79). Cl. cam. supranum. 13 July 1451, sworn 22 Mar. 1455; sec. 21 Oct. 1457. Von Hofmann, *Forschungen*, ii. 92, 115; Frenz, *Kanzlei*, pp. 289–90; Katterbach, *Sussidi*, ii. 46; Forcella, *Iscrizioni*, iv. 506; Davies, *Renascence*, p. 215; R. De Roover, *Il banco Medici dalle origini al declino* (Florence, 1970), 393; Gherardi, *Diario*, pp. 6–7; Kraus, 'Die Sekretäre', p. 33; Ciacconius, *Vitae*, iii. 52;

Theiner, *Codex Diplomaticus*, iii. 481; M. Rosi, *Della Signoria di Francesco Sforza nella Marca secondo le memorie dell'Archivio Recanatense* (Recanati, 1895), 362. His uncle was Archbishop of Ragusa, lieutenant of Ludovico of Treviso ('Scarampo') in the Marches, ibid. 231, 233, 235, 262, 274. See also G. Benaducci, *Della signoria di Francesco Sforza nella Marca e peculiarmente in Tolentino* (Tolentino, 1892), 348; Paschini, *Ludovico Cardinal Camerlengo*, pp. 102–3.

VENIERI, GIOVANNI (d. 1490). Sec. 1487. Von Hofmann, *Forschungen*, ii. 116; Frenz, *Kanzlei*, p. 388, and see also p. 336, no. 808, p. 352, no. 1006. See also *CPL* xi. 486 and *passim*; *CPL* xii. 230–1; Eubel, *Hierarchia*, ii. 243.

VENIERI, JACOPO ANTONIO (d. 1440). Cl. cam. 7 Jan. 1434, decretorum doctor. Arch. Cam. I, vol. 1712, fo. 21ᵛ; see also vol. 1468, fo. 1ᵛ. (audits accounts of F. de Padua, 19 Apr. 1438). Göller, *Päpstliche Poenitentiarie*, i, pt. 1, 122; Eubel, *Hierarchia*, ii. 242; Bååth, 'L'Inventaire', pp. 151, 157; Frenz, 'Problem', p. 272; Theiner, *Codex Diplomaticus*, iii. 325, 392; Hofmann, *Concilium Florentinum*, iii, fasc. 1 (Rome, 1950), 91. Rector of Patrimony of St Peter in Tuscia 15 Mar. 1446. Reg. Vat. 383, fo. 42ᵛ.

VERONA, GASPARE DA (d. 1474). Sec. 17 May 1455. Von Hofmann, *Forschungen*, ii. 113; see also Introduction by Zippel to *Vite di Paolo II*, pp. xxix, xxxi. Signs as secretary before promotion, *CPL* xi. 6 (20 Apr. 1455). See also M. Miglio, 'Note sul manoscritto del primo libro del "De gestis Pauli Secundi" di Gaspare da Verona', *Miscellanea in memoria di Giorgio Cencetti* (Turin, 1973), 271–84; id., *Storiografia pontificia del Quattrocento* (Bologna, 1975); A. Andrews, 'The "Lost" Fifth Book in the Life of Pope Paul II by Gaspar of Verona', *Studies in the Renaissance*, 17 (1970), 7–45; A. J. Dunston, 'Pope Paul II and the Humanists', *Journal of Religious History*, 7 (1973), 287–306.

VISCONTI, AMBROGIO. Cl. cam. 1418. Baix, *La Chambre apostolique*, pp. CCCLXXXI-CCCLXXXII; Kühne, *Repertorium Germanicum*, iii. 28*–29* (protest of the Pisan clerks); Schuchard, *Deutschen Kurie*, p. 79; Partner, *Papal State*, pp. 217–18; Frenz, 'Problem', pp. 263, 270.

WALLER, NICASIUS (dates unknown). Sec. 24 Apr. 1456. Von Hofmann, *Forschungen*, ii. 114. See also Pitz, *Supplikensignatur*, pp. 75, 100; Schwarz, 'Abbreviature Officium', p. 813.

WOLAVIA, NICHOLAS DE (d. 1418/19). Cl. cam. at Constance and under Martin V 14 Mar. 1418. Baix, *La Chambre apostolique*, pp. CCCLII, CCCLXX-CCCLXXI; Von Hofmann, *Forschungen*, i. 240; Schuchard, *Deutschen Kurie*, pp. 81, 82.

Ylperini, Luca, see *Alberini, Luca*.

ZAFFIRI, SIMONE (d. after Aug. 1429). Cl. cam. 19 Nov. 1419. Baix, *La Chambre apostolique*, pp. CCCLXIX-CCCLXX. See also Partner, *Papal State*, pp. 18, 218; Von Hofmann, *Forschungen*, ii. 179; Uginet, *Le Liber Officialium*, pp. 29–30; Clergeac, *La Curie*, p. 110.

ZISTERER, PAUL (dates unknown). Sec. dom.(?) 1523. Von Hofmann, *Forschungen*, ii. 124. See also Pastor, *History*, ix. 121, 166.

HONORIFIC APPOINTMENTS CONNECTED
WITH EMBASSIES

ANDORIA, BENEDICTUS DE. Sec. 1 May 1420. Von Hofmann, *Forschungen*, ii. 110–11. Chancellor of the Doge of Genoa.

CORNINI, GIOVANNI. Sec. 8 Feb. 1418. Von Hofmann, *Forschungen*, ii. 110. Ambassador and secretary of Duke of Milan.

DIAZ, FERNAN. Sec. 22 May 1440. Von Hofmann, *Forschungen*, ii. 112. Referendary of the King of Castile.

FERNAN, PEDRO. Cl. cam. Dec. 1417. Von Hofmann, *Forschungen*, ii. 197. Secretary of the King of Castile.

FERRER, FRANCISCUS. Sec. 19 Nov. 1455. Von Hofmann, *Forschungen*, ii. 114. Proctor of the King of Navarre.

GALINDO, JOHANNES. Cl. cam. Sept. 1418. Von Hofmann, *Forschungen*, ii. 197. Secretary of the King of Navarre.

GAZUL, ANDREA. Sec. 24 Apr. 1447. Von Hofmann, *Forschungen*, ii. 112. Secretary of the King of Aragon. See also Ryder, *Kingdom of Naples*, pp. 220–1, 233, 234.

Bibliography

PRIMARY SOURCES

Acta Pontifica Danica (1904–15).

Albizzi, Rinaldo, see Guasti, C.

Arnold, R. (ed.), *Repertorium Germanicum*, i (Berlin, 1897).

Bååth, L. M., *Diplomatarium Svecanum: Appendix: Acta Pontificum Svecica* (Stockholm, 1936–57).

Burckardi, J., *Liber Notarum*, ed. E. Celani (RRIISS xxii/1).

Calendar of Entries in the Papal Registers: Papal Letters (cited as CPL) i–xiv (London, 1893–1960); xv–xvi (Dublin, 1978–86); vol. xvii, ed. Dr Michael Haren, is forthcoming.

Cherubini, P., *Mandati della reverenda Camera Apostolica (1418–1802)* (Rome, 1988).

Cronache e statuti della città di Viterbo, ed. C. Ciampi (Florence, 1872).

De Vecchis, P. A., *Collectio Constitutionum Chirographorum et Brevium* (Rome, 1732).

Diario romano di Sebastiano di Branca Tedallini (RRIISS, xxiii/3).

Egidi, P., *Necrologi e libri affini della provincia romana* (Rome, 1908–14).

Eubel, C., and others, *Hierarchia Catholica Medii Aevi*, i–iii (Münster, 1898–1923).

Fink, K. A., 'Die politische Korrespondenz Martins V. nach den Brevenregistern', *Quellen*, 26 (1935/6), 172–245.

—— (ed.), *Repertorium Germanicum* (Berlin, 1943–58).

Finke, H., *Acta Concilii Constanciensis* (Münster, 1896–1928).

Forcella, V., *Iscrizioni delle chiese e d'altri edifizi di Roma dal secolo XI fino ai giorni nostri* (Rome, 1869–85).

Fumi, L., *Inventario e spoglio dei registri della tesoreria apostolica di Città di Castello dal R. Archivio di Stato in Roma* (Perugia, 1900).

—— *Inventario e spoglio dei registri della tesoreria apostolica di Perugia e Umbria dal R. Archivio di Stato in Roma* (Perugia, 1901).

Gaspare da Verona, *Vita di Paolo II* (RRIISS, NS, iii/16, ed. G. Zippel).

Gherardi, Giacomo, *Dispacci e lettere di Giacomo Gherardi nunzio pontificio a Firenze e Milano (11 settembre 1487–10 ottobre 1490)*, ed. E. Carusi (Vatican City, 1909).

—— *Il diario romano*, ed. E. Carusi (RRIISS xxiii/3).

Guasti, C. (ed.), *I commissioni di Rinaldo degli Albizzi*, i (Florence, 1864).

Hergenroether, J., *Leonis X. Pontificis Maximi Regesta* (Freiburg i.B., 1884).

Hofmann, G. (ed.), *Concilium Florentinum*, iii (Rome, 1950).

Infessura, Stefano, *Diario della città di Roma*, ed. O. Tommasini (Rome, 1890).

Kühne, U. (ed.), *Repertorium Germanicum* (Berlin, 1935).

Litta, P., *Famiglie celebri italiane* (Milan, 1819–58).

Lombardo, M. L., *La Camera urbis* (Rome, 1970).

Mabillon, J., *Iter Italicum*, i (Paris, 1687).

Magnum Bullarium Romanum, i–ii (Luxemburg, 1727).

Medici, Lorenzo de', *Lettere*, ed. N. Rubinstein and others (Florence, 1977–81).

Müntz, E., *Les Arts à la cour des papes pendant le XVe et le XVIe siècles* (Paris, 1878–82).

Nogara, B., Puncuh, D., and Roncallo, A. (eds.), *Suppliche di Martino V relative alla Liguria*, i. *Diocesi di Genova* (Atti della Società Ligure di Storia Patria, 87, NS, 13 (1973).

Ottenthal, E. von, *Die päpstlichen Kanzleiregeln von Johannes XXII. bis Nicolaus V.* (Innsbruck, 1888).

Paschini, P., *Il carteggio fra il cardinale Marco Barbo e Giovanni Lorenzi* (Vatican City, 1948).

Paul II, *Le vite di Paolo II*, ed. G. Zippel (RRIISS iii/16).

Pélissier, L. G., 'Catalogue des documents de la collection Podocataro à la Biblioteca Marciana à Venise', *Centrallblatt für Bibliothekswesen*, 18 (1901), 473–93, 521–41, 576–98.

Piana, C., *Nuove ricerche sulle Università di Bologna e di Parma* (Bologna, 1966).

—— 'Nuovi documenti sull'Università di Bologna e sul Collegio di Spagna', *Studia Albornotiana*, 25 (1976).

—— *Il 'liber secretus iuris Caesarei' dell'Università di Bologna 1451-1500* (Milan, 1984).

—— and Cenci, C., 'Promozioni agli ordini sacri a Bologna e alle dignità ecclesiastiche nel Veneto nei secoli XIV–XV', *Spicilegium Bonaventurianum*, 3 (1968).

Piccolomini, Aeneas Sylvius, *Aeneas Sylvii Epistolae*, ed. J. Cugnoni (Rome, 1883).

Pius II, *Le vite di Pio II*, ed. G. C. Zimolo (RRIISS iii/3).

Poggio Bracciolini, *Les Facéties de Pogge*, ii (Paris, 1878).

Pontani, G., *Diario romano di Gaspare Pontani*, ed. D. Toni (RRIISS iii/2).

Puncuh, D., 'Carteggio di Pileo de Marini arcivescovo di Genova (1400–1429)', *Atti della Società Ligure di Storia Patria*, 85, NS 11 (1971).

Rius Serra, J., *Regesto iberico de Calixto III* (Barcelona, 1948).

Sanudo, *I diarii di Marino Sanuto* (Venice, 1879–1903).

Sciambra, M., Valentini, G., and Parino, I., *Il 'liber brevium' di Callisto III* (Palermo, 1968).

Tangl, M., *Die päpstlichen Kanzleiordnungen von 1200-1500* (Innsbruck, 1894).

Theiner, A., *Codex Diplomaticus Temporalis Sanctae Sedis*, iii (Rome, 1862).

Ubaldini, F., *Vita di Mons. Angelo Colocci*, ed. V. Fanelli (Vatican City, 1969).

Ughelli, F., *Italia Sacra* (Venice, 1717–22).

Uginet, F.-C., *Le Liber officialium de Martin V* (Pubblicazioni degli Archivi di Stato, Fonti e Sussidi, 7; Rome, 1975).

Vespasiano da Bisticci, *Vite di uomini illustri del secolo XV*, ed.
   P. d'Ancona and E. Aeschlimann (Milan, 1951).
Verde, A. F., *Lo studio fiorentino 1473-1503: Ricerche e documenti*
   (Florence, 1973-85).
Zonta, G., and Brotto, G., *Acta Graduum Academicorum Gymnasii
   Patavini ab anno 1406 ad annum 1450* (Padua, 1970).

SECONDARY SOURCES

Alberigo, G., *I vescovi italiani al concilio di Trento* (Florence, 1959).
Ançel, R., 'La Secrétairerie pontificale sous Paul IV', *Revue des
   Questions Historiques*, 79, NS 30 (1906), 408-70.
Antonovics, A. V., 'A Late Fifteenth-Century Division Register of the
   College of Cardinals', *PBSR* 35 (1967), 87-101.
Anzilotti, A., 'Cenni sulle finanze del Patrimonio di S. Pietro in Tuscia
   nel secolo XV', *ASR* 42 (1919).
Bååth, L. M., 'L'Inventaire de la Chambre apostolique de 1440', *Miscel-
   lanea Archivistica Angelo Mercati* (Vatican City, 1952), 135-57.
Baix, F., *La Chambre apostolique et les 'libri annatarum' de Martin V
   (1417-1431)* (Analecta Vaticano-Belgica, 14; 1942).
Barbiche, R., 'Les "Scriptores" de la Chancellerie apostolique sous le
   pontificat de Boniface VIII (1295-1303)', *Bib.Éc.Ch.* 128 (1970),
   115-87.
Barbini, B., 'Fazioni in lotta a Viterbo al tempo di Alessandro VI',
   Biblioteca e Società, 4 (Viterbo, 1982), 17-20.
Bauer, C., 'Die Epochen der Papstfinanz: Ein Versuch', *Historische
   Zeitschrift*, 138 (1927), 457-503.
Baumgarten, P. M., *Untersuchungen und Urkunden über die Camera
   Collegii Cardinalium* (Leipzig, 1898).
—— *Aus Kanzlei und Kammer* (Freiburg, 1907).
Benci, S., *Storia di Montepulciano* (Florence, 1646; another edn.,
   ed. I. Calabresi and P. Tiraboschi, Florence, 1968).
Berengo, M., *Nobili e mercanti nella Lucca del Cinquecento* (Turin,
   1974 repr.).
Bernardo, F. di, *Un vescovo umanista alla corte pontificia: Giannantonio
   Campana (1429-1477)* (Rome, 1975).
Berrigan, R., 'Leonardo Dati: "Hiensal Tragoedia": A Critical Edition
   with Translation', *Human.Lovan.* 25 (1976).
Bicchierai, J., 'Antonio da Noceto', *ASI*, 5th ser., 4 (1889), 34-49.
Bizzocchi, R., *Chiesa e potere nella Toscana del Quattrocento* (Bologna,
   1987).
—— 'Chiesa e aristocrazia nelle Firenze del Quattrocento', *ASI* 143
   (1984), 191-282.
Blet, P., *Histoire de la représentation diplomatique du Saint-Siège des
   origines à l'aube du XIXe siècle* (Vatican City, 1982).
Bourgin, G., 'Les Cardinaux français et le diaire caméral de 1439-76',
   Mélanges, 24 (1904), 277-318.

Bresslau, H., *Handbuch der Urkundenlehre für Deutschland und Italien* (3rd edn., Berlin, 1958).
Brosius, D., 'Die Pfründen des Enea Silvio Piccolomini', *Quellen*, 54 (1974), 271–327.
Brouette, E., 'Les Clercs "mensiers" de la Chambre apostolique sous le pontificat de Sixte IV', *BIHBR* 24 (1962), 405–18.
—— 'Les Clercs "mensiers" de la Chambre apostolique sous les pontificats d'Innocent VIII et d'Alexandre VI (1484–1503)', *Économies et sociétés au Moyen Age: Mélanges offerts à Édouard Perroy* (Paris, 1973), 581–7.
Brown, C. M., '"Lo insaciabile desiderio nostro de cose antique": New Documents for Isabella d'Este's Collection of Antiquities', in C. H. Clough (ed.), *Cultural Aspects of the Italian Renaissance: Essays in honour of Paul Kristeller* (Manchester, 1976), 324–53.
Bullard, M. M., *Filippo Strozzi and the Medici: Favour and Finance in Sixteenth-Century Florence and Rome* (Cambridge, 1980).
—— '"Mercatores Florentini Romanam Curiam Sequentes" in the Early Sixteenth Century', *Journal of Medieval and Renaissance Studies*, 6 (1976), 51–71.
Burkolter, V., *The Patronage System: Theoretical Remarks* (Basle, 1976).
Burroughs, G., 'Below the Angel: An Urbanistic Project in the Rome of Nicholas V', *JWCI* 45 (1982), 94–124.
Camelli, U., 'Il monastero di S. Bartolomeo "de campo fullonum" e i prelati di casa Capranica', *Studia Picena*, 11 (1935), 81–102.
Célier, L., *Les Dataires du XVe siècle et les origines de la Daterie apostolique* (Paris, 1910).
Cerchiari, E., *Capellani Papae et Apostolicae Sedis: Auditores Causarum Sacri Palatii Apostolici seu Sacrae Romana Rota*, ii (Rome, 1921).
Chambers, D. S., *Cardinal Bainbridge in the Court of Rome 1509 to 1514* (Oxford, 1965).
—— 'The Economic Predicament of Renaissance Cardinals', *Studies in Medieval and Renaissance History*, 3 (1966), 289–313.
Ciacconius, A. (Chacón), *Vitae et Res Gestae Pontificum Romanorum et S.R.E. Cardinalium*, iii (Rome, 1677).
Clergeac, A., *La Curie et les bénéfices consistoriaux* (Paris, 1911).
Clough, C. H. (ed.), *Cultural Aspects of the Italian Renaissance: Essays in honour of Paul Kristeller* (Manchester, 1976).
Cosenza, M., *Biographical and Bibliographical Dictionary of the Italian Humanists, 1300–1800* (Boston, 1962).
D'Amico, J. F., *Renaissance Humanism in Papal Rome: Humanists and Churchmen on the Eve of the Reformation* (Baltimore and London, 1983).
Dalla Santa, G., 'Benedetto Soranzo patrizio veneziano; arcivescovo di Cipro, e Girolamo Riario', *Nuovo Archivio Veneto*, NS 25 (1914), 308–87.
Davies, G. S., *Renascence: The Sculptured Tombs of the Fifteenth Century in Rome* (London, 1910).

Dean, T., 'Lords, Vassals and Clients in Renaissance Ferrara', *EHR* 100 (1985), 106–19.

—— *Land and Power in Medieval Ferrara: The Rule of the Este, 1350–1450* (Cambridge, 1988).

Dephoff, J., *Zum Urkunden und Kanzleiwesen des Konzils von Basel*. (Geschichtliche Darstellungen und Quellen, ed. L. Schmitz-Kallenberg, 2; 1930).

Desert, D., *Argent, pouvoir et société au Grand Siècle* (Paris, 1984).

Dorez, L., *La Cour du Pape Paul III* (Paris, 1932).

Dury, C., 'Les Curialistes belges à Rome et l'histoire de la curie romaine, problème de l'histoire de l'église', *BIHBR* 50 (1980), 131–60.

Dykmans, M., 'D'Avignon à Rome: Martin V et le cortège apostolique', *BIHBR* 39 (1968), 203–309.

Emden, A. E., *A Biographical Register of the University of Oxford to A.D. 1500* (Oxford, 1957–9).

Esch, A., *Bonifaz IX. und der Kirchenstaat* (Tübingen, 1969).

—— 'Das Papsttum unter der Herrschaft der Neapolitaner: Die führende Gruppe Neapolitaner Familien an der Kurie während des Schismas 1378–1415', *Festschrift für Hermann Heimpel*, ii (Göttingen, 1972).

Ferrajoli, A., *Il Ruolo della Corte di Leone X*, ed. V. de Caprio (Rome, 1984; originally published by Ferrajoli in the *Archivio della Società Romana*, 1911–18).

Ferrari Moreni, G., 'Vita del Cardinale Gio. Battista Ferrari di Modena', *Atti e Memorie delle RR. Deputazioni di Storia Patria per la Provincie Modenesi e Parmensi*, 8 (1876), 15–63.

Fink, K. A., 'Dominicus Capranica als Legat in Perugia', *Röm.Quart.* 39 (1931), 272–7.

Flamini, F., 'Leonardo di Pietro Dati, poeta latino del sec. XV', *Giornale Storico della Letteratura Italiana*, 16 (1890), 1–107; 22 (1893), 415–17.

Foffano, T., 'La costruzione de Castiglione Olona in un opuscolo inedito di Francesco Pizzolpasso', *Ital.Med.Uman.* 3 (1960), 153–87.

Frenz, T., 'Das Eindringen humanistischer Schriftsformen in die Urkunden und Akten der päpstlichen Kurie im 15. Jahrhundert', *Arch.f.Dipl.* 19 (1973), 287–418.

—— 'Zum Problem der Reduzierung der Zahl der päpstlichen Kanzleischreiber nach dem Konzil von Konstanz', in W. Schlögl and P. Herde (eds.), *Grundwissenschaften und Geschichte* (Münchener historische Studien, Abt. Geschichtliche Hilfswissenschaften, 15; Kallmünz, 1976), 256–73.

—— 'Die verlorenen Brevenregister 1421–1527', *Röm.Quart.* 57 (1977), 354–65.

—— 'Die Gründung des Abbreviatoren-kollegs durch Pius II. und Sixtus IV.', *Miscellanea M. Giusti*, i (Vatican City, 1978), 297–329.

—— 'Armarium XXXIX, vol. 11 im Vatikanischen Archiv: Ein Formelbuch für Breven aus der Zeit Julius II.', in *Hoberg Festschrift*, i (1979), 197–213.

—— *Die Kanzlei der Päpste der Hochrenaissance (1471–1527)* (Tübingen, 1986).

Fubini, R., 'Tra umanesimo e concilio: Note e giunte a una pubblicazione recente su Francesco Pizolpasso (c.1370-1443)', Studi Medievali, 7 (1966), 323-70.

Fuller, A. P., Introduction to the Calendared Letters, in CPL xvi.

Girgensohn, D., 'Wie wird man Kardinal? Kuriale und außerkuriale Karrieren an der Wende des 14. zum 15. Jahrh.', Quellen, 57 (1977), 138-62.

Giusti, M., 'I registri Vaticani e le loro provenienze originali', Miscellanea Archivistica Angelo Mercati (Vatican City, 1952), 383-459.

Göller, E., Der liber taxarum der päpstlichen Kammer: Eine Studie über seine Entstehung und Anlage (Rome, 1905).

—— Die päpstliche Pönitentiarie von ihrem Ursprung bis zu ihrer Umgestaltung unter Pius V. (Rome, 1907-11).

Gorni, G., 'Storia del Certame Coronario', Rinascimento, 2nd ser., 12 (1972), 135-81.

Gottlob, A., Aus der Camera apostolica des 15. Jahrhunderts (Innsbruck, 1889).

Greco, A., 'Vecchi e nuovi elementi nella biografia di Niccolò Perotti', in 'Niccolò Perotti: Atti del Congresso nel quinto centenario della morte', Respublica Litterarum: Studies in the Classical Tradition, iv-v (Lawrence, 1981-2), 77-81.

Gualdo, G., 'Il "liber brevium de curia anni septimi": Contributo allo studio del breve pontificio', Mélanges Tisserant, iv (Vatican City, 1964), 301-45.

—— 'Francesco Filelfo e la curia pontificia: Una carriera mancata', Archivio della Società Romana di Storia Patria, 102 (1979), 189-236.

Guasti, C., 'Gli avanzi dell'archivio di un pratese vescovo di Volterra', ASI, 4th ser., 13 (1884), 20-68.

Guillemain, B., La Cour pontificale d'Avignon 1309-1376: Étude d'une société (Paris, 1962).

Guiraud, J., L'État pontifical après le Grand Schism: Étude de géographie politique (Paris, 1896).

Gundesheimer, W. L., Ferrara: The Style of a Renaissance Despotism (Princeton, 1973).

Haren, M., Introductions to the Calendared Letters, CPL xv, xvii.

Hausmann, F.-R., 'Giovanni Antonio Campano (1429-1477): Erläuterungen und Ergänzungen zu seiner Briefen' (mimeographed diss., Freiburg i.Breisgau, 1968).

—— 'Armarium 39 Tomus 10 des Archivio Segreto Vaticano: Ein Beitrag zum Epistolar des Kardinals Giacomo Ammanati-Piccolomini (1422-1479) und anderer Humanisten', Quellen, 50 (1971), 112-80.

—— 'Die Benefizien des Kardinals Jakopo Ammanati-Piccolomini: Ein Beitrag zur ökonomischen Situation des Kardinalats im Quattrocento', Röm.Hist.Mitt. 13 (1971) 27-80.

Hay, D., The Church in Italy in the Fifteenth Century (Cambridge, 1977).

Hintze, O., Soziologie und Geschichte (Göttingen, 1964).

—— Historical Essays of Otto Hintze, ed. F. Gilbert (New York, 1975).

Hirst, M., *Sebastiano del Piombo* (Oxford, 1981).

Hoberg Festschrift = E. Gatz (ed.), *Römische Kurie, Kirchliche Finanzen, Vatikanisches Archiv: Studien zu Ehren von Herman Hoberg* (Miscellanea Historiae Pontificiae, 45/6; Rome, 1979).

Hofmann, W. von, *Forschungen zur Geschichte der kurialen Behörden vom Schisma bis zur Reformation* (Rome, 1914).

Imbart de la Tour, P., *Les Origines de la Réforme*, ii (2nd edn., Melun, 1946).

Jedin, H., 'Vorschläge und Entwürfe zur Kardinalsreform', in H. Jedin, *Kirche des Glaubens Kirche der Geschichte*, ii (Freiburg, Basle, and Vienna, 1966), 118–47.

Katterbach, B. (ed.), *Sussidi per la consultazione dell'Archivio Vaticano*, ii. *Referendarii utriusque Signaturae a Martino V usque ad Clementem IX* (Vatican City, 1931).

Kettering, S., *Patrons, Brokers and Clients in Seventeenth-Century France* (New York and Oxford, 1986).

Kraus, A., 'Die Sekretäre Pius II.: Ein Beitrag zur Entwicklungsgeschichte des päpstlichen Staatssekretariats', *Röm.Quart.* 53 (1958), 25–80.

—— 'Secretarius und Sekretariat: Der Ursprung der Institution des Staatssekretariats und ihr Einfluß auf die Entwicklung moderner Regierungsformen in Europa', *Röm.Quart.* 55 (1960), 43–84.

—— *Das päpstliche Staatssekretariat unter Urban VIII. 1623–1644* (Rome, Freiburg, and Vienna, 1964).

Kristeller, P. O., *Iter Italicum*, i (Leiden, 1963).

Lee, E., *Sixtus IV and Men of Letters* (Rome, 1978).

Lefèvre, R., 'Fiorentini a Roma nel '400: I Dati', *Studi Romani*, 20 (1972), 187–97.

Lesage, G.-L., 'La Titulaire des envoyés pontificaux sous Pie II (1458–1464)', *Mélanges*, 58 (1941–6), 206–47.

Lightbown, R. W., *Donatello and Michelozzo: An Artistic Partnership and its Patrons in the Early Renaissance* (London, 1980).

Lodolini, E., 'I libri di conti di Antonio Fatati tesoriere generale della Marca (1449–1453) nell'Archivio di Stato', *AMSM*, 8th ser., 4 (1964–5).

Lulvès, J., 'Päpstliche Wahlkapitulationen', *Quellen*, 12 (1909), 212–35.

Lunt, W. E., *Papal Revenues in the Middle Ages* (New York, 1934).

—— *The Financial Relations of the Papacy with England, 1327–1534* (Cambridge, Mass., 1962).

Mabillon, J., *Iter Italicum*, i (Paris, 1687).

McClung Hallman, B., *Italian Cardinals, Reform, and the Church as Property* (Berkeley, Los Angeles, and London, 1985).

Maire Vigeur, J. C., *Les Pâturages de l'Église et la douane de bétail dans la province du Patrimonio (XIVᵉ-XVᵉ siècles)* (Rome, 1981).

Mallett, M., 'Venice and its Condottieri, 1404–54', *Renaissance Venice* (London, 1973), 121–45.

Marchesi Buonaccorsi, G. V., *Antichità e eccellenza del protonotariato apostolico* (Faenza, 1751).

Martines, L., The Social World of the Florentine Humanists (Princeton, 1963).

—— Lawyers and Statecraft in Renaissance Florence (Princeton, 1978).

Mercati, G., Per la cronologia della vita e degli scritti di Niccolò Perotti arcivescovo di Siponto (Rome, 1925).

—— Ultimi contributi alla storia degli umanisti (Vatican City, 1939).

Miglio, M., Storiografia pontificia nel Quattrocento (Bologna, 1975).

Miller, M. C., 'Participation at the Council of Pavia–Siena 1423–1424', AHP 22 (1984), 289–406.

Minnich, N. H., 'The Participants at the Fifth Lateran Council', AHP 12 (1974), 157–206.

Mitteis, L. von, 'Curiale Eidregister', MIÖG, Ergbd. vi (1901).

Mollat, G., The Popes at Avignon 1305–1378 (London, 1963).

Monfasani, J., George of Trebizond: A Biography and a Study of His Rhetoric and Logic (Leiden, 1976).

Musso, C. G., 'Cultura genovese fra Quattro e Cinquecento', Miscellanea di Storia Ligure, 1 (1958), 121–87.

Nasalli Rocca, E., 'La famiglia di Lorenzo Valla e piacentini nella curia di Roma nel sec. XV', Archivio Storico per le Provincie Parmensi, 9 (1957), 227–59.

Nüske, G., 'Untersuchungen über das Personal der päpstlichen Kanzlei, 1254–1304', Arch.f.Dipl. 20 (1974), 39–240; 21 (1975), 249–431.

Ottenthal, E. von, 'Die Bullenregister Martins V. und Eugens IV.', MIÖG, Ergbd. i (1885), 401–589.

Ourliac, P., 'La Pragmatique Sanction et la légation en France du Cardinal d'Estouteville', Mélanges, 55 (1938), 403–32.

Pagliucchi, P., I castellani di Castel S. Angelo (Rome, 1906; repr. 1973).

Palermino, R. J., 'The Roman Academy, the Catacombs, and the Conspiracy of 1468', AHP 18 (1980), 117–55.

Paravicini Bagliani, A., Cardinali di curia e 'familiae' cardinalizie dal 1227 al 1254 (Padua, 1972).

Paredi, A., La biblioteca del Pizzolpasso (Milan, 1961).

Partner, P., 'Camera Papae: Problems of Papal Finance in the Later Middle Ages', JEH 4 (1953), 55–68.

—— The Papal State under Martin V: The Administration and Government of the Temporal Power in the Early Fifteenth Century (London, 1958).

—— 'The "Budget" of the Roman Church in the Renaissance Period', in E. F. Jacob (ed.), Italian Renaissance Studies: A Tribute to the Late C. M. Ady (London, 1960), 256–78.

—— 'Legations', New Catholic Encyclopedia (1967).

—— 'Florence and the Papacy in the Earlier Fifteenth Century', in N. Rubinstein (ed.), Florentine Studies: Politics and Society in Renaissance Florence (London, 1968), 381–402.

—— The Lands of St Peter: The Papal State in the Middle Ages and the Early Renaissance (London, and Berkeley, LA, 1972).

—— 'Papal Financial Policy in the Renaissance and Counter-Reformation', Past and Present, 88 (1980), 17–62.

—— 'Economia, politica, classi sociali e cultura nello Stato della Chiesa nel XV–XVI secolo', *Storia della Società Italiana*, 8 (Milan, 1988).

—— 'Francesco dal Legname: A Curial Bishop in Disgrace', in P. Denley and C. Elam (eds.), *Florence and Italy: Renaissance Studies in honour of Nicolai Rubinstein* (London, 1988), 395–404.

Paschini, P., *Ludovico Cardinal Camerlengo (†1465)* (Lateranum, NS 5; Rome, 1939).

Pastor, L. von, *History of the Popes from the Close of the Middle Ages*, i–xv (1950–1).

Pastura Ruggiero, M. G., *La reverenda Camera Apostolica e i suoi archivi (secoli XV–XVIII)* (Rome, 1987).

Pásztor, L., 'Le cedole consistoriali', *AHP* 11 (1973), 209–68.

Penuti, C., 'Aspetti della politica economica nello stato pontificio sul finire del '500: Le "visite economiche" di Sisto V', *Ann.Ist.Ital.-germ.Tr.* 2 (1976), 183–202.

Pesce, L., 'Cristoforo Garatone trevigiano nuncio di Eugenio IV', *RSCI* 28 (1974), 23–93.

Petersohn, J., *Ein Diplomat des Quattrocento: Angelo Geraldini (1422–1486)* (Tübingen, 1985).

Peverada, E., 'Il vescovo Francesco de Lignamine e il sinodo del clero romano del 1461', *Analecta Pomposiana: Miscellanea di Storia Religiosa delle Diocesi di Ferrara e Comacchio*, 4 (1978), 177–241.

—— *La visita pastorale del vescovo Francesco del Legname a Ferrara (1447–1450)* (Deputazione Provinciale Ferrarese di Storia Patria, ser. monumenti, 8; 1982).

Pieraccini, G., *La stirpe de' Medici di Cafaggiolo*, i (Florence, 1924).

Pitz, E., *Supplikensignatur und Briefexpedition an der römischen Kurie im Pontifikat Papst Calixts III.* (Tübingen, 1972).

Portenari, A., *Della felicità di Padova* (Padua, 1623).

Prete, S., *L'umanista Niccolò Perotti* (Sassoferato, 1980).

Prodi, P., *Il sovrano pontefice: Un corpo e due anime: La monarchia papale nella prima età moderna* (Bologna, 1982). Engl. tr., *Papal Prince—One Body and Two Souls: The Papal Monarchy in Early Modern Europe* (Cambridge, 1988).

A. Prosperi, *Tra evangelismo e controriforma: G. M. Giberti (1495–1543)* (Rome, 1969).

Re, N. del, *La curia romana* (Rome, 1970).

—— *Monsignore Governatore di Roma* (Rome, 1972).

Reinhard, W., 'Papa Pius: Prolegomena zu einer Sozialgeschichte des Papsttums', *Von Constanz nach Trient: Beiträge zur Kirchengeschichte . . . Festgabe für August Franzen* (Paderborn, 1972), 261–99.

—— 'Ämterlaufbahn und Familienstatus: Der Aufstieg des Hauses Borghese 1537–1621', *Quellen*, 54 (1974), 328–427.

—— 'Nepotismus: Der Funktionswandel einer päpstgeschichtlichen Konstanten', *Zeitschrift für Kirchengeschichte*, 86 (1975), 145–85.

Repgen, K., 'Die Finanzen des Nuntius Fabio Chigi: Ein Beitrag zur Sozialgeschichte der römischen Führungsgruppen im 17. Jahrhundert', in E. Hassinger, J. H. Muller, and H. Ott (eds.), *Geschichte*

Wirtschaft Gesellschaft: Festschrift für Clemens Bauer (Berlin, 1974), 229–80.

Richard, P., 'Origines et développement de la Secrétairerie d'État Apostolique (1417–1823)', Revue d'Histoire Ecclésiastique, 11 (1910), 56–72, 505–29, 728–54.

Rietbergen, P. J. A. N., 'Problems of Government: Some Observations upon a Sixteenth-Century "Istruttione per li governatori delle città e luoghi dello Stato ecclesiastico"', Mededelingen van het Nederlands Instituut te Rome, NS 6 (1979), 173–201.

—— 'Pausen, Prelaten, Bureaucraten: Aspekten van de geschiedenis van het Pausschap en de Pauselijke Staat in de 17e Eeuw', doctoral thesis (Nijmegen, 1983).

Rius Serra, J., 'Catalanes y Aragoneses en la corte de Calixto III', Analecta Sacra Tarraconensis, 3 (1927), 193–330.

Robertson, I., 'The Return of Cesena to the Direct Dominion of the Church after the Death of Malatesta Novello', Studi Romagnoli, 16 (1965), 123–61.

Rubinstein, N., Florence and Italy = C. Elam and P. Denley (eds.), Florence and Italy: Renaissance Studies in honour of Nicolai Rubinstein (London, 1988).

Ryder, A., The Kingdom of Naples under Alfonso the Magnanimous: The Making of a Modern State (Oxford, 1976).

Salimei, A., 'Note di topografia romana: Case e torri dei Leni 1286 e 1442', ASR 53–5 (1930–2), 397–404.

Scapinelli, G. B., 'Il memoriale del p. Oliva S.J. al card. Cybo sul nepotismo (1676)', Rivista di Storia della Chiesa in Italia, 2 (1948), 262–73.

Schiavo, A., Il palazzo della Cancelleria (Rome, 1964).

Schlecht, J., Andrea Zamometić und der Basler Konzilversuch vom Jahre 1482 (Paderborn, 1903).

Schuchard, C., Die Deutschen an der päpstlichen Kurie im späten Mittelalter (1378–1447) (Tübingen, 1987).

Schulte, A., Die Fugger in Rom 1495–1523 (Leipzig, 1904).

Schwarz, B., Die Organisation kurialer Schreiberkollegen von ihrer Entstehung bis zur Mitte des 15. Jahrhunderts (Tübingen, 1972).

—— 'Abbreviature officium est assistere vicecancellario in expeditione litterarum apostolicarum: Zur Entwicklung des Abbreviatorenamts etc.', in E. Gatz (ed.), Römische Kurie, kirchliche Finanzen, Vatikanisches Archiv: Studien zu Ehren von Hermann Hoberg (Miscellanea Historiae Pontificiae, 45–6/ii; Rome, 1979), 789–824A.

—— 'Die Abbreviatoren unter Eugen IV.', Quellen, 60 (1980), 200–74.

Scrittura, biblioteche e stampa a Roma nel Quattrocento: Aspetti e problemi, ed. C. Bianca (Vatican City, 1980).

Setton, K. M., The Papacy and the Levant, i–ii (Philadelphia, 1976–8).

Signorelli, G., Viterbo nella storia della Chiesa (Viterbo, 1907–40).

Smith, L. F., 'Lodrisio Crivelli and Aeneas Sylvius', Studies in the Renaissance, 9 (1962), 31–63.

Stephens, J. N., *The Fall of the Florentine Republic 1512-1530* (Oxford, 1983).

Stinger, C. L., *The Renaissance in Rome* (Bloomington, 1985).

Storia di Cesena, ii/2 (Rimini, 1985).

Storti, N., *La storia e il diritto della Dataria Apostolica dalle origini alle nostre giorni* (Naples, 1969).

Tacchi Venturi, P., 'La pietra tombale di Leonardo Dati al Gesù di Roma', *ASR* 52 (1929), 491-500.

Tommasini, O., 'Nuovi documenti illustrativi del diario di Stefano Infessura', *ASR* 12 (1889), 1-36.

Trame, R. H., *Rodrigo Sánchez de Arévalo 1404-1470: Spanish Diplomat and Champion of the Papacy* (Washington, 1958).

Un pontificato e una città: Sisto IV (1471-1484), ed. M. Miglio and others (Vatican City, 1986).

Valois, N., *La France et le Grand Schisme d'Occident*, iv (Paris, 1902).

Wasner, F., 'Tor der Geschichte: Beiträge zum päpstlichen Zeremonienwesen im 15. Jahrhundert', *AHP* 6 (1968), 113-162.

Weber, C., *Kardinäle und Prälaten in den letzten Jahrzehnten des Kirchenstaates: Elite-Rekrutierung, Karriere-Muster und soziale Zusammensetzung der kurialen Führungsschicht der Zeit Pius' IX. (1846-1878)* (Stuttgart, 1978).

Weber, M., *From Max Weber: Essays in Sociology*, ed. H. H. Gerth and C. Wright Mills (New York, 1958).

Westfall, C. W., 'Alberti and the Vatican Palace Type', *Journal of the Society of Architectural Historians*, 33 (1974), 102-3.

Williman, D., *Records of the Papal Right of Spoil (1316-1412)* (Paris, 1974).

Index